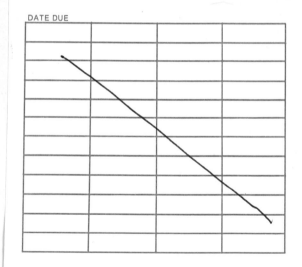

CLASSICAL AND MEDIÆVAL STUDIES IN HONOR OF EDWARD KENNARD RAND

E. K. R.

Bachrach

CLASSICAL AND MEDIÆVAL STUDIES IN HONOR OF EDWARD KENNARD RAND

PRESENTED UPON THE COMPLETION OF
HIS FORTIETH YEAR OF TEACHING

EDITED BY
LESLIE WEBBER JONES

Essay Index Reprint Series

BOOKS FOR LIBRARIES PRESS
FREEPORT, NEW YORK

First Published 1938
Reprinted 1968

LIBRARY OF CONGRESS CATALOG CARD NUMBER:

68-57312

PRINTED IN THE UNITED STATES OF AMERICA

PREFACE

THIS BOOK is a simple expression of gratitude toward a teacher and scholar whose eminence in the classical and mediaeval fields and even in the Renaissance field has already had ample testimony. Most of the essays which it contains have been written by former pupils of Professor Rand; eleven, however, have been produced by others—all colleagues and friends whose work has been closely associated with his own: Prof. C. H. Beeson, Dr. Bernhard Bischoff, Dr. Albert Bruckner, Prof. Lane Cooper, Mme. Olga Dobiaš-Roždestvenskaïa, Prof. J. Wight Duff, Prof. A. Ernout, Dr. Elias Avery Lowe, Giovanni Cardinal Mercati, Prof. Alexander Souter, and Dom André Wilmart, O.S.B. The essays themselves give no adequate idea of the number of scholars who desire to honor the master; many excellent studies have had to be rejected because of limitations of space. They do, however, in their variety fairly symbolize the many interests of Professor Rand.

The editor thanks most heartily all who have helped create the volume; he is particularly indebted to the authors of the studies, the subscribers (a list of whom is printed at the rear of this book), Professor Rand's college classmates, and the following individuals—Prof. F. M. Carey, Prof. Lane Cooper, Dr. Lincoln Davis, Prof. F. H. Fobes, Mr. W. P. Hapgood, Mr. Carl Keller, Dr. Austin Lamont, Mr. Thomas W. Lamont, Mrs. Arthur Lehmann, Mr. J. K. Moffitt, Mr. George Oenslager, Mr. L. I. Prouty, Mr. W. T. Rosen, Prof. Paul Sachs, and Mr. P. W. Wrenn —whose generous donations have ably supplemented the subscriptions. He thanks as well Mr. G. W. Cottrell, Jr. of the Mediaeval Academy of America, Mr. R. F. Gehner of the George Banta Publishing Company, Prof. William Chase Greene of Harvard University, Prof. Dean P. Lockwood of Haverford College, Messrs. Dumas Malone and David T. Pottinger, Director and Associate Director respectively of the Harvard University Press, Prof. Eva M. Sanford of Sweet Briar College, and Dr. B. M. Peebles of Harvard University for their helpful advice and kind offices. He is most grateful to his wife, who has performed services too numerous and too varied to mention here.

It does not seem fitting, finally, to include in this book a bibliography of a man who will undoubtedly write for many years to come. Nor is it practicable to include an index, for the essays are too highly diversified; the descriptive nature of the titles and the relative brevity of the individual essays, however, facilitate reference.

L. W. J.

COLLEGE OF THE CITY OF NEW YORK,
JANUARY 1, 1938.

v

CONTENTS

CONTENTS

LIST OF ILLUSTRATIONS

THE AUTHORSHIP OF 'QUID SIT CEROMA'

CHARLES H. BEESON

ALONG WITH other driftwood of Carolingian learning which has come down to us is a little tract bearing the title 'Quid sit ceroma,' found in a number of MSS, mostly of the tenth and eleventh centuries. The text was printed by Baluze[1] from a Paris codex (B. N. Lat. 8070) and, without knowledge of a previous publication, by Traube,[2] from another Paris MS, (B.N. Lat. 12949). On account of the connection of this MS with Auxerres, Traube suggested that the Fredilo mentioned in the opening sentence of the tract[3] is identical with the Fredilo whom Lupus of Ferrières calls his 'gratissimus auditor' in a letter to the monks of Auxerres[4] and whom he had previously employed as a messenger to them. Traube concluded therefore that it is not impossible that Lupus was the author of the tract.

Dümmler included the tract as the work of an anonymous author among the Additamenta (pp. 115–117) in his edition of the Letters of Lupus. M. Manitius[5] accepted Traube's identification of Fredilo and asserted that the tract was written by Lupus or a member of his circle. The latest editor of the Letters[6] does not include any of Dümmler's Additamenta and makes no mention of 'Quid sit ceroma.'

The oldest MS, Paris 12947, formerly Sangermanensis 1108, saec. IX and X, is miscellaneous, not only as regards contents, but also in makeup. It includes, besides some short scraps of text, the following: 1–11ᵛ Periermeneiae of Aristotle, translated by Boethius (Migne, PL. 64, 296–392); 12–21ᵛ Augustine's Dialectica (*ibid.*, 32, 1409–1420); 24–38 Categoriae of Aristotle, translated by Augustine (*ibid.*, 1419–1440), preceded by the ten introductory verses of Alcuin;[7] 38ᵛ–39ᵛ Quid sit ceroma; 42 a computus table, with the notation at the top of the page, 'Frater iohannis scotti aldelmus fecit istam paginam'; 46–52ᵛ Isagoge of Porphyrius, translated by Boethius (Migne 64, 77–158); 53–56 Boethius De trinitate (*ibid.*,

---

[1] *Miscellaneorum liber IV* (Paris, 1683), 417–420 = Migne, *PL.*, 96, 1385–1388.

[2] *Neues Archiv für ältere deutsche Geschichtskunde*, 18 (1893), 100–102.

[3] 'Quaestiunculam mihi datam a vestra reverentia his diebus attulit familiaris noster Fredilo.'

[4] No. 116 of Dümmler s edition, *MGH Epistolae Karolini aevi*, IV, 99. All references in the following pages are to this edition.

[5] *Geschichte der lateinischen Literatur des Mittelalters*, I, p. 488.

[6] L. Levillain, *Loup de Ferrières, Correspondance, text and translation*, Vol. II (Paris, 1935).

[7] Dümmler, *MGH Poetae Karolini aevi*, I, 295.

1247–1256); 57–58 Boethius Utrum pater et filius ac spiritus sanctus de divinitate substantialiter praedicentur (ibid., 1299–1302); 58–59ᵛ Boethius Quomodo substantiae in eo quod sint, bonae sint cum non sint substantialia bona (ibid., 1311–1314); 59ᵛ–62ᵛ Boethius Brevis fidei christianae complexio (ibid., 1333–1338); 62ᵛ–70ᵛ Boethius De persona et duabus naturis contra Eutychen et Nestorium (ibid., 1337–1354); 71–72ᵛ 'De periermeniis. Sequitur de hanc liber periermenias subtilissimus . . . utiliter introducunt'; 72ᵛ–80 Apuleius Periermeneiae; 80ᵛ–81 Boethius In librum Aristotelis de interpretatione, the beginning and the end only and both greatly abbreviated (Migne 64, 293 D–295 A and 390 D–392 D). Numerous scribes were engaged in the work of copying. Extra strips of parchment have been inserted in various parts of the codex; e.g., 23bisᵛ 'Versus iohanni scotti, Bedae, Virgł' etc.; 27bis twenty-three lines containing extracts from works of Augustine; 52bis five lines containing Boethius' translation of the Categoriae of Aristotle (ibid., 169–175). The hands are slightly different from those found in the rest of the codex. A contemporary scribe added on f. 44ᵛ, which had been left blank, thirteen lines of a text bearing the title De illustribus philosophis eorumque quibusdam sectis. 'Sapientes autem praecipui fuerunt numero VII . . . Heraclitus phisicus propter sermonis obscuritatem σκοτινιος meruit nominari qui per omnem lacrimosis est affectibus persecutus.' Ff. 22ᵛ and 23 are vacant.[8]

Some of the texts in the collection have been annotated. The commentary on Augustine's Dialectica is probably by Heiricus of Auxerres. Heiricus is almost certainly the author of the commentary on the Categoriae of Aristotle (f. 25ᵛ 'Heiricus magister Remigii fecit has glossas,' written by a contemporary hand). The identity of the commentator on the Isagoge is uncertain. Rand[9] suggested Heiricus as a possible though not a probable author. Finally the text of Boethius' De trinitate is accompanied by the glosses of Remigius of Auxerres.[10] The codex furnishes an inter-

[8] E. K. Rand, 'Johannes Scottus,' Ludwig Traube's Quellen und Untersuchungen, I, 2, p. 83, argues that the Categoriae and Dialectica of Augustine and probably the Isagoge of Porphyrius derive from the same source since these works, with identical glosses, once formed a part of another Sangermanensis (No. 613). He rightly objects to Cousin's identification (Oeuvr. inédits d'Abélard, p. LXXX and p. 618) of Sangerm. 613 with Paris 12949. In point of fact the Isagoge, the commentary of Boethius on the Categoriae, the Categoriae without the commentary, and the Dialectica are found in a Leningrad MS (F Cl. Lat. 7), once a part of Sangermanensis 613, along with Leningrad Q XIV 1, in which a seventeenth-century hand entered the Corbie ex libris. According to Olga Dobiaš-Roždestvenskaïa, Histoire de l'atelier graphique de Corbie de 651 à 830 reflétée dans les monuments de Leningrad (Leningrad, 1934), p. 161, the script of F Cl. Lat. 7 resembles that of the Corbie scriptorium and belongs to saec. VIII–IX. The Paris codex, since it is a Sangermanensis, may also have belonged, in part at least, to the library of Corbie.

[9] Op. cit., p. 15.

[10] See Rand, op. cit., pp. 87–106.

esting example of ninth-century scholarship. In it we see the combination of two schools. The central figures are Heiricus and Remigius. Heiricus was first the pupil of Lupus; later he studied at Laon under the Irishman Elias, who was a pupil of Iohannes Scottus. Remigius was a pupil of Heiricus and later received instruction from the Irishman Dunchad.

A palaeographical study of the manuscript supplies abundant evidence of its Irish background, both in the texts (including those found on the inserted strips), and in the commentaries. Insular abbreviations occur throughout the manuscript; their number varies in different texts, and some are confined to one or two texts. A number of them are probably forms that had passed into current use, but others must have been transmitted from the exemplars, since they are clearly imitative. A few belong to the Anglo-Saxon group (e.g., *qñ*, *qūo* for quoniam, *qñđ*, *qñđo* for quando) but most of them are primarily Irish. The list is as follows (folio numbers are given in order to identify the texts in which the symbols are found):

aliquando	*aliqñdo* 11ᵛ *aliqñ* 27bisᵛ	hoc	*h'* 7ᵛ 13 27bisᵛ 57 65 81
apud	*ap̄* 27bisᵛ 39ᵛ		*h̄* 10 (twice) *h* 7ᵛ *h'* 8ᵛ
autem	*the Insular h-symbol* 27bisᵛ		*hº* 67
	52bis 81	homo	*hō* 12 52bis 81 *hº* 60 74ᵛ
caput	*cap̄* 62	homine	*hōe* 46ᵛ 52bis
contra	*reversed c transected* 27bisᵛ	hominem	*hōem* 17ᵛ
	81 (three times)	homines	*hōes* 15ᵛ 27bisᵛ 48
cuius	*c̃* 44ᵛ	huius	*h̃* 58 80 *h'* 25ᵛ (gloss)
dicere	*dr̄e* 81	hunc	*hc̄* 69 *hñc* 67
dicimus	*dm̄s* 81	id est	·|· 12 |÷ 24ᵛ 44ᵛ
dicunt	*dñt* 12	igitur	*gⁱ* 57 81 *igⁱ* 13 46ᵛ 74 77
dicuntur	*dñr* 1ᵛ 28 52bis	inter	+ 27bisᵛ 81
eius	3 27bisᵛ 74ᵛ *(with tongue	mihi	*mⁱ* 14ᵛ 53
	hanging down, imitative)*	modo	*mº* 13 59ᵛ 67 82 *mō* 63ᵛ
	81	nihil	*nł* 27bisᵛ 52bis 59 81
enim	*the H-symbol* 3 12 27bisᵛ 44ᵛ	nisi	*nⁱ* 27bisᵛ 59
	49ᵛ 52bis 53 59ᵛ 74ᵛ 80ᵛ	nomina	*nōa* 15 44ᵛ
ergo	*gº* 27bisᵛ 81	nomine	*nōe* 13ᵛ
est	÷ 1 12 27bisᵛ 54 81 ÷	nominis	*nōis* 19
	45 − 54 54ᵛ · − · 55	numeris	*nūis* 44ᵛ
et	7 8 12 27bisᵛ 38ᵛ 44ᵛ 52bis	numero	*nūo* 27bisᵛ 44ᵛ 52bis
	57 72ᵛ 80ᵛ 81	numeros	*nūos* 27bisᵛ
habens	*hñs* 43	numquam	*ñq* 51ᵛ
habent	*hñt* 58	nunc	*nc̄* 12 55ᵛ 69ᵛ
habere	*hr̄e* 56 60	omne	*oē* 81
habet	*hł* 11ᵛ 12 54 78	omnem	*oēm* 44ᵛ
hae	*h̄* 11ᵛ	omnia	*oā* 27bisᵛ 44ᵛ 81
haec	*h̄* 10 12 56	omnis	*oĩs* 52bis 81

post	*p°* 61 67	quot	*q̄t* 16
propri	*p^i* 45^v	sed	*s̄* 27bis^v 45^v 52bis
propter	*the monogram (pro symbol plus a 'tail')* 44	sine	*sñ* 52bis
		sunt	*s̄t* 12^v 24 50 74^v
qua	*q^a* 27bis^v	tamen	*tm̄* 38^v 59 *tñ* 74^v
quae	*q̄* 12 24^v 27bis^v 52bis 78 81	trans	*t̄s* 27bis^v
quam	*q* 19 *q^ā* 32^v	tunc	*tc̄* 59
quando	*qđo* 5 12 45 48 66^v *qñd* 66	uel	*ł* 1 13 27bis^v 52bis
	qño 55^v 68^v *qñdo* 13 34^v	uero	*u°* 6^v 12 24 27bis^v 52 52bis
	48 52bis 68^v		72^v
quanto	*qñto* 27bis^v		
quare	*q̄re* 65	con	*ɔ* 27bis^v 44^v 74^v 81
quasi	*q̄si* 14^v 53	dem	*d–* 81
qui	*q^i* 1 12 27bis^v 44^v 52bis 81	gra	*g̈* 52bis
quo	*q°* 14^v 27bis^v 52bis	nem	*n–* 81
quod	*the Insular symbol* 12 52bis	pra	*p^a* 27bis^v
	54 81	pri	*p^i* 5 12 27bis^v 61 74 78 81
quomodo	*qm̄o* 69^v	rum	*r̄* 54^v 59^v
quoniam	*qm̄* 1 12 24^v 27bis^v 45 78 81	runt	*r̄t* 12^v 30^v 50
	qũo 3^v (three times) *qñ* 6^v	tra	*t (with diaeresis)* 27 bis^v 81
	7^v 8^v 59^v	tur	*ł* 74^v (twice, once corrected
quoque	*qq̄* 24^v 28 53 81		to *t²*)

Abnormal are the forms *qa, qi, qo* (without strokes) for *qua, qui, quo*. *Finit* is found on f. 39^v and the Insular form of *g* on f. 30^v.

The connection of our MS with Auxerres is indicated by the presence in it of the commentaries of Heiricus and Remigius, whose names also furnish a link between Auxerres and Ferrières. A further link between these two centers is found in Fredilo himself. This young monk figures in another letter of Lupus besides the one mentioned by Traube (No. 116), viz., a fragmentary letter (115a) which ends as follows: 'Ut ergo particeps efficiatur doctrinae memoratus puer, cui iuste consulitis, si licentiam et litteras sui habet episcopi, perducatur ad nos a dilectissimo Remigio IIII Kal. Iul. et, gratia Dei opitulante, conabimur cum aliis illi quoque prodesse.' Levillain[11] is undoubtedly right in identifying the 'memoratus puer' as Fredilo and in assuming that the letter was addressed to the monks of Auxerres. Fredilo was therefore a monk of Auxerres and we can understand why Lupus should have employed him, along with Remigius, on a mission to that place. It is not without significance that in both letters Fredilo is named along with Remigius, to whom Lupus refers as 'carissimus propinquus.'[12] It was probably from Auxerres that

[11] *Op. cit.*, p. 159, ftn. 6.
[12] L. Levillain (*op. cit.*, p. 159, ftn. 4) asserts that Remigius was a monk of Ferrières. But Manitius

the request came through Fredilo to Lupus for information about the meaning of *ceroma*.

Requests for information of this sort were nothing new to Lupus. In a letter to Adalgaudus (No. 8) Lupus discusses matters of metric and grammar, quoting Priscian and Servius.[13] He explains *pater patratus* in a letter to Leotaldus (No. 15); he writes to Altuin (No. 20) at some length about the quantity of the penult where a mute and a liquid are involved and quotes authorities for the accent of certain words; e.g., Martial for *bibliotheca*, Alcuin for *statera*, Prudentius for *blasphemus*, Theodulph for *nundinae*, Vergil and Martial for *fiala;* he quotes Caper on orthography; he comments on the sistrum, adding a citation from Vergil, and discusses the significance of the appearance of a comet, with references to Vergil, Josephus and Trogus. In a second letter to Altuin (No. 34) he expresses impatience at having to devote the small leisure that he finds to explanation of what he already knows rather than to the investigation of subjects he does not know. But he yields to Altuin's insistence and discusses the quantity of the penult of various words, the meaning of *ulciscor* and *vindico*, the spelling of *propitius*, and the perfect tense of *stupeo*. One question he refuses to answer until he has consulted Livy. Finally (No. 37) he instructs Heribold, abbot of Auxerres, in regard to the writings of Caesar and promises to send him a copy of the Commentaries.

The tract 'Quid sit ceroma' is written quite in the manner of Lupus, if one may judge the style of a text which is only sixty-four lines in length, and the exposition is made according to the best philological method. We do not know the name of the person addressed but Manitius[14] calls him a 'Mitglied des höheren Klerus.' One gets the impression that the writer is giving a demonstration of elegant Latinity and classical learning.

There are several similarities of phrasing in the tractate and the Letters of Lupus; e.g., 7.19 *dum altius meas repeto cogitationes* and 115.26 *altius quiddam censeo repetendum;* 45.19 *ab imo ad summum evadere* and 115.18 *a primis ad secunda conscendere;* 7.31 *sapientiae palmam* and 115.14 *palmam Romani eloquii;* 27.40 *commenticiam potestatem* and 115.23 *commenticia tradicio;* 68.14 *ad stabilitatem religionis* and 117.10 *salva stabilitate amicitiae.*

(*op. cit.*, p. 504) identifies him with Remigius of Auxerres. The two letters of Lupus in which Remigius is mentioned were written (861 and 862) shortly before his death and even if Remigius were a monk of Ferrières there is no reason why he should not have gone to Auxerres after the death of Lupus in order to study with Heiricus, the greatest of the pupils of Lupus.

[13] The Servius quotation is at second hand. The real source was a grammatical text resembling that found in Berne 83 (H. Hagen, *Anecdota Helvetica*, p. 179), where a quotation from Juvencus follows the Vergil citation of Servius. The entire passage of Lupus (p. 19, 24-29) is paralleled by Hagen, pp. 179, 5-10.

[14] *Op. cit.*, p. 488.

Another point of contact is the common familiarity with the same authors. The Arithmetic of Boethius is cited on p. 16, lines 26, 30, 35, 37 and on p. 116.28. Traube found in the passage 115. 21, 'Quam ob rem lumen et sensus dilectusque verborum semper a studiosis est habendus,' a parallel with Cicero, De oratore 3.150, 'sed in hoc verborum genere propriorum dilectus est habendus.' We know that Lupus possessed a copy of De oratore, in fact his copy still survives (British Museum, Harleianus 2736.)[15] In the tractate the first word *quaestiunculam* is probably borrowed from De oratore and the expression *ingenuarum artium* instead of *artium liberalium* may be from the same source. Manuscripts of this text were extremely rare in the ninth century.

But it is Aulus Gellius that ties the tractate with Lupus most closely. The first mention of Gellius in the Middle Ages is found in a letter of Lupus, the first in the collection, to Einhard. It was written ca. 830 at Fulda, where Lupus had been sent by the abbot of Ferrières to study under Rhabanus Maurus. In it Lupus asked for the loan of four MSS. It is a notable fact that of these four texts three belonging to Lupus have survived: the De oratore, mentioned above, Cicero's De inventione (Paris 7774A) and Gellius (Vat. Reg. 597).[16] We are justified in assuming that Lupus obtained these texts from Einhard. This is certain in the case of Gellius, for Lupus wrote some six years later explaining why he had not returned the codex (Rhabanus was having a copy made for himself). These MSS were 'edited' by Lupus in his characteristic fashion. Errors were corrected, variant readings entered, syllable-division was revised according to the rules of the mediaeval grammarians, significant passages were indicated by a marginal monogram of N and T (=Nota), and a marginal index was provided. This index listed rare words, an apt word or a neat turn of expression, words where a syntactical construction or assimilation in spelling were involved, or catch-words referring to the contents of a passage (e.g., *Mausolus, Laus Egyptiorum,* etc.). In De oratore Lupus showed his interest in *pater patratus* by listing the words in his marginal index twice; as we have seen he discussed the term in his letter to Leotaldus; *dilectus* is listed in the margin opposite the passage from De oratore quoted above; the word is also indexed in Gellius (17.10, 5). Lupus was quite familiar with the text of Gellius; he revised it more thoroughly than any other of his MSS—he used pen or knife some two thousand times in making changes—and his Gellius marginal index is much the longest. We may infer that some of the rarer words and phrases

---

[15] C. H. Beeson, *Lupus of Ferrières as Scribe and Text Critic, A Study of his Autograph Copy of Cicero's De Oratore* (Cambridge, Mass., 1930).

[16] See Sister Luanne Meagher, *The Gellius Manuscript of Lupus of Ferrières,* University of Chicago dissertation, 1936.

found in his letters were taken from this author; e.g., 38, 5 *diutile* is probably borrowed from Gellius 11.16, 6, where the word appears in the index; similarly *gentilis*, which Lupus twice uses as a substantive (18,8 and 44, 7), is found in Gellius 17.17, 2 where Lupus entered it in the index; 73, 16 *prolixa proturbatio* may have been suggested by Gellius 19.10, 14 *prolixius riderent* where Lupus wrote *prolixius* in the margin. An undoubted borrowing from Gellius is seen in Lupus' Life of St. Wigbert, which was written in 836, while Lupus was still at Fulda. Chapter 26 describes how the saint prevented the burning of a church by the Saxons: 'Videres lignorum simplicem materiam, nec prorsus alumine oblitam, velut amoliri a se ignis potentiam,' etc.[17] Lupus could have learned of this use of *alumen* only from Gellius 15.1, 6, 'Scriptum inveni . . . turrim ligneam defendendi gratia structam, cum ex omni latere circumplexa igni foret, ardere non quisse, quod alumine ab Archelao oblita fuisset.' In his copy of Gellius Lupus registered his interest in the passage by putting the monogram of N and T in the margin opposite.

In the tract on *ceroma* the expression *non incelebres* (115.12) was probably taken from Gellius, who uses the word *inceleber* some half-dozen times, five times with *non*. The most conspicuous case of borrowing is however found at 115.15; here the text reads 'qui nervos et *medullas* ipsumque, ut dicitur, *sanguinem* ex libris antiquorum eliciunt.' We do not need *ut dicitur* to label the passage as a quotation; the striking metaphor bears the ear-mark of antiquity. The original is Gellius 18.4, 2, 'neque primam tantum cutem ac speciem sententiarum, sed *sanguinem* quoque ipsum ac *medullam verborum* eius eruere atque introspicere penitus praedicaret.' The writer chose to excerpt the boldest words of the metaphor. Now in the margin of his Gellius Lupus wrote opposite this passage the words *medullam verborum ac sanguinem*, reversing the order of the words; in the tractate we find the same reversed order. The conclusion is almost inevitable that we are dealing with the work of one and the same writer and that Lupus is therefore the author of 'Quid sit ceroma.'[18]

UNIVERSITY OF CHICAGO.

[17] *Servati Lupi opera*, ed. S. Baluze[2], p. 306.

[18] Besides the MSS of Einhard, Lupus and Rhabanus, which contained only the second half of the Noctes Atticae, we know of only one other possible ninth-century copy, referred to in an anonymous letter written between the years 762–875, possibly at Laon (*MGH Epistolae Karolini aevi*, IV, 187 ff.). But it is uncertain whether this contained the first or the second half of the corpus. The codex used by Dunchad (Manitius, *op. cit.*, p. 526, ftn. 3) contained the first half. It is extremely unlikely that the rare De Oratore together with the rare Gellius could be found in the ninth century outside the circle of Lupus.

ELEMENTARUNTERRICHT UND PROBATIONES PENNAE IN DER ERSTEN HÄLFTE DES MITTELALTERS

BERNHARD BISCHOFF

DER AUSFÜHRLICHEN Erörterung des Lese- und Schreibunterrichts durch den umsichtigen Pädagogen Quintilian,[1] der auch diese 'res necessariae, procul tamen ab ostentatione positae' nicht übergehen will, hat die Literatur des Mittelalters keine ähnlich einlässliche Schilderung an die Seite zu stellen.[2] Auch Originaldokumente von der Art der zahlreichen ägyptischen Funde von Lesetäfelchen und Schreibübungen,[3] die die Unterrichtsmethode auf das glücklichste illustrieren, sind aus den Schulstuben des frühen und hohen Mittelalters kaum erhalten. Versucht man trotzdem, für diese Epoche nach den gelegentlichen Äusserungen der Schriftsteller und nach den sonstigen geringen Anhaltspunkten ein Bild von der Vermittlung und Aneignung von Lesen und Schreiben zu entwerfen, wie es z.B. F. A. Specht[4] und W. Wattenbach[5] getan haben und wie es hier in Anlehnung an die Literatur, aber mit neuem Material unternommen wird, so wird vermutlich das private und irreguläre Erlernen und das Autodidaktentum kaum genügend in Anschlag gebracht werden; gibt es doch auch in Handschriften bisweilen Federproben und sogar längere Einträge in erstaunlich roher und ungehobelter Schrift, sogar mit falscher Bildung von Buchstaben wie dem doppelt gerundeten g, die wohl durch Nachahmung ohne Anleitung und Pflege erklärt werden müssen.

In den Schulen wurde zuerst das Alphabet der gangbaren Minuskel gelehrt und zwar, spätestens vom XII. Jahrhundert ab, nach einem grossen Pergamentblatt, das über eine Holztafel gespannt oder vielleicht auch direkt an der Wand befestigt war. Ein Zeugnis aus einem satirischen Rhythmus führt Wattenbach an;[6] ein zweites steht in den *Sermones dominicales* des Cisterciensers Odo von Cheriton (†1247) in einem der bei den Predigern beliebten Vergleiche zwischen Inhalten der Religion und

---

[1] *Inst. or.* I, 1, 24.

[2] Vgl. auch Dionysius Halicarn., *De comp. verb.*, 25.

[3] Literatur bei K. Preisendanz, *Papyrusfunde und Papyrusforschung* (Leipzig, 1933), S. 307; L. Mitteis-U. Wilcken, *Grundzüge und Chrestomathie der Papyruskunde* (Leipzig u. Berlin, 1912), I, 1, 137.

[4] F. A. Specht, *Geschichte des Unterrichtswesens in Deutschland* (Stuttgart, 1885), SS. 60 f., 67 ff.

[5] W. Wattenbach, *Das Schriftwesen im Mittelalter* (3. Aufl., Leipzig, 1896), SS. 264 ff.

[6] *Loc. cit.*, 269.

Gegenständen des Buchwesens:[7] 'Sicut enim carta, in qua scribitur doctrina parvulorum, quatuor clavis affigitur in poste, sic caro Christi extensa est in cruce . . . cuius quinque vulnera quasi quinque vocales pro nobis ad Patrem per se sonant. Cetere circumstantes sunt consonantes et sicut abecedarium viam aperit in omnem facultatem . . . .'[8] Dass die Buchstaben auch in umgekehrter oder noch sonst veränderter Reihenfolge[9] gedrillt worden wären, wie Quintilian und erhaltene antike Schultafeln es verlangen, dafür liegen keine Beweise vor, auch nicht dafür, dass bei den anschliessenden Silbenübungen[10] eine bestimmte Methode befolgt wurde. Da aber die Silbenreihen *ba be bi bo bu* etc. im Schreibunterricht ihren Platz hatten,[11] ist dasselbe auch für das Lesen anzunehmen.

Das eigentliche Lesebuch des frühen Mittelalters, an dem die Kenntnis der Schrift zuerst erprobt[12] und weiter befestigt wurde, war der Psalter.[13] Dies Buch hatte anscheinend bereits in der christlichen Antike begonnen, die heidnischen Gnomen und Dichterverse aus dem Elementarunterricht zu verdrängen.[14] Einem Zeitalter geistlicher, ja vorwiegend mönchischer Bildung musste er erst recht als der gegebene Lese- und Lernstoff erscheinen; er wurde in den ersten Schuljahren ganz auswendig gelernt.[15] Dank der Unentbehrlichkeit der Psalmen für den Gottesdienst blieb ihre Vorzugsstellung im Unterricht unangetastet, auch wo die Schüler nicht von Hause aus vulgärlateinisch gewöhnt, sondern Germanen oder Kelten waren; hier bedingten die veränderten Sprachverhältnisse eine schwere

---

[7] *Loc. cit.*, 208 f.

[8] *London, B. M., Egerton 2890*, fol. 163 r. Die Kenntnis der Stelle sowie eine Abschrift verdanke ich der Liebenswürdigkeit A. C. Friends.

[9] F. Dornseiff, *Das Alphabet in Mystik und Magie* (2. Aufl., Leipzig u. Berlin, 1925), S. 17, Anm. 2.

[10] Specht, 68; Wattenbach, 268.

[11] Vgl. unten. In *Cotton Titus D. XVIII, s.* XV, foll. 5ᵛ-6ʳ steht zwischen lateinischen und allerlei fremden Alphabeten eine 'Tabula coniunctionum litterarum' ('ba be bi bo bu ca ce . . . , bla ble . . . cla . . . , bra . . . ,' *etc.*), die als besonders nützlich für die Kinder empfohlen wird. Eine Photographie des Stückes verdanke ich der Freundlichkeit von Mlle. G. L. Micheli. Die Einleitung lautet: 'Tabula alphabeti, que multum valet ad instruendum pueros, ut citissime bene ubique legant et litterarum ac sillabarum diversitates in brevi memoria semper sapienter habeant. Et licet quibusdam imprudentibus et minus intelligentibus propter vocum deformitatem vel dissonanciam videntur esse inania et puerilia, tamen scientibus atque intelligentibus eam non parvam conferent sciencie intelligenciam. Nam diutissime possunt legere et forte omnibus diebus vite sue antequam tales inveniant litterarum coniuncciones. Nemo enim (!) in diversarum linguarum libris bene et aperte valet legere, nisi ipsarum litterarum figuras ac formas, potestates et nomina sillabarum et copulaciones studeat prius sagaciter mente intelligere.'

[12] Die Überlegenheit des Lesekundigen über den Analphabeten betont ein Eintrag in *Lucca, Bibl. capit. 21* (Aug., *in ev. Ioh.*, s. X), fol. 182ᵛ: '<h>ic liber caecus est et nullus potest in eo leg<ere> bene nisi sit sapiens litteris.'

[13] Specht, 60 f., 67 ff.; R. Limmer, *Bildungszustände und Bildungsideen des XIII. Jahrhunderts* (München u. Berlin, 1928), SS. 142, 151 f.

[14] W. Schubart, *Einführung in die Papyruskunde* (Berlin, 1918), SS. 382, 474.

[15] Daher war der Psalter das geeignete Übungsbuch für die Erlernung der Tironischen Noten; vgl. Chr. Johnen, *Geschichte der Stenographie* (Berlin, 1911), SS. 211 f.

Hemmung des elementaren Unterrichts selbst bei der Annahme, dass eine gewisse Erläuterung das recht mechanische Auswendiglernen begleitete. Die gleiche unpsychologische Methode ist im Koranunterricht bei den nichtarabischen Muhammedanern noch heute am Leben. Es hiesse aber noch über morgenländischen orthodoxen Schematismus hinausgehen, wollte man mit Specht annehmen, dass die Lehrer den Schülern die 150 Psalmen einprägten, 'noch ehe der Leseunterricht begann';[16] die namhaft gemachten Quellen erzählen vom Auswendiglernen des Psalters in früher Kindheit, aber sie geben keinen Anlass, eine so vernunftwidrige Reihenfolge der beiden Lehrgegenstände anzunehmen. Ein Rest eines Psalters aus dem X. Jahrhundert, an dessen Verwendung im Unterricht kein Zweifel bestehen kann, ist in dem *Fragmentum Augiense 8* in Karlsruhe erhalten: das erste der beiden Folioblätter enthält Teile von Ps. XV und XVI, das zweite auf der Vorderseite Ps. XCIV, mit dem die Handschrift geendet zu haben scheint.[17] Die Schrift ist gross und deutlich, doch nicht ganz frei von Abkürzungen; die Silben sind durch Punkte getrennt, für die auf Bl. 2 bewusst Zwischenräume gelassen wurden. Unter zahlreichen Federproben, zu denen verschiedene Hände die Blätter benutzt haben, findet sich auch der Schulvers 'Ferunt Ophyr' etc., der uns noch später begegnen wird.

Wie sich mit der Säkularisierung des Unterrichts im späteren Mittelalter die Lehrpraxis wandelte, ist in den Einzelheiten noch ganz ungeklärt. Die städtischen Lateinschulen stiessen den Ballast des Psalterlernens ab; in ihnen folgte auf die 'Tabula,'[18] das schmale Pergamentheft mit dem ABC, *Paternoster*, *Ave Maria*, *Credo* und einigen anderen liturgischen Stücken,[19] das wir vom Anfang des XV. Jahrhunderts an verfolgen können, das Lesen des Cato[20] oder des Donat.

Über die Methode des Schreibunterrichts würden die Schreibtäfelchen, auf denen geübt wurde, am besten belehren; aber soviele einst vorhanden waren und verbraucht und weggeworfen wurden, es scheint keines aus unserem Zeitraum erhalten zu sein, und die irischen und Lübecker Tafeln[21]

---

[16] Specht, 60 u. Anm. 5.

[17] A. Holder, *Die Reichenauer Handschriften* (Berlin u. Leipzig, 1914), II, 360, scheint der Meinung gewesen zu sein, dass die Handschrift nur eine Auswahl der Psalmen enthielt.

[18] Der Name wurde wohl von jener grossen ABC-Tafel auf die Lesefibel übertragen.

[19] E. Schulz, 'Das erste Lesebuch an den Lateinschulen des späten Mittelalters,' *Gutenberg-Jahrbuch*, 1929, 18 ff.; Ergänzungen gibt P. Lehmann, 'Sammlungen und Erörterungen von Abkürzungen im Altertum und Mittelalter,' *Abhandlungen d. Bayerischen Akademie d. Wissenschaften, phil.-hist. Abt.*, N. F. III, (1929), 18; *id.*, 'Mitteilungen aus Handschriften II,' *Sitzungsberichte d. Bayer. Akad. d. Wiss., phil.-hist. Abt.*, 1930, S. 5.

[20] Dass die *Disticha Catonis* schon in merovingischer Zeit in der Schule gelesen wurden, zeigen die kursiven Federproben 'Si deus est animus' in *Autun 107*; zur Cato-Lektüre in der späteren Zeit vgl. E. Voigt, 'Das erste Lesebuch des Triviums in den Kloster-und Stiftsschulen des Mittelalters,' *Mitteilungen d. Gesellschaft für deutsche Erziehungs-und Schulgeschichte*, I (1892), 42 ff.

[21] Literatur bei Lehmann, *Sammlungen und Erörterungen*, 18.

aus dem XIV. Jahrhundert stammen nicht von ABC-Schützen. Deren bescheidene Arbeit können wir in einem Abbild erkennen, in den *probationes pennae* oder *probationes incausti;*[22] bei solchen Versuchen floss oft selbst erwachsenen Schreibern in der Schule zum Übermass wiederholtes in die Feder.[23] Einzeln meist ganz wertlos, oft korrupt, oft den angefangenen Vers oder Spruch nach wenigen Buchstaben abbrechend, mit vielen belanglosen Varianten, erlauben sie gesammelt, geworfelt und auf ihre Verbreitung geprüft mancherlei Schlüsse.

Im elementaren Schreibunterricht, der sich naturgemäss zuerst auf die jeweils vorherrschende Schriftart bezogen haben muss, wird der vernünftige Weg von der einfachen virgula ausgehen und über die aus mehreren virgulae zusammengesetzten Buchstaben unter Berücksichtigung der zunehmenden Schwierigkeit zu weiterem fortschreiten.[24] Ein Anzeichen dafür, dass so vorgegangen wurde, ist meines Erachtens in dem häufigen Vorkommen einiger Zeilen zu sehen, die mit wenigen und relativ einfachen Zeichen gebildet sind und auffälligerweise alle mit 'omnis' beginnen:[25]

'omnium inimicorum suorum dominabitur'

(Ps.X, 5, aus 12 Elementen bestehend; *Fulda, Bonif. 3,* fol. 30ᵛ, irisch *saec.* VIII; *Würzburg, Mp. th. q. 2,* fol. 113ᵛ, in englischer Unziale *s.* VIII; *Rom, Vat. Pal. lat. 259,* fol. 97ᵛ, angelsächsisch *s.* VIII–IX; *S. Gallen 904,* p. 77, irisch *s.* IX: 'omnium'; *Wolfenbüttel, Weiss. 53,* fol. 1ʳ, *s.* IX; *München, Clm 14311,* fol. 1ʳ, *s.* XI; nur an letzterer Stelle ist 'dominabitur' hinzugefügt, sodass als Schulübung vielleicht nur die ersten drei Worte mit 8 Elementen anzusehen sind).

'omnis homo primum bonum vinum ponit'

(Ioh.II, 10, 11 Buchstaben; *S. Gallen 157,* p. 1, *s.* X; ich glaube, den Spruch auch in anderen Handschriften gelesen zu haben und ebenso seine leoninische Umformung von 13 Buchstaben, ohne gegenwärtig Belege anführen zu können: 'omnis homo primum preponit nobile vinum').

'omnia sunt bona, sunt, quia tu bonus omnia condis'

(Augustinus, *de anima,* v.1: *Anthologia latina* ed. A. Riese II, 43, no. 489; mit 12 Elementen; *Clm 601,* 60ʳ; *S. Gallen 105,* p. 212, beide *s.* X).

---

[22] Wattenbach, *Schriftwesen,* 231, 234; W. M. Lindsay, *Palaeographia Latina,* II (1923), 29 f.; *S. Gallen 174,* p. 1: 'probatio sipiae' (*s.* X oder XI); *Paris, B. N., lat. 9427,* fol. 47ʳ; 'volo te probare si bona es' (*s.* X).

[23] Von den anderen üblichen Kategorien von Federproben, wie Namen und liturgischen Stücken, sehe ich hier ab.

[24] Dass dem Schüler auch die Hand geführt wurde, erweist Wattenbach, *Schriftwesen,* 267.

[25] Theoretisch könnten auch gewisse raffiniert gefundene Stücke aus dem späteren Mittelalter, die ganz aus den Buchstaben *i m n u* bestehen, hierher gehören: der von W. Meyer, 'Die Buchstabenverbindungen der sogenannten gotischen Schrift,' *Abhandlungen der kgl. Gesellschaft der Wissenschaften zu Göttingen, phil.-hist. Kl.,* N.F., I, 6 (1897), S. 97 f. veröffentlichte Brief der 'mimi numinum niuium' und der Vers 'iui muniui uinum minimum minuiui' in *London, B. M., Royal 17. C. XVII,* vgl. *Catalogue of Royal and King's Manuscripts,* II, 243. Doch entstammen sie höheren Bildungsstufen.

'omnia nocent nimia et omnia mensurata placent'

(13 Buchstaben; *Clm 14311*, fol. 1ʳ; *S. Gallen 9*, p. 300; *ib. 49*, p. 314; *ib. 113*, hinten, in Urkundenschrift *s*. IX; *ib. 155*, p. 402; *ib. 157*, p. 1; *ib. 672*, p. 255; *Zürich, C 68*, vorn; meist *s*. X).

'omnia vincit amor et nos cedamus amori'

(Vergil, *Ecl*. X, 69, mit 14 Buchstaben; Lindsay, *Palaeographia latina* II, 29; häufig, vom IX. Jahrhundert ab).

'omnia cum domino dona redisse suo'

(dieser Pentameter—woher?—, mit 11 Buchstaben, tritt erst im XI. und XII. Jahrhundert auf; *Erlangen 57*, vorn; *Köln, Dombibl. 78*, fol. 96ᵛ; *ib. 211*, fol. 84ᵛ; *Clm 14286*, fol. 212ᵛ; *Clm 15808*, fol. 123ᵛ; *S. Gallen 63*, p. 320; *ib. 135*, p. 467; *ib. 276*, p. 279; *Stuttgart, HB. VI 113*, fol. 223ᵛ; *Würzburg, Mp. th. fol. 34*, fol. 16ᵛ).

In Süddeutschland scheint auch die Zeile

'Infelix vitulus sudibus quam saepe ligatus'

als Schulübung in Umlauf gewesen zu sein (*Augsburg, Ordinariatsbibl. 4*, fol. 62ʳ, *s*. X–XI; *Einsiedeln 18*, p. 333, *s*. X–XI; *Clm 6398*, vorn, *s*. X; *Würzburg, Mp. th. fol. 7*, fol. 71ᵛ, *s*. X). Die beiden Hältfen des Verses finden ihre wörtliche Entsprechung in zwei Versen der *Ecbasis captivi* (248 und 66), deren Dichter also die Schulsentenz verarbeitet hat.[26]

Daneben scheinen aber auch—wie im griechischen Ägypten[27]—systematische Silbenreihen geübt worden zu sein von dem Typus *ba be bi bo bu* etc. (*Berlin, theol. fol. 346*, fol. 277ᵛ, bis *fa*, *s*. X; *Rom, Vat. Reg. lat. 846*, fol. 1ʳ bis *ne*, *s*. IX; *Würzburg, Mp. th. fol. 19*, fol. 1ʳ, bis *du*, *s*. IX und X).[28]

Die Plattform für alle weiteren Studien war erreicht mit der Beherrschung der sämtlichen 23 Buchstaben. Um diese zur Geltung zu bringen und um der trockenen Materie einen Anreiz zu geben, konstruierte wohl in der Zeitenwende vom Altertum zum Mittelalter oder schon früher ein Schulmeister, wie viele andere nach ihm, für den Schreibunterricht einen Hexameter, in dem alle Buchstaben vertreten waren.[29] Es ist nicht festzustellen, ob

'Adnixique globum Zephyri freta kanna secabant'

oder

'Ferunt Ophyr convexa kymba per liquida gazas'

---

[26] Für die Frage nach der Verbreitung der *Ecbasis* (K. Strecker, 'Ecbasisfragen,' *Historische Vierteljahrsschrift*, XXIX, 503) sind die Federproben ohne Gewicht.

[27] Beispiele bei E. Ziebarth, *Aus der antiken Schule* (2. Aufl. Bonn, 1913), S. 3 f.

[28] In *Bern 207* (wohl aus dem Ende des VIII. Jahrhunderts, trotz Lindsays Zweifel, *Palaeographia Lat*. II, 64) steht auf fol. 3ʳ als Probe der irischen Oghamschrift ein Alphabet und eine vollständige Silbenreihe nach dem Muster der lateinischen.

[29] Im Osten wurden schon im ersten nachchristlichen Jahrhundert ähnliche griechische Alphabetverse in der Schule gelernt; vgl. Dornseiff, *Alphabet*, SS. 69 f., der darin eine Sprechübung erblickt.

zuerst auf dem Plan war, oder ob beide andere Vorgänger hatten; für diese Verse setzen die Zeugnisse im VII. Jahrhundert ein, für beide in Spanien. 'Adnixique' wird von Julian von Toledo in seiner Grammatik zitiert;[30] 'adnixiqu' liest man in Halbunziale des VII. Jahrhunderts in *Berlin, Phill. 1761*, fol. 148[r] (aus Lyon). Eine Federprobe in merovingischer Kursive des VIII. Jahrhunderts in *Autun 107*, fol. 24[v], lautet: 'adnixique globum zyppere / freta kanna secchabant / in medio campo'; danach scheint der Vers eine Fortsetzung besessen oder nachträglich erhalten zu haben. Vom IX. bis xum XI. Jahrhundert war er allgemein in Anwendung, jetzt regelmässig mit der Schreibung 'adnexique'; ich fand über 60 Beispiele, aus denen ich wenige herausgreife: *Bern 338*, fol. 5[v]; *Kassel, theol. qu. 6*, fol. 37[r] (eingeritzt); *Manchester, John Rylands Library 12*, fol. 10[r]; *Oxford, Bodley 572*, fol. 58[r]; *S. Gallen 136*, p. 214 (in sehr roher Schrift, von einem Autodidakten ?); *Würzburg, Mp. th. fol. 21*, fol. 50[v]. In *Clm 536* (*s.* XII), *Clm 14731* (*s.* XII), und *Rom, Vat. lat. 822* (*s.* XIV) steht 'Adnexique' von der Hand des Textschreibers in Majuskelbuchstaben zwischen zwei Kreisen am Ende von Honorius *de imagine mundi*. Den Vers durch ein entschieden christliches Beispiel zu ersetzen scheint mit dem zwiefachen Schreibmuster

> 'Te canit adcelebratque polus, rex gazifer, hymnis
> trans Zephyrique globum scandunt tua facta per axem'

(*S. Gallen 913*, p. 89, *s.* VIII, angelsächsisch; zu lesen ist 'kanit', 'skandunt'; vgl. G. Baesecke, *Der Vocabularius S. Galli*, Halle 1933, S. 3)

beabsichtigt gewesen zu sein. Er fand noch andere Nachahmungen:

> 'Dum Zephyri fluctus'

(so unvollständig in *Paris B. N. lat. 17401*, fol. 44[v], *s.* X)

und später:

> 'Exurgens Kaurum duc, Zephyre, flatibus equor'

(*Chartres 39*, *s.* X, fol. 172[v] 'en grande écriture allongée'; *Clm 28363*, fol. 136[v], *s.* XIV; *Oxford, Balliol College 367*, fol. 10[r], *s.* XII).

Der zweite sehr alte Alphabetvers:

> 'Ferunt Ophyr convexa kymba per liquida gazas'

begegnet schon als halbunziale Federprobe in dem Augustinus *de baptismo* des *Escorial* (spanischen Ursprungs; vgl. W. von Hartel, *Bibliotheca patrum latinorum Hispaniensis*, Wien 1886, S. 7: 'ferunt ob iocum fexum cimbe per liquet'). In karolingischer Zeit reicht seine Verbreitung von Corbie bis Regensburg und bis Vercelli: aus 42 mir bekannten Belegen

---

[30] *Anecdota Helvetica* ed. H. Hagen (Lipsiae, 1870), p. CCXXX: 'Da ubi pro duplice (*scil.* x littera): Adnixique etc.'

wähle ich aus: *Cambridge, Fitzwilliam Museum, MacClean Bequest 6;
Karlsruhe, Aug. XCIII*, fol. 2ʳ (mit Neumen); *Köln, Dombibliothek 105*,
fol. 90ʳ; *London, B. M., Harley 5792*, fol. 277ʳ; *Clm 14437*, fol. 12ʳ (eingeritzt); *Paris B. N., lat. 13028*, fol. 1ʳ (in Diplomschrift: 'ferunt ex Ophyr'
etc.); *S. Gallen 278*, p. 514 (in Geheimschrift, die Vokale durch *b f k p x*
ersetzt); *Verona, Capit. XXI* (aus Vercelli), fol. 63ᵛ; *Würzburg, Mp. th.
fol. 41*, fol. 18ʳ.

Elemente von 'Adnexique' und 'Ferunt Ophyr' vereinigt der jüngere
Vers
'Equore cum gelido Zephirus fert xenia kymbis'
(*Durham, B IV 24*, dazu: 'Y quod habens' etc., vgl. unten, davor die Über-
schrift 'In his duobus versibus continentur omnes litterae abecedarii', vgl.
Lindsay, *Pal. lat.* II, 30; *Lambeth 259; ib. 335; ib. 377; London, B.M., Arundel 213*,
foll. 94ᵛ, 101ʳ; *Metz, Coll. Salis 32*, fol. 12ʳ; *Rom, Vat. Regin. lat. 846*, fol. 91ᵛ).

Seine Bezeugung setzt mit den XI. (?) Jahrhundert ein und reicht bis
ins XV. Jahrhundert wie diejenige von 'Exurgens Kaurum' scheint sie
auf französisches und anglonormannisches Gebiet beschränkt.

Eine unabhängige Erfindung wohl des IX. Jahrhunderts, aus Regens-
burg oder Freising, stellt der Vers dar:
'Clam Kraton iudexque Zenophylus abdita fingunt'
(*Clm 6236*, fol. 1ʳ, vollständig, *s.* XI; *Clm 6263*, fol. 178ᵛ; *Clm 6309*, fol. 78ᵛ;
Clm 13038, fol. 1ʳ, *s.*IX; *Clm 14480*, fol. 94ᵛ.)

Die beiden Namen sind nicht willkürlich gewählt: es sind die beiden vor-
nehmen Heiden, die Kaiser Konstantin zu Schiedsrichtern der Disputation zwischen Papst Silvester und den jüdischen Ältesten bestellt; vgl.
Vita s. Silvestri, lib. II, bei B. Mombritius, *Sanctuarium* (Paris 1910) II,
516 *sqq.* Mit Hilfe dieser Namen umfasst auch das Verspaar

'Kraton iudicium iudexque Zenophyle iustum
. . . ibus ambiguis aequo moderamine fertis'

sämtliche Buchstaben (*Einsiedeln 319*, fol. 109ʳ, *s.* X, radiert); es ist wohl
durch 'Clam Kraton' angeregt worden, wie denn zwischen Regensburg
und Einsiedeln recht enge Verbindungen bestanden.
Ganz vereinzelt stehen folgende Zeilen:

'Scribe sagax, Mahtfrid, karis quod plus cano gazis'
(*Berlin, Phill. 1877*, aus S. Vincenz in Metz, fol. 138ᵛ, *s.* IX–X),

'Quam pulchre ymnizat fondens vox Belgika cantum'
(*Trier, Stadtbibliothek 1156/459*, fol. 75ᵛ, *s.* X),

'Mox Ezrae digitis Cypriane . . . quoque facis'
(*S. Gallen 579*, p. 324, *s.* X; die Nachbarschaft der von der gleichen Hand
geschriebenen 'Adnexique' und 'Ferunt Ophyr' legt es nahe, diesen verstümmelt

erhaltenen Vers aufzunehmen. Da *b h k l* noch fehlen, ist die Lücke vielleicht mit 'Balakh'—statt 'Balac,' vgl. Num. XXII ff.—zu schliessen),

'Zelum karnis pax fugat quam Eli dinoscebat'

(*S. Gallen, Vad. 337*, letztes Bl., *s.* IX, in französischer Schrift; lies 'Hely.' Die beiden Halbzeilen bestehen aus je 7 Silben),

'Tote viginti tres litere.
Sic fugiens, dux, zelotypos, quam karus haberis'

(*Venedig, Bessar.* 497, *s.* XII: Baehrens, *Poetae latini minores*, III, 169).

Ein Alphabetvers scheint auch in der verderbten, überlangen Zeile

'Zonam namque rubrum calamo pro oc tibi figitur ast strisx'

(*Berlin, Phill. 1716*, fol. 6ᵛ, *s.* X) enthalten. In einigen Versen wird die volle Reihe der Buchstaben mittels Einsetzen der fehlenden statt Worten und Silben hergestellt:

'Y quod habens signat mihi lex profitens katecizat'

(*Durham, B IV 24, s.* XI, vgl. oben zu 'Equore'; hier kann eine Erinnerung an die 'littera Pythagorica' vorgeschwebt haben)

und

'Ymniza Christo pluteo qui pingis in isto
de cuius calamo scribitur .f. .h. deo'

(*Berlin, Phill. 1877*, fol. 138ᵛ, *s.* IX–X, aus S. Vincenz in Metz; xƥo Hs. Das Distichon gibt sich als Inschrift eines Schreibpultes).

All den bisher vorgeführten Versen und Sprüchen steht die Harmlosigkeit an der Stirn geschrieben. Dagegen reicht ein zur Hälfte rhythmischer Spruch, der im IX. und X. Jahrhundert als Federprobe nicht selten erscheint, vielleicht in das Gebiet des Aberglaubens hinein; ist er doch auch in Chiffernschrift und in das griechische Alphabet übertragen worden. Besprechen und Besegnen und das Vertrauen auf geschriebene Talismane waren im Volksglauben sehr lebendig. Der Gebrauch des Alphabets zu magischen Zwecken, den das antike Zauberwesen so reichlich ausgebildet hat, ist zwar im Mittelalter auf geistlichem Gebiet ausserhalb der Kirchenweihe, auf weltlichem ausserhalb der Onomatomantik und des Losens nicht so direkt nachzuweisen,—dass der kadenzierte Text, der im ersten Teile von den Englen zu reden scheint, das ganze Alphabet in sich barg, mochte den Glauben an seine Kraft bestärken. Es erscheint möglich, dass er des ABCs wegen in der Schule gelehrt, von anderen aber als zauberkräftig angesehen wurde, und also nebeneinander eine harmlose und eine hintergründige Existenz führte. Die verbreitetste und wohl ursprüngliche Form lautet:

'Fixa manent,
pectus habent,
ymnum kanent,

quoniam zelum Domini exercituum timor gehenne castigat'

(*Berlin, Phill. 1869*, 139ʳ, *s*. X; *Karlsruhe, Aug. CLV*, fol. 128ʳ, *s*. X; *Aug. CCXXVII*, fol. 254ʳ; *Köln, Dombibliothek 40*, fol. 117ʳ; *Clm 18628*, fol. 95ʳ, in Geheimschrift, *s*. X, vollständig; *Paris, B.N., lat. 13038*, fol. 1ᵛ, *s*. IX, teilweise in Diplomschrift, teilweise in Minuskel; *Rom, Vat. Regin. lat. 846*, fol. 79ᵛ, *s*. IX, hinter einem verballhornten griechischen Alphabet, in dieses übertragen, und in Minuskel, vollständig; *S. Gallen 2*, pp. 1, 2, *s*. IX; *ib. 156*, hinten, *s*. IX; *Stuttgart, HB. II. 54*, fol. 259ᵛ, *s*. IX; 'kanent' ist regelmässig). ·

Eine andere Fassung verändert die rhythmische Form, ist jedoch vielleicht nicht vollständig überliefert, da ein Wort mit *b* fehlt bezw. das von *Harley 5792* gebotene 'habent' aus der ersten Fassung den Rhythmus zerstört:

> 'Fixa manent pectora
> hymnizantes karmina
> iungunt zelo faciem
> dicunt que superna'

(*Berlin, lat. fol. 746*, 127ʳ, *s*. X, aus S. Maximin in Trier; *Leipzig, Stadtbibl. Rep. II fol. 6*, fol. 1ʳ, *s*. IX, bis 'zelo faciemque,' aus Hildesheim; *London, B. M. Harley 5792*, fol. 277ʳ: einmal 'pectora habent ymn. carm. iung. cum iocunditate exhibitis,' *s*. IX oder X, einmal 'f.m.p. habent hym,' in Diplomschrift *s*. IX oder X).

Die witzigste Einkleidung hat der so zählebige schriftpädagogische Gedanke, das Alphabet in einem Hexameter zusammenzufassen, im XII. Jahrhundert auf niederdeutschem Boden gefunden. Wie ein Märchen liest sich die Geschichte von den sechs Brüdern und den sechs Schwestern mit den merkwürdigen, 'heidnischen' Namen. Sie ist von der Art, dass ein Kind ihr lauschen könnte, ohne anfangs die erzieherische Absicht zu durchschauen, bis es plötzlich am Ende sich überlistet sähe, wenn die braven Kinder schreiben gelernt haben. Das Gedicht ist aus Werden an der Ruhr überliefert (in *Berlin, theol. lat. fol. 367*, fol. 1ʳ, *s*. XII) und mag, nach den Namen zu urteilen—soweit sie nicht aus Verlegenheit gebildet wurden wie Exquenamoth—im Umkreis dieses Stiftes entstanden sein; am Anfang ist es infolge Rasur einer Zeile unvollständig. Es lautet (nach V. Rose, *Verzeichnis der lateinischen Handschriften der k. Bibliothek zu Berlin* II, 1, S. 175):

'. . . . .
nomina Christicolis quamquam[31] gentilia nobis.
Sic sunt sex fratres dicti sex atque sorores:
Uffing, Saxrichus, Merkbold, Tyzo, Bobbo, Quirichus,
Exquenamoth, Frethuhild, Thietburg, Kanka, Azila, Spothild.
5   Uffing duxerat Exquenamoth, Saxrich Frethuhildam,

---

[31] Für eine Kollation habe ich Norbert Fickermann zu danken. 1 'quēquā' (a *aus* e *korr. m. 1*) cod., Rose 4 'Exque namoth' 12 'c̄sangᵘ¹nitatē' korr. m. 1.

Merkbold Thietburgam, pulcher pulchram Tyzo Kankam,
Bobbo Azilam gnarus, Spothildam scriba Quirichus.
Bis terni fratres senas duxere sorores
uxores, mox et natis ex his generatis—
10   quisque unum natum natam generavit et unam—
dant natis patres, dant natabus sua matres
nomina; multiplicem recolunt consanguinitatem.
Edocuere patres sua scribere nomina natos,
sic matresque suas quamque omnia scribere natas.
15   Sic omnes sunt scribendi facti bene gnari.
Haec qui scribere scit, quicquid vult scribere novit.
hic abecedarium quia scribitur omne Latinum;
scribere quod discat, compte quicumque cupiscat.

Ein eigenartiges Nachleben war dem Verse

'Gaza frequens Lybicos duxit Karthago triumphos'

beschieden. Entstanden zu einer Zeit, als die Gattung schon abstarb, vielleicht nach dem Vorbilde von 'Ferunt Ophyr,' war er bis zur grossen Revolution nicht in Vergessenheit geraten. Der früheste Beleg, aus dem XII. Jahrhundert, findet sich in *Clm 29063 b*, aus Schäftlarn, einem liturgischen Fragment, das ungeübten Händen zur Niederschrift einer Legende vom Kreuzesholz und zu Federproben gedient hat. Aus dem XIV. bis XVI. Jahrhundert stammen die Einträge in *Merseburg 67*, *Clm 14787*, fol. 500ᵛ; *Clm, 26888* (auf einem lose inliegenden Blatt); *Schlägl 4. Cpl. 161*, fol. 84ʳ; *Wien, lat. 4120*, fol. 206ᵛ; *Zwettl 115*, fol. 61ʳ. Mit diesem Hexameter beginnt ein spätes grammatisches Gedicht, das in *Clm 19661*, vom Jahre 1430, fol. 2ʳ bis 48ᵛ und *Wien, lat. 5171*, *s.* XV, fol. 19ʳ bis 266ʳ (?) überliefert ist; ein Commentator gibt die Begründung 'Eo quod presens speculacio est tractare de quatuor speciebus artis gramatice, quarum prima dicitur orthographia, cuius subiectum est littera, ergo primum ponitur metrum scilicet "Gaza" etc. continens numerum litterarum' (*Clm 19661*, fol. 2ʳ). In einer Anleitung, das Lateinische mit hebräischen Buchstaben zu schreiben, in *Clm 641 s.* XV bedient sich der Autor des Verses, um die Übertragung sämtlicher lateinischer Buchstaben in das fremde Alphabet, das gelegentlich als Geheimschrift diente, an einem praktischen Beispiel zu zeigen.[32] Mit einigen Abweichungen in der Wahl der Buchstaben und in der Punktierung steht eine hebräische Umschrift auch in *Einsiedeln 377*, *s.* XII–XIII, pp. 72/73. Diese mittelalterlichen Belege weisen alle auf den deutschen Kulturkreis als Verbreitungsgebiet. Die Tradition der Schreibmeister hat den Vers

---

[32] B. Walde, *Christliche Hebraisten Deutschlands am Ausgang des Mittelalters* (Münster i. W., 1916) S. 170.

offenbar weitergetragen. Noch 1789 gibt ihn Domingo Maria de Servidori in seinen *Reflexiones sobre la verdadera arte de escribir* (Madrid 1789) als Muster.[33]

Der Gedanke des Schulmeisters, der vielleicht gar nicht einmal originell, sondern der hellenistischen Unterrichtspraxis entlehnt war, hatte also einen erstaunlichen Erfolg. Wie andere Zeitalter etwa an modischen Rätseln eine Freude haben, so wurde das Ausklügeln neuer Alphabetverse mit einem gewissen sportlichen Eifer betrieben, oft ohne Rücksicht auf einen verständlichen Sinn. Bequeme Wörter wie: 'gaza,' 'kymba,' 'Zephirus,' 'hymnus' erbten sich dabei fort. Nach der handschriftlichen Überlieferung scheinen diese pädagogischen Spielereien etwa im VII. Jahrhundert von Spanien und Südfrankreich aus ihren Zug durch die Schulen anzutreten. In dem regen Schulleben der Karolingerzeit gedeihen und wuchern sie; viele der damals ausgetiftelten Verse sind nie in Umlauf gekommen. Über das XI. Jahrhundert hinaus retten sich nur wenige, und der jüngste, 'Gaza frequens,' ist wohl im XII. Jahrhundert ausgedacht worden; es nimmt wunder, dass gerade das späte Mittelalter, dem jeder Rest einer Scheu vor dem Missbrauch der metrischen Form geschwunden war, nichts mehr von der Art hervorgebracht hat.[34]

ANHANG

Anhangsweise stelle ich solche Einträge aus dem IX. bis XII. Jahrhundert zusammen, die dazu anspornen, das Schreiben zu lernen oder zu üben. Der Form nach meist Monostichen variieren sie vielfach den Gedanken des griechischen Schulspruches φιλοπόνει, ὦ παῖ, μὴ δαρῇς und wie dieser[35] sind sie auch wohl selbst zum Nachschreiben aufgegeben worden. Der erste richtet sich ausdrücklich an den Anfänger, der noch auf der Wachstafel übt.

'Disce, puer, tabulis, quo possis scribere kartis'
(*Karlsruhe, Aug. CCXX*, fol. 1ᵛ, s. X; *Aug. XIV*, fol. 109ᵛ, s. IX oder X, mit: 'disse,' 'tauulis,' 'quod,' 'cartis')

'Iam, dilecte puer, penna sit pinger⟨e⟩ notas'
(*S. Gallen 9*, p. 266, ca. s. IX–X).

'Disce, puer, nigras depingere'
(*Karlsruhe, Aug. CCLV*, fol. 53ᵛ, s. IX, unvollständig; vgl. 'Disce, puer, varias rerum depingere formas' bei Wattenbach, *Schriftwesen*, 267).

'Disce, puer, manibus mercedem quaerere doctis'
(*S. Gallen 6*, p. 14; *ib. 876*, p. 338, danach: 'Ut lasso requies sit tibi virga, puer,' beide s. IX).

[33] H. Degering, *Die Schrift* (Berlin, 1929), Taf. 233.
[34] In Deutschland scheinen im XIV. und XV. Jahrhundert den Spruch 'Homo quidam fecit cenam magnam' (Luc. XIV, 16) bevorzugt haben, da er sich so oft als Federprobe findet (z. B.: *Clm 2535; Clm 12741; Trier, Stadtbibl. 170*).
[35] E. Ziebarth, *Aus der antiken Schule* (2. Aufl.), S. 6.

'Si bene non scribis, cutem meam denique perdis'
(sagt das Pergament; *Clm 14513*, fol. 95ʳ, s. XI).

'Si bene non scribis, verbera dura capis'
(*Clm 6236*, fol. 1ʳ, s. XI).

'Si bene non scribis, dorsum laceraberis'
(*Fulda, Aa 13*, fol. 1ʳ, s. XI).

'Pusio mi dulcis, cur sic non congrua scribis'
(*Clm 14368*, fol. 94ʳ, s. XI).

'Pinge, precor, similes apicum, mi pusio, formas,
ne te iam notis flagra petant odiis.'

'Hoc vigilanter ara studio votoque sagaci,
ne sulcet terram hinc mea palma tuam'
(*Darmstadt 739*, fol. 55ʳ, s. IX, aus S. Jakob in Lüttich).

'Scribe, puer, scribe, qui nomen habes Herimanne'
(*Einsiedeln 298*, p. 143, s. X oder XI).

'Scribere disce, puer, ne sis per singula pauper'
(*S. Gallen 579*, p. 323, s. XI).

'Scribere disce, puer, nec te'
(*Stuttgart, HB.* VII. *38*, fol. 97ᵛ, s. XII, 'disse' *cod.*; der Vers sollte vermutlich enden:
'ne te derideat alter,' Cato, *Dist.* III, 7).

'Scribere cum penna doceat me sancta Maria'
(*Clm 14471*, fol. 127ᵛ; *S. Gallen 207*, hinten; beide s.XII: Wattenbach, *Schriftwesen*,
SS. 228, 492).

'Artem scribendi comitatur cura timendi'
(*Clm 8104*, fol. 71, s. X–XI; P. Lehmann in Lindsay, *Palaeographia Latina*, IV (1925), S. 28).

Von dieser eintönigen Reihe hebt sich mit erfrischender Derbheit ab:

'Asinum vivo, qui scribere nescio'
(*Erlangen 217*, fol. 33ʳ, s. IX).

PLANEGG BEI MÜNCHEN.

HORACE: THE BEGINNING OF THE SILVER AGE

John Bridge

It is rash indeed to attempt to say anything new about Horace at this late date, nor can I, in truth, lay claim to novelty. It has long been known that literature did not flourish under the empire and that the principal cause was absence of freedom. My only excuse for the present venture is that most of those who have written of Horace since Sellar,[1] to whose classic treatment the present contribution aspires to be no more than a footnote, appear to be content with the mere mention of changed conditions. Since the principate was not overtly tyrannical, there is a tendency to assume that restrictions were not felt by writers of the Augustan age.[2] Such a view overlooks the circumstance that the essence of imperial restriction lies not so much in the character of the ruler as in the nature of the rule itself.

The main thesis of this paper is that literature is most vital when it makes articulate the thoughts, aims, and aspirations of a group; in short, when it is social. Moreover, the larger the group, the more nearly literature approaches the universal. When it fails to do this, when, instead of reflecting a social movement, it seeks merely to relieve the tedium of life and becomes an escapist device, or when it stoops to flattery of a ruler or a ruling class and degenerates into a decorative art, then the life has gone out of it. For readers of a subsequent era, as for those of its own time, it has two uses: it may continue to afford amusement, and it may serve as valuable evidence of the condition of the society that produced it. The vital element of activity is lacking. Such literature belongs, at its best, to an age of silver.

It was this social quality that was to a large degree responsible for the peculiar glories of Greek literature. In the words of Professor Ferguson:[3] 'her (Greece's) eminence in art, literature and philosophy was attained, not by the unaided efforts of solitary genius, nor yet alone by the upward movement of the masses; but her uniqueness resulted from the peculiar opportunities for working together of these two forces.' . . . 'The finest

---

[1] W. Y. Sellar, 'Horace and the Elegiac Poets,' *The Roman Poets of the Augustan Age* (2nd ed., 1899).

[2] E.g., T. Frank, *Catullus and Horace* (New York: Henry Holt and Co., 1928), p. 116, admits the influence of change, but minimizes it: 'it took generations of the imperial regime before men actually felt any restraining hand.'

[3] W. S. Ferguson, *Hellenistic Athens* (New York, 1911), p. i. & p. 1.

poetry and the noblest art, however individual in character and attribution, always appeared as the outcome of a popular interest or as the inevitable consequence of a social custom.'

Wherein, precisely, lies the greatness of Cicero? Is it not that in every line he wrote there is a reflection of an intense activity, an activity directed to the service of a nation in which he felt himself a vital element? That he identified the interests of the nation with the interests of the small privileged groups with which he was most closely associated is unimportant. The important thing is that he saw and felt that unless the antagonisms of these groups, the Senatorial aristocracy and the Equites, could be reconciled and his *concordia ordinum* made a reality within the existing framework of the state, the freedom of both groups would be gone, and gone with it whatever freedom existed within the state.

But Cicero lost, and it is with the effects of that loss that this paper is chiefly concerned. The victory of Caesar Octavianus was the culmination of a long period of struggle and civil war. From the outset the rule of the Senatorial landholders was doomed; victory of one of the military adventurers, supported by legionaries, debtors, and proletarians, was inevitable. More and more the men of business looked with favor on the idea of a strong man who, by restoring order to the state, would make it possible for them to carry on their business enterprises with a feeling of security. Such a man they found in Augustus whose consolidation of power in a strong, centralized government made the Roman world safe for men of affairs.

That the differences between the landholding aristocracy and the traders and financiers of the equestrian order had been reconciled was an indisputable fact. But the reconciliation was bought at a price more costly than Cicero would have been willing to pay. For the *concordia ordinum* of Augustus destroyed the privileged position of the *ordines* as the rulers of the state by creating and setting above them a new *ordo*, and that was the principate. That this was, in the then existing conditions of production, a gain must be granted. Economically the Roman world prospered under the principate. The cessation of civil war, the reorganization of the provinces, the security guaranteed agriculture and business, made the Augustan age, for landholders and businessmen, a golden age indeed.

But what of the world of letters? Why is it that so many have felt the great poetic achievement of the age to be a splendid failure? What lies behind the gentle pessimism of Virgil, the tears of things? Why is it that the most brilliant of the Augustan poets, Ovid, is, in the last analysis, an entertainer, a splendid entertainer, but, save when his entertainment enters the field of satire, little more? Why is it that the poet of greatest promise and the most clearseeing mind of the age failed to realize his promise and lapsed into silence at a time when his powers should have been undiminished? Why is it that the poetry of the age excels principally in craftsmanship, that substance is so frequently subordinate to style?

It is the contention of this paper that such tendencies of Augustan literature are directly due to the surrender of all real power into the hands of Augustus, that when the identity of prince and state became an unadmitted fact, the corollary was a transformation of citizens into subjects. The result of such a transformation was to shift emphasis from the community to the individual.[4] With the affairs of the nation safely in the hands of the leader, men had no need to be concerned with anything save their own individual interests.

This change in the nature of the state is reflected in the literature of the times. The transformation, however, did not take place in a single moment. It is for this reason that Horace is so valuable a guide to what took place. For in the changes that took place in him we can see the changes that came over literature as a whole. It is in the contradiction between his desires and potentialities on the one hand and his achievements on the other that we can discover why it was that the golden age did not continue with untarnished lustre to 14 A.D., but was entering the transmutation to silver at the very outset of the Augustan era.

Let us now see how Horace fitted into this changing scene and what effect the changes produced in his writings. His first contact with affairs of state of which we have definite knowledge was in Athens in 44 B.C., when the young poet took what was, perhaps, the most momentous step of his life and joined Brutus and the republicans in their effort to rescue the state from the hands of dictators. Youthful enthusiasm and the charm of Brutus may have influenced his decision, but there are other factors to be considered. In the first place, Horace was not only the son of a freedman, but also of a freedman who, as *praeco*, had followed a means of livelihood that by the *Lex Julia Municipalis* of the dictator Caesar served to bar a man from entry into the municipal magistracy and senate.[5] Secondly, as he himself tells us, he had received from his father the education of a son of the ruling class:[6]

[4] Cf. E. Zeller, *Stoics, Epicureans and Sceptics* (Eng. Trans. by O. J. Reichel, London, 1880), pp. 15–16: 'Greek philosophy, like Greek art, is the offspring of Greek political freedom. . . . With the decline of political independence . . . the mental powers of the nation received a fatal blow . . . weaned from the habit of working for the commonweal, the majority gave themselves up to the petty interests of private life and their personal affairs.'

[5] *Corpus Inscriptionum Latinarum*, I, 206.

[6] Sat., I, 6, 76–78.

sed puerum est ausus Romam portare, docendum
artis quas doceat quivis eques atque senator
semet prognatos.

Not only this education, but also the rustic background of Venusia, where
his father had apparently retired to the land, had contrived to give him a
certain community of feeling with the landed class, if not all of their prejudices.[7]

It is not surprising then that he chose to follow Brutus and the senatorial faction in an effort to restore the republic. The son of the ex-slave,
educated as one of the ruling class, now for the first time had an opportunity to stand on equal footing with the sons of that class and participate
with them in a common venture. It was an experience that made a deep
impression on him.

It is, perhaps, from this time that Horace's interest in the state of his
country dates, and the conflict between his awakened interest and the
subsequently changing conditions may explain much of his later literary
development. The conditions, moreover, began to change rapidly. The
brief period with Brutus soon came to an end. The hopes of the republicans were dashed at Philippi. Horace, not wishing to continue a hopeless
struggle, returned to Italy, a disillusioned and disappointed man. For
it is only upon the assumption that the struggle did appear hopeless and
that he was disillusioned that we can account for the mood of such poems
as the 16th and 8th epodes and the 2nd satire of the first book.

The 16th epode, one of his finest poems, can see no hope for the future
and proposes that Rome's better part leave Italy to its own destruction
and set forth upon the western seas to find a new home in some happy
islands. Familiar as the theme was, and despite a few idyllic details, the
proposal should not be dismissed as mere idle fantasy. The whole history
of Mediterranean development was a history of such departures from the
homeland in search of new shores, and the proposal may have been no
more unreal to Horace than the proposals that led our forefathers to for-
sake the shores of Europe for the new world.

Furthermore the poem has contact with reality at another point. We
see in the conditions of the new colony an outlook that runs like a main
thread through all of the works of Horace. For the life of this new world
is exclusively agricultural. That to which the poet turns yearning eyes is
the peasant economy of the great days of old. To make the point crystal
clear, he closes with a statement that the ship Argo had never reached
this land, nor Sidonian sailors. The naming of Phoenician traders makes
it clear that the Argo and the quest of the Golden Fleece are to be under-

---

[7] For this agrarian feeling see Epode 16, to be discussed later.

stood in this place as an allegory of trade. For it is trade and money that breed that destroyer of cities and men, the avarice he never wearies of assailing.[8] Such an outlook makes it easier to understand why his heart failed to warm to the principate which conferred its greatest benefits on the middle class.

But deeply felt as his *sollicitum taedium* was, there were no listeners. The poet stood alone in Rome, thrown back upon his own resources, his beloved land gone, his only source of livelihood the clerkship in the treasury office that he had managed to secure. It was a great descent from the experience of the preceding years. For a brief time he had participated with others in an attempt to influence and alter the life of his nation, one of a group transmuting common aspirations into action. Now, back in Rome, the ties are cut; he is divorced from the group spirit, an individual in the most disheartening sense of the word. From a colonel in the republican army he has become a treasury clerk, a mechanical part of office routine. It is not strange then that he became contemptuous of principles and causes, that his thoughts were turned inward upon his own personal problems and to mere pleasure seeking. It was no doubt in this period of revulsion from high enterprise that he set down the cynical observations on sexual morality of the second satire of book one. In his disillusionment he may also have toyed with the idea of marriage to some rich and libidinous old woman, and then turned from the thought with the feelings of disgust and loathing to which he gives voice in the eighth epode.

Nor is it at all unlikely that Horace's attacks on Stoic doctrine, such as appear in the third satire of book two, and the strictures upon too rigid a concept of virtue in the third of the first book also date from this period and are reflections of his disappointment with the republican cause. It has long been an accepted view that Stoicism was the unofficial philosophy of the Roman aristocracy.[9] Furthermore the outstanding symbol of principled support of the republic was the Stoic saint, Cato, who was the uncle and father-in-law of Brutus and whose son fought and died at Philippi.

We do not know definitely that the philosophic schools of Horace's time served as centers for the dissemination of political propaganda to the extent that they did in the times of Nero and Domitian,[10] though the remark of Plutarch[11] that Cicero's *Cato* and Caesar's reply both had their

---

[8] This obviously is the meaning of the last four lines: the age of gold is made corrupt by *aere*, i.e. money, and by *aere* the hearts of men are hardened to iron, i.e. to war.

[9] Ferguson, *Hellenistic Athens*, p. 341.

[10] M. Rostovtzeff, *Social and Economic History of the Roman Empire* (Oxford, 1926), pp. 109 ff.

[11] Caesar, 54.

ardent supporters would seem to indicate that in that period too philosophy had its practical applications.

If then, after Philippi, the Stoics are best represented by a survival of Cato's stern unyielding spirit of opposition, and if the Stoic position rested on the assumption that the 'foundation of all government rests upon a divine sanction,'[12] then Horace in abandoning opposition must of necessity have been at variance with the Stoics' uncompromising attitude. Hence in the third satire of the first book, where Horace ridicules a puritanic application of virtue and makes a plea for tolerance toward peccadillos, we may see a reflection of the struggle in his own mind and a justification of his withdrawal from the political conflict. It is but another aspect of what we see in Satires: I, 6, 19–22, where he renounces all claim to the right to participate in public affairs.

If Horace's epistles are a reflection of his whole experience, the lines:[13]

> Nunc agilis fio et mersor civilibus undis,
> virtutis verae custos rigidusque satelles,
> nunc in Aristippi furtim praecepta relabor
> et mihi res, non me rebus subiungere conor

take on new meaning. Horace's fluctuations between Stoicism and Epicureanism are due not merely to transitory moods, but reflect his relations to political conditions.[14]

His reaction from the disappointment of his republican venture not only turned him against the rigidity of Stoic principles, but also sent him into the camp of the Epicureans, where he served 'non sine gloria.' For this school, with its discouragement of all political ambition and all disinterested efforts to improve the condition of the people by legislation,[15] offered a welcome haven to those thrown upon their own resources. Hence Horace's many exquisite and delightful trivialities, exquisite and delightful trifles for which we may be deeply grateful, but trifles none the less.

Thus we may account for Horace's early reaction against Stoicism. Later, when the principate was an established fact and the wartime struggles ended, the Stoics had a new part to play. Against the earthly reality they could set up their ideal king, both as a means of justifying the existing rule and as a standard whereby they could measure the earthly man. With this changed situation Horace's later Stoic moments become understandable and appear not inconsistent with his former attitude. The

---

[12] G. H. Sabine and S. B. Smith, *Cicero on the Commonwealth* (Columbus, Ohio: Ohio State University Press, 1929), p. 48.

[13] Epistles: I, 1, 16–19.

[14] Horace refers to the period of the civil wars in metaphors drawn from the sea in Od., II, 7 15–16, and also in the Ship of State, Od., I, 14.

[15] A. W. Benn, *The Greek Philosophers* (London, 1914), p. 379.

Stoic ideal had then become a means whereby Augustus could be reminded of his duties as a ruler. The figure of Phraates in the second ode of book II, for example, must have suggested to the contemporary reader a figure much nearer home. Augustus too might be excluded from the number of the blessed if he failed to meet the standards set by Virtue, a conclusion that grows upon the reader when he observes that the ode corresponds in position to the second ode of the first book, which is clearly an admonition to Augustus not to abuse his power and position.

But let us return to the poet's development. The mood of despair did not endure. He made new friends in the city, and above all aroused the interest of Maecenas. The gift of the Sabine farm, solving as it did his own personal problem by granting him that rustic paradise to which he had turned longing eyes in the sixteenth epode, must have gone far toward making the inevitable acceptable to him. The republic was gone, but life still remained and there was work to be done. Accordingly Horace attempted to plunge into the current of life and serve his country as teacher and satirist, even as Aristophanes and the writers of old comedy had done before him.

But it is just at this point that the contradiction between desires and conditions begins to make itself felt. For now, his brief experience of public life ended, he is compelled to live as an individual. It was a logical consequence that in his writings he should deal with individualistic themes the behavior of individuals in daily life, their social relations, but all from the point of view of securing the happiness of the individual.

Yet Horace does not appear to be fully conscious of the individualistic nature of his writings. He feels that the writer is a social force.[16] He does not yet realize that the social force of a writer restricted largely to the field of individual behavior differs from the social force of a writer who concerns himself with the organizations of human society. For, when in the fourth satire of the first book he cites the literary ancestry of his satire, he names Aristophanes and the writers of old comedy as chief among his progenitors. These are the men, he says, from whom his master, Lucilius, stems. There is an important omission in this family tree, for Aristophanes and his contemporaries were political satirists and a vital force in the affairs of state, while Horace is most closely akin to the writers of new comedy who dealt with types and manners of men in their day to day relations to one another, but not at all with men in their relations to the state or to society as a whole. Hence the 'timelessness' of the new comedy and of much of Horace. For when men are gathered together, they do eat and drink, love, quarrel, and jest, and give way to

[16] For his statements see Od. III, 1, 1–4 & Epis. II, 1, 124 ff.

peccadillos in much the same manner in all ages and climes. These things are inevitable and not at all important to the rulers of states—nor important for the progress and development of society. Hence the fact that they can appear in the literature of all times and places.

Horace, I say, overlooks this really vital factor in his literary inheritance and the omission can perhaps be explained by his experience. Though he is excluded from public life, the force of his brief period of activity remains. He imagines that, like Aristophanes or Lucilius, he may still be a vital factor in Roman life, and is not yet fully aware of the restrictions imposed by conditions materially different from those under which Aristophanes or Lucilius wrote. This lack of awareness seems to be substantiated by the fact that when in the same satire (I, 4, 48–52) he deals with the substance of comedy, the scene is clearly drawn from new comedy.

The awareness, however, grew upon him; more and more as his craftsmanship and technical excellence forced themselves on the attention of readers, so did the contradiction between his potentialities and his actual achievements become apparent. For Horace, as is demonstrated by almost every line he wrote, was a man who could do what he wished with words. Yet in what he actually produced, something was lacking and not only did he know it, but the Romans who read his works knew it as well, and called for something better. Again and again comes the call, and the promise. The reply to his critics in the dialogue with Trebatius (Sat. II, 1) and the latter's laconic admonition *quiescas* (unless something better be forthcoming); his protestations of lack of ability to handle great themes, recurring with monotonous frequency throughout his works; the references to the hostile attitude of public and critics,[17] all point to one and the same conclusion, that Horace was a man to whom his own ironic reproach to the philosophic Iccius could be applied, *pollicitus meliora*.[18]

Nor is the reason for this failure to live up to promises far to seek. Horace knew the things that were essential for poetry destined to awake an answering chord in the reader's mind. He tells us quite clearly in the *Ars Poetica* (99–103):

> Non satis est pulchra esse poemata; dulcia sunto,
> et, quocumque volent, animum auditoris agunto.
> Ut ridentibus arrident, ita flentibus adsunt
> humani voltus: *si vis me flere, dolendum est
> primum ipsi tibi;*

[17] Epis. I, 19, 35 ff. This hostility may well underlie the attack on public indifference to contemporary voices in Epis. II, 1.

[18] Od. I, 29, 16.

That is, a poet must feel before he writes; he must be in the grip of an emotion in order to call forth an emotional response. Moreover, Horace, for all his philosophic detachment, his wit and urbanity, his acceptance of the maxim *nil admirari*, was a man who could and did feel deeply.

What then prevented him from setting this feeling free in his poetry, from writing the great songs that would have made him the great poet of his promises? The answer that we can deduce from the evidence of his works is that the things about which he felt deeply were, with few exceptions, things that were not acceptable to the ruling powers. For the dearest thing to Horace's heart was the fate of his country, and his thoughts of his country were linked up with a past that contrasted strongly with the present reality.[19]

Why is it that two of the poems in which he displays his strongest emotions close with a sudden retreat in which he reproaches his muse for attempting serious strains? When in the odes (I, 6) he first renounces all claim to epic ability and, after complimenting Agrippa by indirection, concludes with the words:

> nos convivia, nos proelia virginum
> sectis in iuvenes unguibus acrium
> cantamus vacui, sive quid urimur,
> non praeter solitum leves

we might accept the disclaimer at face value and look no further. But in the two other poems it is a different matter. For in the first ode of the second book Horace's feelings seem for the first time to overpower him, and the theme that arouses this strong emotion is none other than the fall of the republic, *periculosae plenum opus aleae*, with its attendant ruin of civil war. The stanzas:

> Quis non Latino sanguine pinguior
> campus sepulcris impia proelia
>   testatur auditumque Medis
>   Hesperiae sonitum ruinae?

> Qui gurges aut quae flumina lugubris
> ignara belli? Quod mare Dauniae
>   non decoloravere caedes?
>   Quae caret ora cruore nostro?

are among the strongest he ever wrote. Immediately after them, however, stands the rebuke to his muse:

> Sed ne relictis, musa procax, iocis
> Ceae retractes munera neniae;

[19] Horace, as the irony of his fulsome tribute to Augustus in the first epistle of the second book shows, was too clearheaded a man to mistake the Augustan 'revival' for reality.

mecum Dionaeo sub antro
quaere modos leviore plectro.

Surely this is more than a conventional device of contrast borrowed from his lyric predecessors. Horace seems suddenly to remember his present situation and to be reminded that by his acceptance of the *status quo* he had said goodbye to all that.

Again in the third ode of book three we find a similar conclusion. When we study this ode, we find that it too is a poem of great strength dealing with the destiny of the nation. Whether the speech of Juno which constitutes the body of the poem is to be interpreted as a warning against removing the seat of government to the East or against establishing an oriental despotism in Rome need not concern us here. The main point is that the intense feeling of the poet speaks out in tones of no uncertain admonition. Why, then, did he add the concluding stanza, so similar in spirit to that of the ode to Pollio:

Non hoc iocosae conveniet lyrae:
quo, musa, tendis ? Desine pervicax
referre sermones deorum et
magna modis tenuare parvis.

unless he were conscious of a lack of freedom and felt that the participation of citizens in matters for which responsibility rested solely in the hands of Augustus was no longer welcome or desired.

When we turn now to two other odes of great power, odes in which the promises of the poet are fully realized, we note that although the odes are even more serious in strain and nobler in thought, there is no note of apology, no concluding reminder that he is a poet of lighter themes. The reason may well be that these poems dealt with themes that a poet could handle without fear of giving offence. For these two poems, which are perhaps his greatest, draw their inspiration from the great days of old. Nor does one feel as one reads them that the noble past lives again in the present. In the one, the famous fifth of the third book, the heroic figure of Regulus is made to stand out in intentional contrast with the corruption of the present. The other, the Pindaric fourth of book four, is in honor of the young Drusus, but it is the victory of Metaurus river and the dismay of Hannibal as he receives the news of his brother's death that stir the reader; the Pindaric technique has, perhaps, been too successful and Drusus is all but forgotten.

It would seem then that Horace, in order to give free rein to his poetic feelings and to write that for which he felt no need of apologizing, was compelled to turn to the past. There are, to be sure, exceptions to this, but exceptions which upon examination support rather than weaken such a conclusion. The most noteworthy is the Cleopatra ode which celebrates the events following upon the victory at Actium. Here, indeed, we have a poem of considerable power, inspired by a contemporary event, and that event none other than the greatest victory of Augustus. Yet it is significant that not only does the poem derive its greatness, not from Caesar, the pursuer, but from the tragic figure of the defeated queen who stands forth at the end in stately grandeur, *non humilis mulier triumpho*, but also that it is a second attempt. For the words *nunc est bibendum . . . antehac nefas depromere Caecubum* clearly look to the opening of the ninth epode,

> Quando repostum Caecubum ad festas dapes
> victore laetus Caesare
> tecum sub alta (sic Iovi gratum) domo
> beate Maecenas, bibam?

Moreover, the earlier poem shows how far from inspired Horace really was by that victory. Indeed the concluding lines with their hint of the unpleasant consequences of too much celebration, *vel quod fluentem nauseam coerceat*, make the compliment to Caesar somewhat short of perfect.

And there again we run up against the obstacle that seems to have barred the way to the fulfillment of Horace's promise. The motto of literature in the Augustan age might well have been *aut Caesar aut nullus*. The poet to fulfill his mission should deal with the contemporary scene and the contemporary scene was dominated by Augustus and his circle. Horace did his best but the odes in praise of Augustus are all noticeable for their lack of warmth and inspiration. For the rest, he was confronted by two alternatives, moral preachings and the lighter trivialities. In his didactic pieces he could and did vigorously assail the avarice that did so much to bring on the civil wars. The lesson, however, was simple and too much repetition became monotonous. The trivialities are pleasing, but there is a limit to their power to please. It is not strange then that Horace felt the burden of increasing years weigh heavily upon him and sought to put aside his playthings.

He was grateful to Augustus for one thing, the restoration of peace, and he expresses his gratitude well in the fourteenth ode of book three:

> ego nec tumultum
> nec mori per vim metuam tenente
> Caesare terras.

Augustus had done much, but the peace and security of the age were purchased at the price of a transformation of citizens into subjects. Since this was so, there was nothing else to do but accept the situation, and leave everything in Caesar's hands. This is the note that runs through the poet's peaceful and somewhat weary farewell to the reader in the final ode of the fourth book, which sums up the achievements of Augustus in the words beginning, *Tua, Caesar, aetas*, and closes with the pleasing suggestion of the concluding stanzas:

Nosque et profestis lucibus et sacris
inter iocosi munera Liberi,
    cum prole matronisque nostris
    rite deos prius adprecati,

virtute functos more patrum duces
Lydis remixto carmine tibiis
    Troiamque et Anchisen et almae
    progeniem Veneris canemus.

that the greatest achievement of the age was the epic of his friend Virgil.

So let it be. Peace reigns and young and old shall sing, the glories of the past. Horace was tired, because there was no more work that he could do and keep his self-respect. He was almost superfluous. Roman life as an adventure of the Roman people was at an end. The state and the people had become separate. The state was Caesar and when individuals participated in the routine of the state, they did so as Caesar's subjects. The people of course continued in their daily life, but that life finds its expression only in terms of their relations one to another, an expression that we see reflected in Horace's concern with ethical themes. It is not without significance that the only branch of literature that did not lose its vitality under the empire was one which was able to give free expression to this relationship of individuals, a branch not commonly included in the category of literature, the writings of the jurists. For the rest, the gold was already turning to silver, and the silver rapidly lost its lustre.

COLLEGE OF THE CITY OF NEW YORK.

ZUR GESCHICHTE DER STIFTS-
BIBLIOTHEK VON ST. PETER
ZU BASEL

ALBERT BRUCKNER

UNTER DEN mittelalterlichen Bibliotheken Basels ist diejenige des ehemaligen, zwischen 1230 und 1233 errichteten und 1529 säkularisierten Chorherrenstiftes zu St. Peter bis jetzt kaum nennenswert bekannt. Die Geschichte des Chorherrenstifts St. Peter zu Basel selbst ist noch nicht geschrieben.[1] Ein reiches Archiv wird die Möglichkeit bieten, insbesondere die wirtschaftlichen Verhältnisses des Stiftes gründlich aufzuhellen.[2] Doch auch für die kulturgeschichtliche Seite ist den Akten und Urkunden Wertvolles abzugewinnen. So beleuchten denn gerade die verchiedenen Jahrzeitbücher, Testamente, Akten und Briefe auch die Geschichte der Bücherei; die Universitätsbibliothek Basel bietet in ihren Beständen dazu manchen, bis jetzt nicht näher lokalisierten Codex des alten Stifts.[3]

Die früheste mir bekannte Bücherschenkung an das Stift stammt aus der Mitte des 14. Jhs. Am 26. Juli 1358 machte der Thesaurar von St. Peter, *Johannes Sintz*, Spross einer alten Basler Familie, eine umfassende

---

[1] Vgl. etwa K. Lichtenhahn, 'Die Secularisation der Klöster und Stifter Basels,' in *Beiträge zur vaterländischen Geschichte*, 1 (Basel, 1839), 94–139 *passim*; R. Wackernagel, 'Das Kirchen- und Schulgut des Kantons Basel-Stadt,' *ibidem* 13 (*NF.* 3) (Basel, 1893), bes. 126–129 und *passim*; Joh. Bernoulli, 'Die Kirchgemeinden Basels vor der Reformation,' in *Basler Jahrbuch*, 1894, 228 f.; P. Ganz, 'Wandmalereien zu St. Peter in Basel,' in *Basler Zeitschrift für Geschichte und Altertumskunde*, 2 (Basel, 1903) 106–121; Ed. Schweizer, 'Das Basler Kirchen- und Schulgut in seiner Entwicklung bis zur Gegenwart,' *ibidem* 9 (1910), 177–346, bes. 340; R. Wackernagel, *Geschichte der Stadt Basel*, Bd. 1–3 (Basel, 1907–1924); E. A. Stückelberg, 'Die Wandgemälde der Predigerkirche,' in *Histor. Museum zu Basel, Jahresberichte und Rechnungen.... Jahr 1914*, (Basel, 1915), 12–13; idem, 'Die Wand- und Deckengemälde der Tresskammer zu St. Peter,' *ibidem*, 14–19; idem, in *Die Schweiz* (1915), p. 382; idem, 'Die Pfarr- und Stiftskirche St. Peter,' in *Basler Kirchen*, 2 (Basel, 1918), 54–82; idem, 'Die erhaltenen Wand- und Deckengemälde des Mittelalters in Basel,' in *Die Garbe* (1918); C. Roth, Artikel 'St. Peter,' in *Histor.-biograph. Lexikon der Schweiz*, 6 (Neuenburg, 1931), 77; Aug. Burckhardt, 'Junker Matthias Eberler, der Typus des reichen und kunstliebenden Baslers aus dem Ende des XV. Jahrhunderts,' in *Freiwillige Basler Denkmalpflege*, 1933, (Basel, 1934), 12–30 (vgl. auch diese Berichte Jg. 1927, 6–9, sowie 1933, 5).—Handschriftlich: R. Wackernagel, *Kollektaneen zur Geschichte der Basler Gotteshäuser, 5. St. Peter* (Staatsarchiv Basel, Handbibliothek B f 16).

[2] Vgl. am besten *Repertorium des Staatsarchivs zu Basel* (Basel, 1904), 491–502, St. Peter.

[3] Infolge beschränkten Raumes kann ich nicht näher auf die noch vorhandenen, bis jetzt nicht zusammengestellten Codices zu St. Peter eingehen. Ich hoffe, dies an anderer Stelle einmal nachholen zu können.

Vergabung zu Gunsten seiner Kirche.[4] Darin werden aufgeführt u.a.: Item libri sui orales qui sunt in duobus voluminibus et antiphonarium in eisdem libris notatum per usum, quos emit a domino Johanne de Meskilch[5] cum viginti septem florenis auri de Florentia ut dicebat.[6] Dieses Legat ergänzte er am 21. August 1361 zu Gunsten seiner natürlichen Töchter.[7] Ihnen vergabte er neben anderem scolasticam historiam scilicet librum scolastice historie et librum parvum horalem, doch sollte die Peterskirche librum suum horalem maiorem sowie alii libri sui zu ihrem Eigentum nehmen.[8]

Der bedeutende Chorherr zu St. Peter, *Heinrich von Rumersheim*,[9] Nachfolger Heinrichs von Nördlingen als Beichtvater der Gottesfreundin Margaretha zum goldenen Ring,[10] wies 1399 in einem umfangreichen Legat seinem Stift auch verschiedenes an Büchern zu: Item legavit, donavit et ordinavit psalterium suum mangnum ecclesie S. Petri Basiliensi sic tamen, quod affingatur kathene et apponatur in chorum eiusdem ecclesie S. Petri Basiliensis. Item legavit, deputavit et ordinavit libros suos orales, videlicet nocturnale et diurnale, discreto viro domino Nicolao de Durlistorffe,[11] canonico dicte ecclesie S. Petri Basiliensis.[12]

Von erheblicher Wichtigkeit für die Stiftsbibliothek war 1402 das grossartige Vermächtnis der *Adelheid Biedermann*,[13] die ob ihrer Gebefreudigkeit als reparatrix ecclesie S. Petri lange Zeit geehrt wurde. Die bibliotheksgeschichtlichen Einzelheiten lauten: Item ordinavit scribi quatuor antiphonarios, quorum tres sunt hyemales et unus estivalis, qui constant CCXX florenos. Item ordinavit scribi duo psalteria, qui constant XXXVIII libras. Item tradidit XXX florenos in subsidium ad scribendum novum missale spectans ad maius altare. . . . Item contulit prebende seu cappellanie eidem unum librum missale. Item duos horales

---

[4] Johannes Sintz wird erstmals 1342 als Kustos erwähnt. Er begegnet in dieser Funktion bis 1351 und erscheint bis 1361 als Thesaurar. Ueber die Familie W. Merz, *Die Burgen des Sisgaus*, 3 (Arau, 1911), 230 ff. und Stammtafel 15.

[5] Etwa Johannes von Messkilch, 1336 Priester in Endingen, 1343, 1347 Mittelmesser zu St. Martin ebenda? Vgl. *Oberbadisches Geschlechterbuch*, 3 (Heidelberg, 1919), 61.

[6] St. Peter Urkunde 478.

[7] Diese Töchter, Dorothea alias Thyna, Nesa (gest. 1360), Elisabeth und Anna waren Klosterfrauen zu Blotzheim im Elsass.

[8] St. Peter Urkunde 507.

[9] Ueber ihn R. Wackernagel, *Geschichte der Stadt Basel*, II, 791, 810. Er begegnet als Chorherr von St. Peter von 1377 bis 1425. Er starb 1434, vgl. St. Peter F (Anniversar des 15. Jhs.) Anhang 56.

[10] R. Wackernagel, *a.a.O.*, II, 791. Nach dem Tode der Gottesfreundin übergab Rumersheim den Einsiedler Waldschwestern zwei deutsche Mystikerhandschriften als ihr Vermächtnis, vgl. G. Morel, *Offenbarung der Mechtold von Magdeburg*, VI, VII; O. Ringholz, *Geschichte des Stifts Einsiedeln*: 1 (Einsiedeln, 1904), 324.

[11] Seit 1407 Chorherr, seit 1427 Scholasticus zu St. Peter.

[12] St. Peter Urkunde 720, 1399 feria Va proxima post dedicationem ecclesie Basiliensis.

[13] Zu Adelheid Biedermann R. Wackernagel, *a.a.O.*, II, 623, 708, 778, bes. 793, 796.

videlicet unum hyemale et alium estivale et psalterium. Item unum diurnale cum psalterio ... Item tria volumina librorum quorum unus est textus sententiarum, alia duo sunt glose desuper.[14]

Am 24. Mai 1436 stattete *Greda Lutringer*, die Frau des verstorbenen Conrad Lutringer alias zem Tor, ihre auf dem Altar zum hl. Kreuz in St. Peter gestiftete neue Präbende mit einem Missale im Werte von 28 Gulden aus,[15] und 1480 wurde die Stiftsbibliothek von dem Kustos *Johannes Husgow*[16] kurz vor seinem Tode mit einem Missale und zwei Gebetbüchern in Pergament beschenkt.[17]

Die inzwischen angewachsene Bibliothek wurde 1484 nach dem Standort der Bücher auf drei Pulten katalogisiert. Es handelt sich um rund 60 Bände, die im ganzen wenig bemerkenswertes bieten.[18] Aus eben dieser Zeit finden sich vereinzelte Aufzeichnungen über Kostbarkeiten und Bücher einzelner Kaplaneien zu St. Peter. Eine 'Bona et redditus Capplanie S. Marie versus ambitum' betitelte Liste verzeichnet neben anderem unum antiquum missale in pergameno und notiert: Item dominus Volricus Wetter ordinavit Cappellanie suum proprium missale inligatum in coreo rubeo,[19] die 'Redditus pro Cappelania prima sanctorum Cosme et Damiani ecclesie S. Petri Basiliensis' enthalten u.a. duos libros orales in pergameno scilicet estivale et hyemale, unum librum missale in pergameno,[20] ein mit 'Avisamenta' überschriebenes gefaltetes Papierblatt führt libri aut psalteria, directorium auf.[21] Wohl derselben Zeit gehört ein Verzeichnis von allerhand Geschenken an, in dem am Schluss erwähnt wird: her *Niclaus Keffler* der truckerher dat 1 messbůch.[22] Ebendamals werden der Liber vitae, der Liber statutorum gelegentlich in den Akten erwähnt.

1486 stiftete der Doktor beider Rechte, Chorherr *Gerhard in Curia de Bercka*, 10 Gulden pro subsidio psalterii legendum annuatim veneris sancta.[23] Der Propst zu St. Peter, *Eustachius Funck*,[24] decretorum doctor,

---

[14] Das Testament St. Peter E (Anniversar) 217 ff., die Bücherzitate besonders 219–220. Das Stück verdient in extenso veröffentlicht zu werden, so ungemein reichhaltig ist es für die Kenntnis des religiösen und kulturellen Lebens der Zeit.

[15] Testamentum honeste domine Grede Lutringerin St. Peter E 229v.

[16] Johannes Husgow erscheint seit 1446 als Chorherr, von 1447 bis 1470 als Cantor oder Senger von 1474 bis zu seinem Tode, Februar 1480, als Kustos.

[17] St. Peter F 51v: Item ordinavit eidem cappellanie unum missale, duos libros orales in pergameno.

[18] Abdruck vgl. unten Beilage I.

[19] St. Peter JJJ 4, undatiert.

[20] St. Peter JJJ 4, undatiert.

[21] St. Peter JJJ 1, undatiert.

[22] St. Peter JJJ 1, undatiert.

[23] St. Peter F 63v.

[24] Eustachius Funck (gest. 1500, vgl. St. Peter F (Anniversar) zum 21. Februar) war Propst von 1496 bis 1500. Vgl. auch Wackernagel, *a.a.O.*, II, 827.

bedachte gleichfalls, am 14. Januar 1500, in seinem Testament die Bibliothek:[25] Idem dominus testatur, ordinavit etiam et deputavit librum suum
missalem manu sua propria scriptum futuro domino preposito et illius
successoribus pro tempore ipsa conditione adiecta, quod ille idem liber
in clausura domini prepositi in quodam reservaculo in sacristigia domino-
rum contento semper manere et ab eodem, dum necesse fuerit, uti debeat,
sed si aliquo tempore contigerit, eundem dominum prepositum a Basilea
fore absentem et apud suam preposituram unam residentiam facere per-
sonalem, extunc communitas tam canonicorum quam cappellanorum illo
libro missali utatur. Seine übrigen Bücher sollten dagegen verkauft werden.[26]

Direkte Zeugnisse über die Bibliothek nach 1500 finden sich nur noch
vereinzelt. Aus den nächsten Jahrzehnten ist ein bisher unbekannter
Brief des Strassburger Reformators *Martin Butzer* an den Vorsteher der
Kirche zu St. Leonhard, Markus Bertschi[27] von Aufschluss, in dem
jener um Abschrift eines liber decretorum ecclesiasticorum der Stiftsbibliothek von St. Peter ersucht.[28]

Nicht ohne Interesse sind zur Ergänzung obiger Notizen Angaben über
die privaten Bibliotheken einzelner Chorherren, wie sie sich teilweise
in Nachlassinventaren erhalten haben. In dem 'Inventarium bonorum
derelictorum domni *Henrici Thorers*[29] cappellani ecclesie S. Petri sexta
post Barnabe (d.i. 12. Juni) conscriptum anno 1500 per dominos magistros Thobald Ouglij cantorem, Marcum Vogel et Joannem Gebwiler'
finden sich die folgenden Gemälde, Schreibutensilien, Bücher usw.:[30] 1
Däfelin de Passione Christi; 1 Grossen brieff de Passione Christi; 1 Alt
vigil; 1 Dintenkruglin; 1 Schribmesserlin; 1 Schribzug; 1 Confessar von
Friderich Körnlin von Memigen; 2 Brevier in parva forma; Preceptorium
Joannis Nider; 1 Postill; 1 Directorium; 1 Switzer Kronick; 2 Klein roti
betbüchli; 1 Mess beate virginis, uningebunden; Allerley gsang und 1
musig; 1 Praemostratz zu dutsch; Dutsch sprüch in eim buch; Viola

---

[25] St. Peter JJJ 10, 1500 Januar 14.

[26] Vgl. die Bestimmung in dessen Testament: voluit ipse dominus testator, ut excepto vita finita
sine mora omnes et singuli sui libri devoto libro missali ac rebus prescriptis . . . atque multa sua bona
mobilia . . . vendantur.

[27] Markus Bertschi 1523–1566 Pfarrer zu S. Leonhard, vgl. Wackernagel, *a.a.O.*, III, 340; K. Gauss,
Basilea reformata (Basel, 1930) 46f.—Anmerkungsweise sei hier auf ein Aktenstück verwiesen, worin
Andreas Bodenstein gen. Karlstadt (ca. 1480–1541), Pfarrer zu St. Peter 1535(1534)–1541, vgl.
Gauss, *a.a.O.*, 96, bekennt, dass er verschiedene Stücke in der Stiftsbehausung zu St. Peter nicht an-
spreche als sein Eigentum, u.a.: Item den grossen bücherschafft in der grössere[n] stuben (Staatsarchiv
Basel, Bau-Akten MM 19, sine dato).

[28] Vgl. unten *Beilage*, II.

[29] Heinrich Thorer, Kaplan, gest. 1500. Diebolt Ouglin, Kantor bis um 1526. Markus Vogel und
Johannes Gebwiler waren Magister um 1500.

[30] St. Peter JJJ 10.

sanctorum; Canon in pergameno; Conpendium theologie videtur; Liber
secretorum Alberti Magni; Libellus de vita Salvatoris; Sulpicius.-Reicher
an Büchern erweist sich die Hinterlassenschaft des Dekans zu St. Peter,
Tiebald Westhoffer,[31] dessen 'verlossen gut im hus zum Tiergarten uff
S. Pettersberg' beschrieben wurde.[32] Im 'Nebentstubly' befanden sich
'LXXVIII bucher clein und gros in bretter gepunden, VIII bucher sunst
ingepunden . . . und sunst allerhand bücher.' Im 'hindern Stubly' lagen
'ein buch nit ingepunden, II bucher in pritter gepunden, 1 schribzug, IIII
bucher oningepunden und sunst allerhand bucher.' Dazu '1 register in
einm betbuchlin mit eim berlin knopff, 1 laden, ist der universitet und
darin: 1 bermentin urfecht in instrumentswys gemacht, die reversbrief
von Ludwig Schachen, allerley missiffen, so man zu ziten eim rector
geschriben hat.' Ebenda ist verzeichnet 'ein buch ff. vetus,' ausserdem
eine weitere Lade, Eigentum der Universität, in der aufbewahrt wurden
'1 fryheit als min herren der universitet in fryheit bestettiget haben, 1
confirmacion irer fryheit vom bapst, libellus statutorum universitatis,
der universitet statuten, etlich coppyen der universitet gultbriefen, der
universitet pligi sigel,' mit andern Worten gewiss Teile des Basler Uni-
versitätsarchivs, was bei der engen Zugehörigkeit des St. Petersstiftes
zur ersteren wohl verständlich wäre.[33] Die 1506 inventierte Verlassenschaft
des Kanonikers *Augustin Alantsee*[34] umfasst 'ein troglin mit alten buchern,' in der 'Understuben XXXX bucher ingebunden klein und gross,'
ausserdem ein Notariatsprotokollbuch und 'IIII bücher in berment pun-
den.'[35]—Eine bedeutende Bibliothek nannte der Propst *Bernhart Müller*[36]
sein eigen. Nach seinem Tode verzeichnete das Gericht in seinem Haus,
3.II.1513, 'LXXXVIII buch, dazu 1 schrybschyber zu buchern, IX
grosser bücher jur.'[37]

Beilagen

I.

Katalog der Stiftsbibliothek zu St. Peter, 1484.[38]

Notandum quod sequentes libri 1484 die mercurii post assumpcionis Marie
reperti sunt in libraria ecclesie collegiate S. Petri Basiliensis.

[31] Thiebald Westhoffer, Canonum Doctor, Dekan 1499–1506, gest. 1506 (vgl. St. Peter F zum 3.X.)

[32] Gerichtsarchiv K 3a, 99ff.

[33] Das St. Peterstift war teilweise der Basler Universität inkorporiert und stellte verschiedene
Pfründen für die Professoren. Vgl. Näheres bei W. Vischer, *Geschichte der Universität Basel von der
Gründung 1460 bis zur Reformation 1529* (Basel, 1860), 48 ff. und *passim*; R. Thommen, *Geschichte
der Universität Basel 1532–1632* (Basel, 1889), *passim*, vgl. 374 sub Basel.

[34] Zu Aug. Alantsee Wackernagel, *a.a.O.*, II, 616, 850, 855, 914, 919.

[35] Gerichtsarchiv K 3a, 75 ff.

[36] Bernhart Müller, Kustos 1479–1505, Propst 1506–1513, gest. 1513. Wackernagel, II, 615, 726.

[37] Gerichtsarchiv K 4, sub dato.

[38] St. Peter MM, 13. und 12. Blatt am Schluss des Bandes. Urspr. gelbbrauner Ledereinband (ca.
22, 5×32 cm) mit Holzdeckeln, einfach gepresst; 3 Bünde; die urspr. Metallschliessen abgerissen.

1. Canones antiqui et aliquot notabiles epistole synodales cum pluribus doctrinis salutaribus.

2. Questiones secundum primum et secundum librum sentenciarum fratris Hugonis de Novo Castro.

3. Textus sentenciarum.

4. Tractatus longus de contractibus et quidam sermones [. . .][39] textorum.

5. Exerpta quaedam de summa sacramentorum. Libellus de infancia salvatoris. Item passio domini Jesu secundum Ancelmum.

6. Item ludus de resurrectione domini. Item ludus de ascensione domini. Item alius ludus. Item de cena domini. Item de resurrectione Lazari.

7. Sermones de tempore et de sanctis.

8. Sermones dominicales. Item de contractu de viciis cum tabula.

9. Pastorale S. Gregorii, pulcherrimus libellus in pergameno.

10. Compendium theologice veritatis quod incipit Veritatis theologice, libellus pulcher.

11. Summa fratris Raymundi cum commento, pulcher liber.

12. Apocalipsis textus cum glosa et plurima alia.

13. Liber vocabulorum dictus pueritius a Johanne de Mera conpilatus.

14. Liber trenorum cum glosa.

15. Summa Raymundi cum glosa notabili et cum tabula secundum ordinem alphabeti in fine.

16. Summa confessorum et tractatus magistri Hugonis de S. Victore.

17. Sermones per se loquentes sive sermones Wilhelmi Parisiensis.

18. Omelie S. Augustini et aliorum sanctorum.

19. Sermones Guilberti de Tornaco qui agnomine dicuntur Boneventura de diversis statibus. Item in principio ponitur formula honeste vite S. Benedicti.

20. Vocabularius de 'Sermones biblie.' Item cronica Martiniana.

In secundo pulpto proximo

21. Prima pars Jordanis et incipit Jordanis ripas alvei sui.

22. Sermones de materiis generalibus secundum varietatem festorum magnorum et temporum, ut patet in fine libri.

23. Prima pars rationalis divinorum officiorum Guilhelmi Durantis, in pappiro.

24. Sexta pars de officiis dominicarum specialite[r] etc. rationalis.

25. Sermones ab adventu domini usque ad cenam domini.

Umfangreiche Papierhandschrift. Auf dem Vorderdeckel die Aufschrift: B Continentur hic census libri vitę ab anno 1400 usque ad annum 1435. Emptiones et reemptiones officiorum ab anno 1495. B. Auf dem Rückdeckel: Liber reemptionum anno domini MCCCCXCV. Auf dem Spiegelblatt: Liber B, auf dem Vorsatzblatt: Continentur hoc libro census libri vite ab anno 1400 usque ad annum 1435. Item census anni 1445 etc. libri vite. Emptiones et reemptiones omnium offitiorum ab anno 1495 B liber, alles von Händen ca. 1500. Das Verzeichnis erwähnen P. Lehmann, 'Johannes Sichardus und die von ihm benutzten Bibliotheken und Handschriften,' in L. Traube, *Quellen und Untersuchungen zur lateinischen Philologie des Mittelalters*, 4, Heft 1 (München, 1912), 92–93, sowie Wackernagel, *a.a.O.*, II, 615.

[39] Lücke im Original.

26. Pastorale novellanum.
27. Rigstrum orandi secundum varietatem litterarum dominicalium.
28. Sermones cuiusdam de tempore.
29. Sermones Socti et est pars hyemalis.
30. Vocabularius singularissimus cum aliis in ibi contentis pulchris.
31. Secunda pars Jordanis et est pars estivalis.
32. Digestum vetus cum glosa in pergameno.

Secunda pars eiusdem pulpti

33. Prima pars summe Hostiensis.
34. Secunda pars summe Hostiensis quae dicitur copiosa.
35. Codex novem librorum et pendet in fine pulpti.
36. Archidyaconus circa sextos decretales.
37. Summa viciorum.[40]
38. Cronica Martini.
39. Compendium theologie.
40. Passionale sanctorum multorum Blasii, Hylarii, Agnetis etc.
41. Summa Pysana.
42. Secunda pars Jordanis et est de materia 21 B.
43. Sermones et incipit Jordanis ripas.
44. Preciosus liber et incipit Liber de gubernacione dei et hominum.
45. Questiones primi et tercii libri sentenciarum, in pergameno.
46. Sermones Jacobi de Voragine quadragesimale.
47. Sermones de tempore et de sanctis, in pergameno.[41]

Tertii pulpti

48. Byblia preciosa cum prologo beati Jacobi et capitula in fine, in pergameno.
49. Tractatus diversi primo Hugonis de sacramentis, de modo audiendi confessiones, de virtutibus misse, de antecristo.
50. Grecismus seu Eberhardus cum commento.
51. Sermones dupliciter de sanctis, in pergameno.
52. Sermones dominicales Jacobi de Voragine, in pergameno.
53. Glosula circa ecclesiastes. Item de episcopis sacerdotibus etc.
54. Breviloquium conditum a Bonaventura ad intelligenciam sacre scripture.
55. Opusculum de missa.
56. Opusculum rarum exemplorum variorum simul collectorum.
57. Liber miraculorum.
58. Passionale sive Lampartica legenda.
59. Excerpta byblie, in pergameno.
60. Liber exepcionum ecclesiasticarum regularum.
61. Racionale divinorum Willhelmi Durantis, liber bonus in pergameno.
62. Legenda de sanctis, in pergameno.

[40] Von anderer Hand ist hinzugefügt: receptorium (?) fugam per dominum canonicum, dessen Sinn mir fraglich ist.
[41] Hinzugefügt ist: plebanus habet. . . .

63. Martilogium. Item metra de contenis in byblia.
64. Legenda sanctorum notabilis, in pergameno.

II.

Domino Marco pastori ecclesiae apud D. Leonhardi uno pro et docto amico singulari B.[42]

Salve charissime Marce. Cum nuper Selestadium transirem, illinc domum rediens prodidit mihi Beatus Rhenanus librum decretorum ecclesiasticorum authore quodam episcopo Wormaciensi, quem asservat D. Nicolaus Briefer,[43] decanus S. Petri. Insunt ei libro quaedam, quae modo necessario mihi essent, quorumque causa et D. Beatum consulueram. Oro itaque te, per hunc vectorem, eius libri mihi copiam facias, nisi possis id commodius et maturius committendo eum alicui amico nam descensuro. Tantam erga me humanitatem exhibuit D. Briefferus Bernae,[44] ut spero haud quoque contradicturum. Curabo etiam librum intra breve tempus illesum remittere. Id etiam adquod libro in ipso, non uni forsan ecclesiae proderit. Obsecro cura, ut sanctorum patrum toti corpus cudetur. Optime vale. Argentorati pridie calendas martias. Salutant te fratres. D. Nicolao me officiose commenda.

M. Bucerus tuus.

Nachtrag von der Hand Briefers:
Hunc librum dedi domino Marco Bårczschy plebano S. Leonardi mittendum ad D. M. Bucerum anno 1531 4a Marcii N. Brieffer. Hic liber exigui pretii erat.

BASEL.

[42] St. Peter JJJ 1 sub dato. Originalpapierbrief, Spuren des Petschaftsiegels. Für freundliche Lesehilfe spreche ich Herrn Dr. H. G. Wackernagel meinen besten Dank aus.

[43] Nikolaus Briefer († 1546), Magister artium et philosophiae, Lic. jur., Kanonikus zu St. Peter, später Dekan; Rektor der Universität Basel 1511, 1521, 1523, 1539. Vgl. R. Thommen, 'Die Rektoren der Universität Basel von 1460-1910,' in *Festschrift zur Feier des 450j. Bestehens der Univ. Basel* (Basel, 1910), 23, 25, 29; Wackernagel, *a.a.O.*, III, 163, 325, 339, 428, 492.

[44] Anspielung auf die Berner Disputation von 1528?

THE SCRIPTORIUM OF REIMS DURING THE ARCHBISHOPRIC OF HINCMAR (845-882 A.D.)

Frederick M. Carey

During the past half century the School of Reims has assumed a most important role in the theories of those who are interested in the history of Carolingian miniatures.[1] Almost every one who writes an article in this field has some new psalter or gospels to add to the ever-growing list of Reims manuscripts. From the comparative certainty of the Utrecht Psalter, the Gospels of Hincmar, St. Thierry, and Loisel, we are led to the somewhat less sure ground of the Douce Psalter, the Psalter of Troyes, the Gospels of Beauvais, Blois, Düsseldorf, Kleve, Yates Thompson, and the so-called *schola Palatina*[2] (Gospels of Aachen, Xanten, and the Vienna Schatzkammer), to mention only the most famous. Further attributions to Reims are made for Terence by Jones and Morey,[3] and for Prudentius by Helen Woodruff.[4] The script of Reims, on the other hand, has received almost no attention at all; unlike her sisters at Tours and Cologne she has had no suitors. Some fifteen years ago when I was casting about for other *scriptoria* in order to find a basis of comparison for the study of manuscripts of Fleury, I noticed that about twenty manuscripts of Reims were marked with the *ex-dono* of Hincmar, the celebrated Archbishop of Reims from 845-882. So large a group of dated manuscripts of the ninth century from a single *scriptorium* seemed quite

For visiting European libraries and collecting materials concerning various *scriptoria* I am greatly indebted to the American Council of Learned Societies for a Fellowship and for other grants.

[1] For works of particular interest for their treatment of Reims cf.: Adolph Goldschmidt, 'Der Utrechtpsalter,' *Repertorium für Kunstwissenschaft*, XV (1892), 156-169. Paul Durrieu, 'L'origine du manuscrit célèbre dit le *Psautier d'Utrecht*,' *Mélanges Julien Havet* (Paris: 1895), pp. 639-657. J. J. Tikkanen, *Die Psalterillustration im Mittelalter* (Helsingfors: 1895-1900). Georg Swarzenski, 'Die karolingische Malerei und Plastik in Reims,' *Jahrbuch der königlich preussischen Kunstsammlungen*, XXIII (1902), 81-100. Amédée Boinet, *La miniature carolingienne* (Paris: 1910). A. M. Friend, 'Carolingian Art in the Abbey of St. Denis,' *Art Studies*, I (1923), 67-75. Helen Woodruff, 'The Physiologus of Bern,' *Art Bulletin*, XII (1930), 226-253. G. R. Benson and D. T. Tselos, 'New Light on the Origin of the Utrecht Psalter: I. (Benson) The Latin Tradition and the Reims Style in the Utrecht Psalter,' *Art Bulletin*, XIII (1931), 13-53. L. W. Jones and C. R. Morey, *The Miniatures of the Mss. of Terence prior to the 13th century* (Princeton: 1931). E. T. DeWald, *The Illustrations of the Utrecht Psalter* (Princeton: 1932). Wilhelm Köhler, *Die Karolingischen Miniaturen: I. Die Schule von Tours. Des Textes zweiter Teil: Die Bilder* (Berlin: 1933), pp. 293-298.

[2] H. Janitschek, *Die Trierer Ada-handschrift* (Leipzig: 1889), *passim*.

[3] Op. cit., pp. 62-67, 100-101, 213-214.

[4] *The Illuminated Mss. of Prudentius* (Harvard Univ. Pr.: 1930), p. 10.

unparalleled. Accordingly, I included Reims, as well as St. Denis of Paris and St. Germain of Auxerre, among the *scriptoria* to be compared with Fleury. I soon decided, however, to complete the study of the script of Reims first, as it was comparatively free from the complexities in which the other centers were involved. The impulse to the study of these schools came from Professor Edward Kennard Rand, under whose guidance I had written a doctoral thesis on the script of Fleury, and in whose honor these studies are published; to his subtle scholarship and wide learning in many fields I am forever under obligation.

The purpose of this article is to give an account in the limited space at my disposal of all known manuscripts of Reims which bear the *ex-dono* of Hincmar, as well as to offer a hand-list of all Reims manuscripts known to me which I consider to be the products of that *scriptorium*. Under the category of Reims manuscripts I include those of the three main sources, the Cathedral Chapter and the monasteries of St. Remi and St. Thierry, with occasional books from the monasteries of St. Denis, St. Nicaise, and Hautvillers. Furthermore, on account of the lack of any history of the Reims libraries, I shall give a brief introductory account of them. The foot-notes will provide a fairly complete bibliography of the subject, bringing up to date the notes of Delisle,[5] Gottlieb,[6] and Weinberger.[7] In order to supplement the description of the manuscripts and to help paleographers in identifying books of Reims the editor has allowed me to offer two specimens of the script of the period of Hincmar. While there are many reproductions of miniatures of this school, there are almost no fac-similes of the script, without which any attempt to describe the writing would be useless. In fact, the script of Reims is as easily recognizable, if not so easily described, as that of Tours.[8]

The history of the Cathedral and monasteries, to say nothing of the libraries, of Reims up to the beginning of the ninth century is largely a matter of uncertainty and legend, in spite of the fact that we have a particular work on the subject by a monk of the tenth century, Flodoard's *Historia Remensis Ecclesiae*.[9] From him we have a meagre notice from

[5] *Le Cabinet des Mss. de la Bibliothèque Nationale* (Paris: 1868–1881), II 15, 404, 411–413.

[6] *Ueber Mittelalterliche Bibliotheken* (Leipzig: 1890), pp. 338–344.

[7] 'Wegweiser durch die Sammlungen altphilologischer Hss.,' *Akademie d. Wissenschaften in Wien. Sitzungsber. 209. Band; 4. Abhandlung. Sitzung vom 13. Februar 1929.*

[8] It is to be hoped that scholars who are aware of the existence of other mss. of Reims provenience will send me that information, as I am engaged on a larger work on this subject.

[9] For the history of the cathedral and monasteries of Reims cf.: *Gallia Christiana* (Paris: 1751), IX, cols. 1–332; instrum. 1–94. Guillaume Marlot, *Histoire de la ville, cité, et université de Reims* (Reims: 1843–46), 4 vols. Georges Boussinesq and Gustave Laurent, *Histoire de Reims* (Reims: 1933) 2 vols. in 3. T. P. Armand, *Histoire de Saint Remi* (Paris: 1846). J. C. Poussin, *Monographie de l'abbaye et de l'église de St.-Remi de Reims* (Reims: 1857).

For editions of Flodoard cf.: Migne, *Patrologia Latina*, vol. 135. M. Lajeune, *Histoire de l'église de Reims par Flodoard* (Reims: 1854), text and translation.

the times of Archbishop Tilpin (753–800):[10] Flodoard, II, 17: *Sed et sacrarum codicibus scripturarum, quibus adhuc aliquibus quoque utimur, hanc instruxit ecclesiam.* There is also an interesting item about a sacramentary, which seems to have been destroyed in the burning of the monastery of St. Remi in 1774. It was written by Lambertus under the direction of the priest Gaudelgaudus, who had offered it to the church of St. Remi; the transcription began on March 22, 798, and was finished on July 23 (or August 1), 800.[11] Of the literary activity of the two succeeding bishops, Vulfarius (808–816) and Ebo (816–835), Flodoard has nothing to say. Mabillon gives specimens of two manuscripts of St. Augustine from the monastery of St. Remi which are lost to-day, undoubtedly destroyed in the fire just mentioned; one of these was written at the command of Vulfarius, the other at the order of Ebo.[12] The best known manuscript of the time of Ebo is the so-called *Ebo Gospels*, written probably between 816 and 835, now *Ms. 1* in the municipal library of Epernay; it is famous for the influence of its miniatures.[13] These three books attest the activity of the Reims *scriptorium* during the first half of the ninth century; some sixteen others will be added in the hand-list at the end of this article.

Nearly half of Flodoard's *History of the Church at Reims* is devoted to its greatest bishop, Hincmar (845–882), who was one of the foremost men of the ninth century.[14] This is not the place to go into his struggles with princes both temporal and spiritual, his quarrels with Godescalc, with his nephew, Hincmar of Laon, his interest in the Church Fathers and Canon Law, although all these elements have left their stamp on the studies of the schools of Reims.[15] For although Hincmar was not definitely

[10] The dates of all bishops mentioned in this article are taken from Pius Bonifacius Gams, *Series episcoporum* (Ratisbon: 1873), p. 608.

[11] Léopold Delisle, 'Mémoire sur d'anciens sacramentaires,' *Mémoires de l'Institut national de France*, XXXII (1886), 87–89. Ulysse Chevalier, *Sacramentaire et martyrologe de l'abbaye de saint-Remy* (Paris: 1900), pp. vi–xii.

[12] Jean Mabillon, *De Re Diplomatica* (Paris: 1681), p. 362, tab. x¹ and tab. x². Details in Gottlieb, *op. cit.*, p. 341.

[13] Edouard Aubert, 'Ms. de l'Abbaye d'Hautvillers dit *Évangélaire d'Ébon*,' *Mémoires de la Société nationale des Antiquaires de France*, X, 4ᵉ série (1879), 111–127. Consult also in particular the articles of Goldschmidt, Durrieu, Swarzenski, and Köhler, mentioned in Note 1.

[14] On Hincmar of Reims cf.: Flodoard, Book III. Abbé Auguste Vidieu, *Hincmar de Reims* (Paris: 1875). C. v. Noorden, *Hinkmar, Erzbischof von Rheims* (Bonn: 1863). Heinrich Schrörs, *Hinkmar, Erzbischof von Reims* (Freiburg im Breisgau: 1884). Max Manitius, *Geschichte der lateinischen Literatur des Mitelalters* (München: 1911), I, 339–354. For his extensive works cf.: Migne, *Patr. lat.*, vols. 125–6.

[15] Guy Carleton Lee, *Hincmar; an introduction to the study of the revolution of the church in the ninth century* (Baltimore: 1897) (reprinted from vol. VIII of the Papers of the American Society of Church History). Ferdinand Lot and Louis Halphen, *Le Règne de Charles le Chauve (840–877)*, première partie (840–851) (Paris: 1909). (Fascicule 175 de la Bibliothèque de l'École des hautes Études).

hostile to the study of the Classics, the practicality of his interests probably explains the absence of manuscripts of the Classics at Reims in our period.[16] To quote from one of his biographers.[17]

'Seine Latinität zeigt keine Spur, dass er klassische Muster hätte auf sich einwirken lassen. Die Diktion lehnt sich stellenweise mehr an die des Volkes an, aus dessen Munde er manche sprichwörtliche Redensarten aufnahm. Er ist einer der ersten, bei dem (sic) sich ein Eindringen der *"lingua rustica"* in die Schriftsprache zeigt.'

Hincmar's zeal for the welfare of the Cathedral and the monasteries, and for the discipline and education of the monks is often illustrated in Flodoard; three passages in particular concern us here.

Flodoard, III, 1: Is siquidem Hincmarus, a pueritia in monasterio Sancti Dyonysii sub Hilduino abbate monasteriali religione nutritus et studiis litterarum imbutus, indeque pro sui tam generis quam sensus nobilitate, in palatium Ludovici imperatoris deductus, et familiarem ipsius notitiam adeptus fuerat; ibique, prout potuit, cum imperatore et praefato abbate, sub episcoporum auctoritate laboravit, ut ordo monasticus in praedicto monasterio quorumdam voluptuosa factione diu delapsus, restauraretur.[18]

Flodoard, III, 5: Evangelium aureis argenteisque describi fecit litteris, aureisque munivit tabulis, et gemmis distinxit pretiosis. His quoque versibus insignivit:

> Sancta Dei Genitrix et semper virgo Maria,
> Hincmarus praesul defero dona tibi.
> Haec pia quae gessit, docuit nos Christus Iesus,
> Editus ex utero, casta puella, tuo.

Librum quoque sacramentorum sed et lectionarium quos scribi fecit, ebore argentoque decoravit.

Flodoard, III, 9: Evangelium aureis litteris insignivit, ac parietibus aureis gemmarumque nitore distinctis munivit, versibus etiam auro inclytis praetitulavit. . . . Librum quoque sacramentorum sub eburneis tabulis, argento praesignitis; sed et lectionarium ad missas librum, pari decore venustatum, ibidem contulit, aliosque libros et ornamenta nonnulla eidem venerabili loco delegavit.

[16] For the emphasis laid on practical subjects cf.: Les Actes de la Province ecclésiastique de Reims, ou Canons et Décrets des Conciles, Constitutions, Statuts, et Lettres des Évêques des différents Diocèses qui dépendent ou qui dépendaient autrefois de la Métropole de Reims. Publiés par Mgr. Th. Gousset, Archévêque de Reims, primat de la Gaule Belgique, etc. 4 vols. (Tome premier, Reims: 1842) I 204 ff.

For Hincmar's knowledge of the Classics cf. Schrörs, *op. cit.*, pp. 466–7; Manitius, *op. cit.*, pp. 346, 349.

[17] Schrörs, *op. cit.*, pp. 469–470.

[18] Paris, *Bibl. Nat. Ms. Lat. 13090*, fols. 70 ff. gives an account of an act of association between monks of St. Denis of Paris and St. Remi of Reims of the year 838. It is printed in d'Achery, *Spicilegium*, IV 229 (shorter edition of 1723: III 333/4). This *societas precum*, as it is styled, should be of interest to those who are trying to trace the spread of the Franco-Saxon type of illumination.

It happens that among the fifty or so manuscripts belonging to this period, of which twenty-two bear Hincmar's *ex-dono*, there are two which are written in gold or silver letters: *Morgan 728* and *Reims 11*.

The schools of Reims continued to flourish after our period under Archbishop Fulco (883–900), when Hucbald of St. Amand and Heiric of Auxerre could be counted among their teachers, under Archbishop Gerbert (991–998), and generally through the later Middle Ages.[19]

Except for the catalogue of the books belonging to Vulfadus, the friend of John the Scot, in Paris *Bibl. Mazarine Ms. 561*, fol. 219[v], written towards the end of the ninth century,[20] and the tenth-century catalogue of the manuscripts of the monastery of St. Thierry,[21] which the editor of the *Catalogue général des Mss. des bibliothèques publiques de France*, vols. XXXVIII and XXXIX, promised to publish in his preface, which never appeared, there seem to be no ancient catalogues of Reims libraries. In the thirteenth century a librarian of the monastery of St. Remi numbered the volumes of the library in red ink, usually at the top of the first page and again in one other place farther along in the book. About seventy manuscripts thus numbered in red have survived, of which two different manuscripts occasionally bear the same number. Before listing them I offer a single example from *Paris, B. N., lat. Ms. 4789*, fols. 1[r] and 32[v]: Lib(er) s(an)c(t)i Rem(igii) vol(umen) vii[xx] et ii. It will be immediately observed that the exponent *xx* survives to-day only in the French word for 'eighty'—quatre-vingt.

SAEC. XIII

NUMBER	PRESENT NUMBER	BRIEF DESCRIPTION OF CONTENTS
1	Berlin lat. 84 (Phillipps 1743)	concilia Galliae; paparum epp.
2	Reims 90	Augustinus in psalmos 50–100.
	" 228	Missale.
4	Paris 4280A? cf. No. 9.	Canones, capitularia, etc.
	" 9347	Sedulius, Fortunatus, Juvencus, etc.
5	Vatic. Regin. lat. 1046	Niceni concilii secundi acta.
6	Paris 2866	Hincmarus de divortio Lotharii.

[19] For the schools of Reims cf.: P. L. Péchenard, *De Schola Remensi Decimo Saeculo* (Reims: 1876). Abbé E. Cauly, *Histoire du Collège des Bons-Enfants de l'Université de Reims* (Reims: 1885).

[20] *Palaeographische Forschungen von Ludwig Traube. Fünfter Teil.* 'Autographen des Johannes Scottus' *aus dem Nachlass herausgegeben von Edward K. Rand. Mit 12 Tafeln. Abhandl. d. könig. bayerisch. Akad. d. Wiss. Philos.-philol. und hist. Kl. XXVI. Band. 1. Abhandl. Vorgelegt am 13. Januar 1912*, pp. 1–12. Plate XII gives fol. 219[v] of *Mazarine Ms. 561* on which this catalogue of about twenty books appears; they can almost all be duplicated among extant books of Reims. Other mss. of the 'circle of John the Scot' which are treated in this article are: *Reims 875; Laon 81; Paris B. N. lat. 12964; Bamberg H. J. IV. 5 (Philos. 2) and Q. VI. 32 (Patrist. 46).* See also, as a corrective, the palinode: E. K. Rand, 'The supposed autographa of John the Scot,' *Univ. of California Publications in Class. Philol.* V, no. 8, pp. 135–141. Plates 1–11 give reproductions of *Reims 875.*

[21] *Reims Ms. 427*, fols. 12[r]–13[v]. *Cat. gén.*, t. XXXVIII (1904) 570.

7	Paris 14194	Bernardus Silvestris; Hildebertus, etc.
	Reims 225	Missale.
8	" 123	Claudius Taurinen. super Leviticum.
9	Paris 4280A? cf. No. 4	
10	" 13764, pars 3.	Passio S. Eugenii; Hincmari Epp. iv.
	Reims 226	Missale.
11	" 25	Biblia.
	" 671	Dionysii Exigui Canones.
15	" 26	Biblia.
19	Paris 13764, pars 6	Vitae SS. Chrysanti et Dariae; Goaris.
21	Reims 27	Biblia.
24	Berlin 82 (Phill. 1741)	Dionysii Exigui Canones.
	Paris 13764, pars 1	Vita S. Basoli.
25	Reims 132	Expos. Remigii super Psalterium.
26	Reims 91	August. sup. Psalmos grad.; homiliae.
31	" 16	Pars veteris et novi Testamenti.
32	" 17	" " " " "
33	" 19	" " " " "
34	" 18	Pars veteris Testamenti.
	" 146	Radulphus de Flaix super Leviticum.
38	" 93	August. super Evangelium S. Iohannis.
39	" 109	Gregorii Moralia in Iob.
40	" 108	" " " "
	Vat. Regin. lat. 417	Caroli Magni Capitularium.
45	Reims 94	August. super Evangelium S. Iohannis.
49	Bern 427	Fulgentius; Dares Phrygius.
50	Bern 83	Nonius Marcellus, etc.
53	Reims 29	Novum Testamentum.
54	Paris 4668	Leges Visigothorum.
59	Reims 1343	Josephus.
	Bern 427 ? cf. No. 49	
60	Reims 1344	Josephus.
61	" 1345	Josephus.
	Paris 7691	Glossarium B-P (Abstrusa).
65	Reims 424	Gregorii epistolae.
68	Leiden B.P. 114	Isidori Etymologiae.
69	Leiden Vos. Q. 60	Liber Pontificalis.
	Reims 674	Burchardi Wormaten. Decreta.
78	" 412	Leonis papae homiliae et epistolae.
	Vat. Regin. lat. 418	Concilia etc.
92	Paris 5609	Vita S. Huberti.
101	Reims 1091	Papiae elementarium doctrin.
106	" 300	Lectionarium.
127	Vat. Regin. 213	Hilarion; Eusebii Chron.; Hier.; Fredeg.
	Paris 8728 ? cf. No. 147	Hyginus.

133	Reims 47	Concordia evangelistarum.
139	" 140	Excerpta Alulfi ex Gregorio.
142	Paris 4789	Liber legis Salicae.
143	" 13763	Vitae SS.
	Reims 28	Libri prophetarum.
145	Brit. Mus. Addit. 9046	Liber Psalmorum notis Tironianis.
147	Paris 8728 ? cf. No. 127	
150	Reims 137	Gilbertus de S. Amando in epp. Pauli.
164	Reims 691	Compilatio tertia decretalium.
165	" 690	Breviarium decreti.
168	Paris 7974 ?	Horatius.
177	Vat. Regin. 994	Isaac Lingonen. canonum collectio.
179	Paris 5569 ?	Vita S. Dion.; Hincmarus: Gesta Dagob.
184	Bern 522	Ars Petri grammatica.
205	Brit. Mus. Reg. 15 B XIX	Beda, etc.
208	Vat. Regin. 272	Alcuini epistolae.
217	Paris 1597A	Synodi.
272	Vat. Regin. 191	Isidorus, etc.
275	Berlin 135 (Phill. 1886)	Paulus Diaconus.
284	Reims 1094	Priscianus.

It is difficult to determine on what principle the enumeration was made on account of the many gaps in the series, but both size and content seem to have played a part; the series starts with sacred books (including canon law and councils) and ends with secular works (Horace, Priscian, etc.). At the beginning of the 18th century we are informed by two Benedictines that the library of St. Remi was the richest in the city of Reims, possessing between five and six hundred manuscripts, of which some were Greek.[22] The fact that *Reims Ms. 1306* bears the old library number *558* would tend to bear out this statement. During the night of January 15, 1774, the monastery of St. Remi was destroyed by fire, an eye-witness of which, Dom Chastelain, says that from fifty to sixty manuscripts out of a total number of a thousand were thrown from a window of the library.[23] An inventory of the property of the monastery for the year 1790 lists 248 manuscripts as against 1500 for the period before the fire.[24] Whatever the truth may be, there are at present in the public library at Reims only about 100 manuscripts from the library of St. Remi. Among those which were burned were the famous Phaedrus[25] and the two to which Mabillon

[22] Edmond Martène and Ursin Durand, *Voyage littéraire de deux Bénédictins de la Congrégation de Saint Maur* (Paris: 1717), I, partie ii, 79–84.

[23] Henri Jadart, 'Journal de Dom Pierre Chastelain, Bénédictin Rémois, 1709–1782,' *Travaux de l'Académie nationale de Reims*, 110 (1900–1), II, 130–2.

[24] 'Abbaye de Saint-Remi de Reims. Inventaire des 28, 29, et 30 avril 1790.' Document inédit publié par M. l'Abbé Favret. *Travaux de l'Académie nationale de Reims*, 131 (1913–4), I, 378.

[25] Anton v. Premerstein, 'Zum Codex Remensis des Phaedrus und Querolus,' *Mittheilungen des österreichischen Vereines für Bibliothekswesen*, I (1897) 1–7 (with one fac-simile).

refers.[26] The manuscripts of the Cathedral Chapter and of the monastery of St. Thierry seem to have come down without great loss. At the opening of the nineteenth century all these various collections were united in the present public library of Reims.[27]

The script of Reims in the Hincmarian period is distinguished by its very traitlessness. There is no hierarchy of scripts like that which is found in manuscripts of Tours; at most, alternating lines of uncials and rustic capitals constitute the headings. There is a tendency towards the elimination of uncials; of the twenty-two books studied here thirteen show almost no trace of them. The form of uncial *A* calls for especial observation. The form of small letter *a* is practically always of the small uncial type, the loop generally making a fairly large belly. The two loops of the letter *g* are usually open, the letter itself often being connected to the following letter by a stroke. Ligatures, except for *et*, do not occur commonly; there seems to have been a conscious effort to abolish them. The ligature for *st* is found more often than those for *ct*, *nt*, and *rt*. Figure 2 is often used as the abbreviation for -*ur*; the apostrophe occurs in only one manuscript of the group, *Reims 434* (No. 21 *infra*), which is perhaps to be dated earlier than this period on other grounds. There are occasional abbreviations for -*bunt*, -*runt*, *sunt*, in the form of *bt*, *rt*, *st*, with a supra-script line. The letters are usually carefully formed and stand fairly straight. There is a tendency towards clubbing, but not the artificial type which was practised in the tenth century. Indications of this kind, however, do no go far towards solving the secrets of the Reims script; one had better form one's own alphabet from a study of fac-similes.

As for the rulings, with the exception of *Reims 434*, which I have mentioned as anomalous, they are all of the regular type when one leaf is ruled at a time, with groove confronting groove, and ridge confronting ridge.[28] If one letters the eight leaves of a quaternion A-H, then the following surfaces will be ruled: A^r; B^v; C^r; D^v; E^r; F^v; G^r; H^v. I have heard that Dom Wilmart has invented a new system to indicate rulings by means of carets lying on their sides, their points showing the grooves. In his system the rulings for a single quaternion in these Hincmarian manuscripts would appear as follows, with each caret standing for a single folio: > < > < | > < > <. For the sake of brevity I have omitted

---

[26] Cf. note 12.

[27] Henri Jadart, *Les anciennes Bibliothèques de Reims, leur sort en 1790–91, et la formation de la Bibliothèque publique* (Reims: 1891).

[28] I will confess here that I do not look for correspondences in rulings. The study of pin-prickings seems to be the latest refinement of paleographers. Much could be learned from the system of marks by which glosses and notes are related to the *lemmata*. *Probationes pennae* are also important; there is one of *saec*. xii and later which occurs often in Reims mss.: *Omnis homo primum bonum vinum ponit.* It belongs naturally to mss. from the Champagne country!

references to the signatures, as they do not seem to contribute any significant criteria for our script.

Hincmar's book-mark appears in the lower margins of the manuscripts, usually at the beginning, and then in the middle or at the end of various quaternions. It is almost always written in contemporary brown rustic capitals in the following form: HINCMARUS ARCHIEPISCOPUS DEDIT / SCAE MARIAE REMENSI or SCAE MARIAE REMENSIS ECCLESIAE. The first three words appear on the verso of one folio and the rest on the recto of the following folio; where reference to but one folio is given, it is to be inferred that half the inscription is lacking. The book-mark is abbreviated in various ways.

A DESCRIPTION OF TWENTY-TWO MANUSCRIPTS OF REIMS WHICH BEAR THE *EX-DONO* OF ARCHBISHOP HINCMAR (845–882 A.D.)

1. CAMBRIDGE, Pembroke 308. (Ex dono Lanceloti Andrews epi. Wintoniensis.) *Rhabanus Maurus. (Enarrationum in epistolas S. Pauli libri IX–XIX.)* 256 leaves. 296×214. 1 col., 228×150. 35 (rarely 36) lines. BOOK-MARKS. The regular Hincmar book-mark on fols. 1^r, 8^v, 17^v-18^r, 25^v-26^r, 33^v-34^r, 41^v-42^r, 55^v-56^r, 63^v-64^r, 71^v-72^r, 79^v-80^r, 87^v-88^r, 103^v-104^r, 129^v-130^r, 137^v-138^r, 153^v-154^r, 161^v-162^r, 177^v-178^r, 193^v-194^r, 203^v-204^r, 220^v-221^r, 236^v-237^r, 244^v-245^r, 255^v-256^r. On the guard-leaf, fol. A^v, in a *saec.* xv *inc.* hand (also on fol. 256^v): *Iste liber pertinet ecclesie eliensi.* SCRIPT. Many varieties of a small, careful Caroline minuscule of the school of Reims, probably written early in Hincmar's period. There are many hands, one for almost every quaternion; in spite of the assertions of the scribes, they do not finish their portions. The signatures are so interesting that I give them in full. fol. 1^r (lower left) *hic incoat port(io) iotsmari.* fol. 47^v (lower right) *et hic finit.* fol. 48^r (lower left) *hic incip(it) port(io) saluioni.* fol. 71^v (lower right) *et hic finit.* fol. 72^r *hic incip. port. hrānigili.* fol. 95^v *et hic finit.* fol. 96^r *hic incip. port. bernardi.* fol. 121^v *et hic finit.* fol. 122^r *incip. port. hrotaldi.* fol. 153^v *finit port. hrotaldi.* fol. 154^r *incip. port. haimoni.* fol. 177^v *et hic finit.* fol. 178^r *incip. port. adelradi.* fol. 205^r *incip. port. ausoldi.* fol. 229^r *incip. port. comūnis.* Abbreviations and ligatures are not uncommon. Small uncial *a* occurs frequently; open *a* rarely. Some hands abolish ligatures like *st.* ILLUMINATION. None. The headings are in brown rustic capitals. REFERENCES. Montague Rhodes James, *A descriptive catalogue of the Mss. in the library of Pembroke College, Cambridge* (Cambr. Univ. Pr.: 1905), 275–6. Migne, *Patr. lat.*, vol. 112. *New Paleographical Society* (London: 1912), I 236, 237 gives plates of fols. 77^r, 154^v, 154^r, 178^r.

2. REIMS, Bibliothèque de la Ville 1. (Chapitre B, ord. 1, no. 1.) *Bible.* (*Genesis—Job.*) *Reims 2* forms the second part of this work. 248 leaves (numbered 249, but fol. 134 was skipped in the enumeration). 425×350. 2 cols., 343×267. 47 lines. BOOK-MARKS. The regular Hincmar book-mark, with occasional minor mutilations, on fols. 27^v-28^r, 54^r, 152^r-153^r, 160^v-161^r, 168^v-169^r,

178^v-179^r, 186^v-187^r, 194^v-195^r, 202^v-203^r, 212^v-213^r, 218^v-219^r, 231^v-232^r. SCRIPT. Clear, ample Caroline minuscule, with occasional pages of small writing for capitula and prologues. Various hands of a very similar type. Almost complete elimination of abbreviations and ligatures except for *et*. Small uncial *a* throughout. Occasional ligature *st*, especially in hand B (fols. 1–34^r). Fols. 1–7 and 170–1 are added c. 1000 A.D. to fill gaps. ILLUMINATION. Large interlaced initials of the embellished Franco-Saxon type, especially on fols. 8^r, 27^r, 44^r, 55^r, 91^r, 105^r, 118^r, 153^r. Contents indicated at tops of pages throughout in red rustic capitals. Headings in red and brown capitals, rustic capitals, and uncials. FOL. 219^r (in a scribble hand of *saec.* xiii) *omnis homo primum bonum vinum ponit*. cf. note 28. REFERENCES. *Catalogue général des Mss. des Bibliothèques Publiques de France*, XXXVIII (1904), pp. 1–3. Samuel Berger, *Histoire de la Vulgate pendant les premiers siècles du Moyen Âge* (Paris: 1893), 281, 412. Durrieu, *op. cit.* (note 1), p. 650, note 4.

   3. REIMS, Bibl. de la Ville 2. (Chap. B, ord. 1, no. 2.) *Bible.* (*Psalms—Apocalypse.*) This Ms. is a continuation of *Reims 1*. The two are often referred to as 'Hincmar's Bible.' 200 leaves. 424×320. 2 cols., 340×265. 47 lines. BOOK-MARKS. The regular Hincmar book-mark (with minor mutilations) on fols. 17^v–18^r, 37^v–38^r, 51^v–52^r, 114^v–115^r, 132^v–133^r, 173^v–174^r, 195^v–196^r. SCRIPT. Same type as in *Reims 1*, but with more small writing at the beginning of the book. On fols. 111^r–115^r one hand appears in which open *a* occurs, a novelty in this period; perhaps it was only the more formal book hand which eliminated it. ILLUMINATION. Same type as in *Reims 1*. Cf. fols. 1^r, 19^r, 37^r, 113^r–114^v (large colophons of the four gospels), 115^r, 125^r, 132^r, 143^r. REFERENCES. *Cat. gén.* XXXVIII, 3–4. Berger, *op. cit.*, pp. 281, 412.

   4. REIMS, Bibl. de la Ville 7. (St. Thierry, no. 9.) *Gospels.* This Ms. is often called the 'Gospels of St. Thierry.' 173 leaves. 300×222. 1 col., 204×138. 27 lines. BOOK-MARKS. Slightly different in this book. HINCMARUS ABBA / DEDIT SCO THEODERICO. On fols. 21^v–22^r, 29^v–30^r, 37^v–38^r, 45^v–46^r, 53^v–54^r. Hincmar was also abbot of St. Thierry and St. Remi. SCRIPT. Straight, careful, clear Caroline minuscule, free from ligatures and abbreviations. Brown to dark brown ink. Fols. 1–7 are later (*saec.* xii^{ex}), containing the gospel to be read at the washing of the feet on Holy Thursday. ILLUMINATION. Large interlaced initials, like those in *Reims 1* and *2*, on fols. 22^r, 64^r, 92^r, and 135^r. Fols. 21^r contains a remarkable portrait of St. Matthew in dull colors. Colophons on fols. 14^v–20^r. Headings in bright red capitals, rustic capitals, and uncials. REFERENCES. *Cat. gén.* XXXVIII, 8–9. Boinet, *op. cit.* (note 1), Pl. LXXV–VII. Durrieu, *op. cit.*, p. 650, note 4.

   5. REIMS, Bibl. de la Ville 46. (Chap. A, ord. 2, no. 13.) *Victor of Capua.* (*Interpretatio harmoniarum Ammonii Alexandrini et Diatessaron Tatiani in quattuor evangelia:* Migne, *Patr. lat.* vol. 68, cols. 251 ff.) 113 leaves. 232×190. 1 col., 151×103. 24 lines. BOOK-MARKS. The regular Hincmar book-mark on fols. 1^r, 22^v–23^r, 62^v–63^r, 86^v–87^r, 112^v–113^r. SCRIPT. The common, traitless Caroline minuscule of Reims, fairly similar to the script of *Reims 7*. Few ligatures or abbreviations; no *st* ligature. The manuscript is horribly disfigured by marginal

and interlinear glosses of *saec.* xii. Capitula on fols. 15^r–17^r are in a tiny hand. ILLUMINATION. Two lines of red uncials followed by two lines of red rustic capitals precede the beginning of the text on fol. 1^r. The colophons are simple and not illuminated. Headings in brown rustic capitals. The uncials and rustic capitals are not yet fancy with finials. REFERENCE. *Cat. gén.* XXXVIII, 41–2.

6. REIMS, Bibl. de la Ville 70. (Chap. A, ord. 1, no. 9.) *St. Augustine, Bede, St. Jerome.* fol. 1^r–22^r *Praedestinatus,* sive *Praedestinatorum liber.* fol. 22^r–25^v *liber nonagesimae heresis.* fol. 25^v–51^v *sub nomine Augustini liber contra hereticos.* fol. 52^r–119^v *expositio ven. Bedae in libro Salomonis quod* (sic) *dicitur Proverbia.* fol. 119^v–168^v *expositio Hieronymi in libro Ecclesiaste.* fol. 169^v–171^v *expositio Bedae in librum Tobiae* (mutil.). 172 leaves (156 bis). 291×238. 1 col., 207×164. 29 lines. BOOK-MARKS. The regular Hincmar book-mark on fols. 1^r, 24^v–25^r, 48^v–49^r, 72^v–73^r, 96^v–97^r, 118^v–119^r, 142^v–143^r, 163^v–164^r. SCRIPT. The typical straight, clear, solemn Caroline minuscule of Reims. Two or more main hands: A (1^r–51^v), B (52^r–end, more or less). Hand B is less impressive but offers the same traitless type of script. Few abbreviations and almost no ligatures. A few glosses of about the year 900. ILLUMINATION. Headings in bright red uncials and rustic capitals. The uncials often have delicate finials. On fol. 1^r there is a characteristic Reims initial *Q* in red and brown with a long understroke. REFERENCE. *Cat. gén.* XXXVIII, 69–70.

7. REIMS, Bibl. de la Ville 83. (Chap. A, ord. 1, no. 5.) *St. Augustine.* fols. 1^r–25^v *Augustini Retractationum libri VII in Genesi etc.* fols. 25^v–149^r *Augustini Quaestiones in eisdem libris.* 150 leaves (74 bis). 316×267. 2 cols., 237×198. 34 lines. BOOK-MARKS. The regular Hincmar book-mark on fols. 1^r, 8^v–9^r, 16^v–17^r, 40^v–41^r, 72^v–73^r, 111^v–112^r, 139^v–140^r, 148^v–149^r. SCRIPT. Small Caroline minuscule of the Reims type but of varying style. Three main hands: A (1^r–97^v, more or less), B (97^v–127^v, 144^r–149^r, more or less), C (128^r–143^v). Hand A is fairly small and carefully spaced, with slightly rounding clubbings in the ligatures *ra, ct, rt, st.* Hand B is also fairly small but more cursive. Hand C, while more irregular than the other two, has more of the look of Reims. The scholia are in the ordinary Hincmarian style. This book shows more ligatures and abbreviations than most books of the period. ILLUMINATION. Headings, *explicits-incipits* in red or brown rustic capitals. There seem to be no uncials in the book. REFERENCE. *Cat. gén.* XXXVIII, 82–3.

8. REIMS, Bibl. de la Ville 99. (Chap. A, ord. 1, no. 7.) *St. Gregory.* (*Moralium in Job libri I–V.*) This Ms. plus *Reims 100* and *101* form one work and belong together. 172 leaves. 298×223. 1 col., 211×144. 24 lines. BOOK-MARKS. The regular Hincmar book-mark on fols. 8^v–9^r, 10^v–11^r, 24^v–25^r, 32^v–33^r, 40^v–41^r, 56^v–57^r, 64^v–65^r, 72^v–73^r, 80^v–81^r, 88^v–89^r, 96^v–97^r, 104^v–105^r, 112^v–113^r, 120^v–121^r, 128^v–129^r, 136^v–137^r, 144^v–145^r, 152^v–153^r, 160^v–161^r, 168^v–169^r, 171^v–172^r. SCRIPT. Full, ample, rich Caroline minuscule, the 'cream' of Reims. Three main hands: A (1^r–49^v, 65^r–137^v), B (49^r–56^v), C (57^r–64^v, 137^v–172^r). Hand A and C are of the good Reims type with careful, straight script, with almost no ligatures or abbreviations. Hand B is less ample and contains some *st* ligatures. ILLUMINATION. There seems to be but one line of uncials in the entire book and

that in red at the very beginning of fol. 1ʳ. It is followed by two lines of red rustic capitals and a line of red capitals. There is also a large initial D of the interlaced Reims type in red and yellow with many red dots on fol. 1ʳ. The first eight and the last two leaves of the book are somewhat stained and damaged. There are red rustic *explicits-incipits passim* (fols. 36ʳ, 72ʳ, 98ᵛ, 134ʳ). The red is of the ordinary bright variety so characteristic of this school. A few notes of *saec.* x. REFERENCE. *Cat. gén.* XXXVIII, 95–6.

9. REIMS, Bibl. de la Ville 100. (Chap. A, ord. 2, no. 24.) *St. Gregory. (Moralium in Job libri VI–X.)* This Ms. belongs with *Reims 99* and *101*. 167 leaves. 276×220. 1 col., 178×155. 22 lines. BOOK-MARKS. This book does not have the regular Hincmar book-mark; since *Reims 101* does not have it either, it is very probable that Hincmar regarded the three volumes as a single manuscript. Instead we read (with some mutilations): SCAE MARIAE / REMENSIS on fols. 16ᵛ–17ʳ, 19ᵛ–20ʳ, 40ᵛ–41ʳ, 60ᵛ–61ʳ, 78ᵛ–79ʳ, 92ᵛ–93ʳ, 106ᵛ–107ʳ, 130ᵛ–131ʳ, 143ᵛ–144ʳ. SCRIPT. Small, somewhat crabbed Caroline minuscule, similar to that of *Reims 83*. Three main hands (hands A, C, and D, which fill the gaps, are of *saec.* x): B (2ʳ–40ᵛ, 101ʳ–108ᵛ), E (61ʳ–100ᵛ, more or less), F (109ʳ–167ᵛ). The hands are fairly similar, although hand E is more in the normal style of the period with its elimination of ligatures and abbreviations. Marginalia of *saec.* x. ILLUMINATION. There seem to be no uncials in the book. The *explicits-incipits* are in bright red rustic capitals. FOLS. 1 and 41–60, which fill in gaps, are of *saec.* x. REFERENCE. *Cat. gén.* XXXVIII, 96.

10. REIMS, Bibl. de la Ville 101. (Chap. A, ord. 2, no. 25.) *St. Gregory. (Moralium in Job libri XI–XVI.)* 181 leaves. 285×184. 1 col., 205×126. 29 lines. BOOK-MARKS. Like the preceding manuscript this book does not have the regular Hincmar book-mark. Instead we find: SCAE MARIAE / REMENSIS ECCLAE on fols. 8ᵛ–9ʳ, 86ᵛ–87ʳ, 176ᵛ–177ʳ. SCRIPT. Several types of Caroline minuscule common at Reims. Five main hands, more or less: A (1ʳ–40ᵛ, 125ʳ–128ᵛ, more or less), B (41ʳ–112ᵛ, more or less), C (113ʳ–124ᵛ, more or less), D (129ʳ–146ᵛ, more or less), E (147ʳ–181ᵛ more or less). Hands A–C are in a fairsized, flowing, open style of the formal Reims type; ligatures and abbreviations occur fairly commonly, however. Hands D–E are somewhat more crabbed and angular, like those of *Reims 83* and *100*. ILLUMINATION. Bright red uncial *explicits-incipits* are more common than those in rustic capitals in this book. REFERENCE. *Cat. gén.* XXXVIII, 96–7.

11. REIMS, Bibl. de la Ville 118. (Chap. A, ord. 2, no. 16.) *Bede, St. Jerome, St. Gregory, Alcuin.* fol. 1ʳ–37ᵛ *Bedae expositio in Psalmos.* fol. 38ʳ–53ʳ *Hieronymi quaestiones in libris Regum.* fol. 53ʳ–67ʳ *Hieronymi expositio in Paralipomenon.* fol. 67ʳ–79ʳ *Bedae quaestiones in libros Regum.* fol. 79ʳ–81ᵛ *Bedae expositio de nominibus locorum quae leguntur in Actibus Apostolorum.* fol. 81ᵛ–90ᵛ *Gregorii Concordia quorumdam testimoniorum sacrae Script.* fol. 90ᵛ–102ᵛ *Gregorii expositio super Cantica Canticorum.* fol. 103ʳ–115ʳ *Alcuini expositio in VII Psalmos poenitentiales.* fol. 116ʳ–124ʳ *Alcuini expositio in psalmos graduales.* fol. 124ʳ–140ᵛ *cuiusdam incerti expositio in quosdam psalmos.* 140 leaves. 278×225. 1 col., 201×160. 29 lines. BOOK-MARKS. This does not have the regular Hincmar book-

mark. Instead we read: HINCMARUS DIACONUS DEDIT STEPHANO on fols. I^r, 58^v–59^r, 140^v–B^r (B is a guard-leaf at the end of the volume). The capital letter *H* with a vertical stroke like an *I* through the cross-bar occurs on fols. I^r, 4^r, 38^r, 103^r. When it occurs in Mss. of Reims, I have found no difficulty in assuming that it stands for Hincmar. On fol. 4^r we find: STEPHANUS DEDIT SCAE MARIAE REMENSI. On fols. II^v–12^r we find: LIBER SCAE MA-RIAE / REMENSIS ECCLAE (perhaps later, *saec* ix). I have no doubt that the Hincmar in question is the famous bishop; in *Reims 7* he calls himself 'abba' in giving a book to the monastery of St. Thierry. For Stephanus *vide Reims 74* and *875*. SCRIPT. Various similar hands of a small, close, careful type, with ligatures and abbreviations almost abolished. Eight main hands: A (I^r–2^v, a preface hand, the 'milk' of Reims), B (4^r–4^v, 28^r–37^v), C (4^v–27^v), D (38^r–71^v, 128^r–140^v), E (72^r–102^v), F (103^r–104^r), G (104^v–115^v), H (116^r 127^v). Hand D is the only one which admits ligatures to any extent. ILLUMINATION. Headings and *explicits-incipits* are in brown rustic capitals. There is no red in the book, nor do there seem to be any uncials. FOL. A (a guard-leaf at the beginning) Scribble: *Rodulfus*. The same scribble occurs in another book written by a Stephanus of the same period: *Reims 74*, fol. 121^v. *Reims 875*, the famous book of John the Scot, was also given to the Cathedral Library by a Stephanus of this same period. REFERENCE. *Cat. gén.* XXXVIII, 109–112.

12. REIMS, Bibl. de la Ville 376. (Chap. A, ord. 3, no. 32.) *St. Ambrose, opuscula.* fol. I^r–10^r *Ambrosii dicta de Salomone.* fol. 10^r–27^r *Ambrosii de divinis mysteriis.* fol. 27^v–33^v *Ambrosii de Gedeon* (*prologus tractatus de Spiritu Sancto*). fol. 33^v–66^v *Ambrosii de vinea Nabuthae Israelitae.* fol. 66^v–109^r *Ambrosii apologia David.* fol. 109^r–112^v *Ambrosii de Pascha.* 112 leaves. 235×183. 1 col., 147×112. 19 lines. BOOK-MARKS. The regular Hincmar book-mark (occasionally mutilated) on fols. I^r, 27^v–28^r, 32^v–33^r, 62^v–63^r, 86^v–87^r, 112^v. SCRIPT. Clear, open, traitless Caroline minuscule of Reims. Some *st* ligatures, but few on the whole. Few abbreviations. One hand throughout. ILLUMINATION. Bright red uncial and rustic capital headings and *explicits-incipits*. Simple initials in red and yellow on fols. I^r, 10^v, 34^r, 66^v, 109^r. Fine white parchment with rulings in brown crayon. REFERENCE. *Cat. gén.* XXXVIII, 484–6.

13. REIMS, Bibl. de la Ville 377. (Chap. A, ord. 2, no. 16.) *St. Ambrose, Rufinus of Aquileia, Victor of Tonnenna.* fol. I^r–10^v *Ambrosii liber de mysteriis.* fol. 10^v–32^r *Ambrosii libri VI de sacramentis.* fol. 32^r–62^v *Ambrosii libri de Paradiso.* fol. 63^r–81^r *Ambrosii de virginibus liber I et II.* fol. 81^r–108^r *Rufini Commentarii in symbolis apostolorum* (here called: *tractatus epi. Augustini de fide simboli ad Laurentium Papam.*) Migne, *P.L.*, vol. 21, cols. 335 ff. fol. 109^r–139^v *S. Victoris Tonensis epi. historiographi de Delapsis.* 140 leaves (112 bis). 254×222. 1 col., 162×142. 23 lines. BOOK-MARKS. The regular Hincmar book-mark (occasionally mutilated) on fols. I^r, 48^v–49^r, 72^v–73^r, 76^v–77^r. On fol. 139^v the same mark in contemporary brown minuscules, an unusual occurrence; but *vide Reims 393*. On fol. I^r in the extreme lower left-hand corner we read: *pars huberti*. In a similar place on fol. 63^r: *incip*(*it*) *pars aderhardi*; and on fol. 109^r: *pars berulfi*. Cf. *Cambridge, Pembroke College 308* for similar signatures of scribes.

SCRIPT. Moderately small, careful but somewhat crabbed and uneven Caroline minuscule. Few ligatures and abbreviations. Some Tironian notes on fols. 44^v, 47^v, 48^v, etc. Three hands, as indicated above: A (*pars Huberti*, 1^r–62^v), B (*pars Aderhardi*, 63^r–108^v), C (*pars Berulfi*, 109^r–139^v). Open *a* occurs in glosses. ILLUMINATION. Red rustic capital *explicits-incipits* on fols. 10^v, 32^r, 62^v, 63^r, 81^r. A few red uncials (fol. 1^r). REFERENCES. *Cat. gén.* XXXVIII, 486–7. *CSEL* XXXII^1 (1897), LV.

14. REIMS, Bibl. de la Ville 382. (Saint-Thierry no. 36.) *St. Augustine.* (*Retractationum libri II. Contra Academicos libri III. De ordine libri II.*) Fols. 1–78, *saec.* xi^{ex}, I disregard. 93 leaves (fols. 79–171). 270×191. 1 col., 195×122. 26 lines. BOOK-MARKS. The regular Hincmar book-mark on fols. 101^v–102^r, 123^v–124^r, 147^v–148^r, 163^v–164^r. (The first half of the book, fols. 1–78, which I disregard, has three marks of the library of St. Thierry of *saec.* xii–xiv.) SCRIPT. Various hands ranging from mediocre to good Caroline minuscule. Eight main hands: A (79^r–80^r), B (80^v–85^v), C (86^r–117^v), D (118^r–123^v), E (124^r–129^v), F (130^r–131^v), G (132^r–165^r), H (165^r–171^v). Hands A and F have no *st* ligatures and otherwise show regular Reims style. The other hands are mostly small and somewhat uneven. Open *a* occurs in glosses (fol. 81^r). ILLUMINATION. Brown and red rustic capitals in headings and *explicits-incipits* on fols. 107^r, 115^r, 134^v, 149^v, 171^v. Uncials seem not to occur. REFERENCE. *Cat. gén.* XXXVIII, 499–500.

15. REIMS, Bibl. de la Ville 384. (Chap. A, ord. 3, no. 35.) *Tichonius.* (*libri VII Regularum.*) 37 leaves. 238×200. 2 cols., 183×148. 28 lines. BOOK-MARKS. The regular Hincmar book-mark on fols. 1^r, 16^v, 17^r, 35^v. SCRIPT. Fine open, spaced, clear, rounding Caroline minuscule, the 'milk' of Reims. One hand throughout. Few ligatures and abbreviations. ILLUMINATION. Headings and *explicits-incipits* in red rustic capitals. Uncials seem not to occur. REFERENCE. *Cat. gén.* XXXVIII, 503–4.

16. REIMS, Bibl. de la Ville 385. (Chap. A, ord. 3, no. 33.) *St. Jerome, Alcuin,* etc. fol. 1^r–14^r *Hieronymi tract. contra Luciferianos.* fol. 14^v–60^v *Altercatio Athanasii contra Arrium* etc. fol. 61^r–95^v *Acta concilii Francofurtensis contra Elipantum.* fol. 95^v–154^r *Alcuini et Elipanti epp. et opuscula quaedam.* fol. 154^r–158^r *Confessio Fidei Felicis, Urgellitani epi.* 160 leaves. 246×192. 1 col., 190×137. 28 lines. BOOK-MARKS. The regular Hincmar book-mark on fols. 1^r, 24^v–25^r, 46^v–47^r, 70^v–71^r, 94^v–95^r, 118^v–119^r, 142^v–143^r, 156^v–157^r. SCRIPT. Several varieties of small and medium-sized Caroline minuscule. Eight main hands: A (1^r–50^v, more or less), B (50^v–70^v), C (71^r–78^v, 95^r–105^r, 111^r–136^v, 157^r–160^r), D (79^r–94^v), E (105^r–110^v), F (136^v–142^v), G (143^r–149^v), H (149^v–155^v). Ligatures and abbreviations are not uncommon in this book. Some of the writing is rather crabbed and stiff. Hand B most nearly approaches the normal style of the period. ILLUMINATION. The headings and *explicits-incipits* seem to be in bright red rustic capitals only. REFERENCES. *Cat. gén.* XXXVIII, 504–8. Albert Werminghoff, *Neues Archiv* 26 (1901), 24.

17. REIMS, Bibl. de la Ville 390. (Chap. A, ord. 1, no. 6.) *St. Augustine.* (*De Trinitate libri XV.*) 136 leaves. 299×262. 2 cols., 215×187. BOOK-MARKS. The

regular Hincmar book-mark on fols. 1ᵛ–2ʳ, 4ᵛ–5ʳ, 12ᵛ–13ʳ, 20ᵛ–21ʳ, 44ᵛ–45ʳ, 68ᵛ–69ʳ, 92ᵛ–93ʳ, 116ᵛ–117ʳ, 133ᵛ–134ʳ. SCRIPT. Ordinary undistinguished Caroline minuscle. One main hand (or possibly two hands) for fols. 5ʳ–108ᵛ. Ligatures and abbreviations are not uncommon. Some of the letters show signs of clubbing. ILLUMINATION. In the capitula on fols. 1ᵛ–4ʳ an abundance of brown and red rustic capitals, as also in the *explicits-incipits* throughout the book. There is a single line of uncials in red on fol. 5ʳ. REFERENCE. *Cat. gén.* XXXVIII, 519–20.

18. REIMS, Bibl. de la Ville 392. (Chap. A, ord. 4, no. 21.) *St. Augustine, opuscula. (Liber de magistro. De sancta virginitate. Regula. Sermo Arrianorum et libellus contra eundem sermonem. Epistola de cavendo Iudaismo et de recipiendis Donatistis.* 120 leaves (plus A, a guard-leaf with a contemporary index on the verso). 2 cols. (fols. 1–31ʳ); 1 col. (fols. 31ᵛ–end), 158×122. 22 lines. BOOK-MARKS. The regular Hincmar book-mark on fols. Aᵛ–1ʳ, 30ᵛ–31ʳ, 48ᵛ–49ʳ, 64ᵛ–65ʳ, 96ᵛ–97ʳ, 119ᵛ–120ʳ. All these press-marks stand in complete erasures on both pages, but the book is certainly Hincmarian. SCRIPT. Various sorts of ordinary, careful Caroline minuscule of the Reims type, straight and fairly well spaced. Some ligatures and abbreviations. Four main hands: A (1ʳ–11ʳ), B (11ʳ–48ᵛ), C (49ʳ–59ʳ), (59ʳ–120ʳ, more or less). ILLUMINATION. Red uncials and red and brown rustic capitals in headings and *explicits-incipits*. REFERENCE. *Cat. gén.* XXXVIII, 522–3.

19. REIMS, Bibl. de la Ville 393. (Chap. A, ord. 2, no. 20.) *St. Augustine, opuscula. (Epistola ad Eutropium et Paulum. De natura et gratia ad Valentinum epistolae duae. De gratia et libero arbitrio. De correptione et gratia. De Praedestinatione. De dono perseverantiae. De bono coniugali. De sancta virginitate. De Nuptiis et concupiscentia.)* 172 leaves. 265×222. 1 col., 193×147. 31 lines. BOOK-MARKS. The regular Hincmar book-mark (with mutilations) on fols. 1ʳ, 72ᵛ–73ʳ. On fols. 171ᵛ–172ʳ the same mark in contemporary brown minuscules, as in *Reims 377*. SCRIPT. Various types of small to medium Caroline minuscule of the Reims school. Four main hands: A (1ʳ–109ʳ, more or less), B (110ʳ–118ʳ), C (118ʳ–149ᵛ), D (150ʳ–172ᵛ, more or less). In Part I (fols. 1–109) many short glosses and Tironian notes occur; in Part II there are some Tironian notes, but few glosses, and these late; in the scholia of Part I open *a* is frequent. Hands A-C show few abbreviations or ligatures; hand D is somewhat free and cursive. ILLUMINATION. Red and brown rustic capitals dominate headings and *explicits-incipits*. I see only two lines of red uncials (fols. 13ᵛ and 74ʳ). On fols. 110ʳ, 140ᵛ, and 154ʳ blank spaces have been left for the rubricator. REFERENCES. *Cat. gén.* XXXVIII, 523–6. *CSEL* XXXXII (1902), IIII–V. CSEL LX (1913), X.

20. REIMS, Bibl. de la Ville 425. (Chap. A, ord. 1, no. 8.) *Isidore, Etymologiae* and *Glossae;* '*Cicero,*' *Synonyma.* 272 leaves. 302×259. 2 cols. (fols. 1ʳ–205); 4 cols. (fols. 206ʳ–266ᵛ); 8 cols. (fols. 266ᵛ–272ᵛ), *circa* 219×191. 30 lines. BOOK-MARKS. The regular Hincmar book-mark (occasionally mutilated) on fols. 1ʳ, 16ᵛ–17ʳ, 48ᵛ–49ʳ, 88ᵛ–89ʳ, 104ᵛ–105ʳ, 128ᵛ–129ʳ, 144ᵛ–145ʳ, 176ᵛ–177ʳ, 205ʳ, 216ᵛ–217ʳ, 235ʳ, 238ᵛ–239ʳ, 272ᵛ. SCRIPT. Varying types of Caroline minuscule of Reims, both mediocre and good. Three main hands: A (1ʳ–24ᵛ), B (25ʳ–232ᵛ, 238ʳ–241ᵛ, more or less), C (233ʳ–237ᵛ, 242ʳ–272ᵛ). Hand A shows more ligatures and ab-

breviations than the other two; hand C is most characteristic of Reims. There are a good many notes of the middle of the tenth century. ILLUMINATION. Many bright red rustic capital headings. REFERENCE. *Cat. gén.* XXXVIII, 566–8.

21. REIMS, Bibl. de la Ville 434. (Chap. A, ord. 1, no. 10.) *Bede.* (*De gratia Dei. Expositio super Cantica Canticorum in V libris. De opusculis Gregorii Papae liber sextus in Cantico Canticorum collectus.*) 133 leaves (13 bis). 300×220. 2 cols., 210–220×153. 27–32 lines. RULING. The only exceptional Ms. of this group. Quire VI ruled two leaves at a time from the outside: $\gg|\gg\|\ll|\ll$. Quire X ruled two leaves at a time from the outside (A on B), and then two leaves at a time from the inside (D^v on C^v): $\gg|\ll\|\gg|\ll$. Quire VII (irregularly): B^v on A^v; C; D^v. $\ll|>|<\|$. Quire VIII (irregularly): A; B^v; D^v on C^v. $>|<|\ll\|$. BOOK-MARKS. The regular Hincmar book-mark on fols. 49^v–50^r, 65^v–66^r, 73^v–74^r, 89^v–90^r, 97^r–98^r, 105^v–106^r, 113^v–114^r, 121^v–122^r, 129^v–130^r, 131^v. SCRIPT. Several varieties of medium to small Caroline minuscule, early in the Hincmarian period, if not before it. Open *a* is common. Both the apostrophe and the figure *2* abbreviation for *-ur* appear, sometimes with the former changed into the latter. Ligatures and abbreviations are fairly frequent, although Hand B (4^r–36^v) has abolished most of them. There are nine or more hands. This is an anomalous book and may well have been written earlier than our period and presented by Hincmar some time later than its writing. ILLUMINATION. Four lines of red uncials give the heading on fol. 4^r. Otherwise brown uncials and rustic capitals are used in the *explicits-incipits.* REFERENCE. *Cat. gén.* XXXVIII, 587–8.

22. PARIS, Bibliothèque Nationale, Ms. Lat. 5609. (Colbert 5543; Regius 4432.7) *Vita S. Huberti episcopi Leodiensis, auctore Iona episcopo.* 68 leaves. 202×175. 1 col., 118×92. 15 lines. BOOK-MARKS. The regular Hincmar book-mark does not appear; instead we have: fols. 2^v–3^r. HINCMARUS ARCHIEPS/ DEDIT SCO REMIGIO (then in a hand of *saec.* xii) *qui ei abstulerit anathema sit.* On fols. 1^r and 35^r in the upper margin in a hand of *saec.* xiii appears the regular red book-mark of the library of St. Remi: *Lib. sci. Remigii Rem. vol. iiii^{xx} et xii* (i.e., quatre-vingt-douze, or 92). SCRIPT. The ordinary full, flowing Caroline minuscule of Reims with few abbreviations or ligatures. One hand throughout. Fols. 1, 2, 67, and 68 are later, *circa* 1000 A.D. ILLUMINATION. Bright red and brown uncials and rustic capitals in the headings. FOL. 63^v. The year 825 is mentioned in the text. According to Potthast this life was written in 825.

*   *   *

In the following list of Reims manuscripts I have marked with an asterisk those books which I have not seen and which I know only from photographs or the descriptions of others. The capital letter within parentheses, which follows the title of a manuscript, designates its provenience, so far as it is known, and is thus to be interpreted: (B) monastery of St. Basol; (C) Cathedral Chapter of Reims; (H) monastery of Hautvillers; (N) monastery of St. Nicaise; (R) monastery of St. Remi; (T) monastery of St. Thierry. In the few instances where facsimiles are available, I have added a brief reference. It is hardly necessary to say that this list represents the results of long study and thought and contains my present opinions on the school of Reims. Some periods, however, like those of 825–845 and 882–900, offer peculiar difficulties and may involve changes later. At the end of the main list I have included a list of doubtful and of rejected manuscripts for the sake of completeness.

A HAND-LIST OF MANUSCRIPTS OF REIMS WRITTEN BEFORE 1100 A.D.

saec. vi/vii
Reims 1424

saec. vii
Reims 132, fol. C.   (R)

saec. viii
Berlin 84 (Phillipps 1743)   (R)
Leiden, Bibl. Pub. Leid. 114   (R)
Paris, Bibl. Nat. 7691   (R)
Reims   8 fols. 1–2.   (T)
"   123 fol. B.   (R)

800–825 A.D.
Bern 522   (R)
*Épernay 1   (H)
Leiden Voss. Q. 60   (R)
Paris, Bibl. Nat. 8780   (R)
Reims   5   (T)
"   8 fols. 3–102.   (T)
"   73   (T)
"   75   (C)
"   76   (R)
"   110   (T)
"   413   (C)
"   414 fols. 49–79.   (T)
"   415   (T)
"   426 fols. 1–117.   (T)
"   435   (T)
"   443   (C)
"   671   (R)
Rome, Vat. Regin. lat. 191   (R)

825–845 A.D.
Bamberg Patrist. 21 (E. III. 21)
fols. 37–146.   (C)
Bern 318
*Leningrad Oct. I. 5.   (R)[29]

Paris, Bibl. Nat. 8728   (R)
Reims   10   (C)
"   123   (R)
"   130   (C)
"   373   (T)
"   374 fols. 16–51.   (C)
"   414 fols. 80–111.   (T)
Rome, Vat. Regin. lat. 213   (R)
*Utrecht, Universitätsbibliothek
F. IV. (The Utrecht Psalter).

845–882 A.D. Period of Hincmar
Bamberg Philos. 2 (HJ. IV. 5 and
6; 2 vols.)
Berlin 82 (Phill. 1741) & Rome,
Vat. Regin. lat. 1283 fols. 95–
96.   (R)
Berlin 163 (Phill. 1762)   (R)
Bern 427   (R)
Cambridge, Pembroke College
308   (C)
*Laon 81
London, Brit. Mus. Addit. 9046   (R)
New York, Morgan 728
*Paris, Bibl. Mazarine 561
"   Bibl. Nat.   5609   (R)
"   "   "   10758 pages 1–
136.
Paris, Bibl. Nat. 12445
"   "   "   13090 fols. 70–
77b.   (R)
Paris, Bibl. Nat. 13764 fols. 73–
89.   (R)
*Paris, Bibl. Nat. 17968 (Loisel
Gospels)
Reims   1   (C)
"   2   (C)

---

[29] Staerk, *Mss. de St. Pétersbourg*, II, Pl. 42–3.

Reims 3 (C)
" 7 (T)
" 11 (C)
" 46 (C)
" 70 (C)
" 74 (C)
" 83 (C)
" 85 (T)
" 99 (C)
" 100 (C)
" 101 (C)
" 116 fols. 1-126. (T)
" 118 (C)
" 123 (R)
" 376 (C)
" 377 (C)
" 382 (T)
" 384 (C)
" 385 (C)
" 390 (C)
" 391 (C)
" 392 (C)
" 393 (C)
" 414 fols. 80-111. (T)
" 425 (C)
" 434 (C)
" 1351 (C)
Rome,Vat. Regin. lat. 272 (R)
" " " " 845 (R)
" " " " 1046 (R)
" " " " 1283 fols. 95-96 & Berlin 82 (Phill. 1741).

882-900 A.D.

Bamberg Patrist. 46 (Q. VI. 36)
Bern 83 (R)
" 370 (C)
" 425 (R)
" 584 (R)
London, Brit. Mus., Reg. 15. A. XXXIII. (R)
London, Brit. Mus., Reg. 15. B. XIX fols. 37-102, 111-196. (R)
*Montpellier, Bibl. de l'École de Méd. 126 (Chatelain, Pl. CLXVI²). (T)

Oxford, Bodleian 157 (R)
Paris, Bibl. Nat. 1594
" " " 1597A (R)
" " " 2865
" " " 2866 (R)
" " " 4668 (R)
" " " 5569 (R)
" " " 7899
" " " 10758 pages 137-340.
Paris, Bibl. Nat. 11884 fols. 1-4.
" " " 12964
" " " 13763 fols. 1-102. (R)
Reims 77 (C)
" 116 fols. 127-223. (T)
" 126 (C)
" 129 (C)
" 296 fols. 1-65. (T)
" 369 (C)
" 396 (H)
" 414 fols. 1-48. (T)
" 438 (T)
" 875 (C)
Rome, Vat. lat. 326 (R)
Rome, Vat. Regin. lat. 994 (R)
" " " " 1650 (R)

900-950 A.D.

Bamberg Class. 8 (HJ. IV. 13)
Leiden, Voss. Q. 71 (C)
Paris, Bibl. Nat. 4280A (R)
" " " 7974 (Chatelain, Pl. LXXXIV). (R)
Paris, Bibl. Nat. 9347 (R)
" " " 13764 fols. 60-72.
Reims 132 (R)
" 247 (C)
" 296 fols. 66-135. (T)
" 304 (T)
" 374 fols. 52-59. (C)
" 394 (T)
" 408 fols. 1-98. (T)
" 421 (T)
" 427 fols. 19-132. (T)

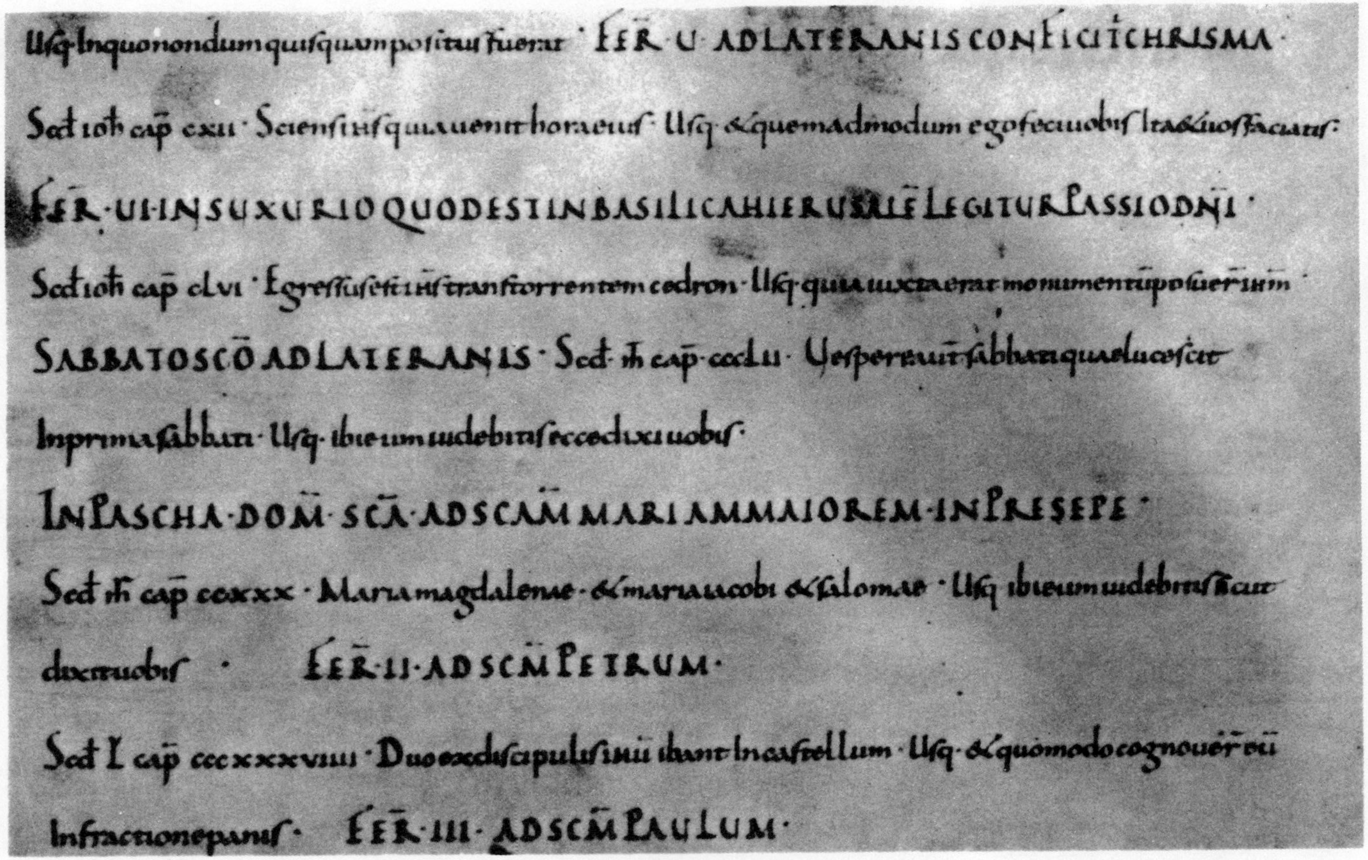
Usq. In quo nondum quisquam positus fuerat · FER. V. AD LATERANIS CONFICIT CHRISMA ·
Sect. ioh. cap. cxii · Sciens ihs quia venit hora eius · Usq. et quemadmodum ego feci vobis ita et vos faciatis ·
FER. VI. IN SUXURIO QUOD EST IN BASILICA HIERUSALE LEGITUR PASSIO DNI ·
Sect. ioh. cap. clvi · Egressus est ihs trans torrentem cedron · Usq. quia iuxta erat monumentu posuer ihm ·
SABBATO SCO AD LATERANIS · Sect. mt cap. cccLii · Vespere aut sabbati quae lucescit
In prima sabbati · Usq. ibi eum videbitis ecce dixi vobis ·
IN PASCHA DOM · SCA AD SCAM MARIAM MAIOREM · IN PRESEPE ·
Sect. mr cap. ccxxx · Maria magdalenae et maria iacobi et salomae · Usq. ibi eum videbitis sicut
dixit vobis · FER. II. AD SCM PETRUM ·
Sect. L cap. cccxxxviiii · Duo ex discipulis ihu ibant in castellum · Usq. et quomodo cognover eu
in fractione panis · FER. III. AD SCM PAULUM ·

PLATE I

New York, Morgan Library, 728, fol. 180v, top.

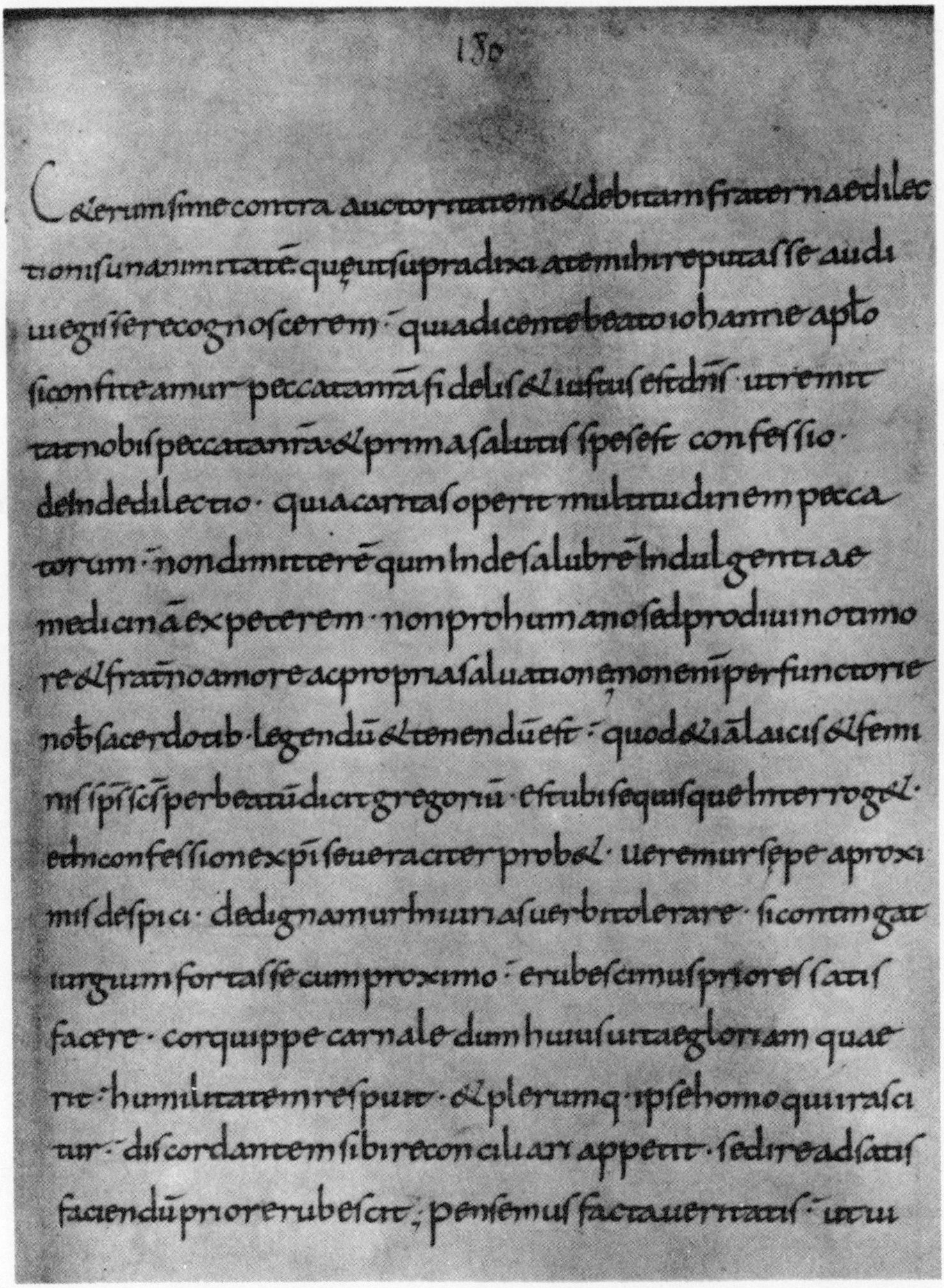

Ceterum sine contra auctoritatem & debitam fraternae dilec
tionis unanimitatem quę ut supradixi a te mihi reputasse audi
ui egi se recognoscerem quia dicente beato iohanne apto
si confiteamur peccata nostra fidelis & iustus est dns ut remit
tat nobis peccata nostra & prima salutis spes est confessio
deinde dilectio quia caritas operit multitudinem pecca
torum non dimittere quin inde salubrem indulgentiae
medicinam expeterem non pro humano sed pro diuino timo
re & fraterno amore ac propria saluatione quę non enim perfunctorie
nobis sacerdotibus legendum & tenendum est quod & ia laicis & femi
nis spus scs per beatum dicit gregorium est ubi se quisque interrogat
& in confessione expii seueraciter probat ut remur sepe a proxi
mis despici dedignamur iniurias uerbi tolerare si contingat
iurgium fortasse cum proximo erubescimus priores satis
facere cor quippe carnale dum huius uitae gloriam quae
rit humilitatem respuit & plerumq ipse homo qui irasci
tur discordantem sibi reconciliari appetit sed ire ad satis
faciendum prior erubescit pensemus facta ueritatis ut ui

PLATE II

Paris, B. N., lat. 2865, fol. 180^r.

Reims 439	(T)	
" 975 fols. 34–75.	(C)	
" 1097	(C)	
" 1395	(C)	
Rome, Vat. Regin. lat. 417	(R)	
" " " " 418	(R)	

950–1000 A.D.

Bamberg Hist. 5 (E. III. 3)	
Berlin 135 (Phill. 1886)	(R)
*Dresden Dc. 182	(C)
Paris, Bibl. Nat. 4789	(R)
" " " 13764 fols. 49–	
59.	(R?)
Reims 4	(T)
" 6	(T)
" 14	(T)
" 96	(T)
" 125	(T)
" 133	(C)
" 214	(T)
" 250	(T)
" 258 fols. 1–145, 153–160.	(T)
" 395 fols. 1–12.	(T)
" 408	(T)
" 427 fols. 137–168.	(T)
" 440	(T)
" 1405	(T)
" 1412	(T)
Rome, Vat. Regin. lat. 561	(R)

1000–1100 A.D.

Paris, Bibl. Nat. 13763 fols. 103–168.	(R?)
Paris, Bibl. Nat. 13764 fols. 1–48.	(R)
Reims 8 fols. 103–111.	(T)
" 12	(T)
" 13 fols. 1–167.	(C)
" 15	(C)
" 78 fols. 7–46.	(T)
" 86 fols. 9–72.	(T)
" 102	(C)
" 134	(T)
" 135	(T)
" 252	(C)
" 258 fols. 161–190.	(T)

Reims 294 fols. 11–281.	(C)
" 295 fols. 1–323.	(C)
" 297	(T)
" 305	(T)
" 340	(C)
" 341	(N)
" 357 fragm. 1.	
" 374 fols. 1–15.	(C)
" 382 fols. 1–78.	(T)
" 395 fols. 41–156.	(T)
" 426 fols. 118–210.	(T)
" 427 fols. 1–13, 133–136.	(T)
" 428	(T)
" 673	(C)
" 975 fols. 1–33.	(C)
" 1329	(C)
" 1352	(T)
" 1354	(T)
" 1402	(C)
" 1403	(C)
" 1406	(T)
" 1412	(T)
" 1413 fols. 20–73.	(T)
" 1429	(C)

Doubtful Mss.
800–825 A.D.

Bern 233	
" 234	
Reims 1094	(H)

845–882 A.D.

Bern 109	(B)
" 705	
Rome, Vat. Regin. lat. 314 fols. 119–140.	
Rome, Vat. Regin. lat. 598 fols. 35–36.	
Rome, Vat. Regin. lat. 980 fols. 19–34.	

882–900 A.D.

Bern 199
Leiden Voss. Q. 116
New York, Morgan 640
Paris, Bibl. Nat. 12255

Paris, Bibl. Nat. 12965
Rome, Vat. Regin. lat. 581 fol. 39.
Rome, Vat. Regin. lat. 1424 fols. 91–98.
Venice, Marcianus 270

900–950 A.D.

Bamberg Hist. 162 (E. III. 5)
  "   Class. 30 (M. V. 18)
Berlin 110 (Phill. 1876)
Paris, Bibl. Nat. 4287   (R?)
  "   "   "   11884 fols. 37–160.
Rome, Vat. Regin. lat. 1669

950–1000 A.D.

Bern 232
Rome, Vat. Regin. lat. 1424 fols. 9–90.

1000–1100 A.D.

Bern 47
  "   626
Berlin 89 (Phill. 1765)
Leiden Voss. Q. 102
  "   Voss. Q. 113
Reims 9   (R)
Rome, Vat. Regin. lat. 1424 fols. 1–8.

Rejected Mss.

saec. viii

Leiden BPL 191 BA
  "   Voss. O 69

UNIVERSITY OF CALIFORNIA AT LOS ANGELES.

800–825 A.D.

Leiden Voss. O. 74

825–845 A.D.

Leiden Voss. F. 62
  "   Voss. O. 29
Reims 789 (St. Omer.)
Rome, Vat. Regin. lat. 669.

845–882 A.D.

Rome, Vat. Regin. lat. 848
  "   "   "   "   849
  "   "   "   "   1128

882–900 A.D.

Leiden BPL 135
  "   Voss. O. 37
Paris, Bibl. Nat. 13764 fols. 118–214.

900–950 A.D.

Leiden BPL 109
  "   Voss. F. 64
  "   Voss. Q. 74

950–1000 A.D.

Bern 720
Leiden Voss. F. 13
  "   Voss. Q. 13
  "   Voss. Q. 18
Paris, Bibl. Nat. 13764 fols. 90–116.
Reims 213 (Noyon).

1000–1100 A.D.

Leiden Voss. O. 7

THE VERBAL 'ORNAMENT' (ΚΟΣΜΟΣ) IN ARISTOTLE'S ART OF POETRY

Lane Cooper

One might suppose that ornamental words would be numerous in poetry; that a Pindaric ode or a Hebrew psalm, or Homeric descriptions, or an ornate work like the Old English *Phoenix* and its source, the Lactantian *Phoenix*, or the Middle English *Pearl*, or 'lapidary' poems in general, would be full of such words and phrases; and that the ordinary names for ordinary things would thereby be reduced in number in these and other poems. But are we to take the term 'ornament' in a wide, or a restricted, sense? The Greek term, κόσμος, in some specific sense, has troubled commentators upon Aristotle's *Art of Poetry* from the days of the Renaissance.

In its widest sense for Aristotle the word κόσμος means what we mean by the cosmos, the ordered universe, for the Greeks as for us a world of beauty. He uses the word thus in various works other than the *Rhetoric* and *Poetics*, as any one may see who will consult the *Index Aristotelicus* of Bonitz. In a narrower sense it means an ornament or decorative element; for Aristotle it is likely almost always to connote order along with beauty. Thus in tragedy (*Poetics* 6.1449^b33) one constituent part must needs be the decorative element of spectacle (ὁ τῆς ὄψεως κόσμος); viewed in one way the whole tragedy is a spectacle, so that spectacle must be a part of the ordering of tragedy, and hence is an adornment. Still more narrowly considered, there is an element of poetic diction which Aristotle has termed κόσμος. And this term according to Gudeman (see his page 361 as mentioned below) offers the utmost difficulty ('die allergrössten Schwierigkeiten') of interpretation, as witness the numerous attempts to throw some light on the obscurity ('die zahlreichen Versuche, das Dunkel zu erhellen').

In this technical sense, for diction, the word 'ornament' (κόσμος) occurs four times in the extant works of Aristotle: once in the *Rhetoric* (3.7.1408^a 14); and thrice in the *Poetics* (21.1457^b2; 22.1458^a33; 22.1459^a14). The term is nowhere explained by him, though illustrated after a fashion in the *Rhetoric* (3.7.1408^a10–16):

Your language will be appropriate if it expresses emotion and character, and if it is in proportion with the subject. By proportion is meant that weighty matters shall not be treated in a slipshod way, nor trivial matters in a solemn way;

nor should ornament [κόσμος] be attached to a commonplace [εὐτελεῖ] word [or 'name-word,' ὀνόματι], or the effect will be comic, as in the poetry of Cleophon. He used phrases as absurd as it would be to say 'O Lady Fig!' [πότνια Συκῆ].

That would be about like saying 'O Lady Sukey!' instead of 'O Lady Psyche!' or 'Hera' or 'Circe.' Further, the manuscripts of the *Poetics* give no evidence of a lacuna where a copyist might have left an explanation out. So far as I know, the best if not the only way now left to explain the doubtful term never has been tried for it, although the method I now recommend has in other cases thrown light on Aristotle's meaning when his principle or statement has seemed dark, or partly so, either because we did not understand his illustration, or because no illustration from him is directly at hand.

The essence of the method here is to search the poets for instances, for positive examples; that is, after duly examining our author's text in order to learn as far as possible what the thing in question is not. So with the term 'enthymeme' in the *Rhetoric*. There is still on occasion some doubt in the minds of students what enthymemes may be, but all doubt should vanish as soon as we study a good speech, and see what the argumentative elements there, as distinguished from all others, really are. When you omit all else, then the arguments actually used by good speakers are the forms of utterance Aristotle has in mind to which he gives the name of enthymemes. That is the way I tried to explain the term 'enthymeme' in the introductory remarks to my translation (1932) of the *Rhetoric*. Accordingly, it is not hard to find enthymemes in profusion; they are as common as speeches because a speech of any length is sure to contain them.

Similarly, then, with the term κόσμος, the verbal 'ornament' in the *Poetics*. It must refer to something that Aristotle had observed in the diction of poets, and should be discoverable there. The searcher should take an ornate passage, as the description of Circe's palace, Alcinous' garden, or the landing-place of Odysseus at Ithaca, all in the *Odyssey*, or take an ornate passage in some other poem, ancient or modern; he should there find what Aristotle calls the current or usual words, the rare (or 'alien') words, if any, the metaphors as such, and the words, if any, invented by the poet, and also any compound, lengthened, shortened, or otherwise 'altered' words; eliminate all these seven kinds, and the remaining words would then be 'ornamental.' The other kinds are all defined or illustrated in the *Poetics*, and this is not, but can be found by the aforesaid method of elimination. Our author thinks that poetic diction is made up of eight kinds of words and phrases; he thinks this list exhaustive, and by his division he is right; if in a poem, or in poetry, we identify *a, b, c, e*, *f*, *g*, and *h*, the seven kinds which he identifies for us, he has, in fact, enabled us to identify *d* as well, the eighth. It comes fourth in his list, and certainly is not lower than fourth in importance. My method will not seem quite as cut and dried as that, for we have to remember that words are plastic, and change color with their surroundings; and yet at bottom that is my procedure.

Meanwhile for utter clearness' sake let us quote from the *Poetics* (21.1457^{b}1–3): ἅπαν δὲ ὄνομά ἐστιν ἢ κύριον ἢ γλῶττα ἢ μεταφορὰ ἢ κόσμος ἢ πεποιημένον ἢ ἐπεκτεταμένον ἢ ἀφῃρημένον ἢ ἐξηλλαγμένον. That is, every ὄνομα is one of the eight species we have just seen listed above. But what does ὄνομα mean? Does it mean 'noun' as Bywater has it, or 'word' as in Gudeman's excellent German translation? In 56^{b}21 Bywater notes its distinction from ῥῆμα, 'verb'; in 61^{a}31 he notes that the sense is extended to include ῥῆμα. In Greek sometimes it is wide enough to mean 'phrase' or 'locution.' We might here do well enough if we called it 'verbal element' —not necessarily restricted to single words. We must also note that κόσμος is not strictly rendered in Bywater's 'an ornamental word,' but is so rendered when we call it simply 'ornament.' In both *Rhetoric* and *Poetics* the Renaissance translator Riccoboni renders the term by the Latin fourth-declension noun *ornatus*. While this article is in galley-proofs, I gratefully learn from Professor Franceschini of Padua that the reading of the anonymous Latin translation of the year 1210 likewise is *ornatus* in all three passages of the *Poetics* here considered. For a discussion of *ornatus*, see in particular Quintilian 8.3.

Gudeman makes fairly clear what κόσμος is not, though he fails to re-mark that it need not mean words taken singly. And between the first and the second occurrence of the term in the *Poetics*, he thinks with Robortelli, Maggi, and others, Aristotle must have explained it at 21.1457^{b}33 after his discussion of the metaphor. It is, however, possible that the lack of a definition in the text is not an accident of time; it may be that the word suggested its own sense fully enough to Aristotle and other Greeks of his day. He often hammers at a small point when he thinks that it may not be clear, and at a large matter if it was then in dispute. Here he may have felt no need to amplify upon the clear word κόσμος.

Gudeman draws no evidence from the Arabic tradition of a possible lacuna, about the existence of which he is in too little doubt; his comment (see his fine edition of the *Poetics*, 1934, pp. 361–2) sums up the history of Aristotelian scholarship on the point, and adequately divides between our traditional knowledge and ignorance about the word, save that he does not join with Vahlen in dwelling on the passage in the *Rhetoric* (see above) where Aristotle shows that he considers πότνια an ornamental word. We know pretty well what κόσμος, as an element in poetic diction, did not mean to Aristotle. It did not mean, for instance, συκῆ (*fig-tree*, or *fig*). It did not mean, thinks Gudeman, the *epitheton*, nor in particular the *epitheton ornans*, since the epithet so often takes the shape of metaphor, and metaphor, as one of the other seven elements, must be something different; similarly, we might argue, it cannot mean the current or the compound word and so on. Gudeman proceeds to show our want of historical light upon any such word as κόσμος among the critical terms employed by later Greek and Latin theorists including Cicero, and indeed the want of traditional light upon it down to Dante; he has missed, however, the *speciosa vocabula* of Horace (*Epist.* 2.2.116). The term receives no further explanation from Aristotle in his *Rhetoric*, unless in 3.2.1405ᵃ 14 ff.—the passage runs to the end of chapter 2—where the verb κοσμεῖν ('adorn') is explained as the process of likening the object you wish to praise to a better object with a fine name; if you wish to belittle your object, compare it to a worse. This substitution of the better synonym represents the sense in which Bywater (ed. *Poetics*, 1909, p. 281) thinks that our term most probably should be taken. But why restrict the term to figurative language? Bywater does not go far enough. And a word is 'ornamental,' not through the comparison, whether express or metaphorically implied, but intrinsically so. Vahlen (*Beiträge zu Aristoteles' Poetik*, 1914, pp. 134–7) feels that the term somehow is more inclusive, but in the end gives up the problem with the hope that others may yet find the solution.

In the *Poetics* the verbal 'ornament,' as we have seen, must simply be distinguished from the other elements of poetic diction; and that is true whether the diction be epic or dramatic (see 22. 1459ᵃ10–14); but, particularly, one might think it ought to be distinguished from the ordinary word (τὸ κύριον) and the metaphor. Further, it is not a word by nature strange or rare ('alien'), compound, curtailed, or lengthened, or altered in some other way, nor yet a word invented by the poet; it is not by nature any of these others—unless it has a dual nature. Or perhaps a given illustration of this term might have a dual or a plural nature? Like the usual or current word (τὸ κύριον), and like metaphors too, the ornamental word is found in prose as well as verse. But Aristotle also says that in hexameter verse—that is, in epic poetry—there is the greatest scope for an embellished diction, and hence to-day our surest hunting-ground for the verbal 'ornament' should be the work of a poet like Homer or Milton. Virgil also ought to be a poet fond of ornamental words. What poet would not sometimes use them, even if, like Skelton or Kipling, he often called a spade a spade or worse?

Meanwhile note that Aristotle does not separate what we call common nouns from proper, and that many proper names are beautiful, as Zephyrus, Boreas, and Maia. Some names, again, like Nymph and Naiad, are midway between the common and the proper noun. Note also that many names for things were once live metaphors, but now are common nouns, and many other metaphors, as Theodore and Margaret, no longer mean the 'Gift of God' and 'Pearl' and so on, but signify an individual man or woman. Moreover, Aristotle's categories need not all of them be mutually exclusive in their application. When we look for actual illustrations of them, an ornamental word might happen to be an epithet as well, or metaphorical, or lengthened or curtailed. Homer's πολυφλοίσβοιο seems to be compounded, lengthened, and also metaphorical, and if it be an *epitheton ornans*, is there any reason why we should not call it *ornamental?* J. D. Lester's 'poluphloisboisterous' epithet for Homer is further lengthened, altered, and turned to comic effect, and is not merely metaphorical.[1] Similarly, if you called a spade, not a spade, but by its finer name, or if by 'Spade' you meant *Spada*, a sword, and had in mind the Ace of Spades, the fine name for the fine thing might well be ornamental. As Aristotle says in his *Rhetoric* (3.2.1405^b 6–8), quoting from the *Rhetoric* of Licymnius, 'The beauty of a word, or its ugliness, will lie either in the sound or in the sense.' He goes on to speak of what we should call the associations of a word, and also holds that, when we aim at beauty, 'our metaphors must be drawn from the province of things that are beautiful in sound, or in effect, or to sight or some other of the senses. It makes a difference whether we say, for instance, "rosy-fingered morn," or "purple-fingered," or, still worse, "red-fingered." ' As I take it, 'rosy-fingered' is a metaphor and a compound word, and 'morn' (in English) is a shortened word, and both of them, ροδοδάκτυλος Ἠώς (see *Iliad* 1.477 and elsewhere), are ornamental words in Greek. It would likewise make a difference, no doubt, to Aristotle, whether you said πότνια Συκῆ, or any of the following from the *Odyssey*: πότνια Ἥρη (4.513); πότνια νύμφη (5.149); πότνια Κίρκη (8.448, 10.394, 549). For us it makes a difference whether one is to say, 'Notre Dame de Paris,' or 'the Widow at Windsor'; one phrase is ornamental, and the other is not. Had Kipling said something like πότνια Νίκη for the Lady of Windsor, he might have received a garland of laurel. For him the damage was done by the first word, 'widow,' since 'Windsor' is or ought to be ornamental. 'Merry Wives' is better than 'Widow.' The courtly Spenser called good Potnia Bess 'the Faerie Queene' and 'Gloriana.' Aristotle nowhere implies that a verbal ornament need be a single word; on occasion it may be that, and at another time a phrase; just as his 'metaphor'

---

[1]   Poluphloisboisterous Homer of old
        Dropped all his augments into the sea.

Cf. *Times Literary Supplement*, London, March 29, 1923, p. 217.

may be one word, but his 'proportional metaphor,' for example, the 'shield of Dionysus' in the sense of a drinking-bowl, takes more than one. That can be true while it is also true that, taken singly, every word in prose or verse falls into one of his eight classes.

So again, if you called a cup, not a cup, but a chalice, or called a crown a diadem, or a hawk a tercelet or a falcon, the name might be an epithet, or metaphorical, and an ornamental word as well. Why a word used as an epithet or a metaphor should not be thought of as ornamental in itself is hard to see:

> Ethereal minstrel! pilgrim of the sky!

The idle question whether κόσμος does or does not mean an adjective or epithet is as old as Vettori and Castelvetro.[2] It is as idle as to say, for instance, that an epithet could not be a compound word like 'rosy-fingered' or a shortened word like 'adventrous' in Milton's 'my adventrous Song,' or to say that for a metaphor a poet could not use a current word like 'hawk' or 'fox' ('Go ye, and tell that fox'—Herod), or a compound, dialectal, coined, lengthened, shortened, or internally altered word. Traditions do not readily die in scholarship, and I do not expect to kill the one I am shooting at unless I shoot at it repeatedly; so I must keep on saying until some one else believes me that Aristotle's eight distinctions do not overlap, but examples of them do. The same example often illustrates more than one of his divisions.

In our search, however, we may first aim at excluding ordinary words, and forms curtailed and lengthened, as also forms that are compounded, and simple metaphors. True similes, in which the likeness is express, and a word of comparison, 'as' or 'like,' is used, need not be excluded, for obviously one thing might be intentionally ennobled by direct comparison with another thing the name of which was to the author ornamental. Thus, among the ornamental passages in the Song of Solomon, we have the description of a beauty

> Terrible as an army with *banners*.

With which compare Wordsworth:

> Before me shone a glorious world—
> Fresh as a banner bright, unfurled
> To music suddenly.[3]

Further, though, to some, Aristotle seems to have 'name-words' in a

---

[2] Castelvetro is sure it does not (*Poetica d'Aristotele Vulgarizzata et Sposta*, Vienna, 1570, p. 254[a]): 'Adunque non è agevol cosa a pervenire al vero di qual maniera di parole intendesse Aristotele per questa voce κόσμος, ma egli è bene agevol cosa a pervenire al vero si come si vede per le cose dette che egli non intese degli aggiunti secondo che vuole Pietro Vittorio.'

[3] *Ruth* 169–71.

narrower sense, that is, what we to-day call adjectives and nouns, primarily in view, still there is no reason why a verb (the name, so to speak, of an action) should not possess the quality of adornment; thus, if to Dante and others a circle is an ornament, the verb as well as the noun should be ornamental: 'A solitary falcon circled on motionless wing.'[4] The very form 'adorning' is an ornamental word; thus Wordsworth on the boreal Aurora, in a passage of elaborate description, where the story is delayed (*Peter Bell* 91–5):

> Haste! and above Siberian snows
> We'll sport amid the boreal morning;
> Will mingle with her lustres gliding
> Among the stars, the stars now hiding,
> And now the stars adorning.

The Aurora with its lustres, and the Siberian snows, are obviously drawn from two rich sources of poetical adornment, geography and the realm of light. This latter realm even more than the other should furnish the poets, Milton and Dante as well as Wordsworth and Homer, with many beautiful words. Thither we ought to betake us. It is Aristotle himself who throughout the *Rhetoric* keeps letting us see that, if we wish to hunt a particular kind of animal or thing, or argument, we should go to the place, the *topos*, where it is likely to be found, its natural habitat. The natural home of beautiful words is not a critical treatise, but the critic may net them in flocks with his quotations. This article quotes enough of them to let the reader make his own induction concerning them.

Yet before all else let us see if another negative consideration will not help us on our way. Take a modern instance in which the poet shows an understanding of the ornamental word by his unexpected choice of one that is not. In Lewis Carroll's short and amusing Art of Poetry which he calls *Poeta Fit, Non Nascitur*, the elderly man of experience advises the budding poet to use words like 'wild,' 'lonely,' 'weary,' 'strange.' 'And will it do,' cries the enthusiastic young one, 'to take them in a lump?'—

> As 'The wild man went his weary way
> To a strange and lonely pump'?

'Lump' and 'pump' are not ornaments for face, ode, or garden. O Lady Lump and Potnia Pump! Nor is 'spade' likely to be a word in this class, nor 'hank'— 'A rag and a bone and a hank of hair.' These last three are in an opposite class, while also to be classed as metaphors. But they serve by opposition to remind us again that the names of ornamental things are likely to be ornamental. And that is the point, if I may say

---

[4] Pseudo-Clemens I.I: Πότνια Ἴρηξ (but because of the gender read Ἴρις?)

so, where my thinking of illustrations for this term began. I was reading
Addison on a certain aspect of *Paradise Lost* which he makes bold to
censure (*Spectator*, No. 297; Cook's *Addison's Criticisms on Paradise
Lost*, pp. 40–1). He objects to Milton's use of technical words, and instances as unsuitable these terms from architecture: 'Doric pillars,' 'pilasters,' 'cornice,' 'frieze,' and 'architrave.' He thinks that 'zenith' also
is too technical.

But are not 'Doric,' 'pillars,' 'pilasters,' 'cornice,' 'frieze,' and 'zenith,'
not only acceptable words in other ways, but also clearly ornamental?
Instinctively defending Milton's well-considered practice against the less
imaginative critic, I thought also of what Aristotle says in a general way
about the embellishment of poetic diction, and especially about the proper place for it. That sort of place, presumably, is where we ought to
hunt. In closing chapter 24 of the *Poetics*, he speaks of the improbabilities
in the episode (*Odyssey* 13. 70ff.) where Odysseus is set ashore, still sleeping, by the Phaeacian crew at Ithaca. It is not likely that the returning
hero would at this point be, or stay, asleep. The poet, says Aristotle,
conceals the improbability by his other excellences, and from what follows it is clear that Aristotle has particularly in mind the excellence of
elaborate diction. The poet should elaborate the *lexis* when there is no
action, and no character or thought to be revealed. And since Odysseus
is asleep, and there can be no action, nor display of *ethos* or *dianoia*, so
far as his activity, and power of choice, and utterance or argument, are
concerned, while the Phaeacians too are silent, we may infer that this
passage of the *Odyssey* will make due use, in Aristotle's view, of ornamental words. Only the poet speaks in description.

What do we find there? We do find elaborate diction, and, among the
words, some perhaps the usual names for things, as the rug (ῥῆγος) and
linen sheet (λίνον) which formed the bed and covering for Odysseus as he
slept upon the deck. And yet in our ignorance of the ordinary names for
things in Homer's day we cannot be sure; in our day Oriental rugs and
the Biblical 'fine linen' might adorn either prose or verse. The two Greek
words seem ornamental in comparison with Kipling's 'rag' and 'bone.'
And 'linen' may be one of a numerous class of words which are the usual
names for things, and ornamental too. In Aristotle's *Rhetoric* the distinction is not made between κύριον and κόσμος, but between κόσμος and
εὐτελή (cheap, shabby, commonplace, mean). The associations of 'fig'
may be worse than shabby. It is true, as he says in the *Poetics* (22.1458ᵃ18–
20), that a style that is all made up of current words, while clear, will be
ταπεινή ('mean,' 'on a low level'); he mentions the poetry of Cleophon in
illustration. Likewise a style full of far-fetched metaphors will be like a
riddle. It is also true that a style made up entirely of ornaments, as the

style of Swinburne, will be cloying. But it is true as well that the words in the 'current' or any other class are not all on one level; the upper range of 'current' words will overlap with the range of the κόσμος. 'Frieze,' 'cornice,' 'rainbow,' 'lilies,' 'iris,' 'lilac,' 'laurel,' 'larch,' 'laburnum,' 'pomegranate,' and 'dulcimer,' are the usual words for all those objects, and every one of them is or can be ornamental. Even the classes of κύριον and κόσμος, then, may overlap, while yet the distinction between them holds. The word 'linen' would be κύριον because it is the usual name for something, and be κόσμος just because the clergyman, the choir-boy, and everybody else so find it. According to Mr. Wilfred J. Funk of the *Literary Digest*, his ten most beautiful words in the English language are these:

Dawn	Luminous
Hush	Chimes
Lullaby	Melody
Murmuring	Golden
Mist	Tranquil

Not one of them is uncommon.

Further, we note in the passage from *Odyssey* 13 some proper nouns, as also lengthened words and shortened, and comparisons rather in the shape of simile than metaphor. Some of the words in the comparisons must be among the ornamental words of the *Poetics*. The stem of the ship leaps under the force of the oarsmen, 'even as on a plain a yoke of four stallions [τετράοροι ἄρσενες] comes springing all together beneath the lash.'[5] The Greek adjective, a compound word, is also ornamental; the translators have aimed at an ornamental word in 'stallions.' In lines 85-7 the adjective (πορφύρεον) applied to the wave, and that (πολυφλοίσβοιο) applied to the sea, and the 'shortened' noun ἴρηξ for the circling (κίρκος) hawk less swift than the ship, seem all to be ornamental words. If we cannot always be sure what was an ordinary word to Homer, and what an ornamental, yet for Aristotle there must be many ornamental words in the lines (93-112) descriptive of the harbor of Phorcys where Odysseus was put ashore asleep: the star (ἀστήρ) that is brightest of all, the Cave of the Winds, the Nymphs, the Naiads, and (for we may now go on to include the adornment by proper nouns) the Dawn ('Ηοῦς),[6] Phorcys himself (Φόρκυνος), yes Ithaca ('Ιθάκης), since we love the name of our own abode, and also Boreas (Βορέαο) and Notus (Νότου), the Winds by which the gates of the Cave are distinguished for mortals and immortals. So Chaucer beautifies the opening of his Prologue to the *Can-*

[5] *Od.* 13. 81-2; translation of Butcher and Lang.

[6] I purposely give the forms as they occur in the text.

terbury Tales with the name of a wind, Zephyrus; and we recall the beauty of names and associations in the landscape of Plato's *Phaedrus*, and how Socrates is made to dwell on them before the argument begins, or when it pauses. Boreas (229 c) is there, and the Nymphs (230 b) soon follow him; but see the whole description of the resting-place of Socrates and Phaedrus beside the stream Ilissus and beneath the lovely plane-tree. It is very important to include the ornamental proper names among ornamental words—Beatrice, Laura, Fiammetta, and all the Muses and Graces. See thirty-three names of the Nereids in ten lines of the *Iliad* (18.39–48), which destructive critics, Nauck and others, would like to exclude from the poem; the list does seem to outrun anything of the kind in *Paradise Lost*, yet consider the list of fallen angels with geographical names intermixed, 129 lines of them, in Book 1 (392–521), and other Miltonic lists in *Paradise Lost* and elsewhere; and compare the catalogue of the Achaeans and the Trojans in *Iliad* 2.484–877. The Hebrews also liked this sort of thing better perhaps than we do, as we see from the book of Numbers; yet we favor ornamental names, as the suffering children know.

My expository aim can now be advanced by quotation from what follows in the episode about sleeping Odysseus, again in the rendering of Butcher and Lang:[7]

And now the vessel in full course ran ashore, half her keel's length high; so well was she sped by the hands of the oarsmen. Then they alighted from the benched ship upon the land, and first they lifted Odysseus from out the hollow ship, all as he was in the sheet of linen and the bright rug [αὐτῷ σύν τε λίνῳ καὶ ῥήγει σιγαλόεντι].

Further, they placed in safety the rich gifts which the Phaeacians had bestowed upon him, the sight of which now specially angers Poseidon:

Gifts out of measure, bronze and gold in plenty, and woven raiment, much store [ἀγλαὰ δῶρα,| χαλκόν τε χρυσόν τε ἅλις ἐσθῆτά θ' ὑφαντήν].

Somewhat casually I have mentioned, or now mention, among words ornamental, suggestive and beautiful names geographical or out of mythology—how often in Greek thought and expression these provinces overlap! Further, add words for fine raiment, as 'purple,' and armor, as 'corslet,' 'glaive,' and 'hauberk,' and all the noble names for things that delight the senses, particularly sight and hearing, as Aristotle notes, but also touch, taste, and smell, and delight the higher sensibilities, and for things with which men and women adorn themselves, their servants, their animals, their houses, public buildings, ships; 'jewel' and the names

[7] *Od.* 13. 113 ff.

of jewels—'beryl,' 'topaz,' 'amethyst,' 'diamond,' 'coral,' 'pearl,' and
'ruby'; words for incense and perfume—'frankincense,' 'spices,' and
'myrrh'; beautiful words from music, 'music' itself, 'melody,' 'harmony,'
'choral,' 'canticle,' 'alleluia,' and the names of instruments, the harp, the
flute, the 'dulcimer' of Coleridge and Nebuchadnezzar, with the rest of
Nebuchadnezzar's Chaldaic orchestra (Dan. 3.5, 7, 15); words from dancing—'dancing' itself and 'choric,' and many a word from Davies' *Orchestra* and Wordsworth's lines, 'I wandered lonely as a cloud'; from sunrise,
sunset, and the starry heavens with their Zodiac and Zenith; from all the
world of nature, birds, trees, flowers (including the cosmos!), clouds, the
hawk, the peacock, and the eagle, from all that realm whence Aristophanes drew titles and the embellishment of comedy; from the architecture and landscape-gardening of God and man. Wherever we find
beauty, there we shall look for ornamental words; the word and its object
belong together. Where shall we begin? With Milton's Oreb, Sinai,
Ormus, Ind, and his longer lists of places from Renaissance maps and
classic myth and Hebrew story? With Homer's Agamemnon and Achilles,
Hector, Nestor, Clytaemnestra, Helen? And what of the names of the
wonderful lands Odysseus saw in his travels? And was it not a geographical name, the blessed word Mesopotamia, with which Garrick or another
said the preacher Whitfield could bring tears to every eye? For Coleridge
the moving names are seen in this:

> It was an Abyssinian maid,
> And on her dulcimer she played,
> Singing of Mount Abora.

Milton had a truer and more ornamental spelling for the mountain:
'Amara.' Or shall we take instances from the Song of Solomon?—'Thy
nose is as the tower of Lebanon which looketh toward Damascus' (7.4).
Truly an Oriental adornation! And where end? With 'glory' for the Bible,
Dante, Milton, Wordsworth?—

> A privacy of glorious light is thine.

With light for blind Homer or blind Milton?—

> Hail holy light, offspring of Heav'n first-born,
> Or of th' Eternal Coeternal beam.

Or with light for Dante? Says Dean Church (*Dante and Other Essays*, 1889,
pp. 163-5):

Light in general is his special and chosen source of poetic beauty. No poet
that we know has shown such singular sensibility to its varied appearances—
has shown that he felt it in itself the cause of a distinct and peculiar pleasure,
delighting the eye apart from form, as music delights the ear apart from words,

and capable, like music, of definite character, of endless variety, and infinite meanings. He must have studied and dwelt upon it like music. His mind is charged with its effects and combinations, and they are rendered with a force, a brevity, a precision, a heedlessness and unconsciousness of ornament, an indifference to circumstance and detail [but there we may doubt Dean Church, for Dante is a most conscious artist, with a sure knowledge when to use, and when to limit ornament]; they flash out with a spontaneous readiness, a suitableness and felicity, which show the familiarity and grasp given only by daily observation, daily thought, daily pleasure. Light everywhere—in the sky and earth and sea, in the star, the flame, the lamp, the gem—broken in the water, reflected from the mirror, transmitted pure through the glass, or colored through the edge of the fractured emerald; dimmed in the mist, the halo, the deep water; streaming through the rent cloud, glowing in the coal, quivering in the lightning, flashing in the topaz and the ruby, veiled behind the pure alabaster, mellowed and clouding itself in the pearl; light contrasted with shadow, shading off and copying itself in the double rainbow, like voice and echo; light seen within light, as voice discerned within voice . . . light from every source, and in all its shapes, illuminates, irradiates, gives its glory to the *Commedia*.

And as Church explains all this with a mixture of customary and ornamental words in prose, so Dante works with all the means at a poet's disposal, including a very large admixture of ornamental words. Or shall we simply end with the Biblical 'beauty of holiness'?

Since, however, we began with Aristotle, and have looked for 'ornamental' words especially in Homer's landscape, we may proceed with illustrations chiefly from that province.

Take, then, not the shield of Achilles in the *Iliad* (18.468–613), which Lessing used for illustration of another point in Homer's art, the method of description by having the divine blacksmith make the object before our eyes; but the passage is a happy hunting-ground for those who seek felicities of diction. Take rather the stream and bank where Nausicaa and her fellows washed the already 'shining raiment' (*Odyssey* 6.85–91):

Now when they were come to the beautiful stream of the river, where truly were the unfailing cisterns, and bright water welled up free from beneath, and flowed past, enough to wash the foulest garments clean, there the girls unharnessed the mules from under the chariot, and turning them loose they drove them along the banks of the eddying river to graze on the honey-sweet clover.

Some of the ornamental words in Butcher and Lang's translation are adjectives and some are nouns ('shining raiment,' 'shining reins'), one ('honey-sweet') is compounded, and Homer's verb τρώγειν (for the two epic poems a *hapax legomenon*), rendered 'graze,' may or may not be included; the notion that 'ornamental' words should also be 'rare' in our modern sense need not be too heavily stressed. We safely infer from a remark in *Poetics* 22.1458ᵇ19–24, on Euripides' use of θοινᾶται in place of the usual word for eating, that Aristotle might well have regarded θοινηθῆναι in *Odyssey* 4.36 as ornamental; and, putting the cases together, we may also infer that when Aristotle calls Euripides' verb a γλῶττα or 'rare' word he is using this term more as we should, and not in the sense of 'alien.' In fact, I should set Euripides' θοινᾶται ('feasts on') pretty clearly among the examples of κόσμος.

The lovely bit of description above, in an episode where Odysseus again is asleep (in his tree), will remind us of other terrestrial paradises. The palace and garden of Alcinous, full of order and ornament, come in the next book (7.86–132); they are described while Odysseus 'stood and gazed,' that is, while the action also is pausing:

Brazen were the walls, . . . and round them was a frieze of blue [Shade of Addison!], and golden were the doors. . . . Silver were the door-posts, . . . and silver the lintel thereupon, and the hook of the door was of gold. And on either side stood golden hounds and silver. . . . And without the courtyard . . . is a great garden. . . . And there grow tall trees blossoming, pear-trees and pomegranates, and apple-trees with bright fruit, and sweet figs, and olives in their bloom.

It was 'a sunny spot on level ground,' reminding us of Circe's home, the island of Calypso, and all the paradises true and false preceding *Paradise Lost*, Book 4, and Coleridge's *Kubla Khan*. The Italian scholar Coli has made a great collection of them in his book on the terrestrial paradise of Dante. Nor may we omit to mention here the little paradise where Socrates and Phaedrus come to rest before the argument or action begins in Plato's dialogue. The reader seeking ornamental words will find abundance of them in the garden at the top of Dante's Purgatorial mount, as in *Paradise Lost*, and he will find the *Paradiso* proper of Dante rich in them. It begins with 'gloria,' is full of color, light, and incense, and beautiful motion, and ends with 'the stars.'

If the reader has been watching, and seen more of the ornamental words in the foregoing passages than I have specifically pointed out, I think he will now be ready to say with me that any word that is ornamental, whether adjective or noun or verb or adverb, is an ornamental word! Aristotle says that they are found in prose as well as verse. Doubtless they are more frequent in impassioned prose like that of Ruskin or De Quincey than in ordinary exposition. At a venture take the tricky paradise of Mark Twain in *A Double-Barreled Detective Story*, chapter 4:

It was a crisp and spicy morning in early October. The lilacs and laburnums, lit with the glory-fires of autumn, hung burning and flashing in the upper air, a fairy bridge provided by kind Nature for the wingless wild things that have their homes in the tree-tops and would visit together; the larch and the pomegranate flung their purple and yellow flames in brilliant broad splashes along the slanting sweep of the woodland; the sensuous fragrance of innumerable deciduous flowers rose upon the swooning atmosphere; far in the empty sky a solitary œsophagus slept upon motionless wing; everywhere brooded stillness, serenity, and the peace of God.

Are not April and October ornamental words for Chaucer and Mark Twain? And what of 'oesophagus'? It is not, as one of my colleagues seems still to regard it, the same as ἴρηξ, a *hapax legomenon*, and a kind of hawk; but surely it is ornamental.[8] And perhaps this choice bit from Mark Twain will send some hunter of verbal ornaments to the *Tale of Sir Thopas* (Topaz—Chaucer's jewel):

> The briddes synge, it is no nay,
> The sparhauk and the papejay,
> That joye it was to heere.

Or, in more serious vein, take Lincoln's 'We cannot dedicate, we cannot consecrate, we cannot hallow this ground.' Are not the ornamental words likely to receive a special stress, whether in prose or verse?—

> With *malice* toward none, with *charity* for all.
>
> Though I speak with the tongues of men and of *angels*.
>
> Calm pleasures there abide, *majestic* pains.[9]

The heavens declare the glory of God, and the firmament showeth his handiwork.

If 'angel' is an ornamental word, and the combination 'Saints and Angels' is an ornament, should we tend to treat the word 'God' as one? It can be more so than the euphemistic substitute 'Adonai.' Yet 'Adonai' is by nature ornamental. It is, in fact, like a kenning, and the kennings of Germanic poetry, Old English and Old Norse, clearly share in the nature and purpose of ornamental words; or at least the beautiful kennings do. The kennings may grow too elaborate or trite. Students of Old English will recall that 'firmamentum' and 'rodor' are kennings for 'heofon,' the heaven, or variations of it.

If these words belong to prose as well as verse, we shall find others in the Bible, words like 'cherubim,' 'tabernacle,' and (Ps. 27.5) 'pavilion' (from the realm of architecture); in the Douai version, 'chalice,' which good Roman Catholics once preferred in Matt. 26.39 to 'cup':

> Father, if it be possible, let this chalice pass from me.

In their Westminster version (1928) we now find 'cup.'

[8] See also my article, *Mark Twain's Lilacs and Laburnums* in *Modern Language Notes* for February, 1932, pp. 85–7.

[9] Wordsworth, *Laodamia* 72.

It may be argued that the ornamental quality of words is in part the outcome of our past associations or of their context at the moment, and again that in its setting a word may sound incongruous when by nature it is too ordinary or too ornamental. It might be over-ornamental in passages of great depth. No doubt Aristotle is right in expecting the poet to use the more elaborate diction when action, character, and thought are in abeyance. We can note the decorative words in preludes before the argument or action begins, in a texture like that of the prelusive strains of a musician, in dedications, eulogies, and psalms.

A term like κόσμος, 'ornament,' may, like other terms in the *Poetics*, be taken in a general sense, and also in a sense that is more specific. But even in its more specific sense it overlaps with other categories of poetic diction. Thus a 'coined' word, the coinage of a single poet, might be ornamental; for instance, very likely the ἐρνύγας ('horns') of *Poetics* 21.1457[b]35 might be so; and surely imitative words when they are beautiful, such as we find in Aristophanes' mimicry of birds and the like in external nature, are properly called ornamental; so also θρεττανελό, presumably the coinage of Philoxenus (see Aristophanes, *Plutus* 290, 296, and Rogers' translation, *Threttanelo! Threttanelo!*), and similar formations mimicking the sound of harps and other instruments. The fine word of one poet may often be accepted by another. Thus from Milton Coleridge takes the adjective 'cedarn,' while Wordsworth does not, and Scott takes it from Coleridge. The verbal gems and beauties of poetry are inherited from age to age, as the fraternity of poets levies on all other ornamental arts for the enrichment of poetic diction.

Paradoxically the usual name for a thing may on occasion be regarded as more ornamental than some finer word. It may be paradoxical to call 'cup' an ornamental word by the side of 'chalice.' But the familiar words for beauty, 'beauty' itself, 'array,' and the like, are ornamental. If you wish to bring a certain quality into your writing, use the words that mean that quality; do as painters do with pigments. Homer, says Matthew Arnold, is 'rapid.' Why not? His hero Achilles is 'swift of foot'; Hermes is speedy, and Iris, who is also the rainbow, is the 'swift' one (ταχεῖα). So when you wish to adorn Circe's palace (*Odyssey* 10.307–17, 348–72), do it with the words for gold and silver; do as Plutarch and Shakespeare after him (*Ant.* 2.2.196 ff.) have done with the Nile-barge of Cleopatra. Similarly, when you wish to convey the impression of beauty, use 'beauty,' 'grace,' and 'charm.' In Greek, use καλός; and when you wish to give the notion of 'adorning,' use κόσμος and κοσμεῖν. Homer uses κόσμῳ in the passage about Odysseus' final voyage and landing (13.77) in the sense of beautiful order. To Aristotle (*Poetics* 7.1450[b]37), beauty depends upon size and order. And when he, too, wishes to convey the notion of beautiful words, he uses κόσμος and κοσμεῖν; for him, I think, τάξις is an ordinary, not an ornamental word. There may be the reason why this notably compact writer, thinking the point obvious and not in dispute, does not define κόσμος in his remarks on diction. The word defines and illustrates itself as other of his terms do not. Thus κύριον and γλῶττα (the customary and the rare word) being themselves Greek metaphors, perhaps not altogether dead, need definition, μεταφορά, the metaphor, needs and receives the longest explanation, and coined and compound, lengthened, shortened, and altered words need illustration. But what sort of words would one count on finding in poetry if not ornamental ones? The remark that they are found in prose as well is needed, and made.

If the *Poetics* as we have it is a set of lecture-notes, or notes for a seminarial discussion, then κόσμος, of all these terms for the elements of poetic diction, would most readily suggest the thing it signifies, and Aristotle could further illustrate it from his memory of other words in the descriptive lines about Odysseus brought to the Ithacan harbor asleep. The author of the *Poetics* would hardly expect this sketchy work to become the subject of textual debate and commentary by future scholars speaking and writing in alien tongues, or by persons who would try to explain his remarks on diction chiefly by his own curt usage without recourse to Homer. He probably would expect any who heard or read him to supply examples of their own. At all events modern notions of him as an 'ancient' author, remote, unpractical, can make difficulties for us where no great cause of trouble exists in his text. We should think of him as a man of great good sense who kept his eye always on his object, and wishes us to do this with him.

And, frankly, it does seem odd to me now that anybody would try to make out what Aristotle meant by enthymenes without consulting more than one good speech for illustrations; or try to study syllogisms, or throw the Aristotelian account of them away, without considering them in the light of actual scientific writing; for I take it he got his theory of the syllogism by the inductive method, out of specimens of rigorous human composition. Just so I take it he found the ornamental word in ornate poetry and prose. Offhand it would seem likely that poetry would teem with such words; that the one kind of word you might certainly expect to find, and could take for granted, in poetry would be this kind. 'Bait your hook with gaudy words,' says Kipling. Keats will 'load every rift with ore.' And 'Longinus,' with both prose and poetry in mind, says that 'beautiful words are the very light of thought.'

Aristotle's distinction between customary words and rare or alien, between κύριον and γλῶττα, suggests one more consideration. To him, the 'rare' is an *alien* word. In one place, Thebes, let us say, the customary word is 'pool'; in another, Athens, it might be 'cistern.' A Theban poet, then, might embellish his style by using the alien or rare word 'cistern,' and in like manner an Athenian poet might use 'pool.' So our translators make Dante (*Inf.* 1.20) say 'in the pool of my heart,' where Wordsworth in the *Prelude* (5.327) uses 'cistern'; compare the reference to the heart in Ecclesiastes 12.6, 'the wheel broken at the cistern.' Our modern distinction between rare and common words in poetry is rather that between the new (*now* current) and the archaic. This difference did not strike Aristotle in the *Poetics*. Why not?

Because, I think, so many words in the Homeric poems, while certainly not current in Attic Greek, were 'ornamental' and, through the popularity of Homer, not unfamiliar. The ornamental πότνια of the *Rhetoric*, as used by Aristotle in deriding Cleophon, occurs some nineteen times in the *Odyssey* alone; it is characteristic also of the later Greek poetic diction. Every one would know such words. They would be ornamental, and yet neither current nor alien.

Let me close with two passages, from Wordsworth and Milton, in which the gentle reader may hunt without pedantic interference for his verbal quarry—more species than one out of Aristotle's eight.

> Mark how the feathered tenants of the flood,
> With grace of motion that might scarcely seem
> Inferior to angelical, prolong
> Their curious pastime! shaping in mid air
> (And sometimes with ambitious wing that soars.
> High as the level of the mountain-tops)
> A circuit ampler than the lake beneath—
> Their own domain; but ever, while intent
> On tracing and retracing that large round,
> Their jubilant activity evolves
> Hundreds of curves and circlets, to and fro,
> Upward and downward, progress intricate
> Yet unperplexed, as if one spirit swayed
> Their indefatigable flight.

> Sabrina fair
>   Listen where thou art sitting
> Under the glassy, cool, translucent wave,
>   In twisted braids of Lillies knitting
> The loose train of thy amber-dropping hair,
>   Listen for dear honour's sake,
>   Goddess of the silver lake,
>   Listen and save.

CORNELL UNIVERSITY.

L'HISTOIRE DES LONGOBARDS, COMMENT FUT-ELLE CONÇUE ET ACHEVÉE?

Olga Dobiaš-Roždestvenskaïa

Le présent article va développer des conclusions historiques qui se dégagent de notre examen paléographique du *Codex Leninopolitanus lat. F v I 7*.[1] Dans les cadres du problème de la minuscule caroline nous insistons au rôle d'un foyer, très modeste, celui de la province d'Italie du VIIIe siècle, foyer qui nous intéresse à trois points de vue.

1. *Ses destinées historiques*. Il s'agit de la ville et de la région de l'ancien Frioul (Cividale actuel) qui, à l'aube même du Moyen Âge, s'est trouvé à une place dangereuse et responsable de l'avant-poste d'Italie, en face des mondes longobard, bavarois, allaman, franc-oriental, slave, avare. Ce foyer a été un des premiers envahis par l'invasion longobarde. Il a été éprouvé par les irruptions avares et slaves. Des influences bavaroises et irlandaises le travaillaient. A la fin du VIIIe siècle il a subi une nouvelle invasion du Nord et se trouva seul à s'insurger contre la domination franque.

2. *Ses destinées littéraires*. Il est lié intimement (nous espérons le démontrer) avec l'énigme de l'œuvre magistrale d'un historien remarquable du VIIIe siècle. Remarquable parce que par lui seul on connaît l'histoire de son peuple. Dans sa belle période cette histoire n'a guère trouvé d'écho sonore. On ne saurait s'y attendre après la ruine définitive de l'état longobard. Et tout de même, au dernier moment, l'indépendance longobarde anéantie, un écrivain de cœur et de talent entre en scène qui a vécu le spectacle et nous en parle. Ce fut, dans la nuit historique, une chance très heureuse que la coïncidence, dans le temps et dans l'espace, du drame final des longobards et d'une conscience claire qui l'a reflété. L'écrivain, dont il est question, c'est le fils de Warnefrid, longobard par ses origines et clerc latin par son ordination, Paul, surnommé le Diacre.

3. Le problème que nous abordons, intéresse l'auteur plus particulièrement, parce qu'une lumière s'y trouve jetée par un *Codex* du VIIIe siècle en dépôt dans notre bibliothèque, la Bibliothèque Publique de Leningrad.

---

[1] Cf. nos études parus aux NN XXV et XXVII des *Memorie Storiche Forogiuliesi* que nous allons citer 'Paul I' et dans le Recueil de l'Académie des Sciences de l' URSS, en russe: Сборник статей по вспомогательным историческим дисциплинам (Ленинград, 1936), que nous allons citer 'Paul II.'

Dans nos études paléographiques, faites sur ce *Codex* nous croyons avoir démontré ceci: il existe deux Mss. que l'on prenait généralement pour les échantillons les plus anciens de l'écriture médiévale de Frioul.[2] Un à Cividale donnant la plus ancienne copie de l'*Historia Langobardorum* par Paul Diacre, l'autre, d'un contenu littéraire mixte, se trouvant au Vatican,[3] mais issu également de l'ancien Frioul. D'après nos investigations[4] il serait impossible de leur attribuer une date avant le début du IXe siècle. Cette date pourtant nous y tenons. Mais, ainsi que nos recherches le montrent,[5] un troisième Ms. existe, que nous croyons être beaucoup plus ancien; savoir: de la fin du VIIIe siècle.

C'est le *Leninopolitanus F v I 7*, écrit en minuscule précaroline d'un foyer modeste et provincial, minuscule curieuse, se replongeant à chaque pas dans une cursive régularisée. Ce *Codex* contient les épîtres de Grégoire le Grand. Le recueil en est précédé d'une épître introductoire du rédacteur, épître qui est adressée *viro dei Adalhardo* et souscrite par *Paulus supplex*. Celui-ci fait connaître comment, empêché par une maladie longue, a-t-il retardé la commande d'Adalhard. En achevant son épître, Paul conclue:

> *Ante suos refluus Rhenus repedabit ad ortus,*
> *ante petet fontem clara Mosella suum,*
> *Quam tuus e nostro, carum ac memorabile semper*
> *dulce Adalard nomen, pectore cedat amor . . .*[6]

Ce *Codex*, pourquoi le datons-nous de la fin du VIIIe siècle, pourquoi l'attribuons-nous à Frioul? Nous croyons avoir démontré—contre Waitz, Bethmann et Hartmann et en accord avec Mabillon[7]—non seulement que sous le nom d'Adalhard il faut voir le célèbre abbé de Corbie et cousin de Charlemagne, et sous la désignation de *Paulus supplex*, Paul Diacre, historien des longobards. Mais encore—ceci, nous l'avons déduit d'un examen paléographique minutieux[8]—que 12 premières lignes de l'épître introductoire *présentent une autographe de Paul*. La fin de l'épître, sous la dictée du maître malade, se trouve écrite par un aide; *clericulus qui haec eadem scripsit*. Celui-ci a commis pas mal de fautes et de bévues, les lignes de Paul se trouvant irréprochables, comme écriture et orthographe. La main de cet aide se révèle ensuite dans l'ensemble de la copie du Recueil,

[2] Cf. les études de Bethmann dans *Pertz-Archiv*, VII, 275 et X, 317; de Waitz dans *NA*, I, 533; et de Bannister, *Paleografia Musicale Vaticana* (1913), p. 89 sqq.

[3] *Reg. lat. 1462.*

[4] Notre étude 'Paul II,' p. 111 sqq.

[5] *Ibid.*, p. 115 sqq.

[6] Le facsimilé de cette épître a été publié plus d'une fois. Tout dernièrement par l'auteur dans son article 'Paul II.'

[7] *Ibid.*, pp. 125–126 et 'Paul I.'

[8] *Ibid.* Cf. également 'Paul I.'

à côté de celles des autres copistes, se servant tous de minuscule analogue et qui dénonce un seul et même atelier graphique.

Paul, fils de Warnefrid, où a-t-il exécuté la commande de son ami? où a-t-il écrit son épître? Dans notre *Codex*, de quel atelier graphique s'agit-il? Sans parler de ce que l'autographe de Paul indique à notre *Codex* la date de la fin du VIIIe siècle, l'atelier graphique dont il s'agit doit être d'une date très haute, la minuscule précaroline et la cursive régularisée y alternant, ainsi que nous l'avons indiqué. Il faut noter aussi une grande simplicité, voire une grossièreté des moyens de l'enluminure, une pauvreté de l'exécution, le petit nombre et la qualité médiocre des copistes, la naïveté des moyens de la ponctuation.[9] Il n'y a que le correcteur postérieur qui les a corrigés. Pas de doute que ce ne fut Adalhard en personne.[10] C'est que dans son épître Paul l'y engage.[11] Et tout cela explique à merveille la plainte qu'énonce Paul dans son épître: *utpote pauper et cui desunt librarii* . . . .[12]

Nous en avons déduit ceci: la copie en question commandée par Adalhard, et où Paul avoue sa 'pauvreté' ne pouvait être exécutée ni dans la riche abbaye de Metz, pendant le séjour de Paul en Gaule, ni dans la célèbre abbaye du Mont Cassin, où Paul se rend, après avoir été 'absous' par Charlemagne.[13] Mais en éliminant les maisons opulentes, où Paul, en hôte honoré, ne pouvait se plaindre de sa pauvreté, nous ne trouvons qu'un seul foyer auquel ces circonstances auraient convenu. Ce serait la ville natale du fils de Warnefrid, où, sur la voie du Mont Cassin il se serait arrêté pour revoir sa famille avant la clôture définitive du Mont Cassin. On le sait: son séjour très long auprès de Charlemagne avait le but principal: l'affranchissement de son frère et de ses concitoyens, emmenés dans la captivité par le vainqueur après l'insurrection de Frioul.[14] Et comme ce but a été atteint,[15] est-ce vraisemblable que, rentré en Italie,

---

[9] Cf. notre étude 'Paul II,' p. 122 sqq.

[10] *Vide* pages 86 sq., 91 sq., et 62 sqq. dans notre investigation: *Histoire de l'atelier graphique de Corbie de 651 à 830 reflétée dans les Mss. de Leningrad* (Leningrad, 1934).

[11] Épître de Paul, ligne 17.

[12] *Ibid.*, l. 7.

[13] Cf. notre étude 'Paul II,' p. 128 sq.

[14] On se souvient de l'épître célèbre de Paul, adressée à Charlemagne en 782–783:

> *Captivus vestris extunc germanus in oris*
> *Est meus, afflicto pectore, nudus, egens . . .*

* * *

> *Captivum patriae redde et civilibus arvis*
> *Cum modicis rebus culmina redde simul.*

(*MGH, Scr. rer. Lang., Historia Langobardorum*, ed. Waitz et Bethmann, p. 15.) Cf. notre étude 'Paul II,' p. 130 sqq.

[15] Cf. l'observation de Pierre de Pise: *fortia qui dudum potuisti solvere vincla, PLAC*, I, 52.

il n'aurait pas cherché l'entrevue avec les amis que ses sollicitations auprès de Charlemagne avaient rendus *civilibus arvis*.[16]

En pèlerin indépendant des liens qui le rattachaient aux abbayes
puissantes, Paul, descendu dans sa ville natale et tombé malade, se trouve
dans cette situation en même temps précaire et libre qui l'oblige à payer
l'exécution de sa promesse (à Adalhard) de sa propre bourse. Il n'y a
que l'arrêt prolongé à Frioul qui explique d'une façon satisfaisante le
phénomène de *Leninopolitanus F v I 7* et tout le contenu de la lettre
mystérieuse.

Il y a pourtant d'autres considérations pour insister à cet arrêt, d'où
une série de conclusions assez intéressantes se dégagent. Dans l'*Histoire
des Longobards*, livre II, chap. 13, à propos des *Carmina* de Fortunat,
Paul indique *en détail* la voie par laquelle celui-là, parti de Ravenne, se
porte vers le tombeau de saint Martin de Tours: *Qui sibi, ut in suis ipse
carminibus refert, illuc properandi per fluenta Tiliamenti et Reunam, perque
Osupum et Alpem Juliam, perque Aguntum castrum, Dravumque et Byrrum
fluvios ac Briones et Augustam civitatem quam Virdo et Lecha fluentant,
iter fuisse describit*. Détails géographiques curieux à noter. Pourquoi Paul
y prend-il intérêt? En partant en 776 avec Charlemagne en Gaule, il
devait, sans doute, prendre une voie différente, plus habituelle aux
pèlerins d'Italie: celle du Grand ou du Petit Saint-Bernard. Mais la
voie en Gaule de Ravenne se trouve indentique à celle de Frioul. Si,
dans la masse énorme des renseignements des *Carmina*, elle a attiré son
attention, *c'est que sans doute, en rentrant de Gaule en 787 il l'a refaite en
sens inverse*. Or, se portant vers le Mont Cassin, il n'a dû choisir ce détour
que pour s'arrêter à Frioul.

Par là nous gagnons, semble-t-il, la réponse à la première question
posée dans le titre de la présente étude: l'idée de l'*Histoire des Longobards*, dans quelles conditions a-t-elle été conçue? Cette œuvre historique
a été beaucoup louée pour le pittoresque de ses récits et la fraîcheur de
son contenu.[17] Tout en s'inspirant de renseignements, secs sans doute, de
son prédécesseur Secundus,[18] dont le texte est perdu—on ne le connaît
que par Paul—celui-ci présente l'histoire de la tribu, riche en épisodes de
couleur, en *sagas* pittoresques et surtout—en traditions et légendes de
Frioul.

Ces légendes, et plus particulièrement celles de la propre famille du
fils de Warnefrid, illustrent de leurs couleurs sauvages son poème historique. Or, cette moisson des récits, d'observations des caractères, *où*

---

[16] Cf. note 6.

[17] Citons seulement, e.g., les Livre II, § 8; VI, §§ 24 et 26; et surtout Livre IV, § 37.

[18] Mort en 612, il a laissé *succinctam de Langobardorum gestis historiam*. Cf. Paul, *Hist. Long.*, III,
29; IV, 27; et IV, 40.

et *quand* l'auteur l'a-t-il recueillie? Serait-ce vraisemblable que, après les avoir rassemblés *avant* son départ avec Charlemagne, Paul les aurait trainés par la Gaule, durant son long séjour dans ce pays, pour ne les mettre en valeur que rentré au Mont Cassin? Ces souvenirs respirent une vie beaucoup trop fraîche pour justifier une pareille conjecture. Non! Ils devaient être réunis en poème historique tout frais, aussitôt recueillis. Cela veut dire: l'*Histoire des Longobards* devait être conçue durant son séjour à Frioul, en 787. C'est devant le spectacle de la ville ruinée, que les souvenirs fiers et tristes du passé ressuscitent dans sa mémoire, qu'il les recueille, les note, au sein de sa famille rentrée au foyer.

L'hypothèse devient vivante en face du chap. IV de son œuvre magistrale. On s'y heurte à l'histoire de la *fara* de Paul: il nous raconte des gestes de ses aïeux, entre autres de son grand-père Arichis. Sa rentrée à Frioul ruiné par la captivité avare suscite une émotion particulière du lecteur qui ne peut s'empêcher de penser à la survie de l'auteur même. Arichis s'approche de la maison paternelle qu'il trouve *déserte*. Le toit enlevé, elle est envahie d'herbes sauvages et de ronces. Après les avoir éloignées, il découvre un foyer énorme, où il met son arc. Ensuite, soutenu par les dons de ses amis, Arichis relève la maison et prend femme. Mais pour le reste de son avoir il ne peut guère le regagner, ni avoir raison de ceux qui l'ont envahi (*invaserunt longa et diuturna possessione*). Lignes impressionnantes, qui vivent d'une vie singulière, tout en faisant résonner dans la mémoire le passage célèbre de Childe-Harold. Ces lignes ont été écrites par Paul sous l'impression récente, sur les traces chaudes de ce qu'il a vécu dans la maison de son frère, jusqu'au meuble (*supellex*) gaspillé par les voisins la perte duquel d'après le témoignage de Paul[19] pleurait en 782 sa belle-sœur.

En résumé. Sur sa voie en Italie, tout en suivant l'itinéraire de Fortunat, Paul s'arrête à Frioul pour revoir sa famille, dans la maison paternelle, restaurée par les soins de son frère. Il y tombe malade et sans doute y prolonge son séjour. C'est là qu'il exécute la promesse donnée à un ami du Nord, ami quitté, dont la 'mémoire ne déserte son cœur, tant que coulent les ondes du Rhin et de la Moselle.' C'est là qu'à l'aide des copistes de Frioul, en minuscule se détachant à peine de la cursive régularisée, il fait écrire le *Codex*—recueil des épîtres de Grégoire le Grand, *nunc Leninopolitanus F v I 7*. C'est là, sur les ruines du passé, couvertes d'*herbes sauvages et de ronces*, que surgit l'idée de restaurer les destinées du royaume. L'ébauche de l'*Historia Langobardorum* fut sans doute tracée pendant le dernier séjour de Paul à Frioul. Se trouvant en accord plus parfait avec la nature tendre et affectueuse de Paul, 'l'épisode de Frioul' explique mieux que tout autre conjecture les points obscurs dans l'his-

---

[19] Cf. l'épître adressée à Charlemagne, *MGH, loc. cit.*

toire de notre *Codex* et, en même temps, dans l'histoire des dernières années de Paul et dans la conception de l'œuvre célèbre. Cette épisode, avons-nous dit ailleurs,[20] éclaire de derniers reflets d'une vie réelle et d'une affection personelle les dernières années du fils de Warnefrid, avant le *silentium* du Mont Cassin.

Telles sont nos considérations sur l'*incipit* de l'*Historia Langobardorum*. Nous voudrions également présenter celles sur son *explicit*. Pourquoi et comment Paul met-il un point à son œuvre? Se trouve-t-elle achevée? Wattenbach regrette (et ce n'est pas lui seul qui le pense) ce qu'elle est restée inachevée: 'leider unvollendet.'[21] Et en effet: le dernier 'principat' longobard qui se trouve décrit par Paul est celui de Liutprand. Ceux de Ratchis, Aïstulphe et Didier, sous lequel l'état longobard a disparu, et Charlemagne s'empare du pouvoir en Italie, sont passés sous un silence. Pourquoi? Est-ce une cause fortuite, dirons-nous la mort de l'auteur qui l'a empêché de poursuivre et l'a obligé de laisser tomber la plume?

Tel n'est point notre avis. Dans son *explicit* Paul semble agir avec une intention transparente, en toute conscience. Tout, dans ce dernier chapitre racontant le règne de Liutprand, s'achemine vers la 'conclusion,' et son canon littéraire est impeccable. Les autres 'principats' sont finis d'une façon abrupte. Ici en déclinant vers la fin, l'auteur trace la silhouette de son héros, dénombre les abbayes et églises qu'il a fondées, résume la chronologie de son règne, fait relation de ses funérailles, pour conclure:

Fuit autem vir multae sapientiae, consilio sagax, pius admodum et pacis amator, belli praepotens, delinquentibus clemens, castus, pudicus, orator pervigil, elemosynis largus, litterarum quidem ignarus, sed philosophis adequandus, nutritor gentis, legum augmentator. Hic initio regni sui Baioariorum plurima castra cepit, plus semper orationibus quam armis fidens, MAXIMA SEMPER CURA FRANCORUM AVA-RUMQUE PACEM CUSTODIENS.

A propos de ce dernier roi, dont il a décrit la vie, Paul insiste sur le faite qu'il s'efforçait 'avec un soin particulier d'observer la paix avec les francs . . . ' Mais Aïstulphe et Didier se trouvaient en guerre avec ceux-ci. N'était-il pas prudent de garder le silence? Si Paul, à l'instar d'une bonne moitié de ses contemporains et prédécesseurs dans la chronique, avait été un homme sans cœur et dignité morale, il aurait raconté, sur un ton de triomphe, la ruine de l'état longobard, il aurait chanté l'éloge du vainqueur. Mais il aimait son peuple. Il souffrait de ses douleurs. Et sans avoir l'audace d'achever son histoire comme, peut-être, il l'aurait voulu, il fait tomber le rideau avant 'la fin du drame.' Il met un point final à son récit en décrivant le règne du dernier roi qui a su conserver une paix sincère avec les francs.

[20] 'Paul I.'

[21] Wattenbach, *Deutschlands Geschichtsquellen im Mittelalter* (Berlin, 1893), Bd. I, ii, § 6.

Le récit de Paul embrasse deux siècles. En abordant l'histoire de son peuple au moment de son entrée en Italie, Paul s'abstient de parler de sa 'fin.' C'eût été impossible et dangereux. L'auteur de sa ruine vivait et régnait. Il s'approchait de la couronne impériale de l'Occident. Peut-être la possédait-il déjà: parce qu'on ignore le moment où le fils de Warnefrid a laissé échapper sa plume, ainsi que l'instant où il est mort. Mais l'humble moine qui écrivait assez près des yeux perspicaces des vainqueurs, dans une abbaye beaucoup visitée par des princes carolingiens et comblée de leurs bienfaits, aurait-il pu oser davantage, tout en racontant les guerres d'Aïstulphe avec Pépin, ou faisant relation des destinées de Didier, emmené dans la captivité de Corbie? Il ne pouvait faire autrement que mettre un point final à son récit en décrivant le règne de Liutprand, en bonne entente avec le peuple vainqueur.

L'histoire des longobards fut écrite par Paul dans le silence du Mont Cassin. Mais relativement peu de temps après—on s'en assure d'après l'existence du *Codex* de Frioul du début du IXe siècle—un clerc intelligent et patriote se trouve à Frioul: preuve d'une floraison nouvelle de cette ville, un clerc qui pénètre à Mont Cassin pour y copier, en minuscule de Frioul, l'œuvre de son citoyen célèbre et pour le déposer dans la sacristie de la cathédrale. C'est dans cette sacristie même qu'en 1851 Bethmann l'a découverte.

Gosudárstvennaya Publíčnaya Bibliotéka,
  Leningrad.

VARIED STRAINS IN MARTIAL

J. Wight Duff

In an author like Martial who makes the true assertion that his writing smacks of mankind (*hominem pagina nostra sapit*), there must inevitably be a wide variety of persons and themes. This clever Spaniard of the first century A.D. had only to use his well-nigh unsurpassed faculty of keen observation in the cosmopolitan Rome where he spent thirty-four years of his life to find infinite material for the epigrams, largely but by no means entirely satiric, in which he proved his mastery. It is the range of human character portrayed in his poems that first and most obviously impresses a reader; for there is little in the Rome of his day that is not set in clear outline before the mind's eye.

Yet to concentrate on this aspect alone would give an imperfect view of his manysidedness. Some years ago in a paper[1] I isolated the tender sentiment which makes so lovable a strain in his nature: and more recently I have discussed his use of the epigram for satire.[2] Here I desire to range more widely over the multiplicity of elements which mixed in him, and throw out a few reminders about his realism, but also about the almost chameleon-like changes of a spirit which could combine cringing and coarseness, hatred and affection, admonition and aspiration; about fluctuations in his literary quality, his deftness in stylistic variation, the composite literary influences acting upon him, his different metres, and his various pronouncements on literature.

In 64 A.D., he came, a young well-educated man, from Spain to Rome with claims on the attention of his fellow-Spaniards, Seneca and Lucan, and although that connection was severed abruptly through their implication in the Pisonian plot against Nero, yet Martial succeeded in maintaining relations, not always as profitable as he would have liked, with many men of high social standing, while at the same time poverty made him acquainted with the lowest grades in the community. In Domitian's reign he could address, amuse, and overpraise the Emperor himself, while studying all ranks of his subjects for 'copy.' The result is a gallery of what in varying proportion to the length or the shortness of a poem may be called portraits, miniatures or mere thumbnail sketches, but all marked by a marvellous realism.

[1] J. Wight Duff, *Martial: Realism and Sentiment in the Epigram* (Cambridge University Press, 1929, printed for Leeds Classical Association).

[2] J. Wight Duff, 'Martial: the Epigram as Satire,' in *Roman Satire: Its Outlook on Social Life* (Berkeley: University of California Press, 1936), 126–146.

It is worth while noting how his figures re-create the society of the times. We meet the senator as well as the swaggerer in senatorial seats who has risen from servitude. So too with the knights—an ex-slave wears the equestrian ring (III, 29), and some people are only pretended knights (V, 35). Social usages lent themselves to comment: dinner-parties, dinner-hunters, mean hosts, legacy-hunters (*captatores*) were traditional subjects for satire. Thus we have the man who never dines at home unless he fails to hook an invitation (V, 47); the systematic diner-out ever hoping for better offers (V, 44) or inventing the latest news (IX, 35); the niggardly patron who has mushrooms served to him, while his guests receive none (I, 20), whereas host and guests in equity and etiquette ought to enjoy the same fare (III, 60); for it is hard at a meal to get perfumes and nothing else (III, 12). There is the terrible literary host whose *recitatio* from his works spoils a dinner (III, 45 and 50), or his fit fellow, the antiquarian bore, chattering about his silver goblets (VIII, 6). But guests also may misbehave by filching dainties (II, 37; VII, 20), or by noisy talkativeness.

The legacy-hunters, courting childless wealthy folk with presents, come in for scathing ridicule. The rich men, whom they secretly wish dead, may go on living, or, worse still, may die without making them heirs (IV, 56 and 61; V, 39; VI, 63; VIII, 27). The morning *levée (salutatio)*, at which patrons received clients in the formal toga, is denounced as a physical burden, an expense, a waste of time (III, 36; V, 22; VII, 39); and the whole Roman day is summarised with inimitable neatness (IV, 8).

Widely various human types—more or less oddities inviting satire—are presented in profusion: the skinflint, parsimonious, although he has inherited two millions (I, 99: cf. I, 103), the acquaintance who gives advice instead of a loan (II, 30), the man who quotes 'Friends go shares' in Greek (κοινὰ φίλων) but fails to put the maxim into practice (II, 43), or one who possesses a well-stocked wardrobe but no clothes for a shivering friend (II, 46), or another whose gifts grow shabbier each December (VIII, 71). There are fussy triflers (*ardaliones*) who know other people's business best (II, 7; IV, 78). There is the nuisance of a fellow who haunts shops, examining countless *objets d'art* and late in the day departs with two small cups bought for a penny (IX, 59); and there is the pretentious dandy who is 'A 1 in cloaks' (*alpha paenulatorum*) but has to pawn his ring to get a dinner (II, 57).

The professions undergo castigation. We meet the advocate who gets and, no doubt, deserves trumpery presents at the Saturnalia (IV, 46), or the surly lawyer incapable of uttering a polite greeting (χαῖρε, V, 51), or your counsel who takes an unconscionable time to say next to nothing

(VIII, 7), or the other who sagaciously blushes in preference to stating his client's case (VIII, 17). In an adaptation of a Greek epigram, an amusing picture is drawn of the pleader in a lawsuit about three she-goats who dragged in with vociferous rhetoric some great names in Roman history and who is at last implored by his client to come back to the three she-goats (VI, 19: cf. *Anth. Pal.* XI, 141). Medical men are no less a theme for jest than they were in Greek epigrams. So Martial laughs at Dr. Doublecourse (*Diaulus*) who exchanged the profession of healing for that of funeral undertaker—the same thing in the end! (I, 47), or the physician who brings a band of students to paw his patient, thereby infecting him with the fever he had not got before (V, 9), or the light-fingered doctor who, after stealing a winecup from his patient, pretends he has done it to keep him teetotal (IX, 96). A remonstrance by an invalid to another doctor declares that he has had one professional visit already and a continuance would make him seriously ill (VIII, 25). The climax comes with the man who died solely because he dreamt about his doctor— another Greek imitation (VI, 53; cf. *Anth. Pal.* XI, 257). Teachers are also subjected to mockery—the schoolmaster whose stridency and whacks before cockcrow prevent folk from sleeping (IX, 68), and the noisy rhetor who, if he does not crack columns, as in Juvenal's exaggeration, at least plagues the ears of others more than he does his own throat (IV, 41). Martial, in a flippant mood, questions the wisdom of his parents in getting him rhetorical instruction (IX, 73, 7–8). Elsewhere he caustically places such money-making arts (*artes pecuniosas*) as an auctioneer's business above a literary education (V, 56); but on those principles we should never have had the epigrams of Martial.

Women make frequent appearance—some attractive, some repulsive. The young bride, good and pretty (IV, 13) and the faithful Arria on the verge of accompanying her husband through the gates of death (I, 13) are offsets to the cruel mistress who beats her slave for one badly arranged curl (II, 66), the much-married woman about to wed her tenth husband (VI, 7), artificial beauties who are all make-up, toothless or nearly toothless crones, an ugly beldame careful to keep a retinue of still uglier creatures so as to shine by contrast, and many others, expert in loathsome vice. Some women were skilled enough in poisoning, as Juvenal reminds us, to be dangerous to a husband, or to lady friends, as was one whom Martial calls Lycoris (IV, 24). A different Lycoris becomes the theme of a frank avowal of altered affections:

> Lycoris, once 'mong women you were queen:
>   Now queen of women Glycera is to me.
> *You* can't be she: *she'll* be what you have been.
>   Time's work! I wanted *you;* but now—'tis *she!*
>
>   (VI, 40).

The common trades of Rome are touched on in their infinite variety, perhaps nowhere more realistically than in the terse catalogue of pedlars on a Roman street, including the hawker who barters pale sulphur matches for broken glass (I, 41).

But it is not only persons to whom Martial directs attention. Concrete things as well as characteristic features of the times demanded record from him. He has an eye for the beautiful, in natural landscape, and in art—the imposing baths of Claudius Etruscus (VI, 42), a winebowl that was a triumph of skill (VIII, 51), an old statuette of Hercules in bronze by Lysippus (IX, 43), or a pretty name like 'Earinos' (IX, 11). Now, he contrasts the nerve-racking din of Rome with rural peace (XII, 57); now, he praises the attractions of his native Spain. He introduces us to most of the prominent writers of the day, and, as we shall see, some of his satire is aimed at literary tendencies like archaizing. Even personal confessions and the author's preferences (a traditional feature in classical satire) tell us much about the characteristics of his age.

It is natural, and certainly most enjoyable and profitable, in surveying Martial's range, to draw instances chiefly from the twelve books which contain his most representative work, produced from 85 to 102 A.D. But one must not overlook his earlier extant writings; firstly, the book of *Spectacula*, as we entitle it, on the games celebrating the opening of the Flavian Amphitheatre by Titus in 80 A.D.; and, secondly, the two collections (*ca.* 83–86 A.D.) of mottoes, mostly in couplets, for gifts to guests, *Xenia* and *Apophoreta*, now numbered, out of due order of composition, as Books XIII and XIV. The *Liber Spectaculorum* has been subjected to a meticulous investigation by Weinreich,[3] and one result brought out is the background of mythological learning which at this period rather beset Martial, though it is striking how he shows independence of originals by a kind of Ovidian gift of variation in expression and motif. The theme of the 'Wonders of the World' in the introductory epigram on the Amphitheatre is an old one freshly handled by Martial. When he takes to writing three elegiac epigrams (*Spect.* 12, 13, 14) about the pregnant sow killed in the imperial hunt, he varies his treatment by using mythology in two of these and dropping it in the third. They are exercises in variation, just as in Book I, by devoting seven poems (six elegiac, one hendecasyllabic) to the incident of the hare spared by a lion, he proves his skill in ringing changes on a single theme. The ingenious rather than thrilling poems on different animals in the arena, including a *pius elephas*, which exhibit instinctive reverence for the Emperor's *numen*, bear a significance for Caesar-worship; and Weinreich left over for a pupil a comparison between the Caesar-cult of Statius and that of

---

[3] O. Weinreich, *Studien zu Martial* (Stuttgart, 1928).

Martial.[4] The *Xenia* might be called one long elaborate menu, for, with four exceptions, the mottoes deal with eatables and drinkables—vegetables, cheeses, savouries, fish, poultry, wines and so forth. The *Apophoreta*, 'things to be taken away,' are concerned, on the whole, with a different sort of gifts, expensive or cheap, such as writing-tablets, dice-box, tooth-pick, sunshade, cloak, table, ivory tusk; but, at the close, we come back to cereal dainties for a very early morning meal:

> Rise! bakers now sell breakfast to the boys—
> Dawn's chaunticleers all round crow out their noise.
>   (XIV, 223).

Mostly in elegiac distichs, with some hendecasyllabics, those two books have a value as showing at once Martial's range of subject and his advance from apprenticeship to skill in that condensed expression which made a factor in his epigrammatic power.

When we study his personality, we are struck with its prodigiously extensive range. Variety of spirit, variety of attitude, lend to his poems an aspect of medley so multifarious as almost to constitute a new kind of *satura*. We find copious indecency wilfully indulged in with the warning that much will shock propriety and with the conventional excuse that a poet can be clean though his verses be filthy. They are another aspect of his realism. Knowing well that lubricity would not please a staid emperor, he feels obliged to make a bowdlerized anthology for Nerva. We suffer too a tedious surfeit in the adulation of Nerva's predecessor, Domitian, disfigured by far-fetched conceits, which, as a rule, are foreign to Martial's forthright and unrhetorical style. Here he pays for insincerity by an artificiality of ideas beyond the verge of absurdity. I give a single instance. In IX, 3 he goes the length of arguing that even the gods could never repay all that Domitian has done for them in the way of temple-building. They are bankrupt debtors, and he assembles Roman business terms (*creditor, auctio, conturbare, decidere*) to elaborate his point. If the deities were to sell off to meet their obligations, Atlas would go smash and Jupiter fail to raise a penny in the shilling (*non erit uncia tota*). Martial is not often so silly, and of such flatteries he explicitly repented under Nerva and Trajan (X, 72).

Other qualities attesting his composite nature are a brutal savagery of attack, mitigated, no doubt, by his censuring under disguised names, and, in contrast, that vein of tender sentiment to which we owe his beautiful poems of friendship and touching tributes of affection to the dead. The genuine accents of a warm heart ring through his verses to friends like Decianus and Julius Martialis no less than through his *In memoriam*

---

[4] F. Sauter, *Der römische Kaiserkult bei Martial und Statius* (Stuttgart, 1934).

poems, lamenting the death of the little slave-girl Erotion (V, 34 and 37; X, 61) or a young friend who will never come back from the East (VI, 85). Death in childhood or youth affects him, as it affected the Greek epigrammatists. But Martial's note is his own. He has a breadth of human sympathy which includes bond and free, as seen in his obituary lines on a slave hairdresser:

> Here lies Pantagathus whose youthful years
> Cut short have brought his master grief and tears.
> His steel that clipped scarce touched each wandering hair
> And trimmed the bearded cheek with deftest care.
> Earth, be thou kind and light as fitteth thee:
> Lighter than his skilled hand thou canst not be.
> (VI, 52).

Allied to this vein of sentiment is his love for beautiful scenery, his raptures over the fine view of the city across the Tiber from the Janiculum, his enjoyment of farm-life on his little property out at Nomentum, his homesick longings for Spain, his distress over the landscape wrecked by the eruption of Vesuvius

> where but late mid vines
> Green shadows played, and noble clusters filled
> The brimming vats.

In that ruined country-side he sees, with poetic imagination, a lost sporting-ground for the fabled creatures of mythology:

> On this same mount the satyrs yesteryear
> Did foot their frolic dance;

and his reflections lead to the melancholy conclusion:

> Now all lies whelmed in fire and ashes dread.
> (IV, 44).[5]

Other poems reveal him in a mood of serious admonition, and here it should be noted that he objects to have his *nugae* and *lusus* dismissed as unconsidered trifles. Thus, he uses epigrams to proffer sound advice. In one he strikes the time-honoured philosophic note that to be 'free' you must have cheap tastes and despise luxury (II, 53); in another, he declares that big purchases argue a small mind (III, 62). He advocates a good use of time (e.g. IV, 54) and sighs with honest aspiration after the leisure essential for an author's work and guaranteed by patronage (I, 107; XI, 3, 6–10), a cardinal point, we shall see, in his literary creed.

Varying strains are further exemplified by the difference of literary

---

[5] The whole poem is translated by J. Wight Duff, *A Literary History of Rome in the Silver Age* (London, 1927), 527.

quality in his epigrams. About this he is disarmingly frank—'some bits are good, some so-so, and more are bad,' he recognizes (I,16): 'that's how a book is made.' It is an implicit and defensive exposure of the hypocritical pretence that abusive criticism, by concentrating wholly on faults in a work, indicates honesty on the part of a critic. Indeed, Martial is still more emphatic in a later book. In VII,90, fastening on the term *inaequalis*, which a critic had applied to his work, he contends that a book to be good must be uneven in quality: *inaequalis*, then, he takes as a compliment (*laudat carmina nostra*); for a dead level means dulness, and no one will charge Martial with that blemish, if his works be taken as a whole. A quite cursory examination confirms his avowal. He is not his best self either in his coarser or in his adulatory pieces; and he cannot always be equally successful in securing polish or point. Some of the dedicatory epigrams are frigid compared with Greek parallels, although there are others where his genius and response to Roman environment have brilliantly eclipsed his models.

The different strains in Martial may be in part set down to the variety of literary influences acting upon him—influences inherited consciously and unconsciously from Greece and Rome. The Roman predecessors to whom he specifies indebtedness are Catullus in Ciceronian times, Domitius Marsus and Albinovanus Pedo, two Augustans, and Lentulus Gaetulicus, put to death by Caligula. The latter is possibly the author of nine epigrams in the Greek anthology under the name Γαιτυλίκου. So insignificant are the fragments of Marsus and Pedo that their influence cannot be disentangled; Catullus, however, is not only quoted and parodied by Martial but is the chief pattern for his hendecasyllabic and choliambic poems. True, he shows metrical independence in restricting the first foot of his hendecasyllables to a spondee; but he owes much to the satiric spirit of Catullus[6] in both of these metres and in elegiac verse. One hendecasyllabic piece, in a tone of withering contempt, might have been written by Catullus to Lesbia after their breach. It shows his method of free adaptation; for he echoes *quot sunt quotque fuere* from Catullus' lines to Cicero (XLIX, 2) and applies the name 'Catulla' to the woman whom he addresses:

> Loveliest of women now or long ago,
> Vilest of all who are or e'er have been,
> Catulla, how I wish that you could grow
> A woman not so lovely but more clean!
> (VIII, 53).

In elegiacs, although influenced by Ovid, he does not accept rigorously

[6] J. Wight Duff, *Roman Satire* (Berkeley: University of California Press, 1936), 128–129.

the Ovidian disyllabic close of the pentameter, but resembles Catullus in endings like *amicitiae* and *ingenio*. For technique and phraseology Martial was also indebted to Virgil and Horace.[7] One influence, however, he never specifies, presumably because it was obvious to his mind. This is the influence of Greek epigrams, long imitated by Latin poets. A generation before Cicero, poets in the circle of Q. Lutatius Catulus freely drew upon them as models.[8] Many distinguished Greek epigrammatists, now represented in the *Anthologia Palatina*, had spent part of their lives in Rome; and it was the ordinary thing for literary men in the coterie of Martial's friend, the younger Pliny, to try their hand at such brief compositions in Latin.[9] It will be conceded that Greek epigrammatic themes and conventions influenced Martial profoundly, although they did not rob him of a free power of adaptation; and some Greek epigrams such as those by Lukillos of the Neronian age, contain resemblances too striking to be dismissed as mere coincidences.[10]

Nor must his variety of metrical form be neglected. It is a variety appropriate to his miscellaneous content. Of his 1561 epigrams, 1235 are elegiac, 238 hendecasyllabic, 77 choliambic: a few are iambic or hexametric. Pieces in hexameters alone are thus comparatively rare; but their importance for him in theory appears to be seldom appreciated. He makes a strong plea for the right to use them in light poetry. An objector in VI, 65 holds that epigrams should be not in continuous hexameters but in distichs. This criticism is intentionally placed immediately after a poem of thirty-two hexameter lines. Martial's defense is that this verse is both permissible and customary: his critic may read distichs only, if he prefers what is short: he may skip (*transire*) long epigrams, provided that Martial is allowed to write them! The significant point is that he virtually places himself, for the moment, alongside of his friend Juvenal, within the domain of *satura*, whose conventional form since the time of Lucilius had been the hexameter. But it was not the high-flown epic hexameter which either of them found to their taste: for Martial it was too much associated with a mythology that had wearied him, and Juvenal makes fun of its style in his description of the Privy Council which deliberated upon the monster-fish presented to Domitian (Satire IV: cf. *consedere duces*, VII, 115, borrowed from Ovid).

[7] E. Wagner, *De M. Valerio Martiale poetarum Augusteae aetatis imitatore* (Regimonti = Königsberg, 1888).

[8] R. Buttner, *Porcius Licinus u. der litterarische Kreis des Q. Lutatius Catulus* (Leipzig, 1893), ch. 9.

[9] J. Wight Duff, *A Lit. Hist. of Rome in Silver Age*, 555–6; cf. p. 536 for Pliny's own light poetry.

[10] O. Autore, *Marziale e l'epigramma greco* (Palermo, 1937) gives a judicious estimate of Martial's debt to Greek epigrams. Cf. K. Prinz, *Martial u. die griechische Epigrammatik* I (Wien, 1910); E. Pertsch, *De Valerio Martiale graecorum poetarum imitatore* (Berlin, 1911); R. Schmook, *De M. Valeri Martialis epigrammatis sepulcralibus et dedicatoriis* (Weidae Thuringorum, 1911).

It remains to indicate his varied views on his own poetry and on literary questions. What he craved for himself was a niche beside Pedo, Marsus and Catullus (V, 5, 5–6). Of these the only rival to his fame in modern times is Catullus, and that for lyric rather than for epigrammatic power. Martial is conscious of his contemporary vogue: his *juvenilia* can still be had (I, 113), and he mentions different booksellers who stock his poems (I, 2 and 117; IV, 72). Rome repeats his verses (VI, 60); but he is known far more widely than in the capital (*toto notus in orbe Martialis* I, 1, 2; cf. III, 95, 7–8; V, 13, 3). He is read or quoted on the Rhone (VII, 88), in Rhaetia (IX, 84), even in distant Britain (XI, 3). His hendecasyllables have brought him notoriety, though, he admits, not equal to that of a circus horse (X, 9): but certainly he is pointed out in the streets (*monstramur digito* IX, 97). He is convinced that his poetry, because it will live, can confer immortality on those mentioned in it (V, 10, 12)— why, then, condescend to mention a snarling detractor (V, 60)? And yet, as regards individuals, he insists that in his censures he avoids personalities (VII, 12, 3; IX, 95 B) and substitutes fictitious names.[11] The principle observed has been

> To spare the sinner, but denounce the sin
> (X, 33, 10),

safeguarding, as he tells us in his valuable prose preface to Book I, the respect due even to persons of lowliest degree (*salva infimarum quoque personarum reverentia*). Thus, he declines to say who 'Postumus' is: and indeed Postumus must be partly a lay figure and parly a Horatian reminiscence when admonished for postponement of 'living' (V, 58). Nor is it likely that the same person is meant by the Postumus, half of whose kisses are still half too much (II, 10); or the over-scented Postumus (II, 12); or the Postumus whose dole as a patron is stingy (IV, 26); or Postumus, the rhetorical advocate who bellows out Roman historical instances in the lawsuit already mentioned (VI, 19). Martial's *ioci* are *innocui*, not meant to hurt (I, 4, 7; V, 15; VII, 12, 9); and they amuse, although they may not pay (I, 76). Naturally, then, he objects to finding scurrilous verses circulated under his name (VII, 72, 12–16; X, 3 and 33); for he is not vitriolic toward actual persons, however bitter in exposing the offender as a type. A poet to whom we owe poems of true friendship and sympathy could not be heartless: indeed, he marks the man without a heart as an object for commiseration (V, 28, 9). Yet this is not to suggest that his poems are compact of sentiment; for he is well aware that epigrams without 'salt' and 'gall' must be insipid (VII, 25).

---

[11] See L. Friedlaender, *M. V. Martialis Epigrammaton libri* (Leipzig, 1886), II, Register 6, 'Wirkliche und fingirte Privatpersonen aus Martials Zeit.'

To his own poetry his attitude is, as we should expect, a varying one: sometimes he stresses the light nature of his *nugae*, sometimes he is anxious to proclaim that he harbours a serious purpose (IV, 49, 1–2). His claim may be conceded, even if he has no constructive system to propound; for an observer so acute and incisive cannot fail to produce a positive effect: his coarsest poems unmask the hideousness of vice and stimulate a revulsion of feeling toward moral health.

A pleasant strain of common sense runs through his literary pronouncements. Writing nice epigrams, he says, looks easy work—yes, but to write a whole book is hard (VII, 85). Conscious that the epigram is his specialty, he naïvely instances an able friend who would no more compete with him in that field than Virgil would compete with Horace in odes or Virgil with Varius in tragedy (VIII, 18). With equal frankness he mentions an admirer who likes his epigrams next to the satires of the now lost Turnus (VII, 97). Patronage he favours because it guarantees leisure for the creation of literature: it might not make Martial a Virgil, but it would at any rate make a Marsus of him (VIII, 56, 24). The same poem summarises this doctrine in one of his familiar lines: *Sint Maecenates, non derunt, Flacce, Marones.*

Writing, however, may be overdone. There is unwisdom in an author's publishing books too frequently—his came out almost annually. The risk is that readers may be satiated:

> What hurts my books, dear Pudens, is the rout
> Of constant issues wearing readers out.
> Rare things delight: first apples charm the more:
> By winter-roses men set ampler store.
> So pride commends the wench that fleeces you:
> An ever-open door keeps no youth true.
> The single book by Persius wins more praise
> Than all light Marsus' epic length of lays.
> Think, when you read again a book by me,
> That it's the only one: more choice 'twill be.
>   (IV, 29).

Some editors have doubted whether the *levis Marsus* of this poem can be the same as the one mentioned among his models. The line *quam levis in tota Marsus Amazonide* is the single extant allusion to his *Amazonis*, an epic apparently in more than one book on a war with the Amazons. It is likely that, had Martial meant a different Marsus, he would have made this clear; and *levis* may be used here not in the derogatory sense of 'trivial' but to suggest that Marsus' province was light poetry like Martial's *nugae*, and that it would have been better if Marsus had shared his distaste for epic.

Prompted either by common sense or by a more penetrating discernment, and conscious of the vital force within him, he states a great literary truth when he declares

> To live, a book must have indwelling power.
> (*Victurus Genium debet habere liber:* VI, 60, 10).

Such is the conviction that entitles him to anticipate literary immortality. He knows that his *métier* is to hold the mirror up to the facts of life. Once—it is in Book VIII—he hesitates whether he should go on writing: five books were surely enough, six or seven rather too much, and now an eighth is in progress. But a rebuke, which is also an encouragement, comes from Thalia, the Muse of light poetry. He has a mission from which she will not discharge him. 'Ingrate!' she exclaims, 'can you abandon your pleasant trifles? What else could Martial compose but *nugae*? Not tragic drama, surely? nor epic?'

> Nay, dye your Roman booklets smart with wit,
> That Life may read and own the portraits fit.
> (VIII, 3, 9–10).

And so there comes in a later book his triumphant proclamation of his literary position. 'Why,' he asks, 'read mythological twaddle about Oedipus or Thyestes, Colchian witches like Medea, or monsters like Scylla?'

> Read this which makes Life say 'It is my own.'
> No Centaurs, Gorgons, Harpies here you'll find:
> My pages have the smack of human-kind.
> (X, 4, 8–10).

This return to the Terentian *humani nil a me alienum puto* reveals the basis of both the pleasant and the unpleasant in Martial. He concludes with the advice: 'if it is not your wish to recognize the manners of men or to know yourself, then take up the study of an Alexandrine mythological poet like Callimachus.'

Such is, definitely announced and in practice maintained, the programme of Realism that explains most of his literary antipathies. He dislikes, we have seen, mythological themes. This hardly needs further illustration; but one short piece may sum up. In V, 53, which is based upon a Greek epigram preserved in *Anth. Pal.* XI, 214, he reasons with Bassus against writing tragedies on Medea, Thyestes, Niobe and Andromache, already overdone in Latin literature (we know of half a dozen attempts at a Thyestes drama).[12] The most suitable *materia* for such work would be Deucalion or Phaëthon: it should, that is to say, be drowned in water or consumed in fire!

---

[12] O. Ribbeck, *Tragicorum Latinorum Reliquiae:* (Leipzig, 1852), index.

He dislikes bombast. This follows from his disclaimer of anything like the epic grand manner, though in the same breath he parodies it:

> Lo! I the man for trifles unsurpassed,
> I mayn't o'erawe you, yet I hold you fast.
> Great themes are for great bards: enough to see
> You oft re-reading my light poetry.
>
> (IX, praef.).

Another of his dislikes is obscurity. Himself preferring the straightforward style of an essential realist, free from the enigmatic and the precious, he was out of sympathy with such Alexandrine poets and such of their imitators as followed that cult of the obscure which is a recurrent ideal of decadents in ancient and modern poetry. A literary contemporary preferred to Virgil the recondite *Zmyrna* of Cinna for its difficulty, and Martial banters him on his hard style:

> It's not a reader but Apollo's light
>   *Your* books require:
> As Cinna, matched with Virgil, was like night,
>   You rank him higher!
>
> (X, 21, 3-4).

Further he felt an objection to compositions written merely to display technical skill—lines of the τεχνοπαίγνιον order such as those that read backward as well as forward or those 'echoic' elegiacs where the words constituting the opening two and a half feet of the hexameter are repeated at the close of the pentameter. Such ingenious trifles he dismisses with the sentence 'silly is the labour spent on puerilities' (*stultus labor est ineptiarum:* II, 86, 10).

Likewise he shares Horace's contempt for slack composition, advocating care in writing, and stigmatizing the glib versifier who tosses off 200 lines per day, but doesn't recite them—for a fool, how wise! (VIII, 20). And he dislikes the archaistic tendencies of some contemporaries, reducing *ad absurdum* the idea that dead poets are necessarily the best (VIII, 69: cf. XI, 90).

His interest in standard poets and prose-writers is shown in couplets suited for copies of their works, in Book XIV, 183-195. It was an interest fostered by friendship with the chief literary men of his day. Most of them he mentions, but he never names Statius, though L. Arruntius Stella was the poet-patron of both (I, 7; IV, 6, 5; V, 11, 2; VII, 14, 5). Statius' mythological poems would not attract Martial: a *Thebaid* or an *Achilleid* were too remote from life around. His concern was not with mythical heroes but with men. One practice, however, he shares with Statius, that of prefixing to some books explanatory prefaces in prose.

Indeed, Statius in certain of his *Silvae* handles the same subjects as Martial in his epigrams: and occasionally they use similar expressions more like borrowings than coincidences (e.g. Mart. I, 41, 4–5; Stat. *Silv.* I, 6, 73). In Martial's aspersions on mythological epics (he does not appear to feel the same objection to Silius' historical epic, the *Punica*), he must have had Statius in mind, just as Statius can hardly have failed to think of Martial, when in his introduction to *Silvae*, Book II, he apologises for some of his own light poems (e.g. on a parrot) as *leves libellos quasi epigrammatis loco scriptos*. What they felt was in all likelihood not deep animosity but incompatibility of taste and temperament.[13]

It is pleasant to take leave of Martial as one of a literary circle, in which his gift for friendship was an asset. He honoured Lucan's memory, keeping the anniversary of his birth and maintaining relations with his widow Polla (VII, 22; X, 64). He respected Silius for the reverence he showed to 'great Virgil's monument' on land he had bought (XI, 48 and 49); as an epic poet he is 'the pride of the Castalian sisterhood' (IV, 14). His activities as advocate, consul and poet are celebrated (VII, 63); and Martial is so proud of his admiration that he asks how a detractor dare carp at poetry valued by Silius (VI, 64, 6–15). To Juvenal he was linked by a share of his satiric outlook and a warm affection (VII, 24 and 90; XII, 18). The younger Pliny, of whose seriousness he affected to be half afraid (X, 19), was another good friend, who supplied him with the expenses of his final journey home to Spain. A common interest in literature animates the friendly note to the prose author Frontinus (X, 58) and the commendation of Sulpicia's writings (X, 35 and 38) as poetry of honourable love and healthy jest. The general effect is that of a versatile man with sympathies broad enough to enable him to understand literature and human beings of the most various types.

Martial is at his best where he is most himself—where he adheres to the theme of humanity which he recognized as his own. When he has beasts of the arena or an imperial *dominus et deus* for his subject he is tempted into artificiality. Here the quest for variety of style makes a display of skill that over-reveals itself. But humanity he can depict, disdain, loathe, pity with a convincing truth which brings into play simple style and fitting metres used with consummate mastery. This realism and his literary genius for reserving to the end the point or sting in many of his most celebrated epigrams are, amidst all his manysidedness, the sure pillars of his fame.

UNIVERSITY OF DURHAM,
    NEWCASTLE-UPON-TYNE.

[13] H. Heuvel, 'De inimicitiarum, quae inter Martialem et Statium fuisse dicuntur, indiciis,' *Mnemosyne* (1937), 299–330.

ACETABULUM

A. Ernout

LES LEXIQUES latin-français publiés par M. Roques[1] donnent une même glose sous trois formes différentes.

Le lexique de Douai a:

11 accetabulum	vaissiaus;

celui du Vatican:

100 acetatorium	sauceron—*esyckkrück*
acetabulum	saucier;

celui de Paris:

109 acetabulum	I. vaicel.

Des diverses graphies qui nous sont attestées, il n'est pas douteux que la bonne ne soit *acetabulum*. Le mot est bien connu en latin, où, dérivé de *acētum*, et spécialisé d'abord dans le sens de vinaigrier, ὀξυβάφιον, il a servi par suite à désigner une mesure de capacité, cf. Caton, Agr. 108, 1: *polentam grandem dimidium acetabuli in caliculum nouum indito*, et Pline, H.N. 21, 85: *cum acetabuli mensura dicitur, significat heminae quartam, id est drachmas XV*; puis un vase quelconque. Traitant de la catachrèse, Quintilien cite le mot comme un exemple de cette figure: '*acetabula*' *quidquid habent*, Inst. Or. VIII, 6, 35.

Mais cette extension du sens a fait relâcher le lien qui unissait *acētabulum* à *acētum*, et l'étymologie populaire a par une association d'idées toute naturelle rapproché le nom du *récipient* du verbe *accipio* 'recevoir.'[2] De là des graphies comme *aceptabulum* (Dioscoride 4, 84; CGL III 553, 15) *acceptabulum* (Dioscor., ibid.; Végèce Ars ueterin., 2, 53; CGL III 612, 22; 586, 22) *acettubula* (leçon du Parisinus 8540 ap. Senec., Ep. ad Luc. 45, 8). La confusion était d'autant plus facile que la prononciation ne distinguait plus le *c* simple du *c* géminé, et que le groupe -*pt*- s'était également réduit à -*t*- en passant par le stade d'assimilation -*tt*- (attesté ici par la graphie *acettubula*; cf. les graphies *accidia*, *accidiare* issues de *acidia*, emprunt au grec ἀκηδία, *bastiterium* 'fons' dans le manuscrit de Douai 179, issu de *batisterium; otimo = optimo* CIL VII, 466, et à l'initiale *Tholomeo = Ptolomaeo* CIL VI, 25961, etc.). Le rapport avec *acētum*

---

[1] Recueil général des lexiques français du Moyen-Age, t. I, Lexiques Alphabétiques; Paris, Champion, 1936.

[2] Cf. le *acceptaculum* de Grégoire le Grand, Epist. 7, 29: *Suadeo ut magnitudo uestra in suo proposito quondam in pauco tempore delectabili acceptaculo* (codd. mel., *receptaculo* dett.) *peregrinationis uiuere studeat.*

n'était pas omis entièrement, car il était conservé par les lexiques et les glossaires qui reproduisaient l'enseignement d'Isidore de Séville, Orig. 20, 4, 12, *acetabulum, quasi acetaferum, quod acetum ferat*,[3] mais il s'est établi dans l'esprit de ceux qui employaient le mot une sorte de compromis entre les deux formes, compromis dont témoigne la note du vocabulaire de Guillaume Briton: *Acetabulum, uel Acetarium uas est aceti. Unde in Exod., cap. 37, ubi fit mentio de Acetabulis, dicit Glossa, quibus Acetum ferebatur. Sed quod numquam uel raro occurrit de oblatione aceti, sic dicit Magister in Hist.: 'Quidam dicunt Acetabula, ubi scilicet fundebantur a Sacerdote quae debebant offerri, ut uiderent utrum accepta, i.e. idonea essent, an non. Graecus interpres τρύβλιον uertit.'*

On voit que le vocabulaire de Briton ajoute un nouveau nom à ceux qui désignent le vinaigrier: *acetarium*. Ce terme à l'origine désigne seulement des légumes accommodés au vinaigre, τρώξιμα, lit-on dans un glossaire, CGL II 13, 41; cf. Pline, N.H. 19, 58: *Horti* (génitif) *maxime placebant quae* (quia codd.) *non egerent igni parcerentque ligno, expedita res et parata semper, unde et acetaria appellantur, facilia concoqui nec oneratura sensus cibo, et quae minime accenderent desiderium panis*; 20, 213 (*porcillaca*) *in acetariis sumpta corroborat*. Mais Apicius et les gloses en font le synonyme de *acetabulum:* on lit *acertarium* (sic): ὀξύβαφον, CGL II 13, 26, et dans Apicius 6, 241 *olei acetarium maiorem, satis modice liquaminis acetabulum minorem*, où *acetarius* et *acetabulus* sont employés dans la même phrase avec le même sens.

On peut se demander si ce n'est pas d'après *acetarius (-ium)*, interprété comme un dérivé de *acceptus* (cf. *mixtarius* de *mixtus* qui désigne justement dans Lucilius un vase à mélanger le vin et l'eau[4]), qu'a été formé *acetatorium* qu'on lit dans le manuscrit du Vatican, et qui peut représenter *acceptatorium*, tiré de *acceptator*, comme *amatorius* de *amator*, et tant d'autres; *acceptatio, acceptator* sont en effet attestés à partir de Tertullien, comme synonymes de *acceptio, acceptor*.

Mais ici la chose est moins sûre. On a vu plus haut qu'Isidore expliquait *acetabulum* par un composé imaginaire, *quasi acetaferum*. Ce mot forgé par Isidore a été recueilli par les glossateurs du moyen-âge; Jean de Gênes le transcrit littéralement; le glossaire d'Ugutio le présente sous

---

[3] Cf. le lexique d'Ugutio: *Acetarium et dicitur Acetabulum* et *Acetaforium quod ferat acetum et appendat XII dragmas;* le lexique de Jean de Gênes a également *acetaferum*.

[4] Nonius 546, 26: mixtarium, quo miscemus. Lucilius lib. V (33):

urceus aut+longe gemino mixtarius paulo+

Le texte est corrompu et a été diversement corrigé. Marx lit avec Lachmann:

urceus haut longe Gemino, mixtarius Paulo

que M. E. Bolisani traduit par: 'L'orciolo non era molto lontano da Gemino, il cratere era vicino a Paolo.' En tout cas l'existence de *mixtarius* est certaine.

la forme *acetaforium* qui a sans doute subi l'influence des mots grecs en
-φόριον comme *pastophorium*, transcription du grec παστοφόριον.

Il n'est pas impossible que *acetatorium* soit une corruption de *acetaforium*, quoique la confusion de *t* et de *f* soit moins facile à expliquer dans
la minuscule que dans la majuscule. Avons-nous affaire à deux mots
différents; ou, s'il n'y en a qu'un, lequel est le bon? Je ne vois pas le
moyen de résoudre avec certitude ce petit problème.

Faculté des Lettres,
Université de Paris.

PLUTARCH AND APPIAN ON TIBERIUS GRACCHUS

RUSSEL MORTIMER GEER

IN 1928 Jérôme Carcopino published under the title *Autour des Gracques* a collection of studies of which the first, 'La Valeur Historique d'Appien,' set forth the thesis that the *Civil War* by Appian was the only trustworthy source for the life of Tiberius Gracchus, and that its excellence was due to the use by Appian, or rather by his immediate authority,[1] of a source unknown both to Plutarch and to Livy and his followers. He thus took issue with the belief that although the sources of Appian and Livy are independent, Plutarch was familiar with both sources, following chiefly that used by Appian and preserving it somewhat more fully, but adding some material, chiefly anecdotal, from the authority used by Livy.

After examining in detail the two accounts of the career of Tiberius given by Appian and Plutarch, Carcopino found that where both tell of the same event they frequently disagree; that where Plutarch presents material not found in Appian, it is usually so inconsistent with Appian that neither can it represent a fuller version of Appian's source, nor could it even have been added by Plutarch from other authorities had he been familiar with, and in the main depending on, that source; and finally, that wherever we can form a judgment on the value of opposing versions, Appian is right and Plutarch wrong. Unfortunately for his theory the contradictions and inconsistencies are, as I hope to point out, almost entirely non-existent, and while it is quite probable that Plutarch has added material from other and possibly inferior sources, there is no reason to assume that he did not use as his main reliance an authority that, if it was not the same as that used by Appian, was essentially similar.

Carcopino (pp. 9–23)[2] first considers the veto of the agrarian law by Octavius and the events immediately connected therewith. According to him, Appian (I, 12) represents the veto as coming suddenly at a meeting of the Assembly, but in Plutarch we have a long period of conflict between the two tribunes occupying the time between the posting of the law and its presentation to the Assembly (10, 1–11, 1). Octavius first interposes

---

[1] Carcopino (pp. 6 and 202 f.) believes that Appian has taken the account of the life of Tiberius almost mechanically from some unknown author, but for the ease in discussion he calls this unknown 'Appian.' I shall do the same. Whenever, therefore, the name Appian is used, the reader is to understand that this immediate source is meant.

[2] References to Carcopino are to pages of his *Autour des Gracques, Études Critiques* (Paris, 1928); those to Appian to his *Civil Wars*, and those to Plutarch to his *Life of Tiberius Gracchus*.

his veto when the law is published (10, 2), then Tiberius substitutes for his original bill another in harsher terms (10, 3), tries to bribe Octavius by offering to repay him for any damage that he may personally suffer through loss of public land (10, 5), and finally endeavors to force the aristocratic party to submit by declaring a *iustitium* (10, 5–7). Then at long last comes the meeting of the Assembly (11, 1), which Appian has reached in a single sentence. The two are entirely independent since Appian's narrative has the conflict between the two men start in the Assembly, but Plutarch has them publicly quarreling for days beforehand. Moreover the events recorded by Plutarch are, in Carcopino's view, improbable in themselves.

Unfortunately for Carcopino's argument Appian is here referring to the first meeting of the Assembly, Plutarch to the second. This second meeting, at which the bill was a second time vetoed by Octavius, which was interrupted by Tiberius' vain appeal to the Senate, and which ended with his threat to raise at the next session the question of recalling Octavius, is clearly described by both writers (Plut. 11, 1–4; Ap. I, 12). Since they are abridging a fuller account they present varying details, but there is no contradiction, nor can there be any question but that both are describing the events of the same day which in Appian is clearly that of the second meeting of the Assembly. At the first meeting Octavius had forbidden the reading of the agrarian bill, and Tiberius had adjourned the Assembly εἰς τὴν ἐπιοῦσαν ἀγοράν, that is, to the next *dies comitialis*, which might be the next day or might be as much as two weeks later.[3] Plutarch does not directly mention the first meeting, but since a measure could not be vetoed until actually presented in the Assembly, this meeting is clearly implied by his narrative, and the events for which Carcopino can find no space fall without difficulty between the two meetings. We cannot even be sure that Appian did not include some of these events in his account since at the very point in his text where they would naturally come the editors for grammatical reasons have indicated a lacuna.

The events themselves present no difficulties. Carcopino's statement (pp. 19–21) that Plutarch shows his ignorance of Roman constitutional usage by having Octavius veto the bill when it was first promulgated is due to his own misunderstanding of Plutarch and calls for no discussion. After the first veto Tiberius, according to Plutarch, withdrew his original bill, introducing another that was harsher toward the occupiers of the public land but more agreeable to the poor. Carcopino (pp. 13–15) objects that it is improbable that Tiberius would antagonize the Senate at the very time that he needed to win it over, and further that since we do not know how the second bill differed from the first there can have

---

[3] Cf. the list of *dies comitiales* in Botsford, *Roman Assemblies* (New York, 1909), 471.

been only one bill. But, as has often been pointed out, Tiberius, finding
no hope of conciliating the aristocrats, might reasonably make the bill
more favorable to the people. That we do not know what changes were
introduced is not surprising since no permanent official records were kept
of proposals that were not made laws, and knowledge of the change and
its general character might easily survive after knowledge of the actual
terms altered had been lost.[4] We have no way of knowing whether the
changes in the law were mentioned in the common source of the two
writers and omitted by Appian following what we shall see to be his
regular practice of ignoring measures proposed but not made laws. Since
the changes are in no way inconsistent with the account in Appian, it
makes no difference for our argument whether Plutarch found them in
the common authority or added them from some other source as is almost
certainly the case with the anecdote of the attempt to bribe Octavius.
Carcopino (p. 15 f.) may well be right in his elaborate explanation of the
origin of this story, but its presence in Plutarch has no bearing on the
immediate question.

Carcopino (pp. 16–18) attacks the next episode, Tiberius' effort to
coerce the aristocrats by prohibiting all public business, as impossible
both on psychological and constitutional grounds. Since there is no other
recorded instance of a *iustitium* declared by a tribune Plutarch must be
following a false tradition. Moreover, if Tiberius had had such a weapon
in his hands, he need only to have used it to the bitter end to have overcome all opposition. Carcopino is possibly right in saying that the tribune
could not formally declare a *iustitium*, but Plutarch does not say that he
did so, and it is certain that the tribune did have the right to forbid the
other magistrates to perform their several functions under pain of punishment.[5] But the efficacy of such a prohibition directed, for example, against
the praetor in his administration of justice would depend solely on the

[4] Carcopino failed to see one valid argument against the possibility of the substituion of one bill
for the other. A bill had to be publicly proposed and a copy deposited in the aerarium a *trinum
nundinum* before it could be acted on. If Mommsen (*Römisches Staatsrecht* [Leipzig, 1887–88] III,
371) is correct, no changes could legally be made in a measure after it was thus promulgated, and
Gracchus must therefore have published an entirely new law and allowed the proper interval before
presenting it for action. I am by no means convinced, however, that Mommsen has established the
existence of a rule forbidding alterations in a law after promulgation, at least at the time of the
Gracchi; and in any case, as he himself admits, there were frequent exceptions to the rule if it existed,
as well as to the whole requirement of a *trinum nundinum* between promulgation and presentation to
the Assembly for action.

[5] The whole question of the obstructive power of the tribunes is discussed by Mommsen (*St.-R.*
[3d ed.], I, 258–292, II, 290–301), who believes (I, 263) that the tribune could decree a *iustitium*.
Niccolini (*Il Tribunato della Plebe* [Milano, 1932], 111 f.), on the other hand, believes that Tiberius
did not risk taking the unprecedented step of formally declaring a *iustitium* on his own authority,
but did accomplish the same end through his undoubted right to prohibit the activity of other magistrates.

ability of the tribune, alone or with his colleagues, to interpose his veto in individual cases as they arose, or on the likelihood that the tribune could make good on the threat of prosecution. Since prosecution was a positive act it was subject to veto by the other tribunes or by any one of them. We can well believe that Tiberius by his prohibition and his threats, probably backed by free use of the veto power, succeeded in bringing public business to a temporary standstill. It must soon, however, have become apparent that his threats were nothing more than threats. Octavius would have been quick to offer his protection to any who ignored the prohibition, and some of the other tribunes, who were soon to show themselves lukewarm supporters of Tiberius, may have followed his example. The confusion that ensued is well described in a fragment of Dio Cassius (Frag. 83, 5–6). Plutarch has certainly exaggerated the success of Tiberius' maneuver, but there is otherwise nothing improbable in his account.[6]

We now come to the actual recall of Octavius. Carcopino (p. 24) here admits that Plutarch (11–12) and Appian (I, 12) are in agreement as to the first events of the second session of the Assembly and that after his vain appeal to the Senate Tiberius decided that he must remove Octavius from office. He continues: 'Seulement, selon Plutarque, il annonce ses intentions dans une première assemblée, et il les réalise dans une seconde, tenue le lendemain. Chez Appien, le geste suit la parole, et une seule *contio plebis*, sollicitée de déposer Octavius, le révoque incontinent.' Actually, if we take Appian's words in their most natural meaning, there is no essential difference between the two accounts. After his vain appeal to the Senators Tiberius 'running back again to the Assembly declared that he would put forward to the next meeting the decision both about the law and about the office of Octavius. . . . And this he did.'[7] Except for the omission by Appian of certain details given by Plutarch only one difference remains in their accounts of the day. In Appian action is put off to the next meeting of the Assembly, which might or might not be

---

[6] Carcopino (pp. 22 f.) believes that Plutarch's narrative, since it combines a *iustitium* (as he calls it) and public mourning, must be an invention of the period following Sulla, implying that this combination first appeared at that dictator's death. Actually we find the two combined at least as early as the First Samnite War (Livy, IX, 7, 7–8). Moreover the assumption of mourning by one party or the other is several times recorded by Livy in his narrative of the struggle between the orders (by patricians, Livy, II, 54, 3, II, 61, 5, III, 58, 1, IV, 42, 8, VI, 20, 1–3; by plebeians, VI, 16, 4). That such details are probably projections into the past of actual events of the late second century makes the argument for the authenticity of Plutarch's story even stronger.

[7] Αὖθις ἐκδραμὼν εἰς τὴν ἀγορὰν ἔφη διαψήφισιν προθήσειν ἐς τὴν ἐπιοῦσαν ἀγορὰν περί τε τοῦ νόμου καὶ τῆς ἀρχῆς τῆς 'Οκταουίου . . . Καὶ ἔπραξεν οὕτως. It is, of course, true that the words of Appian may mean that Tiberius returned to the Forum (the Assembly being already dismissed) and there gave formal notice of a meeting three market days hence at which he would present his motions, but where there are two equally good ways of understanding an ancient writer, one agreeing and one disagreeing with another ancient authority, it is hardly the part of impartial scholarship to insist on bringing about the disagreement.

on the following day depending on the calendar, but Plutarch definitely says that the adjournment is to the following day.[8] Neither account seems to allow for the legal interval required for the introduction of new business.

In their narrative of the voting on the recall of Octavius the two writers seem to be in entire agreement save that Plutarch (12, 1–2) has Tiberius appeal to Octavius before the voting begins and again after the seventeenth tribe has voted, while Appian (I, 12), who agrees as to the time of the second appeal, places the first after the vote of one tribe. Carcopino (pp. 25 f.) rightly lays no stress on the obvious but trivial difference, but he finds on other grounds that Plutarch has entirely misunderstood the procedure of the Assembly and that Appian presents it correctly. According to Fraccaro[9] in elections the tribes voted simultaneously, but separately in legislation. The recall of Octavius was legislation, not election. Therefore the tribes must have voted separately. Appian correctly represents this, but Plutarch, misunderstanding the procedure, has Tiberius appeal to Octavius 'lorsque les votes des 17 premières tribus ont été apportés.' Every one of these statements is subject to question. I have not been able to examine Fraccaro's paper, but we must remember that in either form of voting the vote of each tribe was separately reported to the presiding magistrate and separately announced by him, and that it is therefore almost impossible in our notices to distinguish between the two systems.[10] For example, Appian (I, 14) in describing the election in which Tiberius was a candidate for reelection writes: δύο μὲν ἔφθασαν αἱ πρῶται φυλαὶ Γράκχον ἀποφῆναι, apparently contradicting Fraccaro. It is by no means certain that the recall of Octavius was regarded as a law. It is true that Plutarch (12, 1) calls it a νόμος, and that Diodorus (XXXIV, 7, 1) refers to it as a ψήφισμα, but the fact that it was not vetoed almost forces us to regard it as an election since the election of tribunes seems to have been the only act of the Assembly not subject to the tribunician veto.[11] Finally Plutarch's words, ὡς αἱ δεκαεπτὰ ⟨φυλαὶ⟩ τὴν ψῆφον ἐπενηνόχεισαν, can mean neither more nor less than 'When seventeen tribes had cast their votes,' and are so translated by Perrin in the Loeb edition. Even if the words did have the special meaning required by Carcopino's argument (when the seventeen tribes had reported their votes), they would fit perfectly well with either system of voting.

The first real contradiction between our two authorities occurs in

---

[8] Such adjournment from day to day was possible, e.g. Livy XLV, 36, 2–6.

[9] *Atti dell' Accademia di Torino*, XLIX (1913–14), 600 ff. I take this citation from Carcopino without verification.

[10] Mommsen, *St.-R.* III, 409; Botsford, *Rom. Assemb.* 467.

[11] Mommsen, *St.-R.* (3d ed.) I, 286 f. For an opposite opinion cf. Niccolini, *Tribunato*, p. 116.

their account of events immediately subsequent to the voting. In Appian (I, 12), Octavius quietly withdraws; in Plutarch (12, 4), he is dragged from the bêma by force. Assuming that Appian correctly represents the common authority, Plutarch has here as elsewhere added an anecdote from some other source, but here he has for the first and only time added one that contradicts his main authority.

After Octavius was recalled a new tribune was elected in his place, the agrarian law was passed, and triumvirs to administer it were named. This is the order in Appian (I, 12–13). In Plutarch (13, 1–2) the passage of the law and the election of the commissioners are mentioned, and then the election of a successor to Octavius. Carcopino (p. 28) asserts that the order of Appian is the only one possible because for a law to be free from *vitium* it was necessary that it be enacted in the presence of the entire college of tribunes and with their approval, and because the replacement of Octavius by a new tribune was the sole tangible guarantee against a resurrection of the veto. For the first of these assertions there seems to be no evidence, and the second does not make sense. There thus appear to be no grounds for preferring one order of events to the other, nor does there seem to be any reason to believe that either author is concerned with the chronology of these events. Appian places the election of Mummius first to achieve the natural contrast between the old and the new tribunes: Καὶ ὁ μὲν ᾿Οκτάουιος . . . , Κόιντος δὲ Μούμμιος . . . , καὶ ὁ νόμος. . . . Plutarch mentions the election as something that took place in addition to the other more important matters, not after them: πρὸς τούτοις not μετὰ ταῦτα.

Carcopino devotes five pages (pp. 28–33) to a discussion of events recorded by Plutarch between the appointment of the land commission and the news of the death of Attalus. He admits that in general Plutarch's narrative is historical, that it does not contradict Appian's brief summary, and that it is sometimes supported by it. His objections are confined to details, and since they are almost entirely subjective and therefore incapable of either proof or disproof they need not concern us. It is otherwise with the final legislative program of Tiberius, a series of laws proposed and in some cases officially promulgated by Tiberius in the period preceding the election in which he met his death. None of these measures seems to have been voted on by the Assembly, and Appian mentions none of them. Carcopino rejects them all.

The most important of these were Tiberius' proposals in regard to the legacy of Attalus. According to Plutarch (14, 1 f.), he promulgated a measure that the goods (χρήμητα) of the king should be distributed to those who received land under his bill to enable them to equip themselves, and further announced that he would later introduce a measure for the regulation of the cities included in the kingdom. In Livy (*Ep.*, LVIII) it is stated that he proposed to promulgate a law for the distribution of the king's money (*pecunia*) among those to whom land allotments were due. The author of the *de Viris Illustribus* (64, 5) merely mentions a proposal in regard to the king's estate (*familia*). The differences are to be expected in an account of laws proposed or merely discussed in private but not acted on. If they mean anything, it is that Plutarch here is not following the source used by Livy, and so is presumably preserving an item that Appian neglected in their common source.

Carcopino's chief argument against the whole episode is chronological (pp. 34–39). He argues that Tiberius died not later than the end of July and that Attalus' death was not more than two weeks earlier and could, therefore, not have been known by Tiberius. Both assumed dates need consideration.

It is quite probable that the tribunician elections at this period usually took place during the summer although there is almost no evidence until the time of Cicero, and in 91 B.C., the one year for which we know the date with some precision, they took place in September.[12] Appian places the announcement of candidates for the election of 133 sometime during the summer, but this does not justify one in assigning the election itself to the end of July at the latest. If it were established that the death of Attalus came in mid-July, it would prove, not that Plutarch and Livy are recounting a fable, but that the elections of that year came late in August or early in September.

But I find no reason whatever to believe that Attalus lived until mid-July.[13] The case for this date is based on two inscriptions from Pergamum.[14] One is a decree of the people of that city, passed after the death of Attalus but before word had come from Rome as to the acceptance or rejection of the bequest, and dated on the 19th of Eumeneios. Unfortunately the position of this month in the year is unknown, and therefore no conclusions can be drawn from the inscription as to the date of the Senate's action on the legacy, still less as to the date of Attalus' death. The other inscription is a Greek copy of a *senatus consultum* directing Roman generals who are being sent to Asia to regard as valid certain of Attalus' acts. This decree presupposes the acceptance of the bequest by the Senate. The date is so mutilated that we know only that it was passed between August 18 and December 11, and since it was introduced by a praetor who is otherwise unknown we cannot even be sure of the year. The Senate may have waited weeks or months before acting on the bequest, and there is no reason to place the extant decree in any close chronological relation to the acceptance.[15] A date late in 133 seems

---

[12] This follows from Cic., *de Orat.*, III, 2, 6, and 11. Cf. Niccolini, *Tribunato*, 95 f.

[13] For a discussion of this matter cf. F. B. Marsh, *History of the Roman World from 146 to 30 B.C.* (London, 1935), 380.

[14] Dittenberger, *O.G.I.S.*, 338, 435.

[15] It seems clear from Plutarch's account that the Senate would have invited a tribunician veto had it taken action on this matter during Tiberius' life. If the decree were dated before his death, doubt might be thrown on Plutarch.

probable for the decree, and one in the second half of the next year is not impossible. In any case, the decree gives us no light on the date of Attalus' death, which we may place at any time after the heat of summer had begun[16] leaving plenty of time for Tiberius to form and make known his proposals before the tribunician elections.

The other legislative proposals that Plutarch ascribes to the last days of the tribune's life are not to be rejected lightly. They are typical pre-election promises aimed at securing the favor of all classes in the state except the Senate, and two of them—improvement in military conditions and the extension of the right of appeal—seem to have been the common property of all popular leaders. The third, which dealt with the personnel of the courts, lay in a field which Gaius was to make his own, but the solution proposed by Tiberius is one that, to the best of our knowledge, was not considered by the younger brother. To reject this second program of Tiberius either as unsuitable to the political situation or as an incorrect anticipation of the history of Gaius is far from justifiable. It does not contradict Appian, and since nowhere in his story of the Gracchi does he mention proposals that did not become laws his failure to mention it by no means indicates that it was not in his source.

Carcopino undertook to prove, first, that Plutarch and Appian cannot have used a common source because where they deal with the same material they are often in contradiction, and because Plutarch gives material so inconsistent with Appian that he could not have used it had he had Appian's source before him; and second, that whenever Plutarch varies from Appian he falls into absurdities. This paper has tried to point out that since of all these alleged contradictions only one is valid there is no reason to assume that Appian's sole source was not also the chief authority of Plutarch; and further that the material not in Appian but preserved by Plutarch is reasonable in itself and consistent with the known facts. Carcopino (p. 45 f.) concludes by saying that the work of Appian

vaut mieux à elle seule que les autres réunies; et le devoir s'impose aux modernes, qui songent aujourd'hui à écrire cette histoire, de renverser sans hésitation la balance des valeurs établies, de donner à Appien le premier rang entre tous leurs informateurs, et de n'admettre en leurs synthèses les éléments qui lui manquent que s'ils concordent avec son exposé et rentrent sans effort dans le cadre qu'il y traça de main de maître.

I, on the other hand, suggest that the problem is not so simple, that Plutarch, drawing from the same authority as Appian, has preserved much that Appian has omitted, and has also added from other sources material that must be carefully weighed by the historian.

TULANE UNIVERSITY.

---

[16] He died from heat prostration (Justin, XXXVI, 4). On the day late in May on which I write this there have been two deaths from this cause in Rhode Island.

NOTE ON GEORGICS IV, 491-493

William Chase Greene

> *Ibi omnis*
> *Effusus labor atque immitis rupta tyranni*
> *Foedera, terque fragor stagnis auditus Averni.*

OF THE MATURE art of Virgil there is no more perfect example than the brief epyllion of Orpheus and Eurydice. In economy, in calculated pathos, in the music of anaphora and assonance, in the manipulation of numerals, in the mingling of literary reminiscence and realistic simile to create an atmosphere of wonder made palpable, Virgil here reveals the sure hand of a master. If we see Eurydice only in the half-shadow, Philomela is for once no fabled Greek princess but a wholly real and Italian bird. To measure the extent of Virgil's mastery we need only compare his version of the story with that of Ovid,[1] which owes something to Virgil, but which succeeds only in arousing interest where Virgil awakens wonder and pity.

In nothing do the two versions differ more than in the matter of emphasis. Where Virgil is rapid and allusive, Ovid is explicit and diffuse; where Ovid is bald and brief, Virgil is lavish of picturesque or atmospheric detail. It is Ovid who explains precisely the conditions under which Orpheus was permitted to win his wife again,[2] but who states in three words, *illa relapsa est*, that Eurydice was lost again after the pact was broken; it is Virgil who only hints at any pact,[3] but who characteristically tells us three times over, in the lines that stand at the head of this note, that the pact was broken, before unfolding the tragic consequences.[4]

It is to the last of these three expressions that I draw attention: *terque fragor stagnis auditus Averni.* What was the *fragor* which was heard among the pools of Avernus, and why was it heard thrice? We may dismiss at once the suggestion of Servius, that the *fragor* is the exultation of the shades at the return of Eurydice, supported though the suggestion is by a reference to such a situation in Lucan. J. Martyn rightly pointed out long ago that *fragor* is never used by Virgil of a joyous sound, 'but for some great crash, or horrid noise. I take it in this place to mean a dismal sound given by the earth, or perhaps a clap of thunder, to signify

---

[1] *Metamorphoses* X, 1-85.

[2] Lines 50-52.

[3] *Georgics* IV, 487; 492 f.

[4] On this characteristic of Virgil, Mr. H. W. Garrod has some good remarks in his Introduction to the *Oxford Book of Latin Verse*, pp. xxxiv-xxxvi.

the greatness of the misfortune.'[5] And indeed *fragor* is not only used by Virgil of the crashing of trees or of warriors or of a storm, but is twice employed actually of thunder;[6] in each case the thunder is significant of the approval of a divinity. To these I shall return presently. T. Keightley's comment on *fragor* is to the point: 'probably the signal of return to Eurydice. Virgil perhaps had in view the signal given to Oedipus in Sophocles, *O. C.* 1606.'[7] That, too, I shall consider later. T. E. Page suggests that 'the "crash" is that of subterranean thunder, the words being added to suggest awe and terror.' Like other editors, he refers to Milton's elaborations of the idea;[8] pointing out however that 'in those passages Nature is made to sympathize and share in the suffering caused, whereas here there is no such intention, and the effect is purely dramatic.' He gives no reason for regarding the thunder as 'subterranean.' But that we are here concerned with thunder needs, I think, no further demonstration.

Let us now consider why the crash was heard thrice. Virgil's fondness for numerals is well known.[9] Even within the present epyllion we may note also *noviens*,[10] *tria*,[11] *bis*,[12] and the appropriately Orphic *septem*,[13] to say nothing of the suggestion of number in the anaphora of *te*[14] and the thrice repeated *Eurydicen*,[15] and the suggestion of a mysteriously large number in the simile of the birds.[16] Is there any special significance in the fact that the crash was heard thrice? There were many occasions when circumstances beyond Virgil's control determined his use of particular numerals; this is particularly true of the numeral three in either the adjectival or the adverbial form. In the ritual of magic and religion, above all, we encounter triple objects and thrice repeated acts. So the sorceress in the eighth *Bucolic:*

> terna tibi haec primum triplici diversa colore
> licia circumdo, terque haec altaria circum

---

[5] J. Martyn, ed. *Georgics* (London, 1741). Martyn might have cited Seneca, *Quaestiones Naturales* II, 27, who distinguishes among kinds of thunder *grave murmur, tonitrua venturi imbris,* and *genus acre, hic proprie fragor dicitur, subitus et vehemens,* etc.

[6] *Aeneid* II, 692; VIII, 527.

[7] T. Keightley, ed. *Bucolics and Georgics* (London, 1847).

[8] *Paradise Lost* IX, 782–784; 1000–1004.

[9] It is the subject of a dissertation by C. P. Clark, *Numerical Phraseology in Vergil* (Princeton, 1913).

[10] *Georgics* IV, 480.

[11] Line 483.

[12] Line 504.

[13] Line 507; see Clark, pp. 28 f.

[14] Lines 465 f.

[15] Lines 525–527; this Dryden altogether loses in his translation.

[16] Lines 473 f.

effigiem duco; numero deus impare gaudet.

necte tribus nodis ternos, Amarylli, colores.[17]

Servius has a learned and interesting comment at this point; but most of it involves ideas that were Pythagorean or even later, whereas we have to do here with something quite primitive.[18] Pliny contents himself with asking the question: *Cur impares numeros ad omnia vehementiores credimus?*[19] He suggests no answer. A plausible explanation of the peculiar significance attached by primitive men to the number three is that suggested by H. Diels: that it represents the limit of their ability to count.[20]

Magical three appears in Roman ritual in many well-known forms. Not to go beyond the text of Virgil, and confining our attention to successive acts in time ('thrice,' rather than 'three'), we are reminded of the thrice-repeated lustral procession of the Ambarvalia:

terque novas circum felix eat hostia fruges;[21]

of thrice-repeated libations:

ter liquido ardentem perfundit nectare Vestam,
ter flamma ad summam tecti subiecta reluxit;[22]

of the funeral *decursio* and *conclamatio*:

idem ter socios pura circumtulit unda
spargens rore levi et ramo felicis olivae,
lustravitque viros dixitque novissima verba;[23]

or again:

et magna manis ter voce vocavi;[24]

[17] *Bucolics* VIII, 73–75; 77; cf. *Ciris* 371–373; and for other types of magical three, *Aeneid* VIII, 564–567 (three souls); *Aeneid* II, 174 (the prodigy of the Palladium thrice moving). See further M. C. Sutphen, 'Magic in Theokritos and Vergil,' in *Studies in Honor of Basil L. Gildersleeve* (Baltimore, 1902), 315–327.

[18] Reasoning similar to that of Servius is at work in the Platonic Scholium to *Charmides* 167a (τὸ τρίτον σωτῆρι): τέλειος γὰρ ὁ τρία ἀριθμός, ἐπειδὴ καὶ ἀρχὴν καὶ μέσον καὶ τέλος ἔχει, κτλ.

[19] *Historia Naturalis* XXVIII, 5.

[20] H. Diels, *Archiv für Geschichte der Philosophie* X (1897), 232; also in *Theodor Gomperz Festschrift* (Vienna, 1902), 8, n. 3; so also H. Usener, 'Dreiheit,' *Rheinisches Museum*, N. F. LVIII (1903), 362, agreeing with Diels: 'die typische Geltung der Dreizahl daraus ableitete, dass sie "die ursprungliche Endzahl der primitiven Menschheit war."' This fundamental study by Usener is of great interest for its collections of material with regard to triads or trinities of deities, and other matters; but it yields little for our special inquiry. 'The Number Twenty-seven in Roman Ritual,' by W. Warde Fowler, *Classical Review* XVI (1902), 211 f., and the same author's *Religious Experience of the Roman People* (London, 1911), 328 and note 47; 441 and note 38, illustrate extensions of the idea of magical three.

[21] *Georgics* I, 345.

[22] *Georgics* IV, 384 f.

[23] *Aeneid* VI, 229–231, of the funeral of Misenus.

[24] *Aeneid* VI, 506, of the rites paid to Deïphobus in Troy.

and once more:

> ter circum accensos cincti fulgentibus armis
> decurrere rogos, ter maestum funeris ignem
> lustravere in equis ululatusque ore dedere.[25]

For the *decursio* there is at least one good Homeric precedent, Achilles and the corpse of Patroclus,[26] to which we may perhaps add an Horatian example, as Greek as Roman, of a similar rite:

> licebit
> iniecto ter pulvere curras.[27]

What is implied by *'ter vocavi'* and by the *'novissima verba'* is explained by Servius, who mentions *'vale, vale, vale'* and *'ilicet.'*[28]

Other kinds of ritual also employ the lucky 'thrice'; examples from several poets are collected by D. A. Slater in support of his almost certain emendation of Horace, *Odes* IV, 2, 49, from *teque* (or *tuque*) to *terque*, of a cry at a triumph.[29]

In such cases Virgil describes ritual with the appropriate *ter*. Yet there are many other cases in which he uses it for merely dramatic effect, and this chiefly in imitation of Homer. Achilles had dragged Hector thrice round the walls of Troy;[30] Mezentius rode thrice round Aeneas.[31] Several times a ship in a storm is thrice spun round or tossed, or sucked by Charybdis.[32] Sometimes the *ter* is merely decorative, as when Mezentius whirls his sling thrice, against the best military principles,[33] or as when on the battlefield he hails Aeneas *magna ter voce* for no special reason save that Aeneas has similarly, but more appropriately, hailed dead Deïphobus at his cenotaph.[34] Or again *ter aut quater*, or *ter quaterque*, means merely an indefinite number of times.[35]

Of special interest are the familiar passages in which *ter* is repeated; the first *ter* ordinarily is used of three successive efforts, the second of their frustration. Thus Aeneas seeks in vain to embrace the shade of Creusa:

---

[25] *Aeneid* XI, 188–190, of a general funeral.

[26] *Il.* Ψ 13 f.; cf. *Od.* κ 519; Sophocles, *Antigone* 431.

[27] *Odes* I, 28, 36.

[28] Servius on *Aeneid* II, 644 ('vale, vale, vale'); on *Aeneid* VI, 231: 'novissima verba, id est "ilicet"; nam "vale" dicebatur post tumuli quoque peracta solemnia.' See also on *Aeneid* VI, 229.

[29] *Classical Review* XXIII (1909), 252 f.

[30] *Aeneid* I, 483; cf. *Il.* X 165; 251; Ω 16.

[31] *Aeneid* X, 885 f.; cf. *Od.* δ 277, of Helen and the Wooden Horse.

[32] *Aeneid* I, 116 f.; III, 566 f.; 421; cf. *Od.* μ 105.

[33] *Aeneid* IX, 586 f.; cf. Vegetius II, 23, cited by Cerda and by Conington.

[34] *Aeneid* X, 873; cf. VI, 506, quoted on p. 115 above.

[35] *Georgics* I, 410 f.; cf. Aratus, *Diosemia* 968; 1004; *Aeneid* I, 95; cf. *Od.* ε 306.

ter conatus ibi collo dare bracchia circum;
ter frustra comprensa manus effugit imago,
par levibus ventis volucrisque simillima somno.[36]

Sometimes Virgil uses this figure without complete Homeric sanction, as of the threefold but baffled effort of the giants to scale Heaven,[37] or of the triple attempt of Hercules to enter the cave of Cacus,[38] or of the vain struggles of dying Dido.[39] But the figure need not always imply ultimate frustration; sometimes the second *ter* applies merely to a new series of acts;[40] sometimes the third time succeeds,[41] or if not the third, at any rate the fourth.[42]

If some of this discussion appears to digress from my original inquiry, it may be well to realize that the cumulative effect of these examples, and of many others that might be adduced, is to show how naturally the Greek and Roman mind returned to the idea of an event or act thrice repeated as having a special potency or significance. In some cases Virgil's use of *ter* was determined by the custom of ritual; elsewhere it was mere literary imitation or a sense of the dramatic. So far, however, we have not considered triple thunder. We may return to this subject by way of another example of repeated *ter*, in which Turnus thrice sought to meet Aeneas and was thrice diverted by Juno:

ter conatus utramque viam; ter maxima Iuno
continuit, iuvenemque animi miserata repressit.[43]

No thunder here, to be sure; but if we turn to the Homeric lines which editors have rightly seen to have been in Virgil's mind we discover what he was forced to omit, since the divinity in his episode is not a thunderer:

τρὶς μὲν μερμήριξε κατὰ φρένα καὶ κατὰ θυμόν,
τρὶς δ' ἄρ' ἀπ' Ἰδαίων ὀρέων κτύπε μητίετα Ζεὺς
σῆμα τιθεὶς τρώεσσι, μάχης ἑτεραλκέα νίκην,[44]

---

[36] *Aeneid* II, 792–794, identical with *Aeneid* VI, 700–702, of Aeneas and Anchises, both passages being paraphrases of *Od.* λ 206–208. For further examples of this figure in Homer, see *Il.* Λ 462 f.; Π 702 f.; Σ 155–157; Υ 445 f.; Ψ 817.

[37] *Georgics* I, 281–283, a free treatment of *Od.* λ 313–320.

[38] *Aeneid* VIII, 230–232; here the *ter* is thrice repeated.

[39] *Aeneid* IV, 690–692; see the comment here of A. S. Pease, ed. *Aeneid IV* (Cambridge, Mass., 1935), p. 527.

[40] *Aeneid* XI, 188; cf. *Il.* Σ 228 f.

[41] *Aeneid* XI, 629–635; IX, 799–818.

[42] *Aeneid* VI, 355–357; cf. *Il.* Π 784–786; Φ 176 f.; *Od.* Φ 125–127; Clark, *op. cit.*, p. 56, proposes the term 'limit of endeavor' to cover such cases. Of the two vain efforts of Daedalus to master his emotion, and so to portray his son (*Aeneid* VI, 32 f.), Clark suggests that he 'might have overcome his emotion if he had but tried a third time.'

[43] *Aeneid* X, 685.

[44] *Il.* Θ 169–171.

At last we have reached again the idea of significant and thrice repeated thunder, in this case sent by Zeus as a warning to Diomedes and as a favorable portent for the Trojans, as Hector perceives.[45] In fact Diomedes has just before been warned by a single thunderbolt of Zeus that he should retire from battle for the day, and this omen has been correctly interpreted by Nestor;[46] but his continued hesitation to retire is met by the further triple warning. Other cases of thunder in Homer are not rare: to deter heroes from action, to indicate the direction that a battle is to take, to show that a prayer has been favorably heard. But the thunder is generally equivocal, save as the poet indicates whether it is favorable or unfavorable. In the great battle that follows the return of Achilles, the thunder of Zeus is impartial, and is mingled with the earthquakes of Poseidon, till the Lord of the Lower World himself is terrified.[47] On another occasion the evil thunderings that Zeus sends all night seem to be intended for both the Greeks and the Trojans, feasting separately.[48] It is only the context, in the episode of Zeus and the Golden Scales, that associates the divine thunder with Trojan victory and Greek defeat.[49] But when Apollo aroused Hector to enter the battle over the body of Patroclus, Zeus by his thunder and lightning 'gave victory to the Trojans, and dismayed the Achaeans.'[50] Moreover a prayer of Nestor is immediately answered by thunder, that is, favorably;[51] and in the highly interesting episode in which Odysseus asks Zeus for a double omen, not only does Zeus answer with thunder but an old woman grinding at the mill hears it, notes that it comes from a starry sky, and prays that the omen, clearly intended for some one, may prosper Odysseus; her words are the second omen.[52] Rarely is the lucky side designated by Homer, as right,[53] whereas Virgil frequently designates, in Roman fashion, the lucky left side.[54] Once in Homer,[55] and often in Virgil, we find the good omen of thunder or lightning coming from a clear sky. So the prayer of Aeneas

[45] Line 175.

[46] Lines 130–144; cf. also *Od.* ω 539 f., where Odysseus is similarly deterred from further fighting.

[47] *Il.* Υ 19–66.

[48] *Il.* H 477–482; cf. W. Leaf *ad loc.*: 'There is no reason for confining σφιν to the Greeks alone; Zeus gives both sides alike ominous warning of the coming battles.' In these battles, of course, the Trojans are victorious, thanks to the intervention of Zeus.

[49] *Il.* Θ 69–77.

[50] *Il.* P 593–596.

[51] *Il.* Θ 377.

[52] *Od.* υ 102–121; cf. also the story told of Phidias, and the thunderbolt of Zeus which immediately answered his prayer for a sign approving his work (Pausanias V, 88, 4),—an appropriate token for the sculptor whose statue of Zeus had attempted to suggest the thundering Zeus of *Iliad* A 528–530, as we are told by Strabo (VIII, 3, 30; cf. Valerius Maximus III, 7, ext. 4).

[53] *Il.* B 353; I 236.

[54] *Aeneid* II, 693, and Servius Dan. *ad loc.*; IX, 631, etc.

[55] *Od.* υ 113, cited above, note 52.

to Jupiter and a number of other gods is immediately answered:

> hic pater omnipotens ter caelo clarus ab alto
> intonuit, radiisque ardentem lucis et auro
> ipse manu quatiens ostendit ab aethere nubem.[56]

And the portent is recognized by Aeneas as of great import, and as favorable. Elsewhere[57] the dejection of Aeneas is ended when thunder is sent by Venus not only from a clear sky,[58] but thrice:

> iterum atque iterum fragor increpat ingens.[59]

Yet this token, which Lucretius declares impossible,[60] serves on occasion as an evil omen.[61]

In fact the Greeks, though firmly convinced that thunder is the very language of Zeus,[62] never reduced divination by thunder to anything like a system; and the Etruscans and the Romans, despite the pretentious elaboration of distinctions by which they interpreted lightning and the striking of thunderbolts, as *auspicia oblativa*, made very little use of any signs which the sound of thunder, even if thrice repeated, might be supposed to give.[63] Not very much to our purpose are Seneca's chapters on thunder,[64] attempting to reconcile popular beliefs with Stoic doctrine, or Pliny's chapters in similar vein.[65] Seneca's reference to Caecinna's *fulgura postulatoria quibus sacrificia intermissa aut non rite facta repetuntur* helps only as it suggests that thunder might be a warning that the gods are offended.[66] Subterranean lightning (*fulgura inferna*) is mentioned by

---

[56] *Aeneid* VII, 141–143.

[57] *Aeneid* VIII, 520–540.

[58] Lines 524 f.; 528; cf. *Aeneid* IX, 630.

[59] *Aeneid* VIII, 527.

[60] Lucretius VI, 99; cf. Horace, *Odes* I, 34, 5–8.

[61] *Georgics* I, 487 f.

[62] Cf. [Xenophon], *Apologia Socratis*, 12: βροντὰς δὲ ἀμφιλέξει τις ἢ μὴ φωνεῖν ἢ μὴ μέγιστον οἰωνιστήριον εἶναι; See also Servius Dan. on *Aeneid* I, 230.

[63] A. Bouché-Leclercq, *Histoire de la Divination dans l'Antiquité* (Paris, 1879–1882), I, 199 f., denies the Greeks any *science fulgurale theologique*; C. O. Thulin, *Die Etruskische Disciplin* (Göteborg, 1906), though useful for *Blitzlehre* and *Haruspicin*, yields little as to the lore of thunder, and nothing as to any part that number may have played in it. 'Ob die Etrusker schon aus dem blossen Donner geweissagt haben, können wir nicht entscheiden' (I, p. 56).

[64] Seneca, *Quaestiones Naturales* II, 12–59.

[65] Pliny, *Historia Naturalis* II, 43; 51–56.

[66] Seneca, *op. cit.*, II, 49; cf. Festus, p. 284 Lindsay: *postulatoria fulgura quae votorum ⟨a⟩ut sacrificiorum spretam religionem desiderant.* For other passages, cited by Thulin, I, p. 53, illustrating the fear inspired among the Romans by the sound of thunder, see Cicero, *De Divinatione* II, 18, 42: *Iove tonante, fulgurante, comitia populi nefas* (and see A. S. Pease's comment, ed. *De Div.*, Urbana, Illinois, 1920–23); Servius Dan. on *Aeneid* IV, 161: *murmur autem caeli ad infaustum omen pertinet, quia tonitru dirimuntur auspicia;* Servius Dan. on *Aeneid* IV, 339: *tonuisse: quae res dirimit confarreationes;* but see also the Verona Scholia on *Aeneid* II, 693 (thunder, as well as lightning, on the left, is lucky); also Bouché-Leclercq, *op. cit.*, IV, 44 f.

Seneca as occurring *cum e terra exilivit ignis.*[67] But this means rather more than the sound of thunder: and our authors may really refer to the subterranean rumblings and sulphurous emissions that sometimes in the neighborhood of Naples presage earthquake. That would seem to be at least possible for the 'pools of Avernus,' if not for Rhodope.

Clearly there was such confusion in these matters that Virgil was free to draw what he pleased from the deep well of his memory of Greek poetry, and from popular beliefs, and to use them as best suited his purpose as a poet. His purpose in the story of Orpheus and Eurydice was to mark the frustration of Orpheus, already suggested by the phrases *effusus labor* and *rupta foedera*, as sudden, divinely ordained, and final. By any of his readers, familiar not only with folk-lore but with Homer, thunder would be associated with the divine will; but that it is here hostile would be inferred only from the context. The triple sound would recall those great moments when the destiny of heroes was at stake. The term *fragor*, associated with the pools of Avernus, might suggest subterranean rumblings and the Lower World, but no precise theory of their origin, and could as easily suggest celestial thunder; indeed the vagueness is doubtless as intentional as it is effective. Finally any reader who was familiar with the *Oedipus Coloneus* would remember that the mysterious passing of the blind exile is preceded by three intensely dramatic rolls of thunder,[68] which the Chorus attribute to Zeus yet know not how to interpret, but which Oedipus recognizes as the sign of Zeus that will lead him to Hades;[69] and furthermore that shortly before his disappearance there is heard the thunder of Zeus Chthonios,[70] though his actual end is not violent, nor is it caused by any thunderbolt.[71] The technique of the

[67] Seneca, *Quaestiones Naturales* II, 49.

[68] Sophocles, *Oedipus Coloneus* 1456; 1463; 1478.

[69] Lines 1461 f.; 1472 f.; 1511 f.; 1514 f.; 1540; cf. 95.

[70] Line 1606. Ζεὺς Καταχθόνιος is associated in *Il.* I 457 with Persephone and the Erinyes in the fulfilment of a curse; in Hesiod, *Works and Days* 465, Ζεὺς Χθόνιος is associated with Demeter, as a kindly patron of farmers. (See further L. R. Farnell, *The Cults of the Greek States*, III [Oxford, 1907], 280–288.) For Sophocles the implication of the context would be that he is thinking of a dread but friendly divinity. See also Aeschylus, *Prometheus Vinctus*, 993 f.: βροντήμασι | Χθονίοις; 1082 f.: βρυχία δ'ἠχὼ παραμυκᾶται | βροντῆς; frag. 57 Sidgwick: ὑπογαίου βροντῆς.

[71] *Oedipus Coloneus* 1658 f. H. St. John Thackeray, 'Sophocles and the Perfect Number (A Neglected Nicety), *Proceedings of the British Academy*, XVI (1930), 15–44, collects an extraordinary amount of material in Sophocles in the way of triple alliteration and anaphora and trinities of words, but fails to mention triple thunder. Greek literature, however, is full of such and similar material. The *Hippolytus* of Euripides, for example, reckons with the triple curse granted by Poseidon to Theseus (44; 890; 1315); and the catastrophe is introduced by an ἠχὼ χθόνιος ὡς βροντὴ Διός (1201) and by a τρικυμία (1213; cf. Plato, *Republic* 472a). So also at the end of the Platonic Myth of Er, just before the souls shot to their birth, like stars, there was thunder and an earthquake (βροντήν τε καὶ σεισμὸν γενέσθαι, *Republic* 621b). Nor should we fail to recall that the Gospel accounts of the Crucifixion mention disturbances of nature,—darkness, the rending of the veil of the Temple, and earthquake; 'and the graves were opened, and many bodies of the saints which slept arose' (Matthew

epyllion is more rapid than that of tragedy; what Sophocles elaborates, Virgil suggests in a half-line.

The mind of a poet is sometimes unfathomable; but sometimes he admits his readers to his confidence. Coleridge set down in prose something, but not all, of what was in his waking consciousness just before he had the dream from which he woke to write 'Kubla Khan'; and Professor Lowes has discovered more.[72] I confine my attention to the numerals in the poem. In Purchas's *Pilgrimage*, Coleridge writes, he has read: 'And thus ten miles of fertile ground were inclosed with a wall.' (Actually, the words in Purchas run: 'a stately palace, encompassing sixteene miles of plaine ground with a wall, wherein are fertile Meaddowes. . . .') This becomes in the poem, of course, the far better 'twice five miles of fertile ground.' Bartram's *Travels* mentions 'a creek . . . which meanders six miles through green meadows'; this becomes 'Five miles meandering with a mazy motion | Through wood and dale.' Again the round number 'five' is an improvement on the too precise 'six.' The last four lines of the poem run:

> Weave a circle round him thrice,
> And close your eyes with holy dread,
> For he on honey-dew hath fed,
> And drunk the milk of Paradise.

Why 'thrice'? Not even Professor Lowes has any source for the first two of these four lines; the last two can be traced to Purchas. With the word 'Paradise' given, and placed in the effective last place, it is merely the easy rhyme, I suggest, together with the association of magic, that decided Coleridge in favor of 'thrice.'

Keats, however, had more of a problem in 'La Belle Dame sans Merci.'

> She took me to her elfin grot,
>   And there she wept, and sigh'd full sore,
> And there I shut her wild wild eyes
>   With kisses four.[73]

So Keats wrote; but before these lines were published by Leigh Hunt, a year later, Keats betrayed his uneasiness about them, and they were printed as follows:

> She took me to her elfin grot,
>   And there she gaz'd and sighed deep,
> And there I shut her wild sad eyes—
>   So kiss'd to sleep.

XXVII, 52). These disturbances are still symbolized at the close of the Good Friday services in the Sistine Chapel by the violent banging of prayer-books on benches by the priests.

[72] J. L. Lowes, *The Road to Xanadu²* (Boston, 1930), 356 ff.

[73] Stanza viii.

That is not a change for the better, and later editions have fortunately preserved the original version. What Keats had intended, as Miss Lowell has pointed out, was to follow the old ballad tradition, with its quaint exactness of enumeration. Yet he felt that those not familiar with the tradition might find it ridiculous; so he anticipated criticism not only by changing the lines but before that by writing in defense of them.[74] 'Why four kisses—you will say—why four? Because I wish to restrain the headlong impetuosity of my Muse—she would have fain said "score" without hurting the rhyme—but we must temper the Imagination as the critics say with Judgement. I was obliged to choose an even number that both eyes might have fair play; and to speak truly I think two a piece quite sufficient. Suppose I had said seven; there would have been three and a half a piece—a very awkward affair and well got out on my side.'[75]

So Keats, in playful spirit, analyzed the working of his own mind. Virgil left no letters, and his mind must be read in his poems in the light of the world that he knew. That, and the fascination of the subject, must be my justification for writing so long a note on so few words.

HARVARD UNIVERSITY.

[74] Amy Lowell, *John Keats* (Boston, 1929), II, 227 f.
[75] *Letters of John Keats*, ed. M. B. Forman (Oxford, 1931), II, 357, Letter 114, to George and Georgiana Keats, Feb. 14, 1819.

CURATORES TABULARUM PUBLICARUM

Mason Hammond

THE EARLIEST collection of Latin inscriptions which has been preserved, the primitive ancestor of the *Corpus Inscriptionum Latinarum*, is the *Einsiedeln Codex*, a tenth century copy of a record which some pilgrim to Rome in the late eighth or early ninth century made of the notable inscriptions which he saw.[1] Number 43, which is stated to have been on the Capitol, contains one of the three epigraphical mentions of the curators of the public records at Rome. It reads in the manuscript as follows:

> Ti. claudius dursi · f · Caesar aug. germani
> cus pontif · max · trib · potest · V · cos · III desig.
> IIII · imp · X · p · p · ex S · C · IIII · c · calpetanum
> rantium sedatum metronium · M · petronium
> lurconem · T · satrium decianum curatoris
> tabulariorum publicorum · fac · cur.

The fifteenth century Italian humanist Poggio, who had access to part of the original of the *Einsiedeln Codex*, preserves only one variant, the obvious *Drusi* for *dursi*. The *Corpus* contains two restorations of this inscription, *CIL.*, VI, 1, 1, 916 and VI, 4, 2, 31201. The second and preferable one, by Huelsen, is this:

TI · CLAVDIVS · DRVSI · F · CAESAR · AVG
GERMANICVS · PONTIF · MAX
TRIB · POTEST · V · COS · III · DESIG · IIII
IMP · X · P · P · EX · S · C
per] C · CALPETANVM · RANTIVM · SEDATVM
M · PETRONIVM · LVRCONEM
T · SATRIVM · DECIANVM
CVATOR[*e*]S · TABVLARIORVM · PVBLICORVM
FAC · CVR

The first, probably by Henzen, differs chiefly in the division of the lines, in retaining the ms. *metronium*, though with the note that it is probably a dittography for the following name, and in reading *curatores tabular. public.* This last was Mommsen's correction, of which he later repented.[2]

---

[1] *CIL.*, VI, 1, 1, p. ix.

[2] Mommsen first proposed to read *curat. tabular. publicar.* in *Annali dell'Instituto di Corrispondenza Archaeologica*, XXX (1858), 207–208. He restored the reading of the ms. in his *Staatsrecht*, II (ed. 3, 1887), 1, p. 558, n.3.

Both restorations date the inscription in 46 on the ground that since Claudius was *cos. IIII* in 47, he would have been *cos. desig. IIII* in the previous year. But since Claudius probably received the tribunician power on the day following his elevation by the praetorians, his fifth year ran from Jan. 25, 45 to Jan. 25, 46. Moreover inscriptions record salutations as *imperator* from *VIII* through *XI* with *trib. pot. V* and it is unlikely that he received the last two of these during the twenty-five days of 46 in which he remained *trib. pot. V*. Finally, other inscriptions show that he was *cos. desig. IIII* with *trib. pot. IIII* and even with *trib. pot. III* so that he probably became consul designate upon laying down his third consulship at the end of February, 43. Hence the inscription may safely be dated in 45.[3]

Henzen connected the inscription with a special board which Dio tells us that Claudius established in 42 to recover debts due to the treasury.[4] It is not impossible, but perhaps unlikely, that such a board was still at work two or three years later and that they supervised the erection of a building for Claudius. Mommsen refers it to a board created by Tiberius in 16 to collect and restore the public records.[5] While such a board might well build an addition to the *Tabularium*, Dio's account implies that it was more temporary than would be one which was still functioning almost twenty years later. The literary references to such special boards in connection with the treasury or the public records are six during the first century, as follows:

Dio, LV, 25, 6, in connection with the establishment of the *aerarium militare* by Augustus in 6:

τὰ δ'ἀναλώματα διὰ τριῶν ἀνδρῶν ὑπατευκότων, οὓς ὁ κλῆρος ἀπέφηνε, τὰ μὲν συνέστειλε τὰ δὲ καὶ παντάπασι διέγραψε.

Dio, LVII, 16, 2, under Tiberius in 16:

ἐπεί τε πολλὰ τῶν δημοσίων γραμμάτων τὰ μὲν καὶ παντελῶς ἀπωλώλει, τὰ δὲ ἐξίτηλα γοῦν ὑπὸ τοῦ χρόνου ἐγεγόνει, τρεῖς βουλευταὶ προεχειρίσθησαν ὥστε τά τε ὄντα ἐκγρα-ψάσθαι καὶ τὰ λοιπὰ ἀναζητῆσαι.

Dio, LX, 10, 4, the instance already referred to under Claudius in 42:

καὶ τρεῖς ἄνδρας τῶν ἐστρατηγηκότων πράκτορες τῶν τῷ δημοσίῳ ὀφειλομένων κατέστησε καὶ ῥαβδούχους καὶ τὴν ἄλλην ὑπηρεσίαν αὐτοῖς δούς.

[3] The information is from the articles on Claudius by Groag in Pauly-Wissowa, III (6) s.v. *Claudius* no. 256, cols. 2786, 2794-2800. For *trib. pot. V imp. XI*, cf. *CIL.*, VI, 1, 1, 1252 = Dessau, *Inscriptiones Latinae Selectae*, 205. For *trib. potest. IIII cos. III desig. IIII*, cf. *CIL.*, V, 1, 3326 = Dessau, 204. For *trib. potestat. III cos. de . . .*, cf. *CIL.*, XIII, 1, 2, 4565 = Dessau, 7061. He furthermore appears as *trib. potest. VI cos. desig. IIII*, Dessau, 206-207, before becoming *trib. potest. VI cos. IV*, Dessau, 208, i.e. until the beginning of 47. On Jan. 25, 47, of course, he became *trib. potest. VII cos. IIII*, Dessau, 209-210.

[4] Both this and the next reference to Dio are given in full just below.

[5] *Staatsrecht*, II 1, pp. 558-559. For his earlier views, cf. n. 35.

Tacitus, *Ann.*, XV, 18, 4, under Nero in 62:

tres dein consularis, L. Pisonem, Ducenium Geminum, Pompeium Paulinum vectigalibus publicis praeposuit, cum insectatione priorum principum qui gravitate sumptuum iustos reditus antisset: se annuum sexcenties sestertium rei publicae largiri.

Tacitus, *Hist.*, IV, 40, when Domitian was governing Rome on behalf of Vespasian early in 70:

tum sorte ducti per quos redderentur bello rapta, quique aera legum vetustate delapsa noscerent figerentque, et fastos adulatione temporum foedatos exonerarent, modumque publicis impensis facerent.

Pliny the Younger, *Ep.*, II, 1, 9, in speaking of Verginius Rufus, who had injured himself by a fall during a rehearsal of his speech of thanks to Nerva for the ordinary consulship which he shared with the emperor at the beginning of 97:

quin etiam in hac novissima valetudine veritus, ne forte inter quinqueviros crearetur, qui minuendis publicis sumptibus iudicio senatus constituebantur.

The last three of these passages have been subjects of some discussion. Furneaux,[6] after summarizing various earlier views about the passage from the *Annals*, concludes that *vectigalibus publicis* refers to all the revenues of the *aerarium* but not those of the *fiscus*, that the reference to former princes, i.e. especially Claudius, merely recognizes that the emperor could exercise control over the *aerarium* by his powers of initiating or vetoing senatorial decrees, and that the annual subvention may refer to the transfer of the cost of the free distributions of grain from the *aerarium* to the *fiscus*, a change which occurred under either Claudius or Nero. Spooner[7] shows that the passage from the *Histories* refers back to an earlier discussion, IV, 9, in which the *praetores aerarii*, i.e. the praetorian praefects established by Nero in 56, sought to put a stop to excessive expenditures. Although the consul designate, Valerius Asiaticus, urged awaiting the advice of Vespasian, the republican Helvidius Priscus moved for independent action by the senate. His motion, however, was vetoed by a tribune and thus the later action was taken only after consultation with Domitian. Mommsen[8] thinks that one result of this commission was the short-lived scheme of borrowing sixty million sesterces from private individuals, mentioned in IV, 47.[9] Finally, Nerva's commission has usually been thought to have been established early in his

---

[6] *Annals of Tacitus*, II (ed. 2, 1907), 340, nn. *ad loc.*

[7] *The Histories of Tacitus* (1891), 404, n. *ad. loc.*

[8] *Staatsrecht*, II, 1, p. 642, n. 4.

[9] This task is called a *cura: praepositusque ei curae Pompeius Silvanus.*

brief reign in order to remedy the financial difficulties inherited from Domitian. Syme,[10] however, in an attempt to prove that Domitian's finances were ably managed and that the troubles arose under Nerva's lax control, argues correctly that if Verginius heard about the commission during a long illness following his consulship, the commission must have been created well along in 97, not in 96.[11] He connects with this commission Dio's statement, LXVIII, 2, 3, that Nerva abolished for economy's sake a number of sacrifices, races, and other spectacles.[12] He therefore concludes that the commission effected little except trivial savings. The fears of Verginius show that the members were to be consulars.

The following table will summarize conveniently these six special boards:

DATE	EMPEROR	MEMBERSHIP	SELECTION	PURPOSE
6	Augustus	3 consulars	by lot	reduce expenditures.
16	Tiberius	3 senators, rank not specified	by election	restore public records.
42	Claudius	3 praetorians	by appointment	collect money due the *aerarium*.
62	Nero	3 consulars	by appointment	reduce expenditures.
70	Vespasian (Domitian)	3 senators, rank not specified	by lot	adjust property; restore records; revise official lists; reduce expenditures.
97	Nerva	5 consulars	by election?	reduce expenditures.[13]

[10] R. Syme, 'The Imperial Finances under Domitian, Nerva and Trajan,' *Journal of Roman Studies*, XX (1930), 61.

[11] Though Syme, p. 61, n. 4, envisages the possibility of early 98, Verginius had his funeral oration pronounced by Tacitus as consul, Plin., *Ep.*, II, 1, 6, and it is generally agreed that Tacitus was suffect consul late in 97; cf. M. Schanz-C. Hosius, *Gesch. der Röm. Lit.*, II Teil (ed. 4, 1935), 604, 605; W. Liebenam, *Fasti Consulares Imperii Romani* (Bonn, 1910), 18. If Pliny's panegyric is typical, the *gratiarum actiones* appear to have been pronounced upon assuming the consulship so that there is nothing definite to show whether Verginius' selection to the commission would have been as consul or as consular. Analogy suggests the latter.

[12] This probably inspired Zonares', XI, 20 (ed. Dindorf [Teubner, Leipzig, 1870], vol. III, p. 64, lines 10–11), exaggerated statement that Nerva abolished all gladiatorial combats; Syme, p. 59, n. 6.

[13] There is no doubt of the reading *quinqueviros* in the ms. tradition of Pliny, though on the analogy of the previous boards and other like commissions, *tresviros* might be expected. It is unlikely that an early corruption made *IIIviros*, assuming it to have been so written, into *Vviros*. Probably the financial crisis seemed important enough to justify the larger board. Of the method of selection Pliny uses the verb *crearetur*, which might mean by imperial appointment or by senatorial election, but probably not by lot. Since Pliny goes on to say that Verginius chose him in preference to many older and consular friends *per quem excusaretur*, it is safe to assume that such formal excuses were to be presented to the senate, not the emperor, and that therefore the selection of the members lay with the senate. It is worthy of note, though perhaps accidental, how the methods of selection correspond to the general attitudes of the various emperors towards the senate. Augustus and Vespasian, who desired to encourage independent action by the senate but who were clear-sighted enough to

These senatorial boards, therefore, are all concerned with the finances of
the senate, i.e. the *aerarium*, or with the public records. From an early
date, the Temple of Saturn, in which the public monies were kept, had
also been one of the important store-houses for public records.[14] Even
after the erection in 78 b.c. of the *Tabularium* on the Capitol overlooking the Forum,[15] the quaestors apparently retained some general
supervision of the records and this continued during the first century of
the empire.[16] It was, therefore, entirely natural that the special commissions should be concerned with either or both of these matters.

Finally, two other inscriptions mention the office of curator of the
public records. The first is *CIL.*, XI, 2, 1, 6163 = Dessau, 967:[17]

L. Coiedio L.f. Ani./Candido/tr. mil. leg. VIII Aug., IIIv./capital., quaest./
Ti. Claud. Caes. Aug. Ger.,/quaest. aer. Satur., cur. tab. p./Hunc Ti. Cl. Caes.
Aug. Germ./revers. ex castr. don. mil. don./cor. aur. mur. val. hast. pura,/
eund. cum ha[b]er. inter suos q.,/eod. anno et aer. Sat. q. esse. ius./ Publ.

Groag, in the *Prosopographia*,[18] plausibly suggests that Coiedius was
advanced from *quaestor principis* to *quaestor aerarii Saturni* in 44, the
year in which Claudius replaced Augustus' praetors of the treasury by the
republican quaestors. Since the offices are in ascending sequence, Coiedius
became *cur. tab. p.* soon after 44, though Groag suggests that perhaps a
mention of the praetorship between the quaestorship and the curatorship
was accidentally omitted. Groag, who expands *cur. tab. p.* into *curatori
tabulariorum publicorum*, thus makes Coiedius a member of the board

---

distrust its collective wisdom, use the lot; Tiberius, the most republican of the emperors, despite
Tacitus, in the eyes of modern scholars, and Nerva, the senatorial nominee as emperor, give the
senate full freedom of election; but Claudius and Nero, the chief encroachers upon senatorial preroga-
tives during the Julio-Claudian period, appoint to ensure ability.

[14] Pauly-Wissowa, I(1) s.v. *aerarium*, col. 669; deRuggiero, *Dizionario Epigraphico*, I s.v. *aerarium*,
p. 301.

[15] S. Platner-T. Ashby, *Topographic Dictionary of Ancient Rome* (Oxford, 1929), 506–507.

[16] P.-W., I(1), col. 669; Josephus, *Ant. Jud.*, XIV, 219, and an inscription in Lebas-Foucat-Wad-
dington, *Voyage Archéologique*, III, 1627, are the references to the control of the quaestors over the
records under the empire.

[17] The text is that of Bormann in *CIL.*, the punctuation Dessau's. Dessau indicated some letters
as supplied which are read by Bormann and inserts a *q=que* after *eund.* for which the stone affords no
evidence. The abbreviations in the later part, which do not concern this article, are filled out in Dessau.
W. Weber proposed a similar office by emending an inscription from Pergamum of Julius Quadratus
to read ἐπιμελη[τὴν μονήτη]ς χρυσοῦ ἀργύρου χαράγματος, which he interpreted as a praetorian *curator
monetae auri argenti flandi feriundi* appointed by Domitian upon his reform of the coinage in 84; cf.
Abh. der Preuss. Akad. der Wiss. (Berlin), phil.-phil.-hist. kl., 1932, no. 5, pp. 78–79. But A. von
Premerstein showed conclusively that the reference was simply to the vigintivirate post of *IIIvir
aere argento auro flando feriundo* and should be emended to read ἐπιμελη[τὴν χαλκο]ῦ etc.; cf. *Sitzber.
der Bay. Akad. der Wiss.* (München), phil.-phil.-hist. kl., 1934, heft 3, pp. 24–25. The discussion is
summarized by H. Mattingly in the *Catalogue of Coins of the Rom. Emp. in the Brit. Mus.*, III, p. xviii.

[18] *Prosopographia Imperii Romani*, II (ed. 2, 1926), p. 299, C no. 1257.

established by Claudius, which he presumably identifies with that mentioned in the inscription from which this argument started. In that case, Coiedius must have been a member not merely after 45 but, since the praetorship was held normally five years after the quaestorship,[19] probably some years after. Hence the identification has two weak points: assumption that *pr.*, or probably, since the abbreviations are fuller in the *cursus*, *praet.* was omitted in a man's funeral inscription; and the long existence necessitated for a special *ad hoc* board.

The second inscription is of a far better known figure; *CIL.*, X, 1, 5182 = Dessau, 972:

C. Ummidio C.f. Ter. Durmio/Quadrato cos., XVvir. s.f.,/leg. Ti. Caesaris Aug. prov. Lusit.,/leg. divi Claudi in Illyrico, eiusd. et/Neronis Caesaris Aug. in Syria, procos./provinc. Cypri, q. divi Aug. et T. Caesaris/Aug., aed. cur., pr. aer., Xvir. stlit. iud., curat./tabular. publicar., praef. frum. dandi ex s.c.

Two other fragmentary inscriptions from Casinum, *CIL.*, X, 1, 5180 and 5181, which probably refer to Quadratus, contain the word *curator* . . . . Dessau, in the *Prosopographia*,[20] says that the chief inscription *honores plene enumerat, sed sine ordine*. Nevertheless, there does appear to be an attempt to group them in order of importance: first the two highest offices,[21] then the imperial legateships in ascending order, then his senatorial proconsulship, then his *cursus* in ascending order through the praetorship, then three minor posts. Certain of his offices can be dated: he must have been quaestor of the two emperors in 14; his praetorship of the treasury is dated in 18 by a mention of him in an interesting list of head clerks of the *aerarium*;[22] his legateship of Lusitania, begun under

---

[19] A. H. J. Greenidge, *Roman Public Life* (London, 1901), 364. Dispensations might be made for those with the *ius trium liberorum*. It is also probable that Coiedius would have been aedile or tribune before he became praetor, unless he was a patrician; *Cambridge Ancient History*, X (1934), 164.

[20] *PIR.*, III (ed. 1, 1898), P. 468, V no. 600. The data for the following dates are derived from this account.

[21] The *XVviri sacris faciundis*, one of the *quattuor amplissima collegia*, ranked high throughout the empire. The *XVviri* were for the most part consulars or praetorians and only in the third century do younger men appear among them; cf. Wissowa, *Religion und Kultus der Römer* (ed. 2, 1912), 534–535; Marquardt, *Staatsverwaltung* (ed. 2, 1885), III, 381.

[22] *CIL.* (ed. 2), I, 1, pp. 74–75. Mommsen, whose discussion in *Mittheilungen des römisches Instituts*, VI (1891), 157–162, is summarized in the *Corpus*, shows that these three fragments belong to a list of the *sexprimi* or *curatores* (cf. frag. C; *Eph. Epigr.*, IV (1881), no. 853 = Dessau, 1892; *CIL.*, VI, 1, 1, 1820 = Dessau, 1891) of the *decuriae* of the *scribae quaestorii*. It might be tempting to identify these *curatores* with those of the inscriptions under discussion. However, though Mommsen found that the *scribae* were largely freeborn, only five out of forty being freedmen, *Staatsrecht*, I (ed. 3, 1887), p. 353, n. 4, yet almost none held any magistracy, *ibid.* p. 354, n. 2. Hence they cannot be identical with the men under discussion. For the *scribae*, cf. Kornemann in Pauly-Wissowa, Reihe 2, II (3) s.v. *scribae*, cols. 848–857; Dessau, III. 1, index p. 434 s.v. *scribae*; also, for municipal *scribae*, Mommsen's commentary on the *lex Coloniae Genetivae*, *Eph. Epigr.*, III (1877), pp. 107–108 = *Gesammelte Schriften*, I, 258–260.

Tiberius, lasted until the accession of Gaius in 37.[23] He was legate of Syria from at least 51 until his death in 60.[24] Since this was a consular post, as was the legateship of Illyricum, he must have been consul under Gaius, after 37, or under Claudius, before 51. His proconsulship of Cyprus perhaps preceded his legateship of Lusitania.[25] Of the minor offices, the office of *Xvir stlitibus iudicandis*, one of the so-called vigintivirate posts, preceded his quaestorship and that of *praefectus frumenti dandi* probably followed his praetorship.[26] Though a long enough interval elapsed between his praetorship and his governorship of Lusitania to accommodate easily the curatorship, the praefecture, and the proconsulship of Cyprus, he might equally well have been curator after his quaestorship, like Coiedius.[27] In this case, as far as dates are concerned, he might have been on the board established by Tiberius in 16, but though the rank of the members is not specified by Dio, the analogy of the other commissions suggests that they were at least praetorians. If Quadratus became a member after his praetorship, this commission, as in the other instances, must be assumed to have had an existence of at least three years.

Of the three men on the board of 45, only one appears elsewhere. Groag, in the *Prosopographia*,[28] cites a fragmentary inscription from Dalmatia which Ritterling referred to C. Calpetanus Rantius Sedatus. Since Ritterling concluded that Calpetanus was consular legate of Illyricum under Claudius or Nero, Groag suggests that he was suffect consul in an uncertain year, perhaps before 45. In that case, to relate this board to that established in 42, not only must a long term be assumed but also the rank of its members must be raised from Dio's praetorians to consulars.[29] On the other hand, there is no conclusive evidence that Calpetanus was not in 45 a praetorian or even still a quaestorian. The argument

[23] He administered the oath of allegiance to the people of Aritium, *CIL.*, II, 172 = Dessau, 190. The inscription may omit Gaius' name because of the odium attached to it or because Quadratus was replaced immediately.

[24] Tac., *Ann.*, XII, 45, 6; 48, 1; XIV, 26, 4.

[25] Marquardt, *Staatsverwaltung*, I, 416 (Syria consular); 299 (Illyricum consular); 257 (Lusitania praetorian); 391 (Cyprus had a praetorian proconsul).

[26] The vigintivirate is discussed in most handbooks, cf. conveniently *Cambridge Ancient History*, X, 162. The *praefecti frumenti dandi* were regularly praetorians, rarely aedilician or tribunician, Mommsen, *Staatsrecht* II, 1, p. 673; cf. his article on them in *Hermes*, IV (1870), 364 = *Gesammelte Schriften*, IV, 194.

[27] The suggestion, below p. 130, that the curators were ex-magistrates who had been in charge of the treasury might lend more weight to a date after he was *praetor aerarii*. Dessau so arranges the offices in the *Prosopographia*, *loc. cit.* n. 20.

[28] *PIR.*, II (ed. 2), p. 46, C no. 235. Ritterling's article, cited as in *Bull. Dalm.*, XLVII/XLVIII, 21(2), was not available.

[29] Since the permanent *curae* generally had a consular for chairman, *Cambridge Ancient History*, X, 179, this board might perhaps have comprised Calpetanus as consular chairman and two praetorians.

from silence proves little, but neither of the other two, Petronius and Salvius, appears except on the one inscription so that they were probably not very prominent.[30] Though the literary authorities do not give the members of the various boards, these might be expected to have been relatively experienced and able men, like Verginius Rufus. Of the five curators who have been discussed, Quadratus had a distinguished, but late, career[31] and perhaps Calpetanus amounted to something. On the other hand Coiedius did not get beyond his curatorship.[32] Though Petronius and Salvius may have gone further, the post of curator cannot on the evidence of the inscriptions be called important.

The foregoing argument has demonstrated that the customary identification of the inscriptional curators with the literary special boards has difficulties in respect to dates and to rank. Moreover, though it is probable that the special commissions were called *curae*, there is no evidence for this save the identification. Also, if the appointments to these boards had been something special, the inscriptions might be expected to indicate this by adding *ex s.c.* or the like. As an alternative, it appears possible that there was, apart from the special commissions, a permanent board which, probably under the direction of the quaestors, had charge of the records. In this connection it may be remarked that Tacitus, *Ann.*, XIII, 28, 5, in speaking of Nero's transference of the *aerarium* from the quaestors to praetorian praefects in 56, calls the post *curam tabularum publicarum*. Coiedius was first quaestor of the *aerarium*, then curator, and Quadratus was curator either before or after being praetor of the *aerarium* under the Augustan arrangement. It is possible, therefore, that the board was composed of those who had recently been heads of the treasury as magistrates. Though the forms *tabularia*, meaning records, and *tabularius*, meaning a person, usually a freedman, connected with records of any sort,[33] are common in Latin, the feminine *tabular. publicar.* of Quadratus' inscription, and Tacitus' phrase seem conclusive, despite Mommsen's change

---

[30] *PIR.*, III (ed. 1), p. 27, P no. 210; p. 175, S no. 149.

[31] If he was quaestor in 14 at the earliest possible age, 25 years, he would have been consul after he was 48 (after 37) and governor of Syria at 62 in 51.

[32] Of course, he may have died early but it sounds as though he was a brave soldier who received admission to the senate as a reward from Claudius. Groag, in the *Prosopographia*, *loc. cit.* n. 18, connects his service with the revolt of Scribonianus in Dalmatia in 42 rather than with Claudius' brief and easy campaign in Britain, as did Dessau in his note to his no. 967.

[33] *Tabularium*, "record-office," is attested in inscriptions, cf. Dessau, III, 2, pp. 901–902, index XVII s.v.; *tabularia*, "records," appears mostly in literature, cf. Harper's *Latin Dictionary* s.v.; *tabularius* (also *tabellarius*) is very common for clerks in various kinds of record-offices, cf. Dessau, II, 1, pp. 435–436, index VI s.v. If *tabulariorum* be taken in the last sense, the *curatores* would be reduced to a level with the *curatores scribarum quaestoriorum* mentioned in n. 22! Mommsen meant it in the sense of "records," cf. p. 208 of the discussion cited in n. 2.

of heart, for the emendation *curatores tabularum publicarum* in the *Einsiedeln Codex.*

The chief objection which might be brought against the hypothesis of a permanent *cura tabularum* is the absence of any evidence for it save these three inscriptions. Literary evidence for a minor post might well be lacking. But the major permanent *curae*, that of sacred buildings and public works and property, that of the Tiber bed, that of the aqueducts, and those of the various roads, are well attested in inscriptions.[34] On the other hand, Mommsen accepts the permanence of the post of curator of the acts of the senate, though this is mentioned only twice before Trajan.[35] It is possible that the board was created by Augustus or Tiberius and ceased to exist when Nero reformed the treasury.[36] At least, the proposed hypothesis meets the problems raised by the conflicting evidence of the literary and epigraphic material.[37]

HARVARD UNIVERSITY.

[34] Cf. Dessau, III, 1, pp. 357–360, index VI s.v. *curator.*

[35] *Staatsrecht*, II, 1, p. 901, n. 5. Interesting in this connection are Mommsen's own changes of opinion with respect to the *curatores tabularum publicarum*. In his earliest discussion, *Berichte über die Verhandl. der kön. sächs. Gesellschaft der Wiss. zu Leipzig*, phil.-hist. classe, II (1850), 302, he apparently accepted them as a permanent commission, like the *cura alvei Tiberis* etc. Then, in *Ann. Instit. Arch.* (cf. n. 2), he related them to Claudius' commission in 42 and thought that they might have lasted from then until Nero's reform in 56. Finally, as has been said above, p. 124, he identified them in the *Staatsrecht* (ed. 3) with Tiberius' commission of 16. He apparently separated the commissions on records from those on the *aerarium*, which are discussed in *Staatsrecht*, II, 1, p. 642.

[36] Cf. the phrase of Tacitus, quoted above p. 130.

[37] The only case of a municipal curator resembling those discussed is P. Lucilius Gamala, who was a prominent and public-spirited citizen of Ostia during the second century. Two inscriptions relate his career, *CIL.*, XIV, 375 = Dessau, 6147, and *CIL.*, XIV, 376. In the second of these, lines 8–9, he is called *tabular. et libror./curatori primo constitu[t]* and, lines 13–16, *idem curator pecuniae publicae exi/gendae et attribuendae in comi/tiis factus;* the first mentions only the latter office, lines 9–11, *in comiTis facto cura/[tor]i pecuniae publicae exigen/[d]ae et attribuendae/.* Mommsen, in *Eph. Epigr.*, III (1877), p. 328, parallels these offices to the boards of Tiberius and Claudius respectively. He assumes that there must have been special reasons for the popular election rather than appointment by the decurions. These do appear to be special *ad hoc* offices and like the special boards at Rome in the first century. They perhaps lend support to the title *curator tabularum* for members of such special boards. But this one late instance might equally be modelled on a permanent board at Rome and, in any case, does not help to solve the problems raised in this article.

A LATIN MEDICAL MANUSCRIPT

Herbert B. Hoffleit

Among the books of the late Professor S. L. Millard Rosenberg of the University of California at Los Angeles were a number of rare volumes on subjects illustrative of the history of medicine in which he had a great interest, several of them in Latin. One was a vellum manuscript of apparently the XIIIth century, bound in pigskin but fragmentary at both beginning and end. It appears to have once been in the hands of the well known collector Dr. Vollbehr who numbered it 15683 in his collection and before that to have been at Milan whence it derived a designation Receptorium Milanense. The present writer was asked to translate and partially transcribe the work with a view to extracting whatever might seem worthy of publication with a commentary by Professor Rosenberg. Some preliminary work had been laboriously done[1] without pretense to special knowledge of palaeography or medicine when Professor Rosenberg's death interrupted for good the execution of his larger plan.

Of the value of the manuscript in the history of medicine I am unable to speak, but in 'popular' interest a few curious excerpts may, I hope, not be entirely lacking.

The fragment consists of one incomplete and twenty-two complete gatherings, except that fols. LXXVI and LXXVII are missing. The twelfth gathering has but six leaves, the rest eight each (four sheets). The incomplete gathering at the beginning of the book consists of three leaves (XXXVIII to XL) preceded by a scrap of a fourth (about five inches long next the binding and two wide at the widest); the binding thread is between the last two leaves; the gathering marked by the usual break or interstice at the inside of the binding lacks the customary subscription, in the lower margin, of the initial word of the next page. The eighth, twentieth and twenty-first gatherings likewise lack the subscription, which in some cases is so low on the page as to have been cut in half by the binder. Text and subscriptions appear in two handwritings. The subscription at the end of the book is in both: the one giving the first two words resembling the fine handwriting found perhaps only in the first two subscriptions, in marginal titles on fol. CXXIV^v, CXXV^r, and a corrected rubric on XXXVIIII^r, the other giving the third word below the others in

[1] I wish to thank a friend, Dr. Homer P. Earl of Los Angeles, for helpful suggestions made in the course of his revision of the early part of the work at Prof. Rosenberg's instance.

apparently the same bold hand as appears in this latter part of the text.

Except for troublesome ligatures and abbreviations and a number of blurred or faded passages (the 'flesh-side' of the vellum does not take the ink so well at all times as would be desirable, and incidentally some pages cause the suspicion that the copyist or a student of the book unluckily spilled either his wine or his medicines upon the open page) the writing is admirably clear even to the layman. The first part of the volume displays the smaller, more attractive hand. Foll. CV^v to CXII^r, CXXXIIII^r to CXXXVI^r inclusive, CXXXVII^v to CXXXVIII^r and CXXXXI^v to the end show in comparison a large, almost burly hand. On fol. CXLV^v the writing becomes even bolder than before and continues with hardly perceptible variations to the end of the fragment. Chapter headings are regularly given in red, in a shaky unskilful hand that throughout seems to approximate rather the bolder hand of the latter part of the text. These rubrics usually begin immediately at the end of the preceding paragraph and often break into the paragraph to which they refer, a space being left for them at the right side of the first line or two so that the page presents a solid appearance. Very frequently the title must run into the margin on either or both sides. Paragraph marks alternately in red and blue are used to indicate minor subdivisions with the abbreviation /No. for notandum. Horizontal and vertical rulings are regularly visible. The initials more or less artistically elaborated in blue and red with long figurated patterns, extending up and down the left margin, add to the attractiveness of many pages.

Spelling and grammar are fearfully irregular and inconsistent, proving the illiteracy and carelessness of the scribes. A few Italian words (and the Greek xeri = ξηροῦ) have found their way into the diction of the author or the school. Arabic influence of some slight degree is indicated by the use of at least two words, alcanna (henna) and saracen, and the herbs so called. Its southern provenience is perhaps confessed in a degree by the mention of the word 'ronia' as Salernitan.[2] The author reproduces with naïve corrections here and there, due either to him or to his successors in the transmission, the teaching, oral and written, of a distinguished Doctor or master of the science.[3] His aim and principle of arrangement are

---

[2] Fol. XLI^v ll. 12–14: De Superfluitatibus Ronge. Superfluitas (eruption or suppuration) quidam nascitur in capite qui vulgari Salernitanorum dicitur ronia (cf. It. *rogna*, Fr. *rogne*). Fol. XLII^r ll. 10–12 Ronga quidem est quae apparet in capite ad modum tineae et emittit a se liquorem ad modum mellis.

Fontanella (or fontanea), q. e. retro carnositatem iuxta auriculas, is evidently an Italian word though applied in a different way. Once due stands for duo.

[3] E.g. fol. XL^v ll. 7–8 Nota quodusus argenti vivi non abprobatur a magistro (in an emplastrum for tinea), cf. below, p. 140.

given in the prefatory remarks to his tables of contents, Parts II and III, quoted below. He begins with the head, proceeds to the neck and throat 'quantum ad cirurgiam spectat (surgery)' and divides this part of the subject into the treatment and symptoms, first of wounds, second of abscesses, third of scrofulae, fourth of fistulae, and glands, fifth of tumors, and sixth of internal growths (ailments?). In the first part of the book as it now is, the first subject is depilation, and other treatments of head-scabs immediately follow, then come madness and epilepsy followed by redness of the eyes, unnaturally long lashes, watery eyes, itching of the eyes, pannus of the eyes, bloodshot eyes (treated by incision), fistulae of the eyes, polyps, cancer in the palate, in the gums, and fistulae of the lips, burning of the lips, cuts in the lips, dislocated and fractured jaws and fistulae thereof, toothache, pustules of the face and other eruptions such as ringworm, then ear troubles including foreign substances lodged in the ear. The principle of Celsus' Fourth Book on internal diseases, of taking the parts of the body in order from the head down, is curiously extended to the whole subject of the art of healing. The third part deals with ailments of the trunk and arms. The table of contents of this last, incomplete part with its prefatory remarks again mentions the 'doctor meus' but the recurrence of such words as facere consuevimus —'it is our usual practice'— prove that these precepts, many, if not most of them, dealing with the preparation of salves and powders, are not founded on speculation alone. Indeed the magister is often contradicted. Once the text reads 'I have treated a number of patients in this way with my own hands' (on removing an abscess with the fingers). A phrase, secundum morem veterum has a certain interest in this connection, especially if a common abbreviation in our MS is to be interpreted as having the same meaning: ſ, ꝏ. ꝏ, perhaps secundum operam veterum. Once Hippocrates is mentioned by name as author of a celebrated precept not to employ incision or cauterization in muscular parts where there are intricate arteries and veins. In connection with the four humors curiously melancholia is contrasted as "unnatural colera' producing an abscess (apostema) called cancer with the natural red colera producing as an abscess 'herpes estiomenus' or lupus.

The present-day apothecary's sign ℈ which is common in the MS resembles Isidore's 'Z' in Etym. XVI 27, though the value is different from those given by e.g. Saremberg (Celsus) and Gould. ℞ is also regular in our MS, as also AN(a) for 'each' (ἀνά, aꞥ).

One of the first interesting prescriptions (fol. XXXVIIIᵛ ll. 5–14) shows the Christian practitioner solicitously combining prayer and axle-grease: Et contra morphaeam (cf. 'morphew') contra malum mortuum aptissimae hae orationes sunt: In nomine Patris et Filii et Spiritus Sancti

Amen. Beati Cosmes et Damiane ora pro isto famulo Dei. Et dicite ter Pater noster, Credo ter, et Miserere Mei Deus ter. Oratio ista dicenda est sub caelo divo et retinens axungia in manu super caput ei. His orationibus repetitis ter postea ungue caput cotidie totum dum durat haxungia sed cave ne amittatur de ea postquam incantata est. Another exorcism (entitled a 'coniuratio') reads: cavo cavo cavo recede quia filius dei te maledic̄ upon which follows triple recitation of Paternoster and Mass and use of a candle from the feast of Saint Mary. Elsewhere recourse to magic is had as an alternative method of checking bleeding in a wound: 'write the name 'veronis' in blood on the patient's forehead, or veronissa (v.l. venorisa) written in the patient's own blood beneath his breast checks bleeding.' Again in scrofula it is recommended to take a certain preparation (crispellae radicis spatulae fetidae et raphanus agrestis or rodalda) during the last eleven days of the waning moon: ten crispellae the first day, nine the next and so on, one less each day. If that fails, resort to surgery under certain conditions. But during the watch of the blessed St. John one may heal a scrofula by pricking with a lancet at midnight over a fountain of running water! Once more: against fistula take root of agrimony with a prayer on Sunday, bind to the neck of the patient. When the root dries the disease recedes. And again for an affliction called botium (? a kind of scrofula or tumor): while singing the Pater noster, uproot a nut tree that has not borne fruit, boil the roots with 200 grains of pepper in the best wine and have the patient drink every morning until he is well.

A certain depilatory is to be boiled down (XXXVIIII^r ll. 5–6) until it meets the following impressive test. Signum decoctionis est quando penna immissa et statim abstracta de facili potest depilari.

Folio XL^r is even more horrific. J. Wight Duff in speaking of Celsus employs the term excremental medicine. The scribe of our manuscript achieves a still more startling effect by the accident of a misspelling, writing caput immingas in place of inung(u)as! Si vero habet multos pediculos (l.5) appone argentum vivum mixtum et constrictum cum saliva. Then in the last lines of this fearful page (11–14) there is this prescription to soften the skin and heal tinea. Recipe vetustas soleas combustas stercore bovinum (*sic*, written out, for bovino) ex istis conficitur pulvis et super aspergatur capiti praecedente inunctione cum melle secundum opus est (*sic!*). Stercus bovinum is also used roasted with wine, oil, and honey as an application for bruises and swelling caused by a chance blow, where there is putrefaction by 'overflow of humors.' All this reminds one (maliciously perhaps) of modern cosmetics.

Saliva is an ingredient in several prescriptions; in one it is part of an alternative for a poor man in a case for which balsam is explicitly recommended 'if the patient is a queen or some wealthy personage.'

Stercus humanum is prescribed with bone of sepia and other ingredients for a powder to supply to the eyes and with (dry) parched salt as a quick remedy for cancer and noli-me-tangere. For wounds ass's stercus, dry or fresh, and that of geese for fistulae are mentioned. In abscesses of a certain kind ('colera rubea') the patient is laved with his own urine. Lizards' dung is used for the eyes. Lac muliebre as a prescription contra lippitudines oclorum occurs in our MS and in the 16th Century.[4] In the MS even sow's milk 'after her first litter' finds medical application. For these disgusting remedies one may find parallels in Pliny[5] as well as in later medicine.[6]

Verdigris is exceedingly common as an ingredient in medicines described. Pliny distinguished between two varieties, flos aeris and aerugo, whereas our MS identifies apparently only one under two names, floseris and virideris, i.e. viride aeris.

A method of preparing this closely resembles that given by Pliny N.H. XXXIV 26 by suspending copper over vinegar: our author recommends 'scraping off mould (mucilago or muscillago, once written i'ticillago ex lanimis) from plates suspended over vinegar in an earthen bowl.' Pliny *l.c.* 24–28 has other interesting methods and the application to scurfs and the like, adding that doctors in ignorance risk experiments on their poor patients in order to try out the deceitful recipes of Seplasia! Seplasia was an unguent-sellers' street in Capua: our mediaeval doctor may be said from the copiousness and detail of his recommendations to prove his independence of that quarter. Pliny mentions again elsewhere specifically certain applications of aerugo, verdigris or flos aeris, for instance in XXIX 38 and XXXVI 26 for eye salves, XXVIII 76 in burns.

Trepanning the skull is recommended for ailments of the eyes, 'immobile scrofula,' and 'mania.' In the former (XLIIII') illa cutis tota eradicetur, et separatur (?) circa vero infectum craneum et cum trepano provide perfora et cum spatumine ipsum craneum totum removeas quia vero ipsam superfluitatem a dura ora separare valde difficile est et periculum quod exinde pervenire potest valde timendum est ideo talem curam pocius relinquere quam prosequi desideramus. Next follows Cauterium contra maniam, /No. quod hoc modo debet fieri cauterium contra maniam vel maꝓia (? malitiam or It. matteria, mattia): incidatur cutis in modum C in eo loco ubi sumitas digiti adtingit sive inter fan-

[4] S. L. M. Rosenberg, Sixteenth Century Medicine, reprinted from California and Western Medicine XXXIII July–Sept. 1930, p. 18.

[5] XXVIII 75, XXVIIII 38.

[6] Rosenberg, *op. cit.*

tasticam cellulam et rationalem hic (? or hoc) dico manu apponenti inter duo cilia (brows? 'ciba' in MS) et extensa per medium frontis usque ad crucem capitis et ibi craneum uratur ferro candenti. The object is stated (XLV^r) to be to allow the noxious vapors to exhale. One may compare Celsus III 23, 7: on epilepsy occipitium incidere et cucurbitales admovere, ferro candenti in occipitio quoque et infra, qua summa vertebra cum capite committitur adurere duobus locis, ut per ea perniciosus umor evadat. So our MS gives epilepsy, which is taken up next, similar treatment.[7]

Then comes redness of the eyes (Celsus takes up jaundice characterized by discoloration of the eyes after epilepsy, III 24, 1). Horrific medicine recurs again in this page of the book in dealing with lippitudo: dung of swine male or female according to the sex of the patient is applied warm to the eyes.

To check lacrimation, bloodshot eyes ('redness of eyes') panniculus (pannus, ? panicula, panus) in the eyes, and possibly excess hairs in the eyelids (though the latter seems a mere error in the rubric) an incision of the 'vein of the forehead and the two in the temples' is made. After letting as much blood as he sees fit the practitioner is to tie the vein with a thread and apply bacon to the wound for three days followed by lean pork for ten. When the wound is well cleaned by this 'we draw out the filium' (sic, lege filum). If necessary a strictorium compounded of cantharis beetles (cf. Pliny XI, 35, 41) and goat's fat or axlegrease of pork may be applied to the forehead as supplementary treatment.

Axelgrease is quite commonly named as an ingredient in prescriptions in the book, often distinguished as axlegrease of pork (eight or ten times) or of bear, chicken, goose (at least twice each). Once at least *old* axungia is prescribed. The ailments treated with it vary from chapped lips through cancer and fistula to wounds by a sword or arrow.

If the patient had any suspicion of the nature of some of those compounds he must have either been dreadfully disgusted or been as obtuse to disgust as certain superstitious folk one still meets who combine astrology, vegetarianism, and stercoral methods in our own conceited day. That our authority is not inconsiderate or inhumane in other respects is proved by the measures he not unfrequently offers 'if the patient be delicate' or 'if he be afraid of the fire or the knife,' as in the use of a can(n)ellus (? cannula) or a stuellus (tent).

For toothache we read that it is good to put seeds of leek and others

---

[7] Later on the treatment of a polyp by cautery is similarly given with an explicit reference to the treatment here prescribed for madness and below for the eyes. The 'memorial' cellula is identified apparently with the 'rational': 'the cautery is to be in the same place, i.e. between the fantastic and memorial cellulae.'

called cassilago or leaves of leek and iusquamus (henbane) over hot coals and draw the fumes over the aching tooth, or to chew staphisagria, pyrethrum, and verdigris in a linen sack.

The lowly rabbit proved his value in our mediaeval pharmacopoeia. His blood was smeared warm in cases of morphea alba upon the affected spot after cupping. His hair compounded with unslaked lime and yolk of egg was used to check flow of blood from a serious wound: the alternative is apparently powder (ash) of burnt felt (filtrum) or burnt feathers. Later in the MS white hairs from the belly of the rabbit, cut fine, are specified for this purpose, to be compounded with gummi arabicum and roseoil.

Pigeon's foot or proboscis of a bee is recommended for anthrax unless you prefer consolida minor (consound or comfrey) which ground between two stones will by a 'supernatural action' eradicate the complaint.

'The best tried remedy for cancer and fistula' (and another similar one is used with butter for these and lupus) consists of a powder made of an old toad, puffed up alive, put in a small jar covered with earth and burnt in an oven (furnus). 'Add a little myrrh after pulverizing and strew on the sore.'

Other curious applications contain ink (atramentum) distempered with oxgall, or flour, oil, honey and dry-rot (caries) of wood, or grain chewed in the mouth, or fried snakeskin, or even earthworms.

Curious points in connection with surgery are perhaps worth noting. One is the possibility of using the 'trachea (artery) of some other person grossa admodum intestina (? intestinorum) in place of a cannellus' to repair a wound in the intestines. Another is the insistence that a wound of the lacertus with its nerve or muscle (artery?) is fatal. Certain fatal wounds are wisely not even treated, for the physician could only incur the suspicion that he was responsible for the inevitable. The table of contents to Part III lists cauterization for stomachache.

It may be of some interest to note that treatment sometimes varies according to the time of year. Thus after cautery in cancer yolk of egg is applied regularly, but in summer also white of egg. In wounds and fractures a part of the wound is left open and sprinkled with 'red or (black) berry powder, changed either two or three times a day according to the fitness of the season and the convenience of the patient.' Again, altea (apparently althaea, marshmallow) 'must not be used in summer to mature an abscess, but in winter.' It may stop the pores, causing infistulation. 'In its place may be used mallow (malva) and absinth with pork axlegrease. Add to ripen the abscess a crushed swallow's nest mixed with honey.'

Possibly but not necessarily the last is either a misreading or a popular

designation for swallow-wort (chelidonium, celandine). One draws a similar inference as to the term 'ointment of stag's antlers' for a preparative
to be boiled in wine, oil, and salt. Salt, garlic, soot, anise, and vinegar or
pepper, cinnamon, rose and other compounds strike the layman possibly
more humorously than the physician or chemist. These are all given as
applicatives to mortify fistula; another alternative seems to be unslaked
lime in soapwater (capitellum), which is also applied in a tenta as 'rup-
torium'-ointment for polyp.

We do not wish to be hard upon the scribe; I fancy he knew the principle of comic relief, which may account for some apparent slips. An imaginative reader may therefore thank him when in the midst of the
dreadful subject of curable and incurable polyps he gravely says 'we
treat by inrisio and cautery,' as it were 'with cautery and a smile of de-
precation'? If you insist 'irrision' is rather 'ridicule' we must acquit him
of cruelty and say he intended incisio.

A hot plate of marble is used to test compounds or their ingredients
(e.g., by observing whether they keep their color) or on which to grate
herbs or to liquefy olibanum or laudanum. Gold is used not only in ointment but as an instrument in surgery and cautery. Precious stones and
unpierced pearls (or plants named for them) are used in one form or
another. Natural enough but interesting is the use of a feather to apply
collyrium for the eyes. It depends no doubt upon one's prejudices whether
one sees modernity or primitiveness in such slight details.

That doctors disagreed is evident several times in our fragment, when
an alternative cure may be signalized without change of handwriting with
the remark: 'the treatment here indicated by the author is of no value';
or 'note that black morphea is readily curable whatever the author may
say,' or 'note that on the contrary the bandage must be left on for eleven
days' (instead of twelve hours or a single day), or 'on the contrary they
must be undone at intervals of nine (instead of three) days and not before!' The text at one place reports that if a wound in the thorax is long
'it is not our custom to make a suture' and immediately by way of parenthesis 'on the contrary a suture may very well be made, if the wound is
not deep.' Once the answer is simply 'this is *not* to be done!'

With all its faults it is evident that much serious thought and experience has gone into this astonishing manual. I believe we may say that the
detail and even the superstition prove conscientious work, no matter what
we may think of the scribe who copied it. In its day it may have served as
a guide to many a comforter in disease. Let us in conclusion cite the intro-
ductions to the second and third parts which state both the purpose of
the book and the compiler's apology.

Inasmuch as I have attempted to undertake such a useful work and in orderly fashion reduce the learning of my teacher to the form of a manual of instruction, my devout wish has been rather for the advantage of the present and the future than to consult either my strength or my temporary convenience. Therefore a prudent reader, when time is short and beset by affairs, will rather choose (sc. to consider) something that requires correction by careful reasoning than tear it up because of malice and ill will. I have determined to divide this work in various sections so that it might be possible to ascertain the various cures with greater accuracy in each section and for a careful reader to commit them to memory the more conveniently.[8]

An unpretentious but not undignified statement of a useful object! The other passage is equally dignified and in grammar even more confused:

Nemo prolixitatis *uel* rudis sermonis crime*n* inponatur cum m*u*lta paucis in-plicata obscuritate*m* poti*us et confusione*m* q*uam* com*pendii comoditate*m* parere solea*nt* et ego no*n* solu*m* prouectis s*ed* *etiam* aliis p*roficere* dissposueri*nt.*[9] Quo-circa q*uodcum*q*ue* ab eg*regio* doctore comit*er* et p*riuatim* recipi et d*e* ei*us* sc*riptis* habere ualui *ordine* certo scriptis redige et ut pulcrius elucescat in*corpore* deduces delib*erata* ra*t*ione decreui.

This modesty and good intent deserve credit; for the instruction let us hope the author earned his reward; and if his book now provides us chiefly with entertainment, may that also receive our gratitude, though some of it he must share with his humble scribes.

UNIVERSITY OF CALIFORNIA AT LOS ANGELES.

[8] Foll. CXXXX*v*–CXXXXI*r*, Preface to Part III: ta*nti* operis utilitate*m* tractare te*m*ptaui *et* ordine certo doctoris mei scientia*m* in arte*m* redigere*m* (sic!) desidera*m* (sic!) plus fui*t* d*e* uoto pr*aes*en-tib*us et* futuris p*roficiendi* quam de uiribus aut *tem*poris com*moditate.* Quocirca prouidus lector nego-tiis inminentib*us et* breuitate temporis p*er*obtat corrigendi poti*us* deliberata ra*t*ione quam inuidie liuore rescindat, etc.

[9] Lege fortasse 'disposuerim,' atque infra, 'redigere' et 'in corpus deducere.' Inponatur and recipi are slips for inponat and possibly recepi or recipere. Fol. LXXXVIIII*v*.

THE LIBRARY OF ST. AUBIN'S AT ANGERS IN THE TWELFTH CENTURY

LESLIE WEBBER JONES

FROM 900 TO 1200 A.D. and even later Angers, a suffragan see of the Archdiocese of Tours, was a flourishing ecclesiastical center.[1] In addition to its cathedral (St. Maurice, founded in s.xii) and its numerous churches the city itself possessed no less than five great monasteries—the abbeys of St. Aubin (founded in 549?), Sts. Serge and Bacche (which was founded before 650 at the latest), St. Nicolas (founded by the Count of Anjou, Foulques Nerra in 1020), Toussaint (founded in 1115) and Ronceray (a nunnery for women of noble birth, founded by Foulques Nerra in 1028); and no less than seven 'chapters'—those of the church of Angers ('chapitre de l'église d'Angers,' later the cathedral chapter; founded in s.ix), St. Laud ('chapitre royal de St. Laud,' founded in s.xi by Geoffrey Martel; at first established in the 'enceinte' of the chateau of Angers),[2] St. Martin ('chapitre royal de St. Martin'), St. Pierre, St. Maurille, St. Julien[3] (founded by Foulques Nerra ca. 1020–28), and St. Mainbeuf ('Magnobodus'). Outside the city but within the diocese of Angers were the Abbey of Fontevrault (founded at the close of the eleventh century by Robert d'Arbrissel) and the Abbey of Pontron ('Ponte Otranni,' thirty kilometers west of the city of Angers). This is an impressive list.

It is likely that all of these monasteries and 'chapters' had libraries and that several of them (notably the abbeys of St. Aubin and of Sts. Serge and Bacche) conducted scriptoria from a fairly early period. Of the entire group, however, St. Aubin's stands out as the most important owner and maker of manuscripts. I quote M. Molinier,[4] former librarian of the Municipal Library of Angers:

'La bibliothèque publique d'Angers date de l'époque révolutionnaire. On y recueillit, à l'origine, les livres imprimés et manuscrits provenant des couvents supprimés, ou confisqués sur les émigrés. De tout temps, dès le haut moyen âge, il avait existé à Angers des collections littéraires assez importantes, dignes de la

---

[1] On the history of the ecclesiastical centers of Angers see particularly A. Baudrillart, *Dictionnaire d'Histoire et de Géographie ecclésiastiques* (Paris, Librairie Letouzey et Ané), III (1924), cols. 85–114. See also Tresvaux, *Histoire de l'église et du diocèse d'Angers* (Paris, 1858).

[2] See *Angers, Bib. Mun., mss. 757* and *758.*

[3] Called a monastery rather than a 'chapter' in *The Catholic Encyclopedia*, I (1907), 489.

[4] *Catalogue générale des manuscrits des bibliothèques publiques de France.* XXXIII (1898), p. 188.

vieille réputation de l'école capitulaire de cette ville et de l'école monastique de St. Aubin. Mais, au cours des siècles, ces précieuses librairies avaient subi bien des pertes; d'autre part, plus d'un des volumes catalogués sommairement par Montfaucon dans la *Bibliotheca bibliothecarum* manquait à l'appel, quand le dépôt d'Angers fut ouvert au public en 1798. C'est toutefois cette abbaye bénédictine qui a fourni à la Bibliothèque moderne les meilleurs manuscrits, les plus anciens, et, en tout cas, les plus précieux au point de vue paléographique et littéraire.'

It is a pity that the manuscripts of St. Aubin's have remained so long unstudied, for even a superficial inspection shows what promise awaits the investigator. There are, first of all, codices produced at Tours (?),[5] Fleury (?),[6] the diocese of Poitiers,[7] and other centers,[8]—codices whose writing has in some cases furnished a model for the monks of St. Aubin's.[9] There are, second, specimens of excellent writing, many of them no doubt native adaptations of the Caroline hand.[10] There are, third, two copies of many manuscripts (one at St. Aubin's and one at St. Serge's)—copies which are no doubt closely related.[11] There, are, finally,

[5] *Angers 815* (s.ix) (St. Aubin), a *Martinellus*, was probably written either at Tours or at Angers from a Tours model.

[6] *Angers 91* (s.ix) (St. Aubin), a *Sacramentary* from Fleury(?) has numerous additions made at Angers or Orléans.

[7] *Angers 103* (s.xi), 'Liber capitularius et collectarius divinorum officiorum, ad usum antiquum monasterii Sancti Maxentii, ordinis Sancti Benedicti, Pictavensis diocesis.'

[8] *Angers 476* (s.ix) (St. Aubin), employing a minuscule based on Anglo-Saxon script, may possibly have been written at St. Aubin's itself.

[9] In the case of *Angers 1-2* (s.ix) (St. Aubin), a *Bible*, a monk of Tours took a copy of the Alcuinian Recension to Angers, where he copied part of it and a dozen native scribes the rest; see below under item 141, first note. *Angers 3-4*, a *Bible*, and *Angers 493* (both s.ix; St. Aubin), both use script which resembles that of Tours. In view of this imitation of the style of (St. Martin's of) Tours it is interesting to note that Defensor, the first Bishop of Angers known in history, when present in 372 at the election of the Bishop of Tours, made a determined stand against the nomination of St. Martin. But St. Martin influenced Angers for all that!

For the history of St. Aubin's (and St. Serge's) and their relationship to other monasteries the following mss. from the collection of Monsieur Toussaint Grille are important: *Angers 831* (s.xii-xiv), which contains an 'obituaire, d'un côté, les moines d'abbaye, et de l'autre les moines des maisons associées et les confrères spirituels;' *Angers 836*, part of which is described as 'Pancarte du XII⁰ siècle renfermant la copie des diverses actes interessant l'abbaye;' and *Angers 837* (s.xi) and *Angers 838* (the part of s.xi-xii), which give similar information about St. Serge's.

[10] Note the following mss. of s.ix, e.g. (all St. Aubin): *Angers 19*, 'belle écriture caroline;' *Angers 80*, 'superbe écriture;' *Angers 148*, 'belle écriture régulière;' and *Angers 161*, 'écriture très pure.' Note also two mss. of s.x. (both St. Aubin): *Angers 145* and *Angers 261*, both characterized as having 'belle écriture.'

[11] *Angers 41* (St. Aubin) and *Angers 42* (St. Serge), both s.xii: Angelomus, *Expositio libri Regum*. *Angers 48* (A) and *Angers 47* (S), both s.xii: Peter Lombard, *Commentary on the Psalms*. *Angers 186* (A) and *Angers 187* (S) both s.xi: Gregory, *Moralia in Job*, XVII–XXV. *Angers 234* (A) and *Angers 233* (S), both s.ix, *Exposition of the Epistles and Gospels of the year*. St. Aubin's was occupied by the Benedictines in s.x. and from that date on there was probably a closer connection than before with St. Serge's (also Benedictine).

illuminated initials[12] and canon tables[13] and occasional illustrations.[14]

In this article it is my purpose to survey the ground for a study of the manuscripts which belonged to St. Aubin's and which, in many cases, were written there. Fortunately there exists a twelfth century catalogue of the library of this abbey.[15] I shall attempt below to identify the various items in this catalogue in so far as they can be identified on the basis of published material.[16] The descriptions of Molinier's catalogue (*op. cit.*) for manuscripts now at Angers and of the various other catalogues which I have consulted for manuscripts now at other cities are reasonably complete in most cases. It is of course imperative as the next step that the manuscripts be studied themselves; only then will it be possible to determine whether certain leaves were once part of a codex other than that to which they now belong; only then will it be possible to evaluate the numerous fragments which now appear as fly-leaves; only then will it be possible to discover further Angers products which are now undoubtedly present in other cities.[17]

In my presentation below I give under each item first, the twelfth century catalogue entry *in capitals*; second, the designation of the manuscript or manuscripts in question, each followed by a statement, *in parenthesis*, of its date and, at the end, *in a separate parenthesis*, of the name of the library which owned it immediately before it came to its present resting place. Other details are self-explanatory.

The catalogue and my discussion follow.

NOMINA NOSTRORUM SUNT HIC SIGNATA LIBRORUM,
UT MEMOR ILLORUM SEMPER SIT GREX MONACHORUM

I. DUE PARTES SPALTERII (*sic!*) CASSIODORI: *Angers 43–44* (s.xi), *Cassiodorus' Commentary on the Psalms*, in two volumes. There is a fifteenth

---

[12] Simple colored initials in *Angers 92* (s.x) (St. Aubin); *Angers 144* (s.x) (A); *Angers 148* (s.ix) (A); *Angers 157* (s.x) (A); *Angers 166* (s. ix) (A); *Angers 276* (s.ix) (A); and many others mss. Colored and interlaced initials in *Angers 1-2* (s.ix) (A) and *Angers 5-6* (s.ix) (A). Ornamental initials and letters in *Angers 3-4* (s.ix) (A). A curious initial with interlacings on fol. 1ʳ of *Angers 165* (s.ix) (A). Curious initials in red in *Angers 234* (s.ix) (A). Very interesting painted initials in *Angers 261* (s.x) (A). Beautifully colored initials in *Angers 301* (s.x) (A).

[13] Six curious canon tables in *Angers 3-4* (s.ix) (A).

[14] In *Angers 147* (s.ix) (A), on fol. 137ᵛ in the margin, is an eleventh century drawing of a knight with sword and buckler.

[15] Published by L. Delisle, *Le Cabinet des Manuscrits de la Bibliothèque Nationale*, II (Paris, 1874), 485–487. Delisle notes (p. 485): 'Au mois de septembre 1873, M. Célestin Port a bien voulu me communiquer un feuillet de parchemin sur lequel est écrit, en caractères du XIIᵉ siècle, ce catalogue des livres de l'abbaye de Saint-Aubin d'Angers.' The date of this catalogue must be not long after 1153 A.D., as I demonstrate below under item 96.

[16] I have also used the unpublished summary catalogue of the *Reginenses* by F. M. Carey.

[17] I should expect to find Angers items among the mss. that formerly belonged to Sir Thomas Phillipps and possibly among the residue of that collection now at Cheltenham. Every palaeographer knows the difficulties in tracing books belonging to this collection. Thus far I have had no success with Angers items.

century *ex-libris:* 'De Sancto Albino.' Fragments written during the eleventh century of another copy of the same work appear in both volumes.

2. SPALTERIUM (*sic!*) AUGUSTINI, IN TRIBUS PARTIBUS. The following volumes are doubtlessly meant: *Angers 169* (s.xi), 'Incipit expositio psalmorum a primo usque ad quinquagesimum, digesta a beato Augustino episcopo,' that is, the first part of the *Enarrationes* (St. Aubin); *Angers 170* (s.xi), 'In nomine summi Salvatoris Dei, in hoc corpore continentur expositiones psalmorum quinquaginta sancti Augustini episcopi, id est a quinquagesimo primo usque ad centesimum' (St. Aubin); and *Angers 171* (s.xi), 'In hoc corpore habentur decadae Aurelii Augustini episcopi a centesimo primo psalmo usque in finem centesimi quinquagesimi' (St. Aubin). Note, however, the following duplicate of the second volume: *Angers 1 20* (s.xi), '. . . expositiones psalmorum L^a sancti Augustini episcopi a L^mo psalmo usque ad centesimum' (St. Aubin).[18]

3. AUGUSTINUS DE CIVITATE DEI, II VOL. *Angers 161* (s.ix), which contains Books XVI–XXII of this work, is the second volume. (St. Aubin). The first is missing.

4. AUGUSTINUS SUPER JOHANNEM, I VOL.: *Angers 176* (s.xi), 'In hoc corpore continentur Aurelii Augustini in Johanne evangelista a principio ejusdem evangelii omelie' (St. Aubin).[19]

5. QUESTIONES AUGUSTINI, I VOL.: *Angers 287*, foll. 1–153^v (s.ix), 'Incipiunt questiones Genesis beati Augustini in Eptateucum' (St. Aubin).[20] *Angers 167* (s.xii), 'Incipiunt questiones sancti Augustini super Eptateucum' (St. Aubin), possibly a copy of the first, is no doubt to be dated after the catalogue of the twelfth century.

6. SERMONES AUGUSTINI: perhaps *Angers 281* (s.ix), a collection of sermons for winter, which begins with St. Augustine's 'Legimus sanctum Moysen populo Dei prȩcepta. . . '. (St. Aubin).[21]

7. AUGUSTINUS DE DOCTRINA CHRISTINA, II VOL.: *Angers 278*, foll. 1–124^v (s.x), 'Incipit proemium sancti Augustini episcopi in libro de doctrina christiana' (St. Aubin). Foll. 125–181^v of this manuscript con-

---

[18] The contents of the third volume above appear also in *Angers 173* (s.x. or xi), fol. 150 sqq., (provenience unknown) and in *Angers 172* (s.xii), which bears the following press-mark of the twelfth century: 'Liber Sancte Marie de Ponte Otranni' (Ponte Otranni = Pontron, 30 kilometers west of the city of Angers).

[19] The same work appears in *Angers 175* (s.ix) (ST. SERGE) and in *Angers 177*. The latter bears the following *ex-libris:* 'Iste liber est ecclesie Omnium Sanctorum Andegavis. Quicumque eum furatus fuerit vel celaverit vel titulum istum aboleverit, anathema sit.'

[20] The remainder of the ms. (foll. 154–174^v), containing St. Jerome's 'Prologus locorum' and 'Liber de interpretatione nominum hebraicorum,' belongs to s.xii.

[21] Cf. the collection of sermons on the Gospels of the year, *Angers 235* (s.ix or x), in which St. Augustine is cited among others (St. Serge). This might have been given to St. Serge after the writing of the twelfth century catalogue of St. Aubin's.

tain other items of s.x and xi. St. Augustine's work appears also in *Angers 314* (s.xii) (provenience unknown).

8. AUGUSTINUS UNDE MALUM, I VOL. *Angers 159* (s.xi), bearing the contemporary press-mark 'Hic liber est Sancti Sergii martyris. Feliciter Amen.', contains this work and other works of the same author. There is at least the possibility that this is a gift from St. Aubin's (cf. above under item 6, note).

9. AUGUSTINUS DE TRINITATE, II VOL. One of the copies appears in *Angers 164* (s.xi), 'Incipiunt libri de Trinitate numero quindecim (St. Aubin). The second copy is missing.

10. EPISTOLE AUGUSTINI, I VOL.: perhaps *Angers 160* (s.xii), which contains various opuscula of St. Augustine and, at the end, his letters (St. Aubin).

11. RETRACTATIONES AUGUSTINI, I VOL.: *Angers 157*, foll. 8 sqq. (s.x) (St. Aubin). Foll. 1–6, 'Hic sunt nomina librorum sancti Augustini,' are of s.xii. Six mutilated folios containing part of a collection of masses appear at the end of the manuscript.

12. AUGUSTINUS DE ORDINE RERUM, I VOL.: *Angers 166* (s. ix) (St. Aubin).

13. AUGUSTINUS DE BAPTISMO PARVULORUM, I VOL.[22]

14. AUGUSTINUS CONTRA QUINQUE HERESES, I VOL.: *Angers 179* (s.ix and x), 'Incipit libellus sancti Augustini adversus quinque hereses' (St. Aubin). This manuscript also contains the works 'Adversus Manicheos,' and 'Contra Maximianum.'[23]

15. AUGUSTINUS DE BONO CONJUGALI, I VOL. *Angers 158* (s.x or xi), containing various opuscula of St. Augustine, has this item on foll. 60^r–75^v, but this is hardly the manuscript in question (St. Serge).

16. MUSICA AUGUSTINI, I VOL.: *Angers 486* (s.xi), 'Aurelii Augustini retractatio libri sequentis' . . . and (fol. 2^v) 'Incipit Dialogorum Augustini et Licentii de musica liber primus' etc. (St. Aubin).

17. CONFESSIONES AUGUSTINI, I VOL.: *Angers 163* (s.x), 'Incipit Aurelii Augustini liber primus Confessionum' (St. Aubin).

18. AUGUSTINUS DE ALCAMEDICIS (*sic!*), I VOL.: *Angers 292* (s.xii), 'Aurelii Augustini de Achademicis . . . ' and other works (St. Aubin).

19. EPISTOLA AUGUSTINI AD BEATUM JHERONIMUM, I VOL. *Angers 154* (s.xii), a collection of St. Jerome's letters, contains on fol. 1^r 'Incipit epistola sancti Augustini ad sanctum Ieronimum' and is undoubtedly the volume intended (St. Aubin).

[22] *Angers 277*, a collection of theological works and fragments of s.ix (St. Aubin), contains a *De Baptismo* on foll. 65^r–81^v, but this is hardly the manuscript in question.

[23] Cf. *Angers 180* (s.x–xi) (provenience unknown) which contains these three works and also the 'Contra Pascentium,' and also *Angers 280* (s.xi) (St. Aubin), a collection of theological works, which contains the 'Contra Quinque Hereses' on foll. 189^v–202^r.

20. AUGUSTINUS DE CONSENSU EVANGELISTARUM, I VOL.: *Angers 174* (s.ix or x), 'Aurelii Augustini, episcopi ecclesiae catholicae, incipit liber primus de consensu evangelistarum' (St. Aubin).[24]

21. AUGUSTINUS AD PAULUM ET EUTROPIUM, I VOL. *Angers 276* (s.ix), a collection of works by Fathers of the Church, particularly by St. Augustine, has as its first item 'Ad Paulum et Eutropium de perfectione iustitiae hominis, liber sancti Augustini' (St. Aubin).

22. AUGUSTINUS DE UNICO BAPTISMO, I VOL.

23. AUGUSTINUS[25] SUPER GENESYM, I VOL.: *Angers 168* (s.xii), which begins 'Omnis creatura (*sic!*) bipertita est . . . ' (St. Aubin). The fly-leaves contain fragments of a death roll of St. Aubin's, richly ornamented; a prayer for the abbots GUILLELMUS and JACQUELINUS; and *tituli* of Saint-Jean and Saint Lézin d'Angers.

24. AUGUSTINUS CONTRA FAUSTUM, I VOL.: *Angers 181* (s.xii), 'Aurelii Augustini doctoris liber I contra Faustum manicheum incipit . . . ' (St. Aubin).

25. ENCHERIDION, I VOL. Cf. item 69 (of this list) which is exactly the same work. Very likely one of the two copies of this list is *Angers 291* (s.ix), 'In nomine Domini Haec sunt capitula Enchiridion' (other works by St. Augustine follow) (provenience not designated). It is possible that the other copy is *Angers 308* (s.xii). 'Incipit Aurelii Augustini ad Laurentium primicerium, notarium ecclesię urbis Romae, liber Enchiridion appelatus' (and other contents including passions and lives of saints); the twelfth century press-mark 'Hic liber est Sancte Marie de Laaia' may possibly have been added when (and if) the book was given to St. Mary's. (Cf. item 6, note, and item 8, above.)

26. AMBROSIUS DE VIRGINITATE, I VOL.: possibly *Angers 307*, foll. 89^r–127^v (the end of the ms., where the work is still uncompleted) (s.xii) (St. Aubin). Since fol. 89^r begins with a new hand ('De virginibus'), these folios at the end of the manuscript may represent what was originally all or part of a separate codex, but one now bound with the letters of Ambrose (foll. 1–88^v).[26] The fly-leaves contain fragments of a twelfth century death roll of St. Aubin's.

27. AMBROSIUS SUPER LUCAM, I VOL.: possibly *Angers 306*, foll. 45^r–213^v (s.xii), 'Incipit prefatio sancti Ambrosii episcopi in explanatione evangelii secundum Lucam' (St. Aubin). Since a new hand writes these folios, they may be what was originally all or part of a separate manuscript.[27] The remaining folios of *Angers 306* contain a collection of works

---

[24] In bad condition; some leaves remade in s.xii.

[25] Delisle's report of the twelfth century catalogue bears the following note at this point: 'Avant cet article il y en a un autre, qui avait été soigneusement gratté.'

[26] This possibility will perhaps be established by a careful study of the manuscript itself.

[27] As in the case of *Angers 307* (item 26 above), this manuscript needs study.

by various Church Fathers among whom are St. Augustine and St. John Chrysostom.

28. AMBROSIUS DE PATRIARCHIS, I VOL. *Angers 309* (s.xii), a collection of verse and of theological treatises, contains this work on foll. 12^r–28^r: 'Incipit liber primus Sancti Ambrosii de patriarchis' (St. Aubin). There is no proof, however, that this ever belonged to a separate manuscript; it is probably not the item in question.

29. AMBROSIUS SUPER EPISTOLAM PAULI, I VOL.

30. EXAMERON AMBROSII, I VOL.[28]

31. AMBROSIUS DE OFFICIIS, I VOL. *Angers 296* (s.xii), 'Incipit liber primus de officiis sancti Ambrosii Mediolanensis' (Abbaye de Toussaint), may possibly have been a gift from St. Aubin's to Toussaint after the drawing up of the twelfth century catalogue (cf. items 6, note, 8, and 25 above.)

32. JERONIMUS SUPER YSAIAM, I VOL.: *Angers 150* (s.xii), 'Incipit prologus sancti Hieronimi presbiteri in exposicionem Isaiae prophetẹ' (St. Aubin).

33. JERONIMUS SUPER JHEREMYAM, I VOL.: *Angers 151* (s.xii), which contains 'explanationes in Jeremiam, Osee, Joel, Jonam' and a 'liber prologorum in Veteri Testamento' (St. Aubin).

34. JERONIMUS SUPER JHEZECHIELEM, I VOL.: *Angers 152* (s.xii) (St. Aubin).

35. EPISTOLE JHERONIMI, I VOL.: *Angers 154* (s.xii) (St. Aubin).

36. JERONIMUS SUPER VI PROPHETAS, I VOL.: *Angers 153* (s.xii), commentaries on Habakkuk, Zephaniah, Haggai, Zechariah, Malachi, and Daniel. There is a thirteenth century press-mark: 'Iste liber est Sancti Albini Andegavensis.'

37. JERONIMUS SUPER SECUNDAM PARTEM MORALIUM JOB, I VOL.

38. CONFLICTUS JHERONIMI CONTRA JOVINIANUM, I VOL.: *Angers 155* (s.xii) 'Incipit . . . sancti Ieronimi contra Jovinianum' (St. Aubin).

39. EPISTOLA JHERONIMI AD NEPOTIANUM, I VOL.

40. GREGORIUS SUPER CANTICA CANTICORUM, I VOL.: *Angers 282* (s.x), 'Gregorii papae super cantica canticorum' (St. Aubin). This manuscript also contains other works, among which are fifty sermons of St. Augustine.

41. GREGORIUS SUPER JHEZECHIELEM, I VOL.

42. PASTORALIS GREGORII: *Angers 191* (s.xi), 'Incipit liber pastoralis Gregorii papae, ad Johannem, archiepiscopum Ravennae,' plus other contents (St. Aubin). Cf. item 134 below, where three other copies of this work are discussed.

---

[28] This work appears in *Angers 293* (s.xi), beginning on fol. 94^r and going to the end of the manuscript: 'Exameron sancti Ambrosii' (St. Serge), but *Angers 293* is hardly the book in question.

43. REGISTRUM GREGORII, I VOL.: *Angers 194* (s.xii), 'Symbolum fidei Gregorii papę . . . Regesti (*sic!*) beati Gregorii, papę liber primus incipit, mense septembri per indictionem nonam' (St. Aubin).

44. DIALOGUS GREGORII, I VOL. Could *Angers 811* (s.x–xi) (St. Nicolas d'Angers) have been a gift from St. Aubin's after the drawing up of the twelfth century catalogue? (Cf. items 6, note, 8, 25, and 31 above.)

45. SENTENTIE GENERALES GREGORII DE OPUSCULIS SANCTI JERONIMI, I VOL.: *Angers 275* (s.ix), 'Incipiunt sententie generales de opusculis sancti Ieronimi,' plus other contents which include penitentials, prayers, interpretations, glosses, etc. (St. Aubin). On fol. 110ʳ appears the following entry: 'Nomina episcoporum Rotomagensium. Malonus, . . . Paulus, Wanilo.' (Wanilo died in 871.)

46. RABANUS SUPER MATHEUM, I VOL.: *Angers 58* (s.xi) (St. Aubin). On three preliminary pages appears a short genealogy of the kings of France up to Philip I.

47. RABANUS SUPER EXODUM, I VOL.: *Angers 295* (s.xii), 'Incipit prologus commentariorum Hrabani Mauri in Exodum,' plus other contents (St. Aubin).

48. AIMO SUPER YSAIAM, I VOL.[29]

49. AIMO SUPER EPISTOLAS PAULI, I VOL.: *Angers 67* (s.xi), the commentary on Paul's Letters published under the name of Haymon of Halberstadt.[30] There is a fifteenth century press-mark: 'Pro abbacia Sancti Albini Andegavensis.'

50. BEDA SUPER PARABOLAS SALOMONIS, ET IN EODEM VOLUMINE GESTA ANDEGAVORUM. The first work appears in *Angers 284* (s.xi), a miscellany, on foll. 14ʳ–38ᵛ: 'Tractatus Bede presbiteri super Parabolas Salomonis' (St. Serge), but there is no evidence that this is the item in question. (Cf. item 126.) The Chronicle of St. Aubin's contained in *Angers 827* (s.xii), which came from the manuscripts of Monsieur Toussaint Grille,[31] a collector, may possibly be the second work. Another possible claimant for this honor, though perhaps too late to be considered, is *The Vatican City, Reginensis lat. 711*[1] (=foll. 1–27; s.xii *ex.*), 'Chronicae (*sic!*) S. Albini Andegavensis,' a book which formerly belonged to St. Aubin's.[32]

---

[29] *Angers 817* (s.x *inc.*), a life of St. Benedict (St. Serge), contains, in a fly-leaf, a fragment of a commentary on Isaiah. This *might* prove upon inspection to be part of the item in question.

[30] *Angers 1902*, fragments, contains eleventh century fragments of this work in its title page and fly-leaf.

[31] On Monsieur Grille's collection of antiquities, etc. see *Angers 1702*.

[32] Cf. also two of the seven disconnected parts of *The Vatican City, Reginensis lat. 711*[2] (=foll. 28–114; s.x, xi, and xii); (1) foll. 28ʳ–37ᵛ, 'S. Albini Andegavensis monasterii' (s.xii); and (2) foll. 105ʳ–114ᵛ, 'S. Albini Andegavensis monasterii' (s.xii). The provenience of these parts is not proved, but they may be from St. Aubin's at Angers itself. (The seven parts of this ms. come from various codices. Part II, e.g. (=foll. 38ʳ–45ᵛ), is Quire xxii of *Reg. 318* and Part VI (=foll. 94ʳ–103ᵛ) is Quire xi of the same codex. The hands of Petau and of Daniel appear in various parts of *Reg. 711*[2]). I am

51. BEDA SUPER MARCHUM, I VOL.

52. BEDA SUPER LUCAM, I VOL.: *Angers 63* (s.ix) (St. Aubin).

53. PENITENTIALIS BEDE, I VOL.

54. QUADRIVIUM BEDE, I VOL.[33]

55. QUINQUE PARTES JOB: *Angers 183* (s.xi), Books I–V of Gregory's *Moralia in Job* (St. Aubin); *Angers 184* (s.xii),[34] Books VI–X (St. Aubin);[35] *Angers 185* (s.xi), Books XI–XVI (St. Aubin); *Angers 186* (s.xi), Books XVII–XXV (St. Aubin);[36] *Angers 189* (s.xi), Books XXVI–XXXV (the end) (St. Aubin).[37]

56. APOCALIPSIS, I VOL.[38]

57. YSIDORUS SUPER GENESYM, I VOL.: *Angers 297* (s.xii), 'Incipit opusculum Isidori, Spalensis episcopi, in libris veteris Testamenti' (St. Aubin).[39]

58. YSIDORUS ETHIMOLOGIARUM, I VOL.

59. ORIGENES, I VOL. This item refers, not to the ORIGINES of Isidore which are mentioned above as 'Ethimologiarum,' but to Origen. There is a bare possibility that *Angers 143* (s.xi), 'Incipiunt omeliae Adamantii Origenis, presbiteri, in libro Genesi, numero XVII . . . ' (Abbaye de Pontron), may have belonged to St. Aubin's at the time of the twelfth century catalogue.[40]

60. ANGELOMUS SUPER REGUM, I VOL.: *Angers 41* (s.xii), 'Incipit prefatio Angelomi monachi in expositione libri Regum' (St. Aubin).[41]

61. SERMO DOMINI IN MONTE, I VOL.: *Angers 286* (s.xi and xii), 'libri sancti Augustini episcopi, de sermone Domini in monte libri II; de patientia liber I; etc.' (St. Aubin).[42]

62. BURCARDUS, I VOL.: *Angers 368* (s.xi), 'Incipit liber Brucardi (*sic!*),

---

indebted to F. M. Carey's summary catalogue (unpublished), for the information concerning *Reg. 711*[1] and *Reg. 711*[2].

[33] Cf. *Angers 522* (s.ix), which contains material that might be appropriate for a TRIVIUM: Bede, *De Arte Metrica;* Sedulius; and Priscian (St. Aubin).

[34] Could this possibly be s.xi?

[35] Cf. *Angers 182* (s.ix), which contains the same material.

[36] Cf. *Angers 187* (s.xi or xii), Books XVII–XXV (St. Serge). Could this possibly be a copy of *Angers 186*, written either at St. Aubin's or St. Serge's?

[37] Cf. *Angers 188* (s.xii), Books XI–XXVII (provenience not designated).

[38] Cf. *Angers 74* (s.xiii), foll. 67ʳ–107ᵛ, 'Glose ordinaire sur l'Apocalypse,' according to the departmental catalogue. This can hardly be the item in question.

[39] Cf. *Angers 280* (s.xi), which besides John Chrysostom, Eusebius, etc. contains, on foll. 62ʳ–189ʳ, this same work of Isidore's: 'Incipit praefatio sancti Ysidori, episcopi Spalensis. Historia sacrę legis . . . ' (St. Aubin). Cf. also *Angers 195* (s.ix or x) for this work of Isidore's; this ms. bears a sixteenth-century press-mark: 'Je suys de Sainct Serge et Bach les Angiers; qant de moy vous arez faict, fermez moy, cera bien faict.'

[40] Cf. above, under items 6, note, 8, 25, 31, 44, and 55 (note under *Angers 186*). The Abbaye de Pontron, though not in the city of Angers, belonged to the same diocese.

[41] The same work appears in *Angers 42* (s.xii) (St. Serge).

[42] Cf. *Angers 293* (s.xi) (St. Serge), with similar contents.

episcopi nomine solo Marwortiensis (*sic!*)' = the twenty books of the *Decretum* (St. Aubin).

63. JOSEPHUS ANTIQUITATUM, I VOL.

64. JOSEPHUS HISTORIARUM, I VOL.

65. OROSIUS HISTORIARUM, I VOL.

66. EPISTOLE YVONIS,[43] I VOL.

67. HISTORIA ECCLESIARUM, I VOL.: *Angers 676* (s.xi), 'Incipit praefatio Cassiodori Senatoris . . . Incipiunt tituli ecclesiastice hystoriae cum opere suo ab Epyphanio scolastico . . . translati' (St. Aubin). Less likely a candidate is *Angers 26* (called 's.xiii,' though provided with a *twelfth* century (*sic!*) *ex-libris:* 'Hec istoria ecclesiae sancta vel scolastica pertinet monasterio Sancti Albini Andegavensis. J. Savin'); this manuscript contains 'Pierre le Mangeur,' *Scolastica Historia* (St. Aubin).

68. INSTITUTIONES ECLESIE, I VOL. This might conceivably be *Angers 301* (s.x), which presents Rabanus Maurus' *De Institutione Clericorum* and other contents (St. Aubin).

69. ENCHILIDRION, I VOL. See item 25 above.

70. EFFREN, I VOL. *Angers 284* (s.xi), foll. 73^r–84^r(?), contains five books which start 'Effrem levite incipit hic heremite' and which read at the beginning of Book I 'Dolor me compellit dicere' (St. Serge).[44] An investigation of this manuscript might disclose that foll. 73–84 (?) were originally the beginning of a separate manuscript. The matter requires further study.

71. SPECULUM, I VOL.

72. OMELIE JOHANNIS CRISOTOMI, I VOL.: *Angers 280* (s.xi), 'Omeliae Johannis Chrisostomi' and other contents (St. Aubin). Cf. item 125 and *Angers 147* (s.ix)[45] 'Incipiunt omeliae sancti Johannis, episcopi Constantinopolitani, diversae seu libri . . . ' (St. Aubin).

73. EPISTOLE PLINII, I VOL.

74. EPISTOLE FULBERTI,[46] I VOL.

75. PRUDENTIUS, I VOL.

76. GROSSINI, II VOL.

77. DUE PARTES EPISTOLARUM PAULI: *Angers 65–66* (s.xi), ' . . . in hoc volumine continetur expositio epistolarum beati Pauli apostoli, collecta et in ordinem digesta ex libris sancti Augustini' (St. Aubin).

---

[43] Ivo of Chartres (s.xi).

[44] These words are not those found in the *Vita Sancti Ephraem Syri* (Migne, *P. L.* 73: 321–326), the *Vita Sancti Abrahae* (supposedly founded on the Greek of Ephraem; Migne, *P. L.* 73: 281–294), or the *Vita S. Mariae meretricis* (also supposedly founded on the Greek of Ephraem; Migne, *P. L.* 73: 651–660).

[45] In bad condition; certain parts rewritten, particularly in s.xii.

[46] *Ca.* 975–1029 A.D.

78. EPISTOLE PAULI AD LITTERAM, III VOL.:[47] *Angers 67* (s.xi), a commentary published under the name of Haymon of Halberstadt (Migne, *P. L.*, 117: 361 *sqq.*), containing an *ex-libris* of s.xv: 'Pro abbacia Sancti Albini Andegavensis'; *Angers 68* (s.xii), two incomplete commentaries on Paul's letters, one by Gilbert of St. Amand (provenience undesignated); and *Angers 69* (s.xii), Peter Lombard's commentary (provenience not designated).

79. EPISTOLE PAULI GLOSATE QUINQUE VOL. One of the volumes is probably *Angers 71* (s.xii), which also contains (according to the catalogue description) a commentary by Remigius of Auxerre on the Song of Solomon and the text of the canonical epistles 'avec les arguments ordinaires' (St. Aubin). Cf. also item 88, note, below (the second part of *Angers 300*, s.xii, St. Aubin).

80. GESTA NORMANNORUM, II VOL.[48]

81. PANIGERICUS, I VOL.[49]

82. EPISTOLE SIMACHI, I VOL.

83. VITAS PATRUM, I VOL.: probably *Angers 810* (s.xii) (provenience undesignated).

84. DECRETA PATRUM, II VOL.: *Angers 367* (s.x or xi), the *Decretals* of Pseudo-Isidore, ending with the text of the council of Seville held in the year 658 of the Spanish era by King Sisebut[50] (St. Aubin).

85. VITA PAULI HEREMITE, I VOL. *Angers 154* (s.xii), a collection of St. Jerome's letters, contains, on fol. 276[r] *sqq.* 'Vita S. Pauli primi heremitae' (St. Aubin). If careful study should show that these folios were not originally a part of *Angers 154*, they might be all or part of the item in question. At the present moment it is impossible to decide.

86. CANONES, II VOL. *Paris, B. N., lat. 3837, Canones Apostolorum*, from the Cathedral of Angers, was 'apparently written at Angers before 829 by more than one scribe,' according to W. M. Lindsay, *Notae Latinae*, p. 472. Since the Cathedral chapter was not founded until the ninth century and since few manuscripts appear to have been written there before the twelfth century, *Paris 3837* was probably produced elsewhere. Could it have been at St. Aubin's?[51]

[47] Delisle in his article in *Le Cabinet des Manuscrits de la Bib. Nat.*, Vol. II (1874), 485–487, notes at this point: 'Cet article a été biffé.'

[48] By Dudo of St. Quentin (before 970–1017 A.D.). Cf. M. Manitius, *Geschichte der lateinischen Litteratur des Mittelalters*, II (1923), 264.

[49] Probably the Panegyricus Berengarii of 915–924 A.D. (cf. M. Manitius, *op. cit.*, I (1911), 632–635) and not the Panegyricus Libellus of s.xii (M. Manitius, *op. cit.*, III (1931), 342).

[50] This ms. also contains a letter of St. Augustine's 'de exortatione vitę aeterne' (fol. 1[r]) and a letter written to St. Aurelius by Sts. Alipius and Augustine 'de data ab eo potestate' (fol. 3[v]). The latter is an addition of s.xi.

[51] It was perhaps a gift to the Cathedral chapter. Cf. above, under items 6, note, 8, 25, 31, 44, 55 (note under *Angers 186*), and 59.

87. MUSICA GUIDONIS, I VOL.

88. AMALARIUS DE SACRAMENTIS, I VOL.: *Angers 300* (s.xii), which contains Amalarius, *De Divinis Officiis*, and a commentary on the epistles of Paul[52] (St. Aubin).

89. ALCUINUS, I VOL.: *Angers 279* (s.ix), 'In nomine sanctae Trinitatis, incipiunt capitula primi libri de sancta Trinitate' (the three books of this work follow), plus other works by Alcuin, St. Augustine, and St. Effrem (St. Aubin).

90. EUSEBIUS CESARIENSIS, I VOL.: *Angers 675* (s.ix),[53] 'Incipit prologus in libris historiarum Eusebii Cesariensis' (the eleven books in Rufinus' translation) (St. Aubin).

91. VIGECIUS RENATUS, I VOL.[54]

92. EUSEBIUS EMISENUS, I VOL. Two codices answer this description: *Angers 144* (s.x), 'Incipiunt omelie X de monachis Eusebii Emiseni,' plus twelve homilies for Easter, one 'De Latrone Beato,' two 'De Simbolo,' one 'Omelia de Trinitate generalis'[55] (St. Aubin); and *Angers 145* (s.x),[56] which contains the same homilies (St. Aubin). Apparently only one of these two copies was present at St. Aubin's in the twelfth century when the catalogue was made, though both were present there later. One may very well be the product of a scriptorium other than that of St. Aubin's and may have come to St. Aubin's after the making of the catalogue.

93. AMBROSIUS MACROBIUS[57] DE MENSURA ET LONGITUDINE TERRE, I VOL. Cf. item 114.

94. BENEDICTIONES, I VOL.: *Angers 80* (s.ix), a collection of benedictions for the use of a regular congregation (St. Aubin).

95. HYLARIUS SUPER BEATI IMMACULATI, I VOL.[58]

96. LIBER DEFUNCTI BERNARDI, I VOL.: probably *Angers 239* (s.xii), 'Incipit sermo primus beati Bernardi super Cantica canticorum,' which bears the following note of s. xv: 'Ex dono domini J. Bouhale, scolastici et canonici Andegavensis, utriusque juris doctoris excellentissimi.'[59] This

---

[52] This commentary, if originally part or all of a separate ms., may have been one of the five volumes mentioned in item 79 above.

[53] Foll. 1–5 and 187–194 have been rewritten in s.xi or xii.

[54] I.e., Flavius Vegetius Renatus (end of s.iv or later), *Epitome Rei Militaris.*

[55] And other contents which are missing in *Angers 145:* 'Ieronimus in epistola ad Eliodorum,' 'Ymnus de sancto Nicholao,' 'Sermo Sancti Augustini de natali Domini,' various hymns, 'Gregorius episcopo Neapolitano. Absurdum et inconveniens. . . '.

[56] Foll. 1–40 have been remade somewhat later.

[57] (Aurelius) Macrobius Ambrosius Theodosius, author of the commentary on Cicero's *Somnium Scipionis.*

[58] Another work by this same Hilary, bishop of Poitiers, 'Tractatus psalmi centesimi octavi decimi' appears in the first part of *Angers 289* (s.xi or xii) (St. Aubin).

[59] Cf. *Angers 302* (s.xii) ' . . . hęc ex opusculis venerabilis Bernardi, abbatis Clarevallis—Tractatus super Missus et Gabriel . . . ', etc. (Cathedral of Angers).

work was written by Bernard of Clairvaux (1090–1153), who must have died not long before the making of the twelfth century catalogue, for otherwise the adjective 'DEFUNCTI' in this item would hardly have any motivation.[60] The catalogue itself is, then, probably to be dated not long after 1153 A.D.

97. CIPRIANUS AD DONATUM, I VOL.: *Angers 148* (s.ix),[61] 'Incipit liber sancti Cipriani ad Donatum' (St. Aubin).

98. BOECIUS DE CONSOLACIONE PHILOSOPHYE, I VOL.

99. INSTITUTIONES CASSIANI, I VOL.: *Angers 398* (s.xi), 'Incipiunt Institutiones sancti Cassiani' (St. Aubin).

100. LIBER DE COMPUTATIONE ANNORUM, I VOL.: *Angers 476* (s.ix), a computistical and astronomical treatise beginning 'Ab Adam usque ad diluvium anni II^m et CCXLIII . . . , ' plus Book I and part of Book II of Bede's *De Ratione Temporum* ('Incipit hymnus Bedę, ars calculantis de ratione per ritmus') (St. Aubin).

101. QUINTILIANUS, I VOL.: *Angers 511* (s.xii), 'Marci Fabii Quintiliani cęcus in limine incipit' (the nineteen *Declamationes* or *Causae* ascribed to Quintilian) (provenience not designated).

102. SENTENTIE LONGUOBARDI, I VOL.[62]

103. PSALTERIUM MAGISTRI RICHARDI, I VOL. Who the Richardus was is uncertain. Since the item apparently concerns a psalter without commentary, there are three possibilities: first, *Angers 19* (s.ix), a psalter with its beginning missing[63] and with a special section (fol. 106^r) 'In natali sancti Albini' (St. Aubin); second, *Angers 18* (s.ix), a psalter with various prefatory pieces (provenience not designated); and, third, *Amiens, Lescalopier 2* (s.xi), a psalter with a calendar for the use of the church of Angers (provenience not designated, but probably Angers).[64]

104. DUO LIBRI EJUSDEM MINUTE LITTERE. Perhaps two of the three manuscripts listed in item 103 are to be placed here.[65]

105. GENESYS GLOSATUS, I VOL.

106. HISTO . . . . , I VOL. Cf. item 67 above. One of the two manuscripts there listed may belong here.

[60] Item 96 could hardly refer to Bernard of Angers who flourished *ca.* 1050, since the catalogue is written in a hand of s.xii.

[61] Foll. 1–6 remade in s. xii: 'Incipit de duobus montibus,' an anonymous treatise often attributed to St. Cyprian. Fol. 6^v contains a table of contents.

[62] The *Sententiae* of Petrus Lombardus (*ca.* 1100–1160?).

[63] Richardus' name may have appeared in the part now missing.

[64] Besides the Angers calendar the following sections, placed on additional pages at the beginning of the ms., make it probable that the ms. came from Angers, but not necessarily from St. Aubin's: fol. XIV^v, deliberations of the Angers chapter; fol. XV^r, 'Ordinacio apostolica de ecclesia Andegavensi,' an act of Barthélemy, archbishop of Tours at Angers in 1204. There are seven large miniatures.

[65] Which two have the smaller letters I can not now state. Apparently the Amiens ms. is the most elaborate of the three. This matter requires further investigation.

107. CASSIANUS DE COLLATIONIBUS PATRUM, I VOL.: *Angers 261* (s.x), 'Incipit praefatio Cassiani, viri doctissimi, de decem collationibus patrum' (St. Aubin).

108. . . . ., I VOL.

109. GLOSE SUPER PSALTERIUM, I VOL.: *Angers 50* (s.xii), 'Glose super Psalterium' (the first quire is missing) (provenience not designated). Cf. *Angers 45* (s.xii), an anonymous 'gloss' on the Psalms (= a *Catena*, or collection of extracts from the Fathers of the Church, principally St. Augustine) (St. Aubin);[66] and *Angers 1901* (s.xii), fragments of ten leaves of a 'Catena' on the Psalms.[67] Cf. item 125.

110. ESOPUS ID EST BESTIARIUM, I VOL.

111. CANTICA CANTICORUM, I VOL.: *Angers 290* (s.ix), 'Incipit tractatus in Canticis Canticorum' (a work attributed to Haymon of Halberstadt), plus 'Epistola Paschasii diaconi ad Eugibium presbiterum . . . ' (St. Aubin).

112. GESTA FRANCORUM, I VOL.[68]

113. SIDONIUS, I VOL.[69]

114. MACROBIUS, I VOL. Cf. item 93.

115. EPISTOLARIS NOVUS, I VOL.

116. EPISTOLARIS VETUS, I VOL.

117. SMARAGDUS, I VOL.

118. LIBER EVANGELIORUM, I VOL.: perhaps one of the following, though in every case the provenience is not designated: *Angers 21* (s.ix), *Gospels* with Jerome's preface; *Angers 22* (s.ix), *Gospels* with Jerome's preface; *Angers 23* (s.ix),[70] *Matthew* and *Mark* (*Luke* and *John* are missing entirely). Cf. *Angers 1901* (a collection of fragments), one leaf (s.xi) of an Evangeliary (provenience not designated).

119. MATHEI GLOSATI, II VOL. These volumes have not been identified, but cf. *Angers 1901* (a collection of fragments), one leaf (s.xi) of a commentary on the Gospels.

120. JOHANNIS GLOSATI, II VOL. See item 119.

121. MARCHUS GLOSATUS, I VOL. See item 119.

122. LUCAS ET JOHANNES GLOSATI, I VOL. See item 119.

123. LIBER NUMERI GLOSATUS, I VOL.

124. DEUTERONOMIUM GLOSATUM: *Angers 40* (s.xii), *Deuteronomy* and *Proverbs*, both with the ordinary 'gloss' (St. Aubin).

125. OS AUREUM. This expression, according to the *Glossarium* of Du

---

[66] The fly-leaves contain fragments of a roll of the dead of s.xii, coming probably from St. Aubin's.

[67] Are these two mss. in any way associated? Further study is needed.

[68] The identity of the particular work bearing this title is uncertain.

[69] Sidonius Apollinaris.

[70] Foll. 1–7 have been remade in s.xii. A fragment of *John* (s.xii) appears in the fly-leaves.

Cange,[71] refers either to St. John Chrysostom ('the golden-mouthed') or to St. Gregory ('praeterea dictus Hibernis S. Gregorius M. Cummianus Hibernus de Controv. Paschali . . . '). Perhaps, then, the item in question is *Angers 147* (s.ix), 'Incipiunt omeliae sancti Johannis, episcopi Constantinopolitani, diversae seu libri . . . ' (St. Aubin); see above under item 72. No appropriate work of Gregory's seems to be available. It is barely possible that one of the three following manuscripts is the one in question: *Angers 45* (s.xii), an anonymous commentary ('gloss') on the *Psalms* (a 'Catena,' or collection of extracts from the Fathers of the Church, particularly St. Augustine) (St. Aubin);[72] *Angers 1901* (a collection of fragments), 10 leaves of a 'Catena' on the *Psalms* (s.xii) (provenience not designated); and *Angers 477* (s.ix), Greek-Latin glossary, plus other contents,[73] (provenience not designated). Note that items 119–124 are all 'glosati'; *Angers 45* or the 10 leaves in *Angers 1901* would seem to follow naturally. A Greek-Latin glossary, finally, would also seem to be appropriate here.

126. PARABOLE SALOMONIS AD LITTERAM, II VOL. Cf. item 50 above.

127. VITA SANCTI SILVESTRI, I VOL.: *Angers 802* (s.xi), a collection of lives of saints, including St. Silvester, St. Gregory, etc. (provenience not designated).

128. VITA SANCTI MARTINI, II VOL. One of the volumes is doubtless *Angers 815* (s.ix), *Martinellus* (i.e., Sulpicius Severus' *Life of St. Martin of Tours* and other contents usually associated with this *Life*) (St. Aubin). Was this manuscript copied from a manuscript of Tours or perhaps written at Tours?

129. VITA SANCTI GREGORII, I VOL.: *Angers 819* (s.xi), ' . . . prefatio vitae beati Gregorii papę, edita a Johanne, cardinali diacono urbis Romae . . . ' (St. Aubin).

130. VITA SANCTI MAIOLO, I VOL.: *Angers 820* (s.xi), 'Incipit vita sancti ac venerabilis abbatis Majoli' (St. Aubin).[74] Cf. also *Angers 803* (s.xi and xii), a collection of lives of saints, including Maiolus, Silvester, Samson, Pope Clement, etc. (provenience not designated).

131. VITA SANCTI GIRARDI, I VOL. Can this possibly be *Angers 798* (s.xi), Usuard's *Martyrology*, to which have been prefixed (foll. i–v) a calendar for the use of the diocese of Angers and probably for St. Aubin's in particular and then the 'Depositio sancti Girardi, confessoris' (St. Aubin)? Note that the *Regula* of St. Benedict appears on fol. 69ʳ *sqq.* and that on fol. 102ʳ appears an act in the name of Girard, abbot of St.

---

[71] Edited by L. Favre, 10 vols., Niort, 1883–87.

[72] In the fly-leaves are fragments of rolls of the dead of s.xii coming probably from St. Aubin's.

[73] Astronomical tables; Bede, *De Rerum Natura*; Bede, *De Temporum Ratione*.

[74] Foll. i–v (s.xi), which precede the ms. proper, contain the following: 'Incipit sermo domni abbatis Odonis de sancto Benędicto,' etc.

Aubin (1082–1106), and acts of association. In the spaces left blank and in the margins throughout the manuscript are acts of association between St. Aubin's and other abbeys. These acts ought to be of prime importance in the reconstruction of the history of St. Aubin's.

132. VITE SANCTORUM IN UNO, I VOL.: probably *The Vatican City*, *Reginensis lat. 465* (s.x), *Vitae Sanctorum*, at one time codex 'B. 53' in the library of Paul Petau (apparently from Angers).[75] Cf. however, the following collections of lives of saints:[76] *Angers 802* (s.xi), see item 127 above; *Angers 803* (s.xi and xii), see item 130 above; *Angers 805*, 'Actus S. Johannis evangelistę . . . Passio sancti Sebastiani . . . Vita S. Juliani . . .' etc.; *Angers 806*, fragment of the life of saints Eventius and Theodotus, 'Passio S. Quiriaci' . . . etc.; *Angers 813*, ' . . . S. Christine . . . S. Margarite . . . S. Eustachii . . . ' etc.; *Angers 1559* Fortunatus' life of St. Aubin, Life of St. Mainbeuf (Magnobodus); *Angers 1838*, 'Vita S. Licinii, episcopi Andegavensis' . . . etc.

133. COLLECTANII DUO. It is impossible to state which of the following miscellanies, if any, are the two in question: *Angers 275* (s.ix), see item 45, where this manuscript seems to belong (St. Aubin); *Angers 277* (s.ix), a collection of theological works and fragments, beginning 'Incipit expositio Simboli apostolorum' (St. Aubin) (see item 140 below); *Angers 294* (s.xii), works of St. John Chrysostom, St. Ambrose, St. Augustine, etc. (provenience not designated); *Angers 299* (s.xii), a collection of extracts, chiefly from the Church Fathers: St. Augustine, St. Gregory, etc. (St. Aubin); *Angers 303* (s.xii),[77] a collection of verse and of theological treatises, beginning with Hildebert's metrical life of St. Mary of Egypt; *Angers 306* (s.xii), a collection of works of the Church Fathers: St. Augustine, St. Ambrose, St. John Chrysostom, etc. (St. Aubin); *Angers 309* (s.xii), a collection of verse and of theological treatises, beginning in the same way as *Angers 303* (St. Aubin); *Angers 238* (s.xii), homilies (St. Aubin); *Angers 243*, homilies for the Sundays and holidays of the year (provenience not designated); *Angers 281* (s.ix), fragment of a collection of homilies for winter, etc. (St. Aubin); *Angers 304* (s.xii), a collection of homilies (some by Geoffroi Babion, but ascribed to Hildebert, some by Bruno de Segui, etc.) (St. Aubin); *Angers 1902* (a collection of fragments), two leaves (s.xii) of a collection of homilies.[78] All of the

---

[75] I desire to thank F. M. Carey for his information about this ms., which is listed in his summary catalogue (unpublished) of the *Reginenses*.

[76] All except the first two (*Angers 802* and *803*) are of s.xii. For all without exception the provenience is not designated.

[77] This ms. bears the following press-mark of s.xii or xiii: 'Iste liber est conventus Sancti Albini Andegavensis.'

[78] Cf. also the following three mss., all from St. Serge (though not necessarily written there): *Angers 235* (s.ix or x), a collection of homilies on the Gospels of the year; *Angers 283*, a collection,

manuscripts (except possibly the first) mentioned under item 132 above ought also to be considered here.

134. REGULE TRES: *Angers 192* (s.ix), 'Incipiunt capitula libri regulę pastoralis Gregorii, papę urbis Romae' (provenience not designated); *Angers 193* (s.ix or x), the same work (provenience not designated); and possibly *Angers 400* (s.ix or x), 'Incipit prologus regulae patris eximii Benedicti' (St. Serge).[79] Cf. item 42 above.

135. HYNNERII QUATUOR.

136. ANTIPHONARII VI.

137. GRADALIA VII. Three of these volumes are no doubt the following: *Angers 96* (s.xii), a *Gradual* with neums (St. Aubin);[80] *Angers 97* (s.xii), a *Gradual* with neums, analogous to *Angers 96*, perhaps by the same hand (St. Aubin); and *Angers 1901* (a collection of fragments), four leaves (s.xii) of a *Gradual*.[81]

138. PASSIONARII QUATUOR. The most likely candidate here is *Angers 797* (s.x), Usuard's *Martyrology* (provenience not designated). *Angers 798* (s.xi), with the same contents plus other matters (St. Aubin) has already been suggested as possibly being item 131 above (*q.v.*). *Angers 288* (part of which is s.xii and the rest later) contains Usuard's *Martyrology* (s.xii) on foll. 22 and 126–131.[82] (St. Aubin); though there is no proof that these pages were ever part of a separate manuscript, the matter deserves investigation. Two codices from St. Serge's may possibly belong here:[83] *Angers 801* (s.xi), *Passiones sanctorum* (St. Serge), and *Angers 814* (s.x), 'Passio beatissimorum Christi martyrum Sergii et Bachi'[84] . . . etc. (St. Serge).

139. LECTIONARII TRES. The most likely possibility here is *Angers 121* (s.xi), *Lectionary* (St. Aubin). The remaining two volumes are probably to be selected from the following three: *Angers 124* (s.xii), *Lectionary*, which is no doubt to be selected because of its fifteenth century *ex-libris* on fol. 34^v: 'Cest libvre est au convent de S. Aubin d'Angers'; *Angers 804*, *Lectionary* (provenience not designated); and *Angers 807*, *Lectionary* (provenience not designated). Cf. *Angers 1902*, a collection of fragments, ten

---

coming from St. Serge (a liturgical calendar used at St. Serge appears on pp. 1–10) (Cabinet Toussaint Grille; for Monsieur Grille's collection see item 50, and note, above); *Angers 284* (s.xi), a collection, beginning 'Questiones ab Orosio proposite et a beato Augustino exposite.'

[79] St. Aubin's was founded in s.vi, but was occupied by the Benedictines in s.x. This ms. may have belonged to St. Aubin's at the time of the twelfth century catalogue: cf. above, under items 6, note, 8, 25, 31, 44, 55 (note under *Angers 186*), 59, 86.

[80] The beginning is missing; many leaves have been transposed.

[81] Can these be a part of *Angers 96?*

[82] Plus fragments of an obituary notice of St. Aubin's on foll. 143^r–145^v (s.xii) and other matters.

[83] See above under item 134, note.

[84] This subject seems more appropriate for St. Serge's than for St. Aubin's.

leaves (s.x) of a *Lectionary* (provenience not designated) and *Angers 122*, *Lectionary* (Abbaye de Pontron).[85]

140. EXPOSITORES QUATUOR: *Angers 234* (s.ix), an exposition of the Epistles and Gospels of the year (St. Aubin); *Angers 236* (s.ix), the same work (St. Aubin); *Angers 237* (s.xi or xii), an exposition of the Gospels of the year (St. Aubin); and possibly *Angers 277* (s.ix), a collection of theological works and fragments, beginning 'Incipit expositio Simboli apostolorum' (St. Aubin) (see above under item 133). Cf. *Angers 1902*, a collection of fragments, ten leaves (s.xii) of an exposition of the Gospels of the year (provenience not designated); and *Angers 55* (s.ix), 'Incipiunt quaestiones vel glosae in evangelio nomme (*sic!*)' (a commentary on the Gospels of the year) (provenience not designated). Cf. also *Angers 233* (s.ix), an exposition of the Epistles and Gospels of the year (St. Serge).

141. BIBLIOTHECE QUATUOR. Three of the works in question follow: *Angers 1–2* (s.ix), Latin *Bible* in two volumes, with script resembling that of Tours[86] (St. Aubin);[87] *Angers 3–4* (s.ix), Latin *Bible* in two volumes, with script also resembling that of Tours (St. Aubin); and *Angers 5–6* (s.ix), Latin *Bible* in two volumes (St. Aubin).[88]

142. TROPARII XIIII.[89]

With this item the catalogue ends.

The present identifications will at least provide us with sufficient material with which to begin a study of the script of St. Aubin's at Angers. We must of course distinguish between manuscripts which were merely in the possession of this monastery and those which were actually written there. Unless there is evidence to the contrary in a particular instance, however, a book appearing in the twelfth century catalogue may be considered a product of the scriptorium of St. Aubin's. We must also remember that certain books were produced at this center and sent elsewhere

---

[85] On the Abbaye de Pontron see item 59, and note, above. On the possibility of its having belonged to St. Aubin's see under items 6, note, 8, 25, 31, 44, 55 (note under *Angers 186*), 59, 86, 134.

[86] This *Bible* was originally thought to have been written at Tours by E. K. Rand, *A Survey of the Manuscripts of Tours. Studies in the Script of Tours*, I (Cambridge, Mass., The Mediaeval Academy of America, 1929), p. 131; at Angers by W. Köhler, *Göttingische gelehrte Anzeigen*, 193. Jahrgang (1931), p. 325. Rand now subscribes to Köhler's view and adopts an explanation suggested by me: see E. K. Rand with the assistance of L. W. Jones, *The Earliest Book of Tours with Supplementary Descriptions of Other Manuscripts of Tours. Studies in the Script of Tours*, II (Cambridge, Mass., The Mediaeval Academy of America, 1934), p. 99, note 7: 'I would now accept Köhler's view (*G.G.A.*, p. 325), that this manuscript is of the School of St. Aubin and not that of St. Martin. Perhaps we may say that a monk of Tours (Hand J.) took a copy of the Alcuinian Recension to St. Aubin, where it was copied rapidly by at least a dozen scribes along with the scribe from Tours. . . . '

[87] The following note of s.xv appears on the ms.: 'Macé de Senz, monachus Sancti Albini Andegavensis.'

[88] At the end of this work (Vol. II) is a charter of s.xi, mentioning Vulgrin, abbott of St. Serge of Angers, and then bishop of le Mans, from 1055 to 1064.

[89] Books containing 'tropi' or verses sung at certain festivals, immediately before the 'introitum,' as if they were a sort of preamble.

(to monasteries such as St. Serge's in the same diocese and often to establishments outside the diocese) *before* the date of the twelfth century catalogue. These books, in so far as they are extant, will eventually be discovered.[90] Our immediate task is to study intensively the manuscripts whose provenience is reasonably certain; when their original condition has been established and the nature of their script carefully investigated, we may then proceed to examine less certain items (including fly-leaves and fragments), at Angers and elsewhere.

COLLEGE OF THE CITY OF NEW YORK.

[90] It was formerly thought that *Berlin, Preuss. Staatsbib., lat. 167* (Phillipps 1825) (s.ix), *Commodian*, and *lat. 171* (originally bound in as the first half of *lat. 167*) (s.ix), Sedulius, *Opus Paschale*, were both products of Angers; cf. V. Rose, *Verzeichniss der lateinischen Hss. der Königliche Bibliothek zu Berlin* (1893), I, p. 375, and p. 387, where the attribution rests upon a slender probability. W. Köhler, in *Göttingische gelehrte Anzeigen*, 193. Jahrgang (1931), p. 325, says 'vielleicht Angers' of *Paris, B.N., lat. 4404* (s.ix *inc.*), *Breviarium Alarici*. Aside from these books and those I have already enumerated above in my discussion of the items of the twelfth century catalogue I have little else to mention at present. After 1200 A.D. I may name *Bern 309* (s.xv), possibly Angers; *Edinburgh, University Library, 25* (s.xv, late); *Paris, B.N., lat. 201* (s.xv), *lat. 16250* (s.xv), and *lat. 14344* (anno 1391), all three from the University of Angers. *The Vatican City, Reginensis lat. 1852* (s. xii and xi) contains a St. Serge press-mark of s.xii: 'Liber S. Sergii et Bacchi Andegavens.'

ASTRONOMY IN LUCRETIUS

Harry Joshua Leon

By the first century B. C. astronomical science had advanced about as far as it was to go before the invention of the telescope in comparatively modern times. Receiving their first impulse from the accurate calculations of the Babylonians and, to a lesser extent, the Egyptians,[1] the Greek scientists had already discovered the spherical character of the earth, sun, moon, and planets, the obliquity of the plane of the ecliptic to the axis of the earth, the true nature of eclipses of the sun and moon. In the fourth century B. C. Heraclides of Pontus, a pupil of Plato, had explained the apparent revolution of the heavens as due to the revolution of the earth on its axis. In the third century Aristarchus of Samos had taught that the earth is a planet which with its sister planets revolves about the sun as a center, a doctrine which, scorned by his contemporary astronomers, was eighteen centuries later to be revived by Copernicus. Eratosthenes of Cyrene, who flourished in the late third century B. C., had determined the diameter of the earth to within fifty miles of the reality. Hipparchus of Nicaea, the greatest of the ancient astronomers, had, a century before Lucretius, invented the science of trigonometry for his astronomical calculations, had discovered the precession of the equinoxes, catalogued about one thousand stars and devised a system of latitudes and longitudes for locating them, measured the parallax of the moon and successfully calculated its distance and size, determined accurately the lengths of the tropical and sidereal years, and had in fact established the science of astronomy on so firm a mathematical foundation that when this science was revived in the sixteenth century, it virtually needed only to continue where Hipparchus had left off.

We should have expected therefore that a man of such ardent scientific interests as Lucretius displays in his great poem would be fully abreast of the most advanced astronomical knowledge of his day. Actually, however, his interpretations of astronomical phenomena are for the most part distressingly naive and hardly worthy, we should suppose, of a thinker who could expound such doctrines as the atomic composition of matter, the indestructibility of matter, the evolution of animal and human forms and of human civilization, and, nineteen centuries before Darwin, present the rudiments at least of the biological doctrine of the struggle for existence and the survival of the fittest.

[1] It has been shown that early Greek science owed far more to the Babylonians than to the Egyptians; T. L. Heath, *Greek Astronomy* (London, etc., 1932), xiii-xviii.

It has been pointed out by Woltjer, Giussani, Bailey, and other scholars[2] that Lucretius's explanations of astronomical phenomena are, like most of his other scientific doctrines, derived from earlier philosophers and scientists. Many of his astronomical doctrines seem, in fact, to have been taken directly from Epicurus,[3] who, no astronomer himself, got them from a long line of predecessors, including chiefly Thales, Anaximander, Anaximenes, Pythagoras, and Heraclitus of the sixth century; Empedocles, Anaxagoras, and Democritus of the fifth century. I shall attempt in this paper to restate, as lucidly as I can, Lucretius's views on astronomy, which have received comparatively little attention from the commentators on Lucretius, and to reëxamine the sources for these views.

Lucretius's discussion of astronomical matters is found in the fifth book of *De Rerum Natura*, verses 509–770.[4] In the first part of the fifth book Lucretius had demonstrated that our world is finite and mortal, though part of an infinite and immortal Universe, and that the gods had had no part whatever in its creation. This world, which is only one of the countless worlds which make up the universe, was created out of a chaos of clashing atoms when the heavier atoms assembled at the center, forming the earth and the sea, and forced the lighter atoms to rise up and form the ethereal firmament of fire and the various heavenly bodies. From this point Lucretius proceeds to show in detail that the movements of the heavenly bodies can similarly be explained without bringing in any supernatural beings.

The first astronomical problem to be discussed is the reason for the motion of the stars (509–533). If the entire sphere of the firmament revolves, carrying the stars along in its movement, then there must be some sort of air current, Lucretius thinks, pressing at each pole to keep the sphere steady, while a third air current causes it to revolve by blowing either from above in the direction in which the stars move (that is, from east to west) or from below in the contrary direction, like the river current which moves a water wheel. It is, however, quite possible, he believes, that the firmament itself is motionless, while the stars have an independent movement of their own. In that case, the stellar motion may be caused (1) by fires which are inside the individual stars and propel them onward,

[2] J. Woltjer, *Lucretii Philosophia cum Fontibus Comparata* (Groningen, 1877), 117–136; Carlo Giussani, *T. Lucreti Cari de Rerum Natura Libri Sex* (Turin, 1896), commentary on the passage under discussion; Cyril Bailey, *Epicurus* (Oxford, 1926), 285–299. The various commentaries on Lucretius, such as those of Munro, Kelsey, and Merrill, give some information in this connection.

[3] Epicurus's views on astronomy are summarized in the *Epistle to Pythocles* (in Diogenes Laertius X, 90–98). Because of its extreme compression and the unsatisfactory state of the text, it is often difficult to reconstruct Epicurus's views. His fuller treatment of these matters in the eleventh book of Περὶ Φύσεως is lost. For the text of the *Epistle to Pythocles* with full commentary see Bailey's *Epicurus*.

[4] All references to Lucretius in this paper have to do with the Oxford Text by Cyril Bailey, second edition, 1921.

or (2) by an external air current which drives the fiery stars, or possibly (3) they move of their own accord, like so many grazing sheep, wherever they can discover the fiery food to nurture their fiery bodies. Here the poet insists, as does his master Epicurus,[5] that in astronomical matters it is difficult to determine with certainty the precise cause of any phenomenon, so that one must admit all possible causes which will not conflict with the evidence of the senses. Only one of these causes, to be sure, is the correct one,[6] but the cautious scientist must not be dogmatic where he cannot offer convincing proof.

The theory of air currents supporting and moving the firmament appears to derive ultimately from Anaximenes, who, making air the underlying substance of the Universe, stated that the heavenly bodies are supported by the air[7] and that the courses of the heavenly bodies are due to the resistance of compressed air.[8] The idea that inner fires drive the stars along may have originated with Anaximander, who regarded the stars as wheels filled with fire and emitting flames from small openings.[9] To Anaximenes also may be attributed the view that the individual stars are moved by air currents, although Anaxagoras refers to air currents as driving the sun and moon backward against the current of the firmament.[10] The strange view that the stars browse in search of their fiery food appears to derive from the Stoics, who may have got it essentially from Heraclitus.[11] Lucretius ignores Epicurus's suggestion that if the firmament is stationary, the revolution of the heavenly bodies may be due to a natural impulse which was produced at the genesis of the world.[12] It is noteworthy that in a discussion of the movements of the heavenly bodies Lucretius makes no attempt to distinguish between the planets and the fixed stars.

Lucretius's second astronomical topic (534–563), which fits but loosely into its context,[13] is concerned with the relation of our earth to the rest of the world. While the poet does not definitely describe the shape of the

[5] Often in the *Epistle to Pythocles*, especially Diog. Laert. X, 86–88, 95, 97, 113.

[6] Since the Universe contains an infinite number of worlds, all the possible causes will be exemplified in the various worlds, but it is impossible to determine which cause is operative in our particular world (526–533).

[7] Hermann Diels, *Die Fragmente der Vorsokratiker*, fifth edition by Walther Kranz (Berlin, 1934–5) I, 92, lines 11–13 (=Hippolytus, *Refutatio* I, 7, 4).

[8] Diels-Kranz I, 93, 41–42 (=Aetius, *Placita* II, 23, 1). The texts of Aetius and Hippolytus, apart from the citations in Diels-Kranz, are available in Diels, *Doxographi Graeci* (Berlin and Leipzig, 1929, reprint of the edition of 1879).

[9] Diels-Kranz I, 86, 28–29 (=Aetius II, 13, 7).

[10] Diels-Kranz II, 16, 26–27 (=Hippolytus, *Refutatio*, I, 8, 9).

[11] Bailey, *Epicurus*, p. 291; Woltjer, *Lucretii Philosophia*, p. 121.

[12] Diog. Laert. X, 92.

[13] Most scholars think that this passage originally followed verse 508 and was part of the account of the formation of the world. If this view is correct, the passage would properly fall outside Lucretius's discussion of astronomical matters.

earth, he probably thought of it as a sort of thick, flat disk.[14] The earth lies motionless in the center of the world. Its weight and density gradually diminish as one goes down, so that its rarefied lowest part is akin to the atmosphere on which it rests. The earth, though heavier, does not weigh down upon the air which supports it, because it has grown up together with it, just as in man the head is no burden to the neck nor the body to the legs, since they are parts of the same organism, while alien weights are burdensome. Thus the earth is not alien to the atmosphere, since they have been associated perfectly from the creation of the world. Their close connection is apparent when thunder shakes both the earth and the air above it. In a similar manner the soul, slight though it is in density, sustains and moves the much greater weight of the body, because the two have got used to working together since birth. This argument, as Giussani rightly observes,[15] is an example of the Epicurean abuse of analogy.

This view of the nature of the earth, which Lucretius may have derived from Epicurus,[16] is at variance with the then prevailing scientific view that the earth is a motionless sphere around which the heavens revolve.[17] The doctrine that the earth is flat and rests on air is found in Anaximenes[18] and in Anaxagoras.[19]

Next (564–591) the poet considers the size of the heavenly bodies. He begins this topic with a surprising assertion: 'The wheel of the sun can hardly be greater or its heat less than appears to our senses.'[20] As proof he points out that fires on earth, as long as they are clearly visible and their heat is felt, do not decrease their apparent size. Therefore, since the sun's heat and light reach us effectively, the size and shape of the sun

[14] Epicurus held that the worlds which make up the Universe in infinite number show a variety of shapes (Diog. Laert. X, 74 and the scholium). The extant remains of Epicurus do not reveal what shape he assigned to our earth and our world. From the fact that Lucretius refuses to accept a geocentric world and emphatically denies the existence of antipodes as a ridiculous theory (I, 1052–1082) we may reasonably assume that he accepted the disk-shaped earth of Democritus (Diels-Kranz II, 106, 37 = Aetius III, 10, 5) or the drum-shaped earth of Leucippus (Diels-Kranz II, 70, 25 = Diog. Laert. IX, 30; Diels-Kranz II, 78, 11 = Aetius III, 10, 4); cf. Woltjer, *Lucretii Philosophia*, p. 123.

[15] Vol. IV, 60.

[16] So Woltjer, *op. cit.*, p. 124. That Epicurus regarded the earth as resting on air is indicated by the scholium to Diog. Laert. X, 73.

[17] The doctrine that the earth is a sphere placed at the center of the Universe is found as early as Parmenides (Diels-Kranz I, 218, 1 = Diog. Laert. IX, 21). Diogenes Laertius attributes this view even to Anaximander (Diels-Kranz I, 81, 10–11 = Diog. Laert. II, 1), but other citations indicate that he regarded the earth as a short, cylindrical pillar (Diels-Kranz I, 83, 32–33; 84, 7–8; 87, 37). Because of the authority of Hipparchus and other leading Greek astronomers the concept of a geocentric Universe was maintained through antiquity and the Middle Ages.

[18] Diels-Kranz I, 91, 29–30 (= Pseudo-Plutarch, *Stromata*, 3) and I, 94, 27 (= Aristotle, *De Caelo*, II, 13, 7). Anaximenes regarded the earth as table-shaped (Diels-Kranz I, 94, 22 = Aetius III, 10, 3).

[19] Diels-Kranz II, 16, 9–11 (= Hippolytus, *Refutatio* I, 8, 3).

[20]   Nec nimio solis maior rota nec minor ardor
esse potest, nostris quam sensibus esse videtur.   (V, 564–565)

must be about the same as they appear to be. Similarly, the moon, whether it shines by reflected sunlight or is itself a luminous body, is of no larger size than appears to our eyes. It is true, in fact, of all distant objects that their shapes and outlines become blurred before their apparent size decreases. Since the shape of the moon remains perfectly clear and its outline distinct, it must follow that its size is precisely what it seems to be. Finally, the stars also can be only a trifle smaller[21] or larger than they seem.

This strange idea utterly contradicts the views of the scientists of the day and appears to have been more or less peculiar to Epicurus and his followers.[22] Epicurus apparently got it from Heraclitus, who stated that the sun is no larger than it appears to be[23] and, more specifically, estimated its diameter at one human foot.[24] Even the earliest of the Greek astronomers, as Anaximander[25] and Empedocles,[26] held that the sun is as large as the earth, while Anaxagoras, who regarded the sun as a fiery fragment of the earth,[27] said that it is much larger than the Peloponnesus.[28] Democritus, from whom Epicurus took most of his physical doctrines, also regarded the sun as a large body.[29] It is no wonder that Epicurus's view arouses the ridicule of Cicero, who cites in contrast the statement of the scientists that the sun is more than eighteen times as large as the earth.[30]

[21] The heavenly bodies may actually be smaller than they appear to be, since at a distance terrestrial fires may seem larger than they really are.

[22] Cf. Diog. Laert. X, 91 and the scholium on the passage, from which we learn that the idea was more fully developed in the eleventh book of Epicurus's lost work Περὶ Φύσεως. Bailey (*Epicurus*, p. 287) offers this comment: 'This is one of the most characteristic of Epicurus' doctrines both in its boldness and its childishness. It was of course based primarily on his complete trust in the evidence of sense-perception. We see sun, moon, and stars as of a certain size; we have no right to attempt to go behind the evidence of our senses: therefore they are that size.'

[23] Diels-Kranz I, 141, 12–13 (=Diog. Laert. IX, 7).

[24] Diels-Kranz I, 151, 5–6 (=Aetius II, 21, 4). Cicero (*Acad.* II, 82 and *De Fin.* I, 20) indicates that to Epicurus the diameter of the sun was about one foot (*pedalis*).

[25] Diels-Kranz I, 87, 14–15 (=Aetius II, 21, 1). Actually, Anaximander regarded the sun and moon each as a huge circle like a chariot wheel (or, as we might visualize it, like an automobile tire), hollow and filled with fire; the visible sun or moon is merely that portion which shines through an opening in the wheel. While the visible part of the sun is as large as the earth, its circle is twenty-seven (or twenty-eight) times as large as the earth, while the circle of the moon is nineteen times as large as the earth; see Diels-Kranz I, 84, 13–14 (=Hippolytus, *Refutatio* I, 6, 5); I, 87, 11–13 (=Aetius II, 20, 1); I, 87, 18–21 (=Aetius II, 25, 1).

[26] Diels-Kranz I, 294, 2 (=Aetius II, 21, 2). He also stated that the sun is larger than the moon; Diels-Kranz I, 282, 12 (=Diog. Laert. VIII, 77).

[27] Diels-Kranz II, 23, 25 (=Aetius II, 20, 6); cf. II, 11, 13–14; II, 23, 22–24.

[28] Diels-Kranz II, 23, 26 (=Aetius II, 21, 3); cf. II, 16, 22–23 (=Hippolytus I, 8, 8). Parmenides said that the moon is as large as the sun (Diels-Kranz I, 225, 5 =Aetius II, 26, 2), but there is no indication of the size which he attributed to those bodies.

[29] Cicero, *De Fin.* I, 20.

[30] *Acad.* II, 82; cf. *De Fin.* I, 20. Aristarchus, the greatest of the ancient astronomers, maintained that the diameter of the sun is about seven times that of the earth (more precisely, in a greater ratio

How the sun, small though it is, can send out so large a volume of light and heat as to illumine and warm all the seas, lands, and sky, is readily explained by Lucretius (592–613). Three explanations are offered: (1) The atoms of heat from all parts of the world collect in the vicinity of the sun, which, functioning as a sort of fountainhead, emits a great flow of light and heat, just as a small spring can send forth enough water to drench wide meadows. (2) The sun itself produces a comparatively small amount of fire, which, however, causes the surrounding atmosphere to catch fire, just as the stubble in a field is kindled by a single spark. (3) The sun has about it great quantities of unseen heat, which gives forth no light to betray its presence.

While the extant fragments offer no parallels to these explanations of the sun's heat and light,[31] it is not unlikely that they are derived from Epicurus, as Woltjer suggests.[32] The last of Lucretius's explanations is a kind of anticipation of the modern theory of invisible heat rays. In an article in the *Gentleman's Magazine*[33] E. W. Adams quotes as strikingly parallel the following sentence from Tyndall: 'Besides its luminous rays, the sun pours forth a multitude of other rays, more powerfully calorific than the luminous ones, but entirely unsuited to the purposes of vision.'[34]

No single explanation will account for the annual movement of the sun between the tropics and the monthly course of the moon between the same limits (614–649). Lucretius first offers and apparently favors the theory of Democritus.[35] According to this view, the nearer any celestial body is to the earth, the less involved it is in the swift revolution of the heavens. Therefore the sun, which is lower than the fixed stars, moves forward less rapidly than they and accordingly seems to move backward through the signs of the zodiac. The actual motion of the moon is slower than that of the sun because it is farther from the firmament and nearer the earth. Consequently, the moon's apparent retrograde motion is more rapid than that of the sun, since the starry firmament goes past it more

---

than 19 to 3, but in a less ratio than 43 to 6); Heath, *Greek Astronomy*, p. 103. The later astronomers, however, including Ptolemy, held that the diameter of the sun is about $5\frac{1}{2}$ times that of the earth; Heath, p. 104. All seem to have agreed that the moon is approximately one third the size of the earth.

[31] Anaxagoras's idea that the atmosphere hisses and crackles when heated by the sun (Diels-Kranz II, 24, 8–9 and 13–14) may be compared with Lucretius's suggestion that the sun kindles the surrounding air.

[32] *Lucretii Philosophia*, p. 126.

[33] See *Living Age*, CCII (1894), 733.

[34] The passage may be found in John Tyndall's *Fragments of Science*, Vol. I (New York, 1896), 31. Munro in his note on Lucretius V, 610–613 indicates that Tyndall, calling it 'this remarkable passage,' quotes the Lucretian lines before his essay on Radiation, but this passage is not included in the revision of 1896.

[35] For a full explanation of Democritus's theory see Woltjer, *Lucretii Philosophia*, 128–129. There is no reference to this matter in the fragments of Democritus, but Aetius II, 23, 7 (=Diels-Kranz II, 105, 30–31) alludes to it.

rapidly. It is, however, quite possible, Lucretius suggests, that two air currents, blowing across the sky alternately, drive the sun from the summer signs of the zodiac to the winter solstice and then back again. The same explanation would account for the movements of the moon and the planets.[36] These alternating air currents would be similar in principle to the opposing winds which drive the lower clouds in a different direction from the clouds above them.

In this passage Lucretius makes no clear distinction between the apparent regressive orbit of the sun through the signs of the zodiac and its seasonal oscillation between the tropics. As Giussani has pointed out,[37] the explanation from Democritus would account only for the regressive motion, while the theory of the air currents seeks to explain the motion from tropic to tropic. Lucretius has, unhappily, represented these as alternative explanations of the same phenomenon, whereas actually they are complementary explanations of two different aspects of the sun's movements.[38] The theory of the air currents appears to go back to Anaximenes[39] and Anaxagoras.[40] In the *Epistle to Pythocles*[41] Epicurus offers four possible explanations of the movement of the sun between the tropics: (1) the obliquity of the heavens, an explanation which reflects the correct view of the astronomers, (2) the action of air currents, (3) the successive kindling of the appropriate material, (4) a sort of inherent spiral motion of these heavenly bodies. Lucretius uses only the second of these explanations.[42] Epicurus does not allude in this passage to Democritus's theory of the whirl of the heavens, since he recognized, as Lucretius did not, that it applies only to the retrograde course of the sun and does not account for the movement between the tropics.

[36] In line 643 *stellas* must refer to the planets, since the stars do not move between the tropics like the sun and moon. Nowhere does Lucretius distinguish clearly between stars and planets; he seems to refer to them indiscriminately as *stellae, sidera,* or *signa.* In line 644 *magnos annos* is apparently an allusion to the 'great year' of the astronomers, the period within which the sun, moon, and five planets complete a cycle, returning to the same relative position which they occupied at the beginning of the period. While the number of solar years in the *magnus annus* was a matter of disagreement, in Tacitus, *Dialogus* 16 this period is fixed precisely at 12,954 years. See Alfred Gudeman's notes on this passage in his edition of the *Dialogus* (ed. 2, Leipzig and Berlin, 1914).

[37] Note on V, 613–615 (his numbering). Giussani thinks (note on 619) that Lucretius did not cite Democritus directly, but found his doctrines referred to in Epicurus.

[38] Democritus seems not to have been guilty of the same confusion, as he tried to account also for the tropical movement of the sun as due to the revolution of the firmament; Diels-Kranz II, 105, 30–31 (=Aetius II, 23, 7).

[39] Diels-Kranz I, 93, 41–42 (=Aetius II, 23, 1).

[40] Diels-Kranz II, 16, 26–27 (=Hippolytus I, 8, 9); II 23, 27–28 (=Aetius II, 23, 2). Merrill (note on V, 637) erroneously substitutes Anaximander for Anaxagoras.

[41] Diog. Laert. X, 93.

[42] Woltjer (*Lucretii Philosophia,* p. 131) thinks that Lucretius's explanation is quite different, but Bailey (*Epicurus,* p. 292) rightly, I think, regards the Lucretian passage (V, 637–649) as an amplification of the view alluded to in Epicurus.

Night brings its darkness upon the earth either because the sun's fires, exhausted after the long day's journey through the atmosphere, are extinguished, or because the course of the sun is driven beneath the earth by the same force which brings it above the earth (650–655). Dawn, the poet continues (656–679), spreads its rose-colored light over the sky either because the sun, after passing beneath the earth, now returns, or because new atoms of fire assemble at a fixed time and bring a new sun into being. To prove that this explanation is a plausible one Lucretius cites a phenomenon seen on Mount Ida in the Troad, where at dawn the scattered fires of the sun are actually seen to assemble and form a single globe. The idea that a brand-new sun is born each day is, furthermore, quite in accord with the known processes of nature, for the vegetation springs up regularly each season and then dies, the teeth of children fall out and grow in again, the soft downy beard appears on the face of a youth, the various atmospherical phenomena, as thunder, snow, rain, clouds, winds, recur at fairly definite seasons. In fact, the recurrence of phenomena in a fixed sequence is an important law of nature. This argument is again an example of Lucretius's unscientific use of analogy.

The notion that the sun's fires burn out at the end of the day and that a new sun is born the next morning is found in Heraclitus[43] and Xenophanes[44] and was adopted by Epicurus.[45] That the sun simply passes below the horizon to come up again on the other side was the prevailing view of the astronomers with their concept of a fixed earth and the heavenly spheres revolving about it. Here Lucretius appears to vary somewhat from the alternative explanation offered by Epicurus,[46] following that of Anaximenes,[47] who held that the sun does not pass beneath the earth but only horizontally around it, so that it is hidden from our view by the higher parts of the earth's surface toward the north.

That the days are longer when the nights are shorter and vice versa is due to any one of three causes (680–704): Lucretius first gives the view of the astronomers that the course of the sun is so divided that during the winter a greater portion of its path lies beneath the earth, while in the

[43] Diels-Kranz I, 152, 3–5 (=Arist. *Meteorologica* II, 2, 9); I, 146, 27–28 (=Aetius II, 20, 16). Heraclitus's conception of the extinction and rebirth of the sun each day may have become proverbial; cf. Plato, *Republic* 498a.

[44] Diels-Kranz I, 122, 35 (=Hippolytus I, 14, 3); I, 125, 1–2 (=Aetius II, 24, 4 though Aetius classifies it under eclipses). Xenophanes regarded the sun as consisting of clouds set on fire; Diels-Kranz I, 124, 34 (=Aetius II, 20, 3). He also held that the stars are fiery particles of cloud and that they are extinguished each day to be rekindled at night like coals; Diels-Kranz I, 124, 28–30 (=Aetius II, 13, 14).

[45] Diog. Laert. X, 92.

[46] *Ibid.*

[47] Diels-Kranz I, 92, 16–19 (=Hippolytus I, 7, 6); I. 93, 28–31 (=Arist. *Meteor.* II, 1, 13); I, 93, 27–28 (=Aetius II, 16, 6, on the movement of the stars).

summer its path above the earth is the longer one. When its orbit inter-
sects the equator, that is, at the equinoxes, the days and nights are equal
in length.[48] It may be, however, that the atmosphere is denser in certain
areas, so that the sun takes longer to rise in the winter. Thirdly, if a new
sun is born each day, the fires which form it assemble more slowly or
more quickly, according to the season of the year.

The idea that a denser atmosphere, through which the sun must move,
delays its rising in the winter was probably derived by Lucretius from
Epicurus,[49] who may in turn have got it from Anaximenes.[50] That the
length of the days is dependent on the time it takes for the atoms of
flame to assemble in forming the new-born sun is a corollary of the Hera-
clitean theory that the sun is extinguished and rekindled each day.

No less than four explanations are offered to account for the phases of
the moon (705-750): (1) If the moon gets its light from the sun, it shows
us a larger lighted surface as it gets farther away from the sun, until it
is fully illuminated when it is in opposition, so that it rises when the sun
sets. Then it wanes gradually as it again approaches the sun. This, Lucretius says, is the view of those who believe that the moon is a sphere
with its orbit below that of the sun. Still, (2) it is entirely possible that the
moon shines with its own light, but is accompanied by a dark, invisible
body, which so obstructs it that it shows a succession of phases. It is
possible also (3) that only one half of the moon's globe is luminous, so
that as it revolves the familiar phases appear. This is the view of the
Babylonians, as opposed to that of the astronomers, but Lucretius thinks
that the one theory is just as likely to be right as the other. And finally,
(4) it may well be that a new moon is born each day in a different shape,
only to perish and be reborn the next day. Analogies for such a sequence
may be found in nature. For example, the seasons succeed each other in a
fixed order.

The origins of these explanations of the moon's phases are reasonably
clear.[51] That the moon reflects the sun's light to us at different angles was

[48] Here the poet clearly refers to the obliquity of the plane of the ecliptic to the equator and its
intersection by the equator (689-693); *metas* (690) is to be taken as referring to the tropics. So
Giussani and Merrill and Bailey in his translation (Oxford, 1910), pp. 304-305; Munro interprets
metas as the points where the sun rises and sets at the time of the equinox.

[49] The passage dealing with this matter in the *Epistle to Pythocles* (Diog. Laert. X, 98) is corrupt.
Bailey (*Epicurus*, pp. 297-299) thinks that at least the first two of the reasons offered by Lucretius
are included there and that the third (i.e. the rekindling of the new-born sun at different speeds)
has fallen out in the mss.

[50] So Woltjer (*op. cit.*, p. 132) thinks, citing Aetius II, 23, 1 (= Diels-Kranz I, 93, 41-42), the
passage (cited above, Note 39) in which Anaximenes attributes the turning back of the sun at the
tropics to the resistance of compressed air.

[51] In the *Letter to Pythocles* (Diog. Laert. X, 94) Epicurus impartially offers as explanations of
the phases the revolution of the moon, successive conformations of the atmosphere (so Bailey), or the
interposition of other bodies. The moon may either have its own light or be illuminated by the sun.

the prevailing scientific view, which appears to have been held first by Anaxagoras in the fifth century.[52] That the moon shines with its own light, which is obstructed by an opaque body to form the phases, was the theory of Anaximenes.[53] That the moon is half luminous and half dark was, as Lucretius states, a Babylonian theory, which was introduced to Rome by the Chaldaean astronomer Berosus in the third century, as we learn from Vitruvius, who describes the theory with some detail.[54] A similar idea is found in Heraclitus,[55] who held that the moon, like the other heavenly bodies, is shaped like a bowl, the concave portion of which is filled with fire, while the reverse side is dark. The moon's phases are produced by a gradual turning of the bowl. The theory of the daily rebirth of the moon in a different shape is akin to that of Heraclitus on the daily rebirth of the sun.[56] While the succession of the seasons offers a rather

---

[52] Cf. Heath, *Greek Astronomy*, p. xxxiii; Diels-Kranz II, 16, 23 (=Hippolytus I, 8, 8, but, strangely, a few lines above, in the same passage [§6 = Diels-Kranz II, 16, 16–17], Hippolytus states that Anaxagoras regarded the sun, moon, and all the stars as fiery rocks); Diels-Kranz II, 24, 20–21 (=Plato, *Cratylus* 409a); Diels-Kranz II, 24, 36–37 (=Aetius II, 29, 6); Diels-Kranz II, 41, 6–7 (=Plutarch, *De Facie in Orbe Lunae* 16, p. 929B). The distinction of being the first to teach that the moon's light is derived from the sun was also attributed to various earlier scientists, but seemingly without sufficient reason. Aetius II, 28, 5 (=Diels-Kranz I, 78, 25) attributes it to Thales, but Thales's predictions of eclipses were probably based on the Babylonian method of counting periods of lunations; Heath, p. xix. The honor was assigned also to Anaximenes (Diels-Kranz I, 94, 2–3 = Theo. Smyrn., p. 98, 14 Hill.), but other evidence indicates that he regarded the moon as a fiery body (Diels-Kranz I, 92, 12 = Hippolytus I, 7, 4; Diels-Kranz I, 94, 4 = Aetius II, 25, 2). Aetius attributes it also to Parmenides (II, 26, 2 = Diels-Kranz I, 225, 5; cf. Diels-Kranz I, 225, 6–7 = Aetius II, 28, 5; also Diels-Kranz I, 243, 19; I, 244, 1–3), but Aetius indicates elsewhere (II, 25, 3 = Diels-Kranz I, 225, 4) that Parmenides regarded the moon as a fiery body; also that it is a mixture of air and fire (Aetius II, 7, 1 = Diels-Kranz I, 224, 12–13); yet, in still another passage (II, 20, 8a = Diels-Kranz I, 225, 8–10) he has Parmenides state that the moon is cold because it was separated from the denser element of the Milky Way, while the sun came from a rarefied, hot mixture; but he may mean cold as compared with the sun. Empedocles, a contemporary of Anaxagoras, also seems to have regarded the moon as a dark body illuminated by the sun; Diels-Kranz I, 294, 30–31 (=Aetius II, 28, 5); I, 288, 31–32 (=Pseudo-Plutarch, *Stromata*, frag. 10). Aetius in the passage (II, 28, 5) in which he represents Thales, Parmenides, Empedocles, and Anaxagoras as holding this view also attributes it to Pythagoras.

Giussani rightly points out (note on V, 706, his numbering) that by admitting the possibility that the moon gets its light from the sun, Lucretius is quite inconsistent with his uncompromising view that the sun is no larger than it appears to be, since it would obviously be impossible for so small a sun to illuminate the full moon at midnight when the vast earth lies between these two bodies. Giussani regards this as an indication that Lucretius is here following the astronomers and not Epicurus.

[53] Diels-Kranz I, 93, 24–25 (=Aetius II, 13, 10), stating that all heavenly bodies are fiery and have unseen, earthlike bodies circling around them. Hippolytus, *Refutatio* I, 8, 6 (=Diels-Kranz II, 16, 16–19) attributes a similar idea to Anaxagoras, but this is in contradiction to Anaxagoras's well-attested view that the moon has its light from the sun; cf. the preceding note.

[54] *De Archit.* IX, 2, 1–2.

[55] Diels-Kranz I, 142, 3–4 (=Diog. Laert. IX, 10).

[56] While Heraclitus may have believed that the moon is reborn daily, no reference can be cited from an ancient author. Woltjer (*Lucretii Philosophia*, p. 134) cites Aetius II, 28, 6 (=Diels-Kranz I, 146, 31), but this passage, which treats of the shape and illumination of the sun and moon, does not even imply a daily extinction and rebirth. Such a view would in any case be contrary to Heraclitus's statement that the phases are caused by the revolution of a bowl-shaped moon. Xenophanes

feeble analogy in support of this last theory, it gives Lucretius an opportunity to display his poetic powers after a long stretch of rather prosaic
verse.

The last astronomical problem which Lucretius considers is the explanation of eclipses (751–770). Here again we have (1) the true scientific
explanation that the sun is eclipsed when the interposition of the moon
cuts the sunlight off from the earth. But Lucretius immediately adds (2)
that it is just as likely that some other dark body obstructs the sun.
There is also (3) the possibility that the sun's fires are temporarily extinguished as that body passes through a region inimical to its flames. The
moon is eclipsed (1) when it passes through the cone of the earth's shadow.
It may also be (2) that some other opaque body cuts the sunlight off from
the moon either by passing beneath the moon or by crossing the face of
the sun. And finally, (3) if the moon shines with its own light, it may,
like the eclipsed sun, be extinguished when it passes through a region
hostile to its fires.

The scientific explanation of eclipses goes back probably to Anaxagoras,[57] although Thales, using the Babylonian method of calculating by the
number of lunations,[58] was able to predict eclipses still earlier. This view
had been adopted by Plato, Aristotle, and the Stoics.[59] The Epicureans,
however, while familiar with this explanation, regarded other theories
as equally valid.[60] The tone of Lucretius is, in fact, almost defiant as he
virtually asks, 'Why must we accept the view of the scientists and at the
same time exclude other reasonable possibilities?'[61] The idea that some

---

seems to have held that the moon's phases are due to an extinguishing of its light (Diels-Kranz I,
125, 15 = Aetius II, 29, 5), but the one passage referring to this view is too brief to admit an explanation. Aetius, in fact, places it in the section on eclipses, although the phrase τὴν μηνιαίαν ἀπόκρυψιν
clearly indicates a monthly phenomenon. Cf. Xenophanes's views about the sun (p. 170, above, and
Note 44).

[57] Cf. Heath, *Greek Astronomy*, p. xxxiii. The significant passages are Diels-Kranz II, 16, 24–26
(= Hippolytus I, 8, 9) and II, 24, 37–39 (= Aetius II, 29, 6), where Thales is included among those
who held this view.

[58] So Heath, *op. cit.*, pp. xviii–xix.

[59] Aetius II, 29, 6. In admitting even the possibility that the earth's shadow forms a cone (764),
Lucretius is inconsistent with his view that the earth is a great disk and the sun is a very small
body. This has been pointed out by Giussani in his note on the passage. Bailey in his translation of
Lucretius (pp. 306–307) cites this inconsistency as a proof that Lucretius did not really understand
the astronomical theories which he discusses.

[60] In the *Letter to Pythocles* (Diog. Laert. X, 96) Epicurus explains eclipses as due either to extinction or to the interposition of opaque bodies. Cf. Bailey's commentary on this passage, *Epicurus*,
pp. 294–296. The scholium on the passage indicates that in the eleventh book of Περὶ Φύσεως Epicurus
gave also the scientists' explanation of eclipses.

[61]   nam cur luna queat terram secludere solis
     lumine . . .
     tempore eodem aliud facere id non posse putetur
     corpus . . .   (V, 753–757)
and so throughout the rest of the passage.

unknown dark body covers the sun or moon is found in Anaximenes,[62] and even Anaxagoras, despite his understanding of the true reason, admits that the moon may be eclipsed also by the interposition of other dark bodies beneath it.[63] That the sun or moon is extinguished in a hostile region was probably the opinion of Xenophanes.[64]

After reading Lucretius's strange mixture of true science and childish theorizing, we may well ask why it is that this great author of the epic of the Universe should have fallen far below his scientific and poetic standards in his treatment of astronomy, an aspect of his subject which, we should suppose, ought to have inspired his glowing enthusiasm, his bold imagination, and his unmatched poetic gifts to their noblest results. That he was abundantly capable of treating such a subject in a brilliant and imaginative manner is evident from many passages in other parts of his work. For example, in illustrating the infinity of the Universe, he says, 'Such is the nature of space and the expanse of the vast Universe, that the brilliant lightnings, speeding in their course through the endless stretch of time, cannot traverse it or even reduce one whit from the distance they still must go;—so great is the quantity of matter extending in every direction, deprived of boundaries.'[65] In discussing how calloused people may become even to the most wonderful things after they are accustomed to them, he offers this illustration: 'Consider first the brilliant and clear hue of the sky and all it contains, the stars roaming on every side, and the moon and the splendor of the sun with its glorious light. If all this spectacle were now for the first time revealed on a sudden to the eyes of mortals, what more marvelous vision than this could be described, one that men would never before have dared to believe possible? None, I believe; so amazing would this spectacle have been. Yet now,

---

[62] Diels-Kranz I, 93, 24–25 (= Aetius II, 13, 10). While it does not refer specifically to eclipses, the passage states that unseen, earthlike bodies circle around the heavenly bodies, which are fiery in nature.

[63] Diels-Kranz II, 16, 25 (= Hippolytus I, 8, 9); II, 24, 39–40 (= Aetius II, 29, 7).

[64] Diels-Kranz I, 125, 1–2 (= Aetius II, 24, 4). While Aetius classifies it under eclipses of the sun, the passage may refer rather to the extinction of the sun at its setting, since the author speaks of the rebirth of the sun at its rising (πρὸς ταῖς ἀνατολαῖς); cf. supra, p. 170 and Note 44. Still, the reference to solar eclipses in the following sentence would indicate that the same general explanation applies to both phenomena. Woltjer (op. cit., pp. 135, 136) attributes the theory of the extinction of the sun and the moon during eclipses to Heraclitus, but this philosopher regarded eclipses as due to the turning of the dark, convex sides of the affected bodies toward us; Diels-Kranz I, 142, 2–3 (= Diog Laert. IX, 10); I, 146, 29–30 (= Aetius II, 24, 3); I, 146, 35–36 (= Aetius II, 29, 3); cf. supra, p. 172 and Note 56.

[65]
  est igitur natura loci spatiumque profundi,
  quod neque clara suo percurrere fulmina cursu
  perpetuo possint aevi labentia tractu
  nec prorsum facere ut restet minus ire meando;
  usque adeo passim patet ingens copia rebus
  finibus exemptis in cunctas undique partis. (I, 1002–1007)

sated as we are with beholding it, no one even deigns to look up to the glittering realms of the heavens.'[66] One can cite also his references to the 'gliding emblems of the sky,' to 'the serene stars in the spangled sky,' to 'the austere emblems of night, the night-roaming firebrands, and the winged flames of the sky,' or 'the heavenly realms of the mighty firmament and the aether above studded with the sparkling stars.'[67] Yet hardly a phrase of similar poetic quality can be cited from the astronomical discussion in the fifth book.

Actually, however, Lucretius was not particularly interested in astronomy. The fields of physics, biology, and anthropology appealed to him much more. Nor did he, as we have seen, have a clear understanding of the astronomical views which he discusses. The atomic doctrine, he felt, is essential for our understanding of the nature of the things that surround us and especially of the nature of the soul and the meaning of life and death; the doctrine of the evolution of man and society is necessary for the proper understanding of our contemporary civilization and for refuting the religious dogmas of special creation by some god and the mythological tales of a Golden Age or a Garden-of-Eden stage of civilization, from which mankind has fallen. On the other hand, it seemed to him that the true explanation of the movements of the heavenly bodies mattered but little in the ordering of our lives on earth. In considering this subject at all, his sole purpose was to prove that all astronomical phenomena could be explained as due entirely to natural forces and that the religious doctrines that the celestial bodies were created by gods or operated by gods or were themselves gods were utterly unnecessary and unworthy of belief. The ultimately true explanations of these phenomena he regarded as unattainable, while any explanations which did not involve the power of the gods, which did not contradict the atomic doctrine or the basic

[66]
principio caeli clarum purumque colorem,
quaeque in se cohibet, palantia sidera passim,
lunamque et solis praeclara luce nitorem;
omnia quae nunc si primum mortalibus essent,
ex improviso si sint obiecta repente,
quid magis his rebus poterat mirabile dici
aut minus ante quod auderent fore credere gentes?
nil, ut opinor: ita haec species miranda fuisset.
quam tibi iam nemo, fessus satiate videndi,
suspicere in caeli dignatur lucida templa!   (II, 1030–1039)

[67]
caeli . . . labentia signa   (I, 2)
          . . . caelo stellante serena
sidera . . .   (IV, 212–213)
          . . . noctis signa severa
noctivagaeque faces caeli flammaeque volantes   (V, 1190–1191)
          . . . magni caelestia mundi
templa super stellisque micantibus aethera fixum   (V, 1204–1205)

teachings of Epicureanism, and which were not contrary to known phenomena or the evidence of the senses were acceptable.[68]

We must bear in mind that Greek astronomy, though far developed, was, after all, chiefly theoretical and based on mathematical hypotheses which explained those phenomena that could be observed, but that without such modern instruments as the telescope these hypotheses could not possibly be verified. Lucretius, who seems to have had but little interest in mathematics or understanding of it, felt that one theory was as good as another in a field where verification was impossible, and that in the infinite number of worlds which make up the infinite Universe any of the various causes which he suggested might be exemplified. Consequently, the astronomical speculations of the early Ionian scientists, such as Anaximander, Anaximenes, Xenophanes, and Heraclitus, absurd though they may seem to us, were in Lucretius's opinion quite as adequate as those of the later astronomers for explaining the phenomena; and for the non-mathematician they were certainly easier to understand. That Lucretius was not wholly unacquainted with the teachings of the scientific astronomy of his time is evident from the fact that he gives the current scientific view in discussing the apparent orbit of the sun and in explaining the phases of the moon and eclipses. He is even acquainted with the idea that the earth's shadow is cone-shaped, although, as has been observed, in admitting that possibility he is hardly consistent with his own belief that the earth is a large, flat disk floating on air and that the sun is as small as it looks.

Lucretius is, at least, frank in admitting that his astronomical explanations are only guesses impossible of verification, and he condemns those who accept only one explanation to the exclusion of all others. This is, as one critic points out,[69] 'a very easy-going sort of science,' which only reveals the poet's ignorance of the true theory on which the science of astronomy is based. It is an attitude which would discourage any serious attempt to find out the truth by further research.

While it is thus possible to explain Lucretius's attitude toward astronomy, still, in view of the scientific zeal with which he examines the nature of the Universe and the brilliance and apparent enthusiasm of his scattered references to the glory of the heavens, it is rather a disappointment for an admiring reader to find that in his principal treatment of this subject Lucretius is both unscientific and prosaic.

THE UNIVERSITY OF TEXAS.

---

[68] This was the view of Epicurus; cf. Bailey, *The Greek Atomists and Epicurus* (Oxford, 1928), pp. 369–374.

[69] E. W. Adams, 'Lucretius and his Science,' in *Living Age*, CCII (1894), 734.

IN DOMO RINUCII

Dean P. Lockwood

IN THE twenty-five years that have elapsed since my initial study[1] of Rinucci,[2] there have come to my attention[3] four manuscripts associated in one way or another with Rinucci himself and with a group of scribes who were under his supervision. These manuscripts not only throw new light on the character and activities of Rinucci, but also contribute a bit of chiaroscuro to the picture of humanism as a whole.

I

I begin with the manuscript of Lucan's *Pharsalia* now *lat. 10061* in the Biblioteca Nacional of Madrid,[4] containing 134 unnumbered paper folios,[5] written in a fair book-hand,[6] with marginal and interlinear notes in one or more cursive hands of much smaller size. I have taken the significant phrase 'in domo Rinucii' from its *explicit:*

Lucani liber Vltimus per me MArcellum Calo|philum Rosam De Tarracena Scriptus atque li|gatus[7] Tempore[8] Millesimoquadrigentesimoquadrage|simo-nono Tempore Nicolai pape quinti. Explicit:|in domo domini Rinucii Oratoris clarissimi.

At the bottom of fol. 1ʳ is a monogram.[9]

[1] 'De Rinucio Aretino Graecarum Litterarum Interprete,' *Harvard Studies in Classical Philology*, XXIV (1913), 51–109: referred to hereafter as 'Lockwood.'

[2] I have used the traditional form of the name 'Rinucci,' though the Italian form 'Rinuccio' (as in the *Enciclopedia Italiana*) more clearly indicates the fact that it is a *praenomen*.

[3] Chiefly through the kindness of my friend, Dr. Ludwig Bertalot.

[4] I say 'now' as of 1932. It came to Madrid from the Cathedral Library of Toledo, where it was no. *101-31*. It is described in Octavio de Toledo, *Catálogo de la Librería del Cabildo Toledano*, Part I (Madrid, 1903), p. 123, no. CCLI. Octavio says that it previously belonged to Card. Zelada. Zelada's library, gathered in Rome, was presented to Toledo by Archbishop Lorenzana (cf. G. Valentinelli, 'Delle Biblioteche della Spagna,' *Wiener Akademie der Wissenschaften, Phil.-hist. Klasse, Sitzungsberichte*, XXXIII [1860], p. 88). Zelada must have acquired this ms. from the dispersed library of the Maurists, for at the top of the first page stands 'Ex lib. Cong. S. Mauri Romae,' with the numbers 102 and 336. The Roman office of the Procurator General of the Maurists was maintained from 1633 to 1733 (cf. *Catholic Encyclopedia*). There is no indication as to where the ms. was before it belonged to the Maurists.

[5] A modern hand has numbered, or attempted to number, every ten folios.

[6] Cf. Plate I, 1 (scale considerably reduced).

[7] Rosa's binding was probably practical, not artistic. Unfortunately the question of whether the ms. is still in its original binding escaped my attention while I was in Madrid. Octavio de Toledo, *loc. cit.*, merely states that the binding is 'pergamino.'

[8] 'Tempore' is deleted by a line drawn through it, but the obvious correction, 'Anno Domini,' has not been made.

[9] Cf. Plate I, 2. I have reproduced the monogram with my own hand. Repeated efforts to get a photograph that would include everything on the page were unavailing. There is a very small circle

I can find no other trace of Marcello Rosa nor of the monogram. 'Rosa' is a family name well-known in the Neapolitan region, and 'Calophilus' is surely an appropriate humanistic sobriquet for a calligrapher to assume. The chief problem, however, is to determine the relation of Rosa to Rinucci. Rosa's presence 'in domo Rinucii' was certainly not accidental. Why should such prominence be given thereto, if not to enhance the value of the manuscript? It is tempting to conjecture that Rosa was working as a copyist under Rinucci's supervision; and that Rinucci, therefore, in the Rome of Nicholas V, was eking out his income from the Curia[10] by engaging in the book business. So far as I know, the rôle of *Kopienlieferant* (to use Burckhardt's descriptive term)[11] has not previously been indicated for a genuine humanist, but it has strong inherent probability.[12] Rinucci had but to imitate the scholarly (and only slightly less commercial) pursuits of his life-long friend, Poggio,[13] and the business methods of Vespasiano da Bisticci, in order to become a forerunner of the humanistic editors and publishers of printed books who began to appear within a generation.[14] The relation of minor humanists to the *manuscript* book trade of the XV century is a problem that deserves further investigation.

---

at the right of the monogram, which seems to be an accidental stain. If this monogram is that of the scribe, I can only hazard the reading, MA[rcellus] K[alophilus] T[arracinensis].

[10] The income of lay office-holders in the papal Curia was never great (cf. G. Voigt, *Wiederbelebung des classischen Alterthums* [3rd ed., Berlin: Reimer, 1893], II, 3–4). Nor did minor translators receive lavish honoraria even from Nicholas V (cf. Voigt, *ibid.*, II, 84). That Rinucci considered poverty his lot in life is shown by his early surreptitious translation from Aristophanes, entitled *Penia*—'ut mihi esset ad solamen' (cf. Lockwood, p. 73, *Prooemium*, line 6). Nevertheless in his chronic complaints of ill fortune, he alludes only once to his meager income, namely, *ca.* 1443, in the *Prooemium* to Hippocrates, *Epistula ad Damagetum* (*ibid.*, p. 90, l. 18), where he says, 'cum id pusillum mihi fuit ereptum quo vitam vix tenuem ducebam.' This may refer to a temporary loss of the position of *scriptor*, to which he had been appointed by Eugene IV in Sept. 1440 (cf. W. v. Hofmann, *Forschungen zur Geschichte der kurialen Behörden* [Rome, 1914], II, 114). By the same pope at an unknown date he was made a *custos cancellariae apostolicae*. He held these two minor positions under Nicholas V. Voigt's statement, based on Valla's vague allusion in the *Antidoton in Pogium* (see below, n. 52), that Nicholas V made Rinucci apostolic secretary, is not borne out by Hofmann's records. It was Calixtus III who raised Rinucci to the secretaryship in 1455 and conferred on him for life the 'quarta pars emolumentorum officii custodis.' Ultimately Calixtus raised him to the rank of *secretarius participans* (cf. Hofmann, *op. cit.*, II, 79 and 114).

[11] *Kultur der Renaissance* (9th ed., Leipzig, 1904), I, 110, ftn. 1.

[12] *Explicits* similar to Rosa's are rare, i.e. those which mention scribe and employer (other than owner of the ms.). Wattenbach, *Schriftwesen im Mittelalter* (3rd ed., Leipzig, 1896), p. 487, cites Barptolomeus Johannis who copied Claudian, *De Raptu Proserpinae*, in 1403 'in scholis magistri Matthiae de S. Geminiano electi ad legendam grammaticam Prati.' *Vat. Urb. 383* was copied in 1472 'per Petrum de Traiecto almano (sic) florentiae sub Vespasiano librario.' We must distinguish, as far as possible, between commercial production and private. An example of the latter (if any is needed) is Tortelli's *Suetonius* (*Vat. lat. 1906*), 'Liber Joannis Tortelli quem scribi feci a Joanne Alemanno familiari meo'—not to mention the thousands of manuscripts copied for patrons by professional scribes or even by impecunious scholars.

[13] Cf. E. Walser, *Poggius Florentinus* (Leipzig: Teubner, 1914), 27–28, and B. L. Ullman, 'Poggio's Manuscripts of Livy,' *Classical Philology*, XXVIII (1933), 282–288.

[14] Pomponius Laetus, Aldus Manutius, *et al.*

II

The second manuscript that I have to discuss, *Vat. Chis. H. 181*, belongs to a different category. It is a codex produced by a scholar for his own library. Originally composed of 200 parchment folios in 25 quaternions, it contained nineteen genuine and two spurious orations of Cicero,[15] transcribed by Rinucci with his own hand. At the beginning of orations 1–10 and 20, there are brief rhetorical comments or analyses, presumably Rinucci's own, though perhaps copied from some other source.[16] They are neatly placed in the margins in exactly the same hand as the text[17]—probably written, therefore, at the same time as the text. A peculiar feature of the manuscript—and a useful criterion for identifying other manuscripts copied by Rinucci, if there are any such—is the fact that Greek numerals[18] are used for numbering the folios (α to σ), as well as the gatherings (α to κε). Rinucci also paraded his Greek by using τέρμα for *finis* after each oration,[19] and the longer phrase τέρμα σὺν εὐτυχεία (sic) after the last oration on fol. σ recto. On σ verso, in blue ink, is the note of the illuminator: Ego presbiter nicolaus sanuto hoc volumen, quod amicus meus | intimus rinucius manu propria scripsit, aliena manu miniari[20] | quam mea non sum passus, nostre intime iure amicicie.[21] This is followed by Rinucci's large and flamboyant autograph signature in cursive Greek.

[15] Rinucci's own titles are: (1) de laudibus Gn. Pompeii, (2) pro T. Milone, (3) pro M. Marcello, (4) pro Gn. Plancio, (5) pro P. Quintio, (6) pro Aulo Licinio Archia poeta, (7) pro P. Silla, (8) pro Q. Ligario, (9) pro rege Deiotaro, (10) pro Aulo Cluentio, (11) pro M. Celio, (12) pro L. Cornelio, (13) pro L. Flacco, (14) pro restitutione domus suae ad pontifices, (15) in Clodium pro aruspicum responsis, (16) de provinciis consularibus, (17) ad quirites pridie quam in exilium mitteretur, (18) ad senatum de reditu suo, (19) ad quirites de reditu suo, (20) pro vituperatione Pisonis, (21)—title excised [declamatio in Catilinam].

[16] I give the following two examples:

(a) *pro Milone:* In genere iudiciali est hec oratio. Constitutio secundum Quintilianum libro tertio est coniecturalis, secundum alios iuridicialis assumptiva ex relatione criminis. Exordium secundum alios in genere honesto, secundum alios in genere dubio, nam benivolentiam captat multipliciter in figura gravi.

(b) *pro rege Deiotaro:* Hec oratio in iudiciali genere constituta habet accusationem cum defensione, accusatus enim deyotarus a philippo quod Caesarem voluisset necare, a Cicerone hac oratione defenditur. Constitutio coniecturalis, nam factum negatur, scilicet, deyotarum fecisse contra Caesarem animo inpio. Incidit genus demonstrativum, cum de laudibus deyotari dicitur. Exordium sub dubio genere positum est, nam turpitudo accusatoris cum accusati honestate pugnat.

Cf. also Plate I, 9 for the very brief comment on the *de Laudibus Pompeii.*

[17] Cf. Plate I, 9.

[18] Cf. Plate I, 14 (upper right-hand corner of page) and 8 (Table of contents). The normal line used in the ms. itself over all the Greek numerals will be omitted throughout the present description.

[19] Cf. Plate I, 10.

[20] This refers only to the illuminated initials at the beginning of each oration; the ordinary rubrics are in Rinucci's own hand.

[21] The literary quality of Sanuto's Latin marks him as a scholar; his illuminated initials, moreover, are quite simple and amateurish. Cf. Plate I, 10.

To the text thus completed and annotated Rinucci (so I infer) prefixed a *unio*. These two preliminary folios were left unnumbered, and the first would seem to have been originally left blank. On the recto of the second, at the top of the page, Rinucci inscribed the following *titulus:* Orationes .M.T.Ciceronis mei Rynucii atychi[22] in quibus scribendis | corrigendisque non mediocris quidem mihi labor fuit; and above it he again wrote his Greek signature.[23] On the verso of the same folio he wrote, in his most careful hand, a table of contents, in which each title is followed by a hybrid formula: 'ad Kρ.α.' (= ad cartam.1.), 'ad Kρ.νε.' (= ad cartam.55.), etc.[24]

After he had thus completed the text, with its dozen or so of rhetorical analyses, Rinucci's zeal seems to have flagged somewhat, as the complaint of 'non mediocris mihi labor' in the *titulus* and the increasing haste of his handwriting toward the end[25] would indicate. Moreover certain additions to the commentary were now made in a much more careless style, scrawled clear across the bottom of the page or crowded into the margins with little or no regard for appearances; and—most important evidence of all—Rinucci, merely started the work; its completion he entrusted to two helpers.

The additional material consists primarily of the brief *argumenta* from Antonio Loschi's Commentary on eleven orations of Cicero (the eleven are Rinucci's 1–10, in a different order, and 13). Loschi's argument for the first oration (*de Laudibus Pompeii*) was transcribed by Rinucci himself on the blank portion of the second preliminary folio, beneath the *titulus*, but in a more careless sloping hand and with a finer pen.[26] In the same hasty hand and careless manner he added three rhetorical analyses (to the 14th, 15th,[27] and 16th orations), as well as the very brief notes at the beginning of orations 11, 12, 18, and 19—though one or two of these jottings may belong to the earlier group executed at the same time as the text.

The first helper (whose hand I designate as A), writing rather unevenly across the bottom or top of the page, followed Rinucci's lead by supplying Loschi's *argumenta*[28] for orations 2–10. Furthermore, on the verso of the first preliminary folio, he—or someone with a very similar hand—hastily

[22] The word 'atychi,' though in an erasure and written in slightly larger letters, is probably in Rinucci's own hand, cf. Plate I, 4. The self-imposed epithet *atychus* (sic) is quite in accordance with Rinucci's character and is paralleled by the words 'Rynucius infoelix' in the salutation of the dedicatory epistle to the *First Monodia*, cf. Lockwood, p. 53, ftn. 6.

[23] Cf. Plate I, 4.

[24] Cf. Plate I, 8.

[25] Cf. Plate I, 10.

[26] Cf. Plate I, 16.

[27] Cf. Plate I, 15.

[28] Cf. Plate I, 19, from the argument for the *pro Plancio* on fol. 27ᵛ.

copied another argument for the second oration (*pro Milone*),[29] and on the recto he jotted down brief *initia* of all twenty-one orations.[30]

The second helper (hand B), besides making brief notes and a few corrections throughout the manuscript, supplied (1)—for the thirteenth oration, *pro Flacco*—a brief rhetorical analysis and Loschi's argument (but he inserted this material on fol. ριε as a note to the twelfth oration, *pro Balbo*),[31] and (2)—for the twentieth oration, *in Pisonem*—two extracts from Asconius,[32] namely the *argumentum* and the first *enarratio*.[33]

One more addition to the completed manuscript is of importance: namely, the scraps of writing on fol. σ verso, unconnected though they are with the main contents of the manuscript. Only the first four are of the fifteenth century: (1) perhaps in Rinucci's hand, a definition of *intercalare*, (2) probably in hand A, definitions of *fescennina* and *crepundia*, (3) in a hand[34] (which I call C), not elsewhere found in this manuscript, the first half of Caesar's letter to Cicero (*Epist. ad Atticum*, IX, 16), (4) probably in hand B, a Latin version of the brief epistle from Androcydes to Alexander concerning drunkenness, which at once suggests Rinucci's interest in the Greek epistolographers, especially pseudo-Hippocrates.[35]

Now—to return to hands A and B—who were these helpers? That they actually assisted Rinucci as copyists, and were not merely subsequent owners of the manuscript, is indicated by the fact that they carried on only what Rinucci himself had begun. But this is not all. Their close association with Rinucci is definitely proved by the fact that these two assistants, along with the writer of the letter of Caesar (hand C) are the copyists of *Ms. Florent. Naz. Cent. II–VIII–129*, owned by Rinucci and containing *Rinucciana*.[36] The conclusion is unescapable that we have here three scribes working under Rinucci's supervision. Now Rinucci was surely not so prosperous that he could afford three private secretaries:

[29] Cf. Plate I, 18. This argument, which is much longer than Loschi's (on fol. 11ᵛ), begins 'P. Clodius senator seditiosus erat et tyrannicis moribus . . .' and ends '. . . in thomeas schythiae.'

[30] Cf. Plate I, 17. Hand A is crude, awkward, and variable. Brief samples (as in my plate) tend to accentuate differences rather than establish affinities. I feel only a shade of doubt about assigning 17 and 18 to A.

[31] Cf. Plate I, 22. The 'A' following this footnote is not a clue to the scribe's name, but merely a cross-reference from the similar 'A' on fol. ριη, where the *pro Flacco* begins.

[32] Asconius is cited by Rinucci also, in a brief note preceding the rhetorical analysis of this oration: Ex asconio pediano apparet hoc non esse principium huius orationis, sed aliquantum deesse.

[33] It is possible that B's annotations may have been made at a later date, for his activities seem somewhat more independent than those of A—although, in whatever he did, he may only have carried out Rinucci's instructions. Nevertheless he alone of the helpers supplied one rhetorical analysis; and he apparently corrected Rinucci's own analysis of the first oration, emending the last word (in an erasure) to 'mediocri,' cf. Plate I, 9. There is no doubt, however, that he was associated with Rinucci during the latter's lifetime.

[34] Cf. Plate I, 6.

[35] Cf. Lockwood, pp. 88–94.

[36] See p. 185.

few humanists ever reached that degree of affluence. Nor is it likely that not only three friends, but the same three, would volunteer to act as his amanuenses on two different occasions—and much less likely, as we shall see, in the case of the Florence miscellany than of the Cicero codex. I believe, therefore, that these three helpers were scribes working in his *scriptorium*, and that these scribes occasionally acted as his amanuenses. Marcello Rosa would make a fourth.[37] The three amanuenses, moreover, imitated the hand of their scholarly employer—even though Rosa did not. The imitation was either spontaneous or studied. There is precedent for the latter in Poggio's training of scribes, but Poggio was a calligrapher.[38] It seems more likely that Rinucci's helpers imitated unconsciously, or with a natural desire to flatter. Possibly they were his students.

Rinucci's hand (R) has two outstanding features: (1) complete avoidance of small 's'; only the tall form of this letter[39] is used even at the end of words; (2) the frequent employment in Latin words of certain Greek letters, especially μ (for both capital and small 'm')[40] and final σ, often superposed.[41] The hands of the helpers show these same general traits,[42] they are stronger, however, in A and B than in C.

The chief differentiating features of the various hands are as follows. Hand R invariably uses a ligature for *et* resembling cursive minuscule θ, as tall as 'b,' 'h,' etc. Whether this is another instance of Rinucci's affectation of Greek letters, I cannot say.[43] Hand A has a 'g' with a broad horizontal tail, sometimes absurdly broad.[44] It uses, rather infrequently a ligature for *et* consisting of a horizontal pot-hook with a dependent curved tail, reduced sometimes to a mere wedge.[45] Hand B has a rather variable figure-2 sign for *et*,[46] but its outstanding characteristic is its 'r,' which

---

[37] There is nothing in the text or notes of the Madrid ms. that bears any sure resemblance to the hands of the Chigi and Florence mss., except that certain annotations are in a hand very similar to B —perhaps B itself.

[38] Cf. G. Voigt, *Wiederbelebung des classischen Alterthums* (3rd ed., Berlin: Reimer, 1893), I, 398.

[39] With a tendency to lengthen the horizontal top-stroke, especially in his more cursive hand, cf. Plate I, 9–10 and 15–16.

[40] Cf. Plate I, 10.

[41] Cf. Plate I, 16.

[42] It is this resemblance that led Bertalot to assert that the first 124 fols. of the Florence ms. are in the hand of Rinucci (cf. 'Zwölf Briefe des A. Traversari, *Römische Quartalschrift* [1915], p. *92, ftn. 6). But fols. 51^v (line 15)–55^v of this ms. are surely written by hand B of the Chigi (it is unmistakable), and the remainder of the 124 folios (except part of 3^r and of 5^v–6^v) are probably by hand A of the Chigi. In spite of its variations in size and form, hand A frequently shows, in both mss., the characteristic 'g' and the hooked sign for *et* that differentiate it from R. Cf. Plate I, 11 for the transition from A to B at the middle of fol. 51^v in the Florence ms.

[43] Cf. Plate I, 9–10 and 15–16.

[44] Cf. Plate I, 11 (first half) and 17–21.

[45] Cf. Plate I, 18 and 21.

[46] Cf. Plate I, 22.

often has a long tail hanging below the line, so that it looks like a 'y.'[47] The hand is rather variable and shaky. Hand C, least like Rinucci's of the three, has two striking peculiarities, namely, little curlicues on the vertical strokes of 't,' 'l,' etc. and an outlandish anchor-shaped sign for *et*.[48]

When and why did Rinucci produce this manuscript? As regards the date, there is one significant piece of evidence: the twenty-first oration, of which now (for reasons that I shall explain later) only the concluding four lines remain, was the pseudo-Ciceronian *Declamatio in Catilinam*. On Dec. 31, 1451, Rinucci's old friend and colleague in curial office, Poggio, wrote to an unknown correspondent in Utrecht, requesting a copy of this 'Fifth Oration against Catiline,' which, he declared, was unknown in Italy.[49] If Rinucci, as we may reasonably conjecture, transcribed the text from the copy that Poggio subsequently received, we obtain the date 1452 as a *terminus a quo* for the whole collection—for the manuscript is closely written without variation of style and would seem therefore to have been continuously copied, not gradually assembled over a long period of time. Poggio left Rome in 1453 toward the end of May;[50] if therefore we assume that Rinucci borrowed directly from Poggio, this date becomes our *terminus ad quem*. Otherwise we must extend the time-limit to 1456, the probable date of Rinucci's death.[51] On the whole, however, it seems safe to assign the manuscript to 1452–53.

As regards the purpose of the manuscript, it is clear (as I have already indicated) that it was not, like Rosa's Lucan of 1449, a commercial product of Rinucci's *scriptorium*, but was a labor of love. The contents of the manuscript, however, and especially the rhetorical annotations, throw light on another activity of Rinucci's: Valla apparently refers to his occupying a chair of rhetoric,[52] probably in the University of Rome under Eugene IV. May we not conjecture that he continued, perhaps privately, to profess rhetoric at Rome? Of his earlier pedagogical career we have evidence in his call to the University of Perugia on Nov. 22, 1440, 'ad legendam artem oratoriam et eloquentiam'—though he never actually assumed the chair.[53] In the absence of any evidence that Rinucci shone as a public

[47] Cf. Plate I, 11 (second half) and 22 and the last word in 9 (mediocri).

[48] Cf. Plate I, 5–6.

[49] It was at least unknown to Poggio and the Roman humanists, cf. R. Sabbadini, *Da Codici Braidensi* (Milano, 1908), p. 5 ff.

[50] Cf. Walser, *op. cit.*, p. 222.

[51] Cf. W. v. Hofmann, *Forschungen zur Geschichte der kurialen Behörden* (Rome, 1914), II, 114.

[52] *Antidoton in Pogium*, II, iv (*Opera* [Basileae, 1540], p. 286): Cum enim meum officium vituperas, omnes rhetores vituperas, Guarinum . . . Gasparinum . . . Philelphum . . . Trapezuntium . . . item collegam tuum Rinutium, qui si meliore valitudine esset, adhuc legeret.

[53] Cf. G. B. Vermiglioli, *Memorie di Jac. Antiquarj* (Perugia, 1813), pp. 160 and 164; V. Bini, *Memorie istoriche della Perugina Università* (Perugia, 1816), pp. 548–9.

orator, we may regard Rosa's eulogistic phrase, 'orator clarissimus,' as referring primarily to the profession of rhetoric.[54]

Until the death of Rinucci in 1456 the manuscript undoubtedly occupied an honored place in his library. It must have been a subsequent owner who took offence at the *Declamatio in Catilinam*. He excised its nine folios, including the last page of the preceding oration (*in Pisonem*), but allowed the last four lines of the *Declamatio*, on fol. σ recto, to stand. He also tore off the bottom of Rinucci's table of contents, thus removing not only the offending twenty-first title, but most of the three preceding ones as well, and multilating the *argumentum* in Rinucci's hand on the recto of the same folio.[55] And he erased A's twenty-first *initium*—though it can still be deciphered: Si quid pcbuσ.[56] This mutilation can hardly have been the work of Rinucci himself or of A, even though either of them may have been ultimately disillusioned as to the genuineness of the 'Fifth Oration against Catiline.' A corrector, furthermore (whose rather shaky hand, of *saec.* XV–XVI, is seen in many marginal notes)[57] inserted three whole folios to fill lacunae: one between ϟϛ and ϟϛ to supply the passage 'quendam quasi . . . honestissimorum' in *pro Cluentio* (63, 176–65, 182), two between ρθ and ρι to complete the text of *pro Caelio* from 'De vi . . .' (29, 70) to the end.[58] Finally, the Piccolomini arms with papal

[54] In view of the cumulative evidence of Rinucci's interest in rhetoric, I am now incl.ned to ascribe to him two brief works (unmentioned in my previous study), preserved anonymously in *Ms. Berolin. lat. quart. 558* (cf. Lockwood, p. 59). The first follows immediately after Rinucci's translation of Plutarch's *Quid principem decet* and is entitled 'Isocratis rhetoris quod discipline radix amara sit capitulum' (*inc.* 218ᵛ, 'Isocrates rhetor apud grecos longe clarissimus . . . ,' *expl.* 219ᵛ, ' . . . recte disseruit'). The second (*inc.* 219ᵛ, 'Paupertas sane devitari debet . . . ,' *expl.* 220ᵛ, ' . . . de paupertate precepit') is entitled merely 'Orationis formula,' and is immediately followed by Rinucci's translation of Plato's *Axiochus*. These two *oratiunculae* are actually translations from Aphthonius, to wit, the Χρεία λογική from the third *Progymnasma* and the Γνώμη προτρεπτική from the fourth (cf. Rabe's Teubner text, 1926). Rinucci may have wanted to pass these translations off as his own compositions, just as he did in the case of his *Penia fabula* (=Aristophanes, *Plutus*, 400–626). It is interesting to note that Aphthonius' *Progymnasmata* occur in Greek manuscript collections of oratorical and rhetorical models, i.e. those which contain genuine orations (of Demosthenes, Aeschines, etc.) + pseudo-epistolographers + rhetorical declamations. Such a ms. is *Vat. gr. 67, saec.* XIV (cf. Giov. Mercati, 'Scritti d'Isidoro il card. Ruteno,' *Studi e Testi*, 46 [Roma, 1926], preliminary pp. 1–2). Rinucci, who translated, in whole or in part, five orations of Demosthenes and four collections of pseudo-epistles, may have owned such a manuscript and have drawn his Aphthonius extracts therefrom.

[55] At a much later date someone mended the torn folio and hastily restored the titles of the table of contents—omitting, of course, the twenty-first. The *argumentum* on the recto was left in its mutilated state.

[56] The *p* and *c* are overlined.

[57] Cf. Plate I, 14. Note the Rinuccian influence in 'μetello.'

[58] The modern foliation, in Arabic numerals stamped in the lower right-hand corner, begins with the preliminary folios, 1–2, which were not numbered at all by Rinucci; the folios now numbered 3–98 were Rinucci's 1–96; the present 99, inserted by the corrector, was not in Rinucci's volume at all; the folios now numbered 100–112 were originally 97–109; the present 113 and 114 were inserted by the corrector; the folios now numbered 115–195 were originally 110–190; Rinucci's 191–199

tiara, crowded into the lower margin of fol. *a* recto, indicate that the manuscript was in the collection of Franc. Todeschini (Pius III) in Siena in the second half of the XV century, whence it passed in the XVII century into the 'Chigi Library' of Pope Alexander VII.

III

Under the same roof and on the same book-shelf stood another manuscript, now *Vat. Palat. 1493*, whose contents had lured even the miserly Rinucci[59] to expend five gold florins for its purchase. It contained models for the humanistic study of Greco-Roman oratory: fols. 1–4, Cicero, *de Optimo Genere Oratorum* (a very popular work in the XV century, as being the prototype for *prooemia* to humanistic translations from the Greek); 4–102, seven orations of Cicero;[60] 102–186, Bruni's translation of Demosthenes, *de Corona*, and Aeschines, *in Ctes*. On the following blank folio (187^v) are two items in Rinucci's hand: the price[61] and his signature,[62] 'Mei Raynucii[63] de castroleonis.'[64]

IV

The last of the four manuscripts associated with Rinucci, no. *II–VIII– 129* in the Biblioteca Nazionale of Florence, is a humanistic miscellany,[65] begun under his supervision and copied for him in large part by the same amanuenses (A, B, and C) whose hands appear in the Chigi manuscript.[66] Originally it consisted of seventeen paper gatherings, of which nos.

---

having been removed, the present 196 was Rinucci's 200 (=σ); and a new final folio, numbered 197, has been added.

[59] Cf. the savage attack on his avarice in an epigram by P. C. Decembrio, published by Bertalot, *Römische Quartalschrift* (1915), *92, ftn. 6.

[60] Viz. (1) *pro Ligario*, (2) *pro Marcello*, (3) *pro Rege Deiotaro*, (4) *Pridie quam in exilium iret*, (5) *Cum senatui gratias egit* (a fragment; ends VIII, 20 ' . . . esset sustentavit'; followed by 23 blank folios), (6) *de Laudibus Pompeii*, (7) *pro Milone*.

[61] Cf. Plate I, 12.

[62] Cf. Plate I, 13.

[63] What is the correct form of Rinucci's name? It is, of course, a *praenomen*, appearing most frequently in the form 'Ranuccio' (Ranutius); and our Rinucci is so designated in contemporary documents at Perugia (cf. ftn. 53). 'Raynucius' is either a traditional mediaeval variant, pronounced as spelled; or possibly it is derived from the well-attested form 'Renucius,' through the itacistic Greek Ραινούκιος (pronounced Ρεν-) = Rainucius = Raynucius. Our Rinucci generally used the form 'Rinucius,' which he hellenized as Ρυνούκιος = Rynucius. The name was also unfortunate in lending itself easily to mistakes in copying, so that Rinucius was often wrongly transcribed as 'Rimitius,' Rainucius as 'Raimitius,' etc. *ad lib.* But what was our Rinucci's family name? G. Ghizzi (*Storia d. Terra di Castiglione Fiorentino* [Arezzo, 1883–86], I, 114) asserts, without citing his evidence, that it was Papi!

[64] The place-name 'Castrum-leonis' is obviously a punning version of Castiglione. Rinucci came from Castiglione Aretino (hence 'Rinucius Aretinus'), officially called Castiglione Fiorentino, cf. G. Ghizzi, *op. cit.*

[65] Described by G. Mazzatinti, *Inventari dei Manoscritti delle Biblioteche d'Italia*, XI (1901), pp. 247–8.

[66] Cf. ftn. 42.

1–4, 6–11, 13–16 were *sexterni*, nos. 5 and 17 were 'nines' (18 fols. each), and no. 12 a 'seven' (14 fols.), making a total of 218 fols. These folios were numbered by the use of an alphabet of 26 letters and signs repeated eight times (though the omission of the first 'e' made the first series consist of 25 fols. instead of 26),[67] followed by the first eleven letters of the ninth series—which brought the grand total to 218 fols. The alphabet consists of the 22 Latin minuscule letters from 'a' to 'y,' followed by Byzantine cursive zeta[68] and the three signs 7 (*et*), 9 (*us*), and ꝶ (*rum*). These letters and signs were placed in the lower right-hand corner of the recto of each folio. The use of an alphabet augmented by abbreviation signs (especially when placed in the lower corner) at once suggests the signatures of early printed books, and raises the question whether this curious system of foliation was introduced into the manuscript by a subsequent owner of the late XV or early XVI century, familiar with printers' devices; but against this suppostion is the fact that the letters are not only in an early XV-century hand, but are definitely Rinuccian in form and are therefore to be ascribed to him or to one of his helpers: the angular sign for *et* points to A, who is the initial and the chief scribe of the miscellany. The use of Greek zeta for Latin 'z' is a Rinuccian touch.[69] Moreover a haphazard miscellany of this sort stands in much greater need of folionumbers for ready reference than does a manuscript of a continuous work with numbered books and chapters. The manuscript, therefore, could hardly have long remained without folio-numbers; in fact, if it was bound blank (as a prospective miscellany volume might well be), the folios may have been numbered before any writing was begun—and a few blank folios or those containing rejected material may have been removed without any effect on the existing texts.

There is no trace of any other numbers in the manuscript, except the modern Arabic figures (probably of the XVIII century) in the upper right-hand corners. These numbers run from 1 to 201, for seventeen folios had by that time been lost, namely, two (probably blank) from the twelfth gathering, i.e. x and y of the sixth series between fols. 149 and 150; the entire fifteenth gathering, i.e. y–ꝶ of the seventh series plus a–g of the eighth, between fols. 174 and 175, entailing the loss of most of Bruni's *Dialogus in Petrum Histrum*; two from the sixteenth gathering, i.e. m and t of the eighth series, the first between fols. 178 and 179 and the second between 184 and 185, both from Apuleius, *de Deo Socratis*;[70] and the last

---

[67] The omission must have been a mere error in the numbering, for there is no break in the text, and the gathering is a complete *sexternus*.

[68] For a similar zeta from the Chigi ms. see Plate I, 8.

[69] Is it possible that this alphabet had some affinity in Rinucci's mind to Greek numerals, which consist of the regular Greek alphabet plus three signs—though the total is 27 instead of 26?

[70] I do not know whether anything is missing from the text.

folio (probably blank) from the seventeenth gathering, i.e. 1 of the ninth series. The XVIII-century foliation was probably inserted by Canonico Antonio Bardi, whose signature appears seventeen times in the manuscript; six times (e.g. 48ᵛ) with the date 1745 and twice (e.g. 75ʳ) with the place-name Colle. Finally the manuscript came into the possession of the modern Rinuccini family[71] (who, I suspect, had fallen unto the familiar error[72] of confusing a Rinucci with a Rinuccini), whence it entered the Biblioteca Nazionale Centrale in 1850.

The first point to note about the miscellany is that it falls into two parts, divided by the blank page 145ᵛ. It is the first part only that is associated with Rinucci,[73] as shown by the contents, the scribes, and the Greek subscriptions.

The contents are briefly as follows: (1) fols. 1-15, *Rinucciana*, i.e. a quasi *carteggio Rinucciano* consisting of 23 epistles: three written by Rinucci himself; four addressed to Rinucci (one from F. Barbaro, two from Traversari, one from P.[74] archbishop of Crete); and finally sixteen written by Barbaro, Traversari,[75] Poggio, and others to various correspondents, in which Rinucci is only incidentally mentioned or concerned ('remember me to Rinucci', etc.), i.e. a meager collection of memorabilia flattering to Rinucci's vanity (like a modern album of press-clippings); (2) 15-89, a selected lot of contemporary Latin epistles and orations—standard works of humanistic literature—by Bruni, Leon. Giustiniano, Guarino, Poggio, Cincio, etc.; (3) 91-125, rhetorical material analogous to that in *Palat. 1493*, namely (omitting a few stray unimportant classical excerpts), a selection of thirteen of the well-known model orations of Gasp. Barzizza; ps.-Cicero, *Invect. contra Catilinam* ('non est . . . expuleritis') and ps.-Catiline, *Responsiva* ('Si subtiliter . . . confiteri');[76] Bruni's translation of Demosthenes' *Third Olynthiac;* and brief orthographical and lexicographi-

---

[71] See the modern note on fol. 201ᵛ.

[72] The latest example is T. O. Achelis, who ascribed Alamanno Rinuccini's translation of Philostratus, *de Vita Apollonii*, to Rinucci (cf. 'Die hundert äsop. Fabeln des Rinucci,' *Philologus*, LXXXIII [1928], pp. 55-88).

[73] The second part, though a continuation of the miscellany, has nothing to do with Rinucci. It is written in six or seven successive non-interlocking hands, some of which are much later and all of which are entirely unrelated to those of the first part. These later scribes or owners must have filled up the codex after it had passed out of Rinucci's possession, perhaps after his death. The conventional τ·ε·λ·ο·σ on 199ᵛ is not in Rinucci's hand. The contents suggest no particular associations with Rinucci: 146-149, Guarinus, *de Diphthongis* (?); 150-153, (?) Leonardus Aretinus, *de Litterarum Salutationibus;* 154-162, Guarinus, *contra Nicolaum;* 173-174, Leonardus Aret., *Dial. in Petr. Histrum* (fragmentary); 175-185, Apuleius, *de Deo Socr.;* 185-190, Marrasius, *Angelinetum;* 190-199, Claudivius (?), *de Vita b. Hieronymi.*

[74] Probably Petrus Donatus archiepisc. Candiensis, 1418-26.

[75] In all there are five letters by Traversari (one in Greek). They are edited by L. Bertalot, *loc. cit.*

[76] Cf. L. Laurand, *Berliner Philologische Wochenschrift* (1911), Sp. 504, and L. Bertalot, *ibid.*, Sp. 983.

cal excerpts from Marius Vict., Val. Probus, and Guarino; (4) 127–145, Bruni, *de Summo Bono* (=*Isagog. Moralis Discip.*) and *de Studiis et Litteris*, followed by chap. 47 of Jerome, *contra Jovinianum*, containing the translation from Theophrastus, *de Nuptiis*.

Omitting minor jottings, some of which may have been added later, we find that the first part of the manuscript was written by four scribes:[77] A, B, and C of the Chigi, and a fourth (N) whose brief contribution of less than two pages (5^v line 21–6^v line 5) is relatively insignificant. The chief scribe was A, who wrote 1^r–5^v (line 20),[78] 6^v (line 6)–51^v (line 15),[79] 58^v–124^v. B wrote 51^v (line 15)[80]–55^v. C wrote 127^r–145^r. The following fols. are blank: 56^r–58^r between B and A; 90^v in A's portion (after a page which he seems to have written while suffering from the ague); 125^v–126^r between A and C;[81] and 145^v after C's portion at the end of the first part of the manuscript. It is significant that the portions of A, B, and N are more or less interlocked: N, contributing epistles nos. 11 and 12 to the group of *Rinucciana*, is embedded within A; the transition from A to B at 51^v is in the middle of a sentence in the middle of a work (Giustiniani, *Orat. in funere Car. Zeni*). C, however, is separated from B by two folios.

Finally, this first part of the manuscript, like the Chigi, is tied together by Greek subscriptions (τέλοσ twice, τέρμα eleven times, τέρμα σὺν εὐτυχεία seven times, τέρμα τοῦ λόγου once), probably inserted by Rinucci with his own hand, to wit, at the end of the *Rinucciana* on 15^r within hand A; on 55^v at the conclusion of B's contribution (Giustiniani, *op. cit.*); on 66^v, 75^v, 83^r, 89^r, after various works of the second group, all in hand A; on 92^r, 94^v, 96^v, 97^v, 100^r, 105^v, 106^v, 109^r, 110^r, 111^r, 112^v, 114^r, 115^v (τέρμα τοῦ λόγου), and 120^r, i.e. after almost every piece in the group of *rhetorica*, all in hand A; and on 135^v, within hand C, at the end of Leonardus Aret., *de Summo Bono*, τέρμα σὺν εὐτυχῇ. (sic),[82] followed by a small cursive Greek signature[83] of Rinucci, resembling the larger signatures in the Chigi manuscript.

In regard to the date of the manuscript—and I am here concerned only with the first part—there is no definite clue, but obviously it cannot be far removed from that of the Chigi. The cooperation of Rinucci and his three

[77] See ftn. 42.

[78] Not including the Greek epistle, which is in Rinucci's hand (cf. Plate I, 7, especially ρυνούκιε, and the autograph signature in Plate I, 5).

[79] Cf. Plate I, 11 (first half).

[80] Ditto (second half).

[81] The preceding and following pages, 125^r and 126^v, contain wholly unrelated material, inserted by two XVI-century hands.

[82] This is probably intended for an abbreviated form. I assume that the three marks that follow are mere flourishes. Cf. Plate I, 5. Elsewhere Rinucci wrote εὐτυχεία.

[83] Cf. Plate I, 5.

chief helpers or quasi amanuenses can hardly have preceded the period of
his settled and relatively prosperous years in Rome,[84] *ca.* 1443–1456. If
my interpretation of the evidence offered by the Madrid and the Chigi
manuscripts is correct, the association of Rinucci with certain scribes is
attested for the years 1449–*ca.* 1452; how much earlier it began and how
much longer it continued, I cannot say. These were apparently the years
of Rinucci's greatest renown. The two chief manuscripts of his collected
versions from the Greek were transcribed about this time: *Balliol. 131*
between 1449 and 1454, *Vat. lat. 305* in 1453 or shortly after.[85] Now the
contents of the Rinuccian part of the Florence manuscript, so far as they
are dated or readily datable, cover the period from about 1414 to 1427.
To refer the actual copying of the manuscript to this date (*ca.* 1427) is
unthinkable: in his earlier years of trial and tribulation[86] Rinucci could
hardly have commanded the services of three or four helpers; nor is it
likely that anyone, however fortunate, could retain three amanuenses
for twenty-five years. I am more inclined to the hypothesis that the
Florence manuscript is the latest of the four that I have discussed; that
its contents reflect the reminiscences of an old man; and that the copying
of the first 145 folios, in which Rinucci transcribed the one Greek epistle
and inserted the many Greek subscriptions along with his final signature
of approval and ownership, was completed not long before his death.[87]

HAVERFORD COLLEGE.

---

[84] Cf. Lockwood, p. 55.

[85] Cf. Lockwood, pp. 57 and 59.

[86] Cf. Lockwood, pp. 51–55.

[87] Rinucci's library cannot have been extensive, but in addition to the three Latin manuscripts
that still contain his signature he must have had a few Greek manuscripts in his possession also.
Whether any of these have survived, I cannot say. There is no sure indication of what works he
brought home from Greece or how long he kept them. His reputed codex of Archimedes was a *cause
célèbre*, cf. Sabbadini, *Carteggio di Giovanni Aurispa* (Roma, 1931), pp. 161–162. In the *Prooemium*
to his translation of the *Epistles* of Abaris *et al.* he mentions the miscellany described by Traversari,
Epist. VIII, 28. It—or what was left of it—was therefore still in Rinucci's possession *ca.* 1443 (cf.
Lockwood, p. 60): ' . . . me ad recensendum fragmenta quaedam graece scripta, ne dicam codices,
converti. Haec inter volvendo incidi in trium doctissimorum hominum epistolia tria . . . ' (Traversari
had found the same *epistolia* in the same ms., when he borrowed it from Rinucci, about fifteen years
before.) I have already mentioned (ftn. 54) the possibility that Rinucci owned a corpus of oratorical
and rhetorical models (Demosthenes, pseudo-epistles, and Aphthonius). Sabbadini's assumption,
Le Scoperte (Firenze, 1905), p. 49, that Rinucci owned every Greek author that he translated or even
cited, is unjustified, e.g. Rinucci's allusion to Herodotus in the *Prooemium* to the translation of Plato's
Axiochus (cf. Lockwood, p. 103) is taken from Gellius, XVI, 19.

DESCRIPTION OF PLATE

(Sigla of manuscripts: M = Madrid, Bibl. Nac., *lat. 10061*. F = Florence, Bibl. Naz. Cent., *II–VIII–129*. Vc = *Vat. Chis. H. 181*. Vp = *Vat. Palat. 1493*.)

(Scribes: R = Rinucci. A, B, C = Rinucci's assistants in F and Vc. N = scribe of fol. 6^r in F.)

1. Rosa's hand: M, 1^r.
2. Rosa's (?) monogram: M, 1^r.
3. N's hand: F, 6^r.
4. R's Greek and Latin signatures: Vc, 2^r.
5. C's hand+R's Greek subscription and signature: F, 135^v.
6. C's hand: Vc, 196^v.
7. R's Greek hand: F, 3^r.
8. R's Table of Contents: Vc, 2^v.
9. R's careful text and note+last word (*mediocri*) in B's hand: Vc, 3^r.
10. R's rubric and hasty text and Greek subscription+Sanuto's illuminated initial: Vc, 153^v.
11. Transition from A to B: F, 51^v.
12. R's price-note: Vp, 187^v.
13. R's Latin signature: Vp, 187^v.
14. R's Greek folio-number+Corrector's hand: Vc, 178^r.
15. R's hand in hasty note: Vc, 153^v.
16. R's hand in Argument: Vc, 2^r.
17. A's (?) Initia: Vc, 1^r.
18. A's (?) hand in extra Argument: Vc, 1^v.
19. A's hand in regular Argument: Vc, 27^v.
20. A's hand: F, 3^r.
21. A's hand: F, 9^r.
22. B's in Argument: Vc, 120^r.

R's Latin hands: careful book-hand—4, 8, 9; hasty book-hand—10, 14 (*uerŭt* only); informal hand—12, 13, 15, 16.

R's Greek hands: signatures—4, 5; book-hand—5, 7, 10; numerals—8, 14.

A's hand 11 (first half), 17 (?), 18 (?), 19, 20, 21.

B's hand: 9 (*mediocri* only), 11 (second half), 22.

C's hand: 5 (Latin), 6.

N's hand: 3.

Rosa's hand: 1, 2 (?).

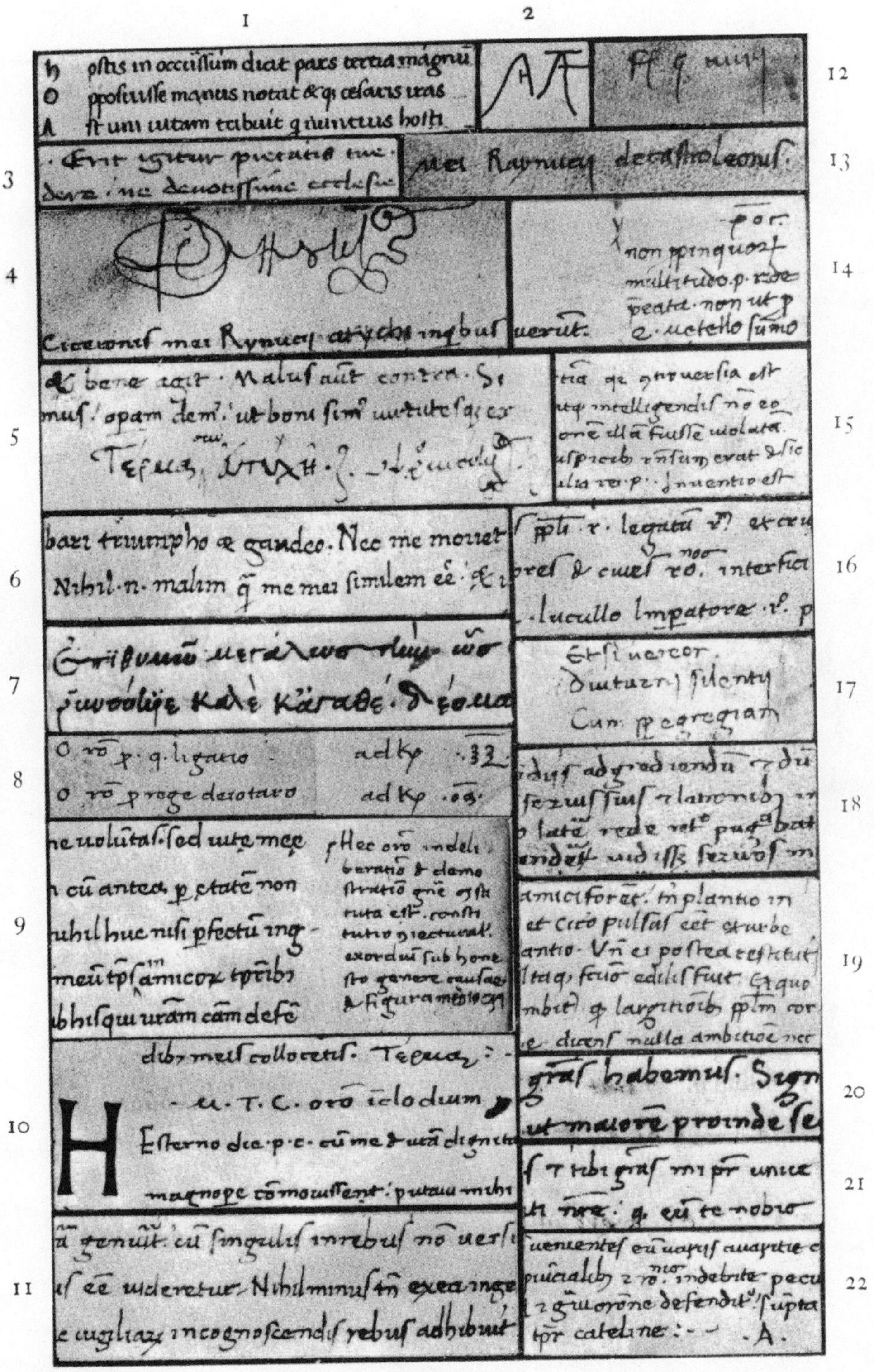

PLATE I

Hands of Rinucci and his Helpers

(See *Description of Plate* appended to article).

A MANUSCRIPT OF ALCUIN IN THE SCRIPT OF TOURS

Elias Avery Lowe

Of the scores of manuscripts that have come down to us in the beautiful script of Tours, few contain the works of Alcuin,—few, that is, considering the popularity of his writings and his eminence in the very centre which produced these masterpieces of calligraphy. In his monumental publication on the script of Tours,[1] Professor Rand describes four Alcuin manuscripts as written in the Tours minuscule. They are, in the order of Rand's series, as follows:

No. 38: *Liber de Virtutibus et de Vitiis* (MS. Troyes 1742) written, according to Köhler, in Alcuin's time.

No. 42: *Expositio in VII Psalmos Paenitentiae et alia* (MS. Cologne CVI). Regarding the Turonian origin of this manuscript Rand entertained doubts: probably it originated at Cologne.[2]

No. 48: *Expositio in Iohannem* (MS. Cologne CVII), reproduced on pl. XLI.3 of Vol. II.[3]

No. 62: *Martinellus*, including Alcuin's sermon on St. Martin (Vatican Regin. 495), written, according to Rand,[4] 'under Alcuin or not long after his death.'

Eight other Alcuin manuscripts had reached the stage of being considered candidates for Tours membership, but on careful examination Rand rejected them: these Ishmaelites are listed under No. 232.[5]

It is therefore of some interest to publish another Alcuin manuscript whose graceful lineaments proclaim it at once a true product of Tours, copied only a few years after Alcuin's death, hardly more than a score or so. The manuscript in question contains Alcuin's *Commentary on Ecclesiastes*[6] and is preserved in the Cathedral Library of Salisbury under the

---

[1] Rand, E. K., *Studies in the Script of Tours*, I, *A Survey of the Manuscripts of Tours* (Cambridge, Mass.: The Mediaeval Academy of America, 1929).

[2] *Ibid.*, p. 115. See Jones, L. W., *The Script of Cologne from Hildebald to Hermann* (Cambridge, Mass.: The Mediaeval Academy of America, 1932), 40–43.

[3] Rand, E. K. and Jones, L. W., *Studies in the Script of Tours*, II, *The Earliest Book of Tours, with Supplementary Descriptions of Other Manuscripts of Tours* (Cambridge, Mass.: The Mediaeval Academy of America, 1934); for the description of the ms. see p. 95.

[4] Vol. I, p. 126.

[5] *Ibid.*, pp. 203–206.

[6] Schenkl, K., *Biblioteca patrum latinorum britannica*, No. 3725.

press-mark 133.[7] It was in very bad condition till it was restored last year. Both the beginning and the end are lost and there are other lacunae, the precise contents being: Cap. II. 14–IV.9; IV.12–IX.10; X.2–9(fragments), and two scraps from X.10.

What follows is a purely paleographic description in the manner employed in *Codices Latini Antiquiores:*

Foll. 47+2 scraps (five folios are missing, one between foll. 14ᵛ and 15, four between 45ᵛ and 46); 245×180 mm. ⟨168×110 mm.⟩ in 19 long lines. Ruling on the hair-side, 2 bifolia at a time; the centre opening and foll. 2ᵛ and 7 of each quire show the direct impression. Double bounding lines. Gatherings probably of eights, with hair-side outside, signed by Roman numerals in the centre of the lower margin (fol. 22ᵛ has the quire-mark IIII). Punctuation: the medial (occasionally the high) point is used for all pauses; the question-mark and some accents over monosyllables are original; many commas, points, and accents were added. Citations are marked by an s-like flourish in the margin opposite each line cited. Abbreviations include *b;*, *q; = bus, que;* the Nomina Sacra *dŝ, dī, dō, dnō, xp̄s,* etc. *= deus, dominus* and cases, *Christus,* etc.; *iśrl = Israel; nr̄o, nr̄is = nostro, nostris; ur̄t, ur̄a = vester, vestra; ·ē·, ·ēē·* (between 2 dots) *= est, esse;* the usual *per, prae,* and *pro* symbols; *ī = ter* at line-ends; *tur* is not abbreviated. Omitted *m* is indicated by a horizontal stroke over the vowel. Spelling: a*d*flictionem, a*d*quirendi, i*n*precatur, yet a*m*moneo. Simple initials alternately red and black project into the margin; on foll. 27ᵛ, 28, 36ᵛ, 37 are black initials crudely filled with red, doubtless by a later illuminator. Parchment is smooth, well prepared, and generally thin. Ink brown. Script is a beautiful Caroline minuscule of the Tours type which flourished under Alcuin's successor Fridugisus and which Rand calls the Perfected Style. Half-uncial of the unmistakably Tours type is used for the Biblical passages commented upon. The shafts of tall letters have sinuous horizontal serifs, which, according to Rand, are a survival of an earlier stage. Here and there the uncial form of *N* occurs. Ligature of *rt* is frequent in the minuscule; ligatures with *e* are very frequent in the half-uncial. Many marginalia in ordinary minuscule (see plate).

Written doubtless at Tours, to judge by the script, probably at the same time as Bamberg H. J. IV. 12, containing [Boethius, *Arithmetica,*[8] with which our ms. agrees in the size of the written space and the number of lines.

Our manuscript supplies a not very accurate text of Alcuin's *Commentary on Ecclesiastes,* but it is in all probability the oldest. Such as it is, this copy survived not in its place of origin, but in England. Precisely when or how it reached Alcuin's native land it is hard to say. There are no ancient Anglo-Saxon annotations in the manuscript to prove that it

---

[7] Thanks are due to Mr. N. R. Ker for calling my attention to this manuscript, and to Canon Christopher Wordsworth and the Chapter of Salisbury for their kindness in sending the manuscript to Oxford.

[8] Rand, *op. cit.,* No. 71, pls. LXXXVII, LXXXVIII.

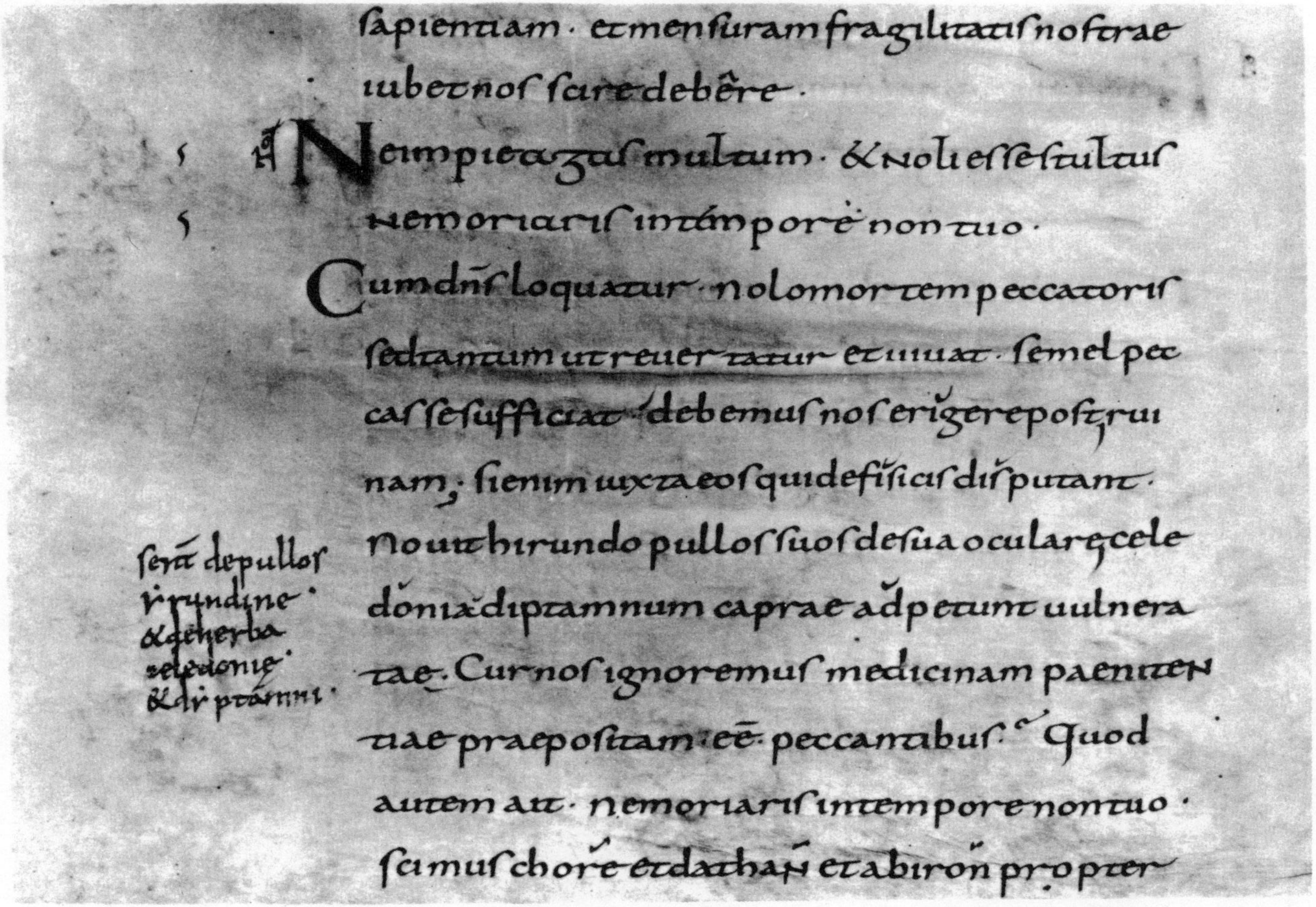

sapientiam. et mensuram fragilitatis nostrae
iubet nos facere debere.

Nempe pietas tumultum. et noli esse tultus
memoriae in tempore non tuo.

Cum dñs loquitur nolo mortem peccatoris
sed tantum ut retribuitur et inveniat semel pec
caret sufficiat. debemus nos erigere post tru
nam; fient unius zaeos quidem efficare dis putant.

Non ut hirundo pullos suos de sua oculare cele
dum ad damnum aprae ad peaunt uulnera
tae. Cur nos ignoremus medicinam praesentem
tae praepositam. cē peccaturus. quod
autem ait. memorari in tempore non tuo.
famus corbore et dia ian et a biron propter

fort de pullo
r inadñe
alphonta
afptonus
& ñ praxmu.

PLATE I
Salisbury, Chapter Library, Ms. 133, fol. 31ᵛ.
Alcuin in Ecclesiasten. Saec. IXᵛ.

had been read in England; but not even that evidence would be conclusive, since Anglo-Saxon was actually written in Alcuin's monastery at Tours—how could it be different, with Alcuin living and writing there?— as may be seen from the Laurentian copy of Donatus on Vergil (MS. XLV.15),[9] and the British Museum manuscript of Jerome on Isaiah (Egerton 2831),[10] manuscripts which prove that Northumbrian and Tours scribes worked side by side at least in Alcuin's time.

INSTITUTE FOR ADVANCED STUDY,
  PRINCETON, NEW JERSEY.

[9] *Ibid.*, pl. XIV.
[10] *Ibid.*, pl. XIII; and Lowe, E. A., *Codices Latini Antiquiores*, II (Oxford, 1935), No. 196.

MODON—A VENETIAN STATION IN MEDIAEVAL GREECE

Stephen B. Luce

PYLOS IS frequently visited by those lovers of the Classics, who, with their Thucydides fresh in their minds, wish to see the scene of the surrender of the Spartans to the Athenians in 425 B.C.; and by modern Philhellenes, who wish to gaze on the site of the battle of Navarino, which decided the independence of Greece as a nation. But they are usually either ignorant, or wilfully neglectful, of the fact that just a short distance to the South, at the tip of the Messenian Cape, is one of the most interesting and imposing ruins to be seen in Greece—a ruin not ancient, to be sure, but quite as picturesque as anything antiquity can offer. To those who can see nothing but the ancient in Hellas, this paper will have but little interest; she had, nevertheless, a romantic and fascinating history in the Middle Ages, and of the mediaeval sites in Greece, few have the appeal and charm of Modon.

Modon, then, lies to the South of Pylos, to which it is connected by a carriage road which can be negotiated by motor in about thirty minutes. This also has the honor of being the first modern road in Greece—it was built in 1828–1829 by the French military engineers of the expeditionary force of Marshal Maison, who occupied the Morea when Ibrahim Pasha evacuated it, after the battle of Navarino.[1]

The interest of Modon is not wholly mediaeval, for under the name of Pedasos it appears in Homer[2] where it is given the significant epithet ἀμπελόεσσα; this epithet, and the name of the group of islands adjacent, Oenussae, and its subsequent name Methone, which Curtius wished to derive from μέθυ,[3] hints that the wine industry was the great feature of the region in antiquity.

It figures in the Peloponnesian War as having been unsuccessfully besieged by the Athenians in 431, who were beaten off, and the town relieved by Brasidas, who first appears in the history of the war at this point.[4]

---

[1] This statement is based on the fact that there were no other modern carriage roads in 1828–29. See Jean Alexandre C. Buchon, *La Grèce Continentale et la Morée*, Paris, 1843, p. 458. The eminent scholar of Mediaeval Greece, Mr. William Miller, in a conversation with the writer, believes this statement to be true.

[2] *Il.*, IX, 152, and 294.

[3] *Peloponnesos*, Gotha, 1851–52, II, 171. 'Die Heroine Methone galt für eine Tochter des Weinmannes Oineus.'

[4] Thucydides, II, 25, Ed. H. S. Jones, Oxford, 1898.

Of its later history in antiquity we need say nothing as it was of little importance. It was besieged and occupied by Agrippa shortly before the Battle of Actium[5] and was visited by Pausanias,[6] who mentions a temple of Athena of the Winds, the image in which was said to have been dedicated by Diomede, and a sanctuary of Artemis and 'a well of water mixed with pitch' which no longer exists.

In 1125 it had become, through the laxity of the Byzantine administration such a dangerous nest of pirates that the Venetian Doge, Domenico Michiel, was obliged, for the safety of the Republic's commerce, to descend on it and raze it to the ground.[7] And so it was apparently unoccupied for nearly one hundred years. There would seem to be some evidence, however, that by 1199 it may have been inhabited and that Venetians were seeking commerical privileges there, for it is specifically mentioned in a treaty in that year between Venice and Byzantium, in which free trade is granted to Venetians at Methone and other places.[8]

The real history of Modon from our point of view begins in 1204. That year which marked the sack of Constantinople by the Latins of the Fourth Crusade and the creation of the Latin Empire of the East, saw the partition of Byzantine territory among the conquerors. To Venice were assigned, among other places, the districts of Patras and Methone with their appurtenances. But Fate had already intervened, and it was not for several years that Venice was able actively to assume her dominion. For in 1204, Geoffroy de Villehardouin, nephew of the famous chronicler of the Fourth Crusade, on his way to join his uncle and his brothers-in-arms, was driven out of his course by contrary winds, and finally found a haven of refuge at Modon.[9] Here he spent the winter of 1204 and made the place his headquarters, from which he proceeded to the conquest of the Morea and the formation of the Principality of Achaia. His first capture was of Coron, and it is from now on that the names of Modon and Coron become inseparable among Latins and Greeks alike—for Curtius[10] notes the Modern Greek term τὰ Μεθωνοκόρωνα. To the period of Villehardouin's brief occupation Buchon[11] assigns part of one of the towers in the wall, but a very superficial examination of the walls of Modon made in 1928, convinces me that the entire wall is Venetian.

    [5] Dio Cassius, L, 11, 3. Ed. Cary, *Loeb Classical Lib.*, 1917. Strabo, VIII, 4, 3. Ed. H. L. Jones, *Loeb Classical Lib.*, 1927.
    [6] IV, 35, trans. J. G. Frazer, London, 1913 (2nd ed.). He calls it Μοθώνη, whence the name Modone or Modon. For a commentary, see J. G. Frazer's *Pausanias*, III, 452 ff. London, 1913 (2nd ed.).
    [7] W. Miller, *The Latins in the Levant* (London, 1908), p. 24, etc.
    [8] Miller, *loc. cit.*, p. 5.
    [9] See the *Chronicle of Villehardouin*, trans. Sir Frank Marzials, London, 1911, p. 85. (*Everyman's Lib. ed.*)
    [10] *Loc. cit.*, p. 195, note 42.
    [11] *La Grèce Continentale et la Morée*, pp. 456–457.

Villehardouin maintained possession of Modon in spite of the Venetian title obtained in 1204, for two years, and then, having by rather questionable means ousted Champlitte, his companion in arms in the conquest of the Morea, he was obliged, in order to make his peace wih Venice, to cede them Modon and Coron in 1206, when their long first occupation began, lasting very nearly three centuries. Of the extant fortifications of Modon, the present enceinte with the exception of the northern, or land wall, belongs to this long period; and I am also inclined to believe that the little island fortress[12] should be dated at this time and not later, though it was unquestionably strengthened by the Turks after their occupation. This makes Modon roughly contemporaneous with Aigues-Mortes, which it somewhat resembles in little, and a visit to Modon enables one to reconstruct the Provençal fortress when it, too, was on the sea, and St. Louis led his crusades out of its harbor.

Modon and Coron were the first territorial possessions of Venice on the Greek mainland, and remained for a long time the most important. As the Eastern trade of the Most Serene Republic increased, Modon, in particular, assumed a great importance in Venetian commercial supremacy. Situated at the tip end of the westernmost of the three capes of the Peloponnese with a fair natural haven protected from the severe westerly winds, harbor works were undertaken, a mole built, and the town supplied with walls, the thickness and strength of which were the admiration of all travellers to and from the East. All the commercial convoys stopped at this port for supplies, to refit, to repair damages from wind or weather, and to take on fresh pilots—to Jaffa on the outward voyage and to Parenzo on the homeward. It is not my purpose to enter very largely upon the history of this Venetian occupation, but rather to quote the accounts of certain travellers to and from the East as they can show something of life in a Venetian colony at the height of the Republic's prosperity.

The numerous wars between Venice and Genoa could not but have an effect upon such important colonies, so we are not surprised to find Modon a naval station for the protection, as an outpost, of the rich and important colony of Crete, and as a place of mobilization for Venetian naval forces. And in all these wars Modon played her rôle and had the humiliation of witnessing the total defeat of the Venetian navy in 1354 in the celebrated battle of Sapienza, named for the large island opposite, when the Genoese took prisoner the Venetian commander, Niccolò Pisani, and six thousand others and captured thirty galleys as prizes, which were sent to Genoa. It will always remain a mystery why Doria, the Genoese commander, did not dash up the Adriatic when Venice herself must needs have fallen

---

[12] The Μόθων λίθος of Pausanias.

into his hands. But as it was, he did not even stop to capture Modon, and it is probable that the victory cost the Genoese dear, as they were willing to arrange a truce of four months. Revenge was obtained fifty years later, however, when in 1403, the Venetians under the famous Carlo Zeno defeated the Genoese fleet under the French Marshal Boucicaut in a bloody battle, off Modon, taking many prisoners and much booty in ships and money. In this battle many recriminations were made against the Venetians by the French and Genoese, who accused them of disloyalty, but the conduct of Boucicaut towards Venetian merchants in Syria, where he had been campaigning against the infidel, had been unnecessarily stupid, severe, and grasping, as there was a nominal state of peace between the two nations.

Our best descriptions of life in Modon come from the accounts of travellers in the fifteenth century, the last hundred years of Venetian occupation. Most of these travellers were pilgrims bound to or from the Holy Land. Venice had the virtual monopoly of the oversea pilgrimage business, and a regular convoy sailed every June to take pilgrims, returning in December. A large number of them were Germans and two, Felix Faber of Ulm, and Bernhard von Breydenbach, wrote their itineraries as a sort of guidebook for pilgrims. Faber, in particular, gives a statement of what a pilgrim needed to carry with him in the way of clothing, money, food, bedding and the like, while von Breydenbach, who was a man of means and substance in his community, took an artist with him, who made drawings (inserted as woodcuts into the book) of the different places visited; and it is thanks to von Breydenbach that our earliest picture of Modon is due—a picture not unlike its appearance today, if one imagines the walled town inhabited. These books belong in the period between 1480 and 1484. Previous to that, however, the Spaniard, Pero Tafúr,[13] had visited Modon in 1436 and describes it as follows: 'On the fourth day (from Corfu) we came in sight of the city of Modone, . . . and there we landed in order to provision the ship, and to enable the master and the passengers to transact certain business there, for they were Venetians and the place belongs to Venice. There are two thousand inhabitants and the sea encloses it on both sides. It is well walled and sufficiently strong, but flat. I saw there numerous gardens supplied with all kinds of fruit, and the soil is very productive, like that of Andalucia. Lodging is good, the language is Greek, but the place is governed from Venice. . . . The Venetians have these possessions in the Morea because they are vital for their trade. The people are very wealthy, for these places are the

---

[13] Pero Tafúr: *Travels and Adventures, 1435–1439*, trans. Malcolm Letts, New York and London, 1926 (In 'The Broadway Travellers' series). For Modon, pp. 49–50, and 153, where he speaks of the town as 'very unhealthy.'

ports of discharge for Greece and the Black Sea for all classes of merchandise. We remained there six days . . . . From Modone to the island of Crete the distance is 350 miles which we compassed in two days and two nights, after which we arrived at the harbor of Candia.'

Our best authority, however, is the worthy pilgrim Felix Faber, whose name originally was doubtless Schmidt, as, being a monk and a scholar he probably Latinized it.[14] He made two pilgrimages to the Holy Land about 1483, and on his return from the second pilgrimage remained ten days in Modon, where they arrived December 9, O.S., as the convoy had met with bad weather and was obliged to undergo repairs. From him we learn that there were several monasteries established by the Roman Catholics at Modon, notably the preaching Friars (Franciscans) with whom he associated while there and where he had many friends as a result of his first pilgrimage. He also mentions a 'house of the Teutonic Lords' where he slept, evidently an establishment like the Fondaco dei Tedeschi at Venice. He speaks of going up to the walls of the town and walking around upon them 'and we admired its impregnable fortifications.' He incidentally mentions that Modon is 'said to be midway between Venice and Jerusalem.'

To understand Faber one must realize that with certain exceptions all the Morea was in the hands of the Turks when he wrote. Those exceptions (Modon, Coron, *Monemvasia*,[15] Nauplia) were in the possession of Venice, which had recently lost Argos and Euboea to the infidel.

Faber gives us a hint as to the kind of houses and streets within the walls in a section that is worth quoting at length. 'On December 12th, through the whole preceding night there was a horrible wind and no one dared to sail. At midnight, as I was wont, I rose to say matins and having said it under the shadow of the Blessed Virgin, I entered the kitchen . . . and saw burning brands glowing under the ashes . . . . I ascribed it to the force of the winds and yet was not strong enough to extinguish them. At daylight when I had read matins . . . I saw such a glow through the door through which I had come out, and in the house also, but thought no more than that someone else had arisen, . . . So I hastened, and entering the house, saw nobody and then looking around in the direction from which the glow had come, saw that the timbers under the fireplace had begun to burn. When I saw this I was alarmed and ran to the room of the host of our inn, where he slept with certain of our knights, awoke him, and asked him to get up and come out with me quickly, just as he was, as

[14] *Fratris Felicis Fabri Evagatorium in Terrae Sanctae, Arabiae, et Egypti Peregrinationem*, ed., C. D. Hassler (Stuttgart, 1849), III, 330–344, (187a–191b). The translations are my own.

[15] Faber speaks of Monemvasia being Turkish and that ship captains gave the town a wide berth. W. Miller (*Essays on the Latin Orient*, p. 239) states that Monemvasia belonged to Venice from 1464 till 1540. What is meant is that the famous vineyards were in Turkish hands.

I had something important to tell him; for I did not wish to mention fire there for fear of starting a panic: as it seemed to me that we could extinguish it without any disturbance. When he came out, I said, "See, master, the house is beginning to catch fire; where is water?" So water was brought and we put out the fire without any noise or disturbance . . . the timbers were burned through the thick foundation, and this was why the brands burned under the ashes, because there was a draught from below. When, then, we had put it all out, the master of the house said to me, "Felix, how fortunate are your matins and vigils! Through them my house and the entire city are saved from fire, and all of us from confusion and danger!" To which I gave answer, "Our help is in the Name of the Lord!". I surely did arise at a good hour, for if I had waited even the sixth of an hour, the whole house would have been in flames, and consequently the adjoining houses: for this house was of wood, and very old, of the dryest kind of timbers and with party walls to similar houses (vallata sibi similibus domibus) in a congested, narrow street, and there was a terrible wind which would have carried the fire through the entire city: we could in no way I know of have escaped the flames, but must have all perished at once; and if there had been a means of escape, the Greeks, seeing their city burned, would doubtless have thrown us into the flames, or cast us in chains to extort a recompense in money to satisfy their loss. All, then, when day broke, gave thanks to the Lord inasmuch as He had delivered us that day from great danger.'

The day following the fire (December 13th) was a feast day of St. Lucia, when mass was celebrated and the pious pilgrims visited the churches and inspected the relics which they contained—going first to the Cathedral, 'which is consecrated to St. John,' and in which was preserved the body of St. Leo, 'a German pilgrim who had died among the Turks, and was renowned among them for many miracles,' the head of Athanasius, bishop of Alexandria, and two fingers of Sts. Cosmas and Damianus. At the end he adds, 'For the churches of the Greeks, which also are there, we cared nothing.' In fact so bitter was the feeling between these two branches of the Christian religion, that the Greeks preferred the rule of Mohammedan Turks to that of Catholic Venetians, and this preference continued during the second Venetian occupation.

The following day, December 14th, another interesting entry occurs which still further illuminates life at Modon in the first Venetian period. 'While we were eating,' he says, 'the heavens darkened and lightning and thunder began to flash and rumble in such wise as I never remember to have heard it: for the earth seemed to quake and the buildings to tremble, and we doubted not that the lightning had struck in some place nearby: and our apprehension was correct, for it struck two galleys and stunned all on board . . . and killed one man . . . the physician and surgeon for the whole fleet. . . . After the thunder and lightning followed a great inundation of rain, so much so that the waters ran through the streets of the city like rapid rivers, for which inundation the inhabitants of Modon were especially glad, as their cisterns were all filled with water; for they had been empty for many months, and they had suffered a dearth of water nor was there in the city any water save that which they brought in from a certain cistern which stood a long way outside, next the convent of the Minorites. For in these parts there are no rivers nor springs, nor frequent rains, and inasmuch as they do not have such a storm more than once or twice in a year, they suffer a very great lack of water.'

Thus we get a fairly complete and very vivid picture. Poor timber houses, closely congested within the walls and fronting on narrow, crooked streets—no water except what some chance rain could provide for the cisterns built to catch it, and yet apparently little disease that is deemed worthy of note. Esteemed and prized by Venice along with Coron, the two being called 'Oculi capitales communis,' it was nevertheless a miserable place to live in and was so considered even then.

On the following day is an item of equal interest. (December 15th) 'We went over to the market, and saw many Turks bargaining with the Christians. For there are Turks, neighbors of the people of Modon, and these Turks raise hogs, and fatten them, and bring them to Modon to sell to the Christians, because, like the Jews, they themselves do not eat pork; and especially when they see a fleet or convoy arrive, they come with their herds of swine, and do such a good business that for less than one mark one may buy a fat porker. The men from the galleys buy and kill them, burn off the hair—saving only the bacon fat, and all the bacon and lard of two or three pigs they cram into the hide of one, sew it up with a needle and so carry it to Venice. . . . I believe that in those days while we remained at Modon over 6000 such hides were brought on board the galleys . . . and every pig was thus equivalent to three or four; for the city of Venice gets its bacon and lard from this place; and sausages are also made there in great quantities, which are sold by the ell.

'Fruit is without value there, so that one can buy a basket full of the best and finest fruits for five or six marks . . . and everybody, even we pilgrims, bought a basket for himself. But of the wine which grows there, what shall I say, since the very thought of it alone delights me! for there there grows a muscat wine whose bouquet and noble name a certain wine has taken to itself which grows in Calabria[16] . . . which in comparison to the wine of Modon is hardly as water. It is plentiful and cheap, and finer than the Cretan wine, wherefore at Ulm, Modon wine is sold at a higher

[16] 'in aulone Tridentino juxta Tramindam villam.'

price than Cretan—and both are called Malmsey. But the market is good for other things also and is exceeding prosperous; and it is extraordinary that the Turks have not long ago destroyed the place; but perhaps they spare it on account of the trade which they have with the Christians, which would cease if they sacked the city.'

Then follows a description of Modon, its fine walls and defences, and of a suburb outside where the markets were held. Of this suburb the principal inhabitants were Gypsies. Within the city the negotiations of the merchants took place as opposed to the noisy market. 'The city,' he continues, 'is the seat of a bishop; the church is humble, the clergy poor, the people divided' ('humilis ecclesia, miser clerus, distractus populus').

On the following day Faber mentions the arrival of pilgrims from Britain who had gone overland to Jerusalem 'by circling the Black Sea,' and were planning to take ship from Modon for Sicily and Rome; 'for at Modon one may find sailings to every port inasmuch as it is, as it were, midway to every land and sea.'

So much for Faber; and I think that he gives a very vivid picture of the importance of Modon during the Venetian occupation as a port of call, and of life within its walls. Another pilgrim who left an account of the place was one Canon Pietro Casola,[17] whose trip was in the year 1494, six years before Modon fell. His itinerary from Venice is given—three weeks were necessary to go from there to Modon, the ship calling at Parenzo, Zara, Lesina, Ragusa and Corfu. Leaving Venice on June 4th, they reached Modon on the 25th, the longest call being that at Ragusa where they arrived on the 14th and left on the 16th. Five days were required from Ragusa to Corfu and four from Corfu to Modon. A stop of two days was made at Modon which they left on the 27th. Casola went ashore and was bitter about the lack of food and lodging to be obtained. He describes the place as follows: 'The city is in a plain. The sea washes the walls and it has a port capable of receiving the largest ships. It has strong walls with drawbridges at every gate which are four according to my reckoning. It is well furnished with towers, and on the towers and the walls there are large pieces of artillery of every size. Towards the mainland it is very strong, and is being continually strengthened. The Signoria is adding there a large moat, and a double line of thick walls and it will be a stupendous thing when it is finished.

'There is a large suburb, also walled. It seems to me that the greater part of the silk industry is carried on in the said suburb; certainly many Jews . . . live there, who work in silk. . . . I entered the city where I did

<hr>

[17] *Canon Pietro Casola's Pilgrimage to Jerusalem in the Year 1494*, trans. M. Margaret Nowett, Manchester, 1907, (Publication of the University of Manchester, Historical Series, no. V). For Modon, see pp. 191–194, 319, 380 notes 65 and 66.

not see either house or palace worthy of description; for its size it has many houses and they are close together. I think there are few inhabitants, for in the finest and widest street there, the houses appeared to be shut up for the most part, and when I stood in the market place, I did not see many people. Those I saw, besides that they are Greeks, . . . are thin and ugly to look at. The majority of the houses are built of timber.'

He speaks with contempt of the churches as 'miserable' and the cathedral as being 'badly kept in every way,' and 'a very wretched affair.'

In Casola's period the wine of Modon had begun to be impregnated with resin, which is done today. 'They say that the wines would not keep otherwise. That odor does not please me.' This is important because apparently in Faber's time it was not resinated. As opposed to Faber he says, 'I did not see much good fruit.' Later he mentions that good Malmsey can be obtained.

'The city,' he continues, 'is governed by a Captain and a Governor of the Castle who are sent by the Signoria, and they are changed every two years.' In his time the Governor was Ser Antonio Venier, the governor of the suburb Ser Pietro Gradenigo.

The account given by Casola shows a decline in Modon's prosperity from the days of Faber. This is doubtless due to the fact that the fear of the Turks was growing more and more acute and that Christian people were leaving for other Venetian posssesions. And six years later, in 1500, Modon and Coron finally fell into the hands of the infidel. The account of the fall of Modon has been made familiar by the graphic account by William Miller.[18] It was bombarded for one month by Sultan Bajazet II, who commanded the Turkish army in person. A foretaste of what was to happen was afforded by the capture of Lepanto (the ancient Naupactos) by the Turks, and at the request of the governor of Modon, Cabriel, additional men, munitions and money had been sent for the defence, and most of the women and children had been removed to Crete. The garrison of 7000 men was in excellent morale, Bajazet's 500 siege guns produced little effect, and his army of over 100,000 could not force the town. So discouraged was he that at the end of a month he was about to raise the siege when the arrival of four Venetian galleys from Corfu with reinforcements and supplies caused the overjoyed garrison to leave their posts and rush to the mole to welcome the new arrivals. The walls were deserted; Bajazet's janissaries swarmed over; and thus the very event that should have saved the city caused its loss. The inhabitants and garrison rushed back to retrieve their lack of discipline, but it was too late; in despair they set fire to the town which burned to the ground, and they fought heroically to the bitter end. Local tradition tells that the survivors

[18] *Latins in the Levant*, p. 495 f.

made their last stand in the little island fortress at the south. The Turks killed all over twelve years old as they found them, even the bishop being slain in cold blood as he was addressing his flock of non-combatants in the Cathedral. The life of the governor was spared, and he was made prisoner, but later escaped. Modon was at once repaired and strengthened by the Turks and repopulated from the Morea, and as its loss brought with it that of Coron, the revenues of the two places were consecrated to Mecca.

The history of Modon during the first Turkish occupation (1500–1686) is eventless, save that an attempt, almost successful, was made in 1531 to capture and hold it by the Knights of Malta, who, however, were only able to sack the city and carry off 1600 prisoners.

Sometime after 1571, when the battle of Lepanto had been fought and won by Christendom, there is some evidence (though it cannot be said to be proven) that a very distinguished stranger visited Modon—perhaps the most distinguished man who ever set foot within its walls. If, as I like to believe, he did enter the town, he was received with scorn and contumely. A Christian slave, captured by Moslem galleys—one among many—would be measured only by what he would bring in the market, and one who was maimed was not regarded as of any great worth. Nevertheless this man, who came into the town in manacles, and with his left hand amputated as a result of his wounds, was the greatest man whom Modon ever received up to then or since—for his name was Miguel de Cervantes.[19]

We now come to the second Venetian period. Morosini landed at Coron in 1684–85 and captured the place, and leaving Modon for the moment, took Kalamata and, aided by the warlike Mainotes, some of the castles in that region. In 1686 he captured the two castles of Old and New Pylos, and then having isolated Modon, started to besiege it. Although well fortified and with excellent artillery and garrisoned by one thousand men, (an English authority, Bernard Randolph, speaks of a total of one hundred guns)[20] it offered but a feeble resistance and capitulated on July 10th, 1686. At that time it had a population of 4000. The division of the rich booty found in the town was the cause of much discontent among the Hanoverian mercenaries in the Venetian service, who were dissatisfied for other reasons as well, and among whom Morosini was personally unpopular for his severity, and was furthermore charged with favoring Venetians at their expense.

[19] It is usually believed that the Story of the Captive in *Don Quixote* is based on the experiences of the author in the period of his enslavement by the Turks—and the Captive was at Modon, which he erroneously describes as an island.

[20] Bernard Randolph: *The Present State of the Morea*, etc., p. 6. Reference is to the Third Edition. London, 1689.

After the capture of the Morea by Morosini, Venice was faced with the problem of administering it, and for fiscal purposes, seven districts were created, Modon being the seat of one. Later these districts were reduced to four and the records of Modon transferred to Navarino. Owing to the cruelty of the Turks in the rest of the Ottoman Empire many refugees were established in the Morea, and we hear of Chiotes and Armenians at Modon, as well as Cretans and even a few Bulgarians. These Chiote refugees, many of whom were Roman Catholics, revived the silk industry which had been allowed to die after the first Venetian occupation had ended. But there was great dissatisfaction among the Greeks, who always preferred Mohammedan domination to that of another Christian sect, and who disliked Catholics worse than outright infidels.[21]

The second Venetian domination lasted only thirty years. In 1715 war was again declared by Turkey and an immense force was assembled under the command of the Grand Vizier Ali Cumurgi to reconquer the Morea. The Venetians decided, owing to the poverty of their resources, to defend only five places—Corinth, Nauplia, the "Castle of the Morea" at the entrance of the Gulf of Corinth, Modon, and Monemvasia. It had been hoped to save Coron, Argos and two castles in Maina as well but Venice had only 8000 men to defend the Morea against at least 70,000, so this further concentration was necessary. But Modon was lost not so much by the lack of strength of her garrison as by the timidity of the Venetian admiral, Delfino, whose fleet lay off Sapienza, but who declined an engagement with the Turkish fleet, fearing a defeat, as his was the only fleet at that time sailing the seas under the lion-banner of St. Mark. Then the garrison mutinied and Modon passed a second time into Turkish hands, and remained under Ottoman rule until it became a part of the independent Greek nation.

There was, indeed, one time when Modon was seriously threatened by a foreign invader who for the first, but not the last time, intervened in the affairs of Greece and exerted influence upon them. In 1770 Russia, under that most extraordinary figure Catherine the Great, declared war upon Turkey, and the Empress' favorite, Alexis Orlov, was given a small expeditionary force to penetrate the Morea and arouse the Greeks against the infidel. Orlov was a handsome man who wore a uniform well, but he was devoid of tact and of the most elementary military capacity. Moreover, his fleet was small and his troops were insufficient and ill equipped. He unconsciously imitated Morosini by selecting Coron as the first place to attack, but he found it impossible to capture. He did, however, succeed in obtaining Navarino and he penetrated the Morea to Mistra and Tri-

[21] For a good account of this period, see W. Miller, *Essays on the Latin Orient*, Cambridge University Press, 1921, pp. 403–427.

polis, both of which places fell to his forces, reinforced by Greek levies. From Navarino he sent Prince Dolgoruki with a small force to reduce Modon, but the arrival of Albanian reinforcements enabled the Turks to defeat Dolgoruki, capture all his artillery and raise the siege.[22]

In the period between the Russian fiasco and the final cession to Greece Modon was visited by various travellers, who fortunately wrote of their travels. Among these may be noted François Auguste René, Vicomte de Chateaubriand (1806),[23] who made here his first landing on 'the classic soil of Greece,' François Charles H. L. Pouqueville[24] (whose book was published in 1827, a good many years after his visit), and, greatest of all, Col. W. M. Leake, who visited the place in 1805 but whose book was not published till 1830.[25] At that time all agree that it was a miserable place. In Pouqueville's time the fortress mounted eighty guns, twenty-four of which had been captured from the Russians. Pouqueville also speaks of the silting up of the harbor, which today is impossible for anything but small craft, the steamers that stop there lying outside the mole. In his day there was a population of about 1600 Turks and outside the walls a Greek population of some 8000 (estimated) who depended on the town, and who lived in 52 small villages. Of these about 1000 (estimated) lived in the outskirts of Modon. In his time the culture of silk had been abandoned and oil, cotton, grain, and wine were the principal products. But the chief trade was in negro slaves.

Leake, who of course was an army officer, comments on the wretched state of the fortifications, and the 'poverty and idleness' of the Turks residing there. In speaking of the granite column in the square, still standing, he tells of the local name for the Venetian lion which formerly surmounted it, 'τὸ ἅγιον σκυλί'—'the sacred dog!'

In the Greek War of Independence Modon was from beginning to end in Turkish hands. The Greeks were never able to obtain it or Coron, and in fact it was at Modon that Ibrahim Pasha, with his Egyptian troops, landed in 1825 to subdue the Morea. The destruction of part of his fleet in the harbor by a daring raid of Miaoulis did not prevent him from achieving most of what he set out to do. As it was, however, after Navarino, when the French landed an expeditionary force in the Morea, Ibrahim surrendered those fortresses in which he held garrisons, to them— his *amour propre* would not permit him to cede them to the Greeks direct.

The first scholar of mediaeval Greece to examine Modon, Buchon,[26]

---

[22] The best account I have seen of the Russian fiasco is in George Finlay, *Greece under Ottoman and Venetian Domination* (Edinburgh, 1856), p. 311 ff.

[23] *Travels in Greece*, Eng. Trans. Phila., 1813, pp. 71–75.

[24] *Voyage de la Grèce*, 2nd ed. Paris, 1826–27, VI, 63 ff., 67 ff., 265.

[25] *Travels in the Morea*, London, 1830, I, 428–434.

[26] *La Grèce Continentale et la Morée*, pp. 455–458.

who visited the town in 1840 or 1841 mentions the column in the square and seeks to see in the inscription on it a reference to Morosini. The reading of Leake, however, is to be preferred and it is not likely that Morosini's name can be read here. Buchon reads MORO (SINI) while for the same place Leake reads BR–. Buchon reads a date of MCCCCLXXXIII (which is impossible for Morosini), Leake . . . MCCCCLXXXXIII a difference of ten years. Furthermore in a Latin inscription Morosini's Latinized name of MAVROCENIVS would have been employed.[27]

Only once more does Modon appear in history and then indirectly. In 1850 at the time of the claims of the notorious Gibraltar Jew, Don Pacifico, against the Greek Government, Great Britain addressed a note to Greece, supporting him and other claimants and finally asserting that the island of Sapienza, opposite Modon, was part of the Ionian Islands, then under British protection. This note was followed by a blockade of the Peiraeus by a British squadron, and the whole affair reflected but little credit on Great Britain, even the historian Finlay, who was one of the claimants concerned, criticizing the violent action of a strong nation against a weak, which all the bluster of Palmerston's 'Civis Romanus sum' speech could not explain away. As for Sapienza, it was handled for Greece by the veteran Leake, who in a most able little pamphlet so completely disposed of the British claim that it was quietly dropped.[28]

Today Modon is but the shadow of its former greatness. Its harbor has silted up so that only the smallest craft can anchor within the mole; the town inside the walls has long been abandoned and is in ruins, while a village of poor houses of some 2000 inhabitants exists to the north of the walls on the site of the Jew and Gypsy suburb of which Faber and Casola speak. The culture of the vine, now as all through its history, appears to be the principal source of income of the inhabitants; and a sound wine is produced, much esteemed by the natives, but owing to its resinated condition, not palatable to many Europeans. If left alone it would be the muscat of which Faber speaks.

The fortress preserves much of its former strength and impressive character. The entrance is from the north, across a deep wide moat which dates from the first Venetian occupation but which was bridged by the Turks. The present northern walls panelled with the lion of St. Mark are dated by their character and by an inscription in the second Venetian period. We pass through a thick gate to a space which shows that the outer northern wall was a curtain with a second wall of earlier date behind

[27] See Buchon, loc. cit., p. 457: (a classic case of making a stone say what you want it to say, at all costs), but see Leake, loc. cit., p. 431, for a more accurate reading.

[28] For this episode, see W. Miller, The Ottoman Empire and its Successors, Cambridge Univ. Press, 1923, pp. 179–181; W. M. Leake, On the Claim to the Islands of Cervi and Sapienza, 1850.

it. Passing through a second gate we enter a square in which is a column standing some 12 feet high, already referred to above, on top of which there was originally the winged Lion of St. Mark. In this square was always the palace of the Governor; here as late as a century ago, Ibrahim Pasha had his headquarters, and after him, Marshal Maison. Today no house remains, nothing but a church, which *may* be on the site of the Venetian cathedral. Beyond, a mass of ruins of houses, churches and cisterns fill the enclosure of the walls. In one church usually identified by travellers with the cathedral, may be seen a number of remains of Roman and Byzantine columns and a Byzantine inscription, while the presence of the base of a minaret shows that it was a mosque in Turkish times. When I visited Modon in 1928 a southwest gale was blowing, the sky was black and threatening, and the surf was dashing up against the crumbling walls and towers on the seaward side, reminding one of Faber's day of the thunderstorm. At the southern end, connected by a short causeway, to which entrance may be obtained through a fine sea gate, is the little fortified islet on which the desperate remnant of the Venetian garrison made their last stand, to be cut down to a man by the Ottoman hordes on that August day in 1500 when Modon fell and her greatness and importance fell with her. Two gates on the east lead to the harbor and these were the gates through which the pilgrims entered or left the town —near the southernmost of these (if I interpret Faber aright) was the German inn, and over one of them may still be seen a medallion of the Venetian Lion, crumbling away like the tower on which he is carved, reminding the chance visitor of a nation which has ceased to exist, and suggesting that in Greece, after all, one may perhaps learn more of the greatness of Venice than in the City on the Lagoons herself.

Boston, Mass.

THE DE SYLLOGISMIS CATEGORICIS[1] AND INTRODUCTIO AD SYLLOGISMOS CATEGORICOS OF BOETHIUS

ARTHUR PATCH McKINLAY

THIS PAPER is an outgrowth of a previous article entitled: *Stylistic Tests and the Chronology of the Works of Boethius*.[2] This earlier work presented accepted data bearing on the chronology of the works of Boethius. It then undertook to apply the method of Wicenty Lutoslawski[3] to fill in the gaps left vacant by other research. The results were striking. By the use of hundreds of stylistic tests embodying thousands of instances I corroborated the findings of Brandt[4] who had utilized the internal evidence and cross references furnished by the works themselves. The query then presented itself: Given a large body of writings, granted that the relative dates of nearly all are definitely known, provided that the tests from style and direct evidence corroborated each other in all known instances, may we not be warranted in making use of stylistic tests to place the few uncertain works? Answering this question in the affirmative, I proceeded to classify the works of Boethius into four periods: *viz.*, first, of non-Greek influence; second, of Greek influence; third, of transition; fourth, of Ciceronian influence. Taking up the uncertain works, contrary to the more or less accepted opinion I separated the *De Arithmetica* and the *De Musica*, putting the former in the first period and the latter in the fourth. Separating the *Analytica*, I put the *Priora* in the second class and the *Posteriora* in the fourth. I concluded that the *Christian Tractates* were not school boy exercises but mature products of the pen. When I came to the *De Syllogismis Categoricis*, I ran up against a snag. The work would not fit in anywhere. This set me thinking: 'Is my whole method wrong? Does this discrepancy invalidate all my findings?'

Musing thus, I noticed that there was something peculiar about the work in question. Its style is noteworthy. It has an introduction far too elaborate in embellishment for the rest of the work. After an exordium stuffed with metaphors taken from road, bridge, and house building,

---

[1] For the plural instead of the singular see Samuel Brandt, 'Entstehungszeit und zeitliche Folge der Werke von Boethius,' *Philologus*, LXII (1903), p. 238, note 4.

[2] *Harvard Studies in Classical Philology*, XVIII (1907), pp. 123–156.

[3] *The Origin and Growth of Plato's Logic, with an Account of Plato's Style and of the Chronology of his Writings* (London: Longmans, 1897).

[4] *Entstehungszeit*, pp. 141–154; 234–279.

209

from edged tools, from groping in fog, from tasting and hearing, three from wrestling, including sweating, struggling, and dodging, from besieging towns and taming horses, Boethius immediately gives notice how barren and unadorned in style his treatment shall be. He keeps his promise, if indeed it is his work, by presenting us a rare collection of barbarisms by the side of which the rest of his works wells forth a spring of Ciceronian Latinity pure and undefiled. Rocco Murari,[5] noticing these peculiarities of style, would make this work, or at least the first book, a medieval reworking. Samuel Brandt[6] found trouble with certain references in the *De Syllogismis Categoricis* to the *Analytica Priora*. Of the references, four are in the past, one in the future. He got out of the difficulty by interpreting the future as a second future, *zweiten futurums*. He translates the passage in question: 'Si qua vero desint, in Analyticis nostris calcatius exprimemus' as follows: 'Wenn etwas fehlen sollte, so wird dafür auch schon gesorgt sein,' or to anglicize, 'if anything should prove lacking (in our treatment), it will have been already provided for in our *Analytica*.' This interpretation is, of course, not a demonstration and merely serves to accentuate our quandary in regard to the *De Syllogismis Categoricis*.

Lastly in my earlier work[7] I had pointed out a confusion in the manuscripts involving the title of the *De Syllogismis Categoricis*. Later manuscripts (s. xii–xiii) have the title of our editions, but early manuscripts (s. ix–x) call it an *Introductio* which is the title of another work of Boethius as it appears in our editions, namely the *Introductio ad Syllogismos Categoricos*. This confusion of the manuscripts and editions concerning the titles of these works is but a reflection of the interrelation of these works that has troubled students, an interrelation which it is the purpose of this paper further to investigate.

To arrive at a clear understanding of the question involved, it will be helpful, first rapidly to survey all the works of Boethius that are related to the works in question, then to take up the theories that deal with them. A large proportion of the writings of our author consisted of translations from Greek authors and of commentaries thereon. No small portion of these dealt wholly or in part with the *Peri Hermeneias* of Aristotle, with much reliance on Porphyry.[8] Five of these are extant. From references in the works of Boethius it has been inferred that two others once existed. To take these up in detail, the most important are *Prior et Secunda Editiones Peri Hermeneias*. The former comprises about two hundred

---

[5] *Dante e Boezio* (Bologna: 1905), p. 92.

[6] *Entstehungszeit*, pp. 252–254.

[7] P. 143.

[8] Bidez J., 'Boèce et Porphyre,' *Revue Belge de Philologie et d'Histoire*, II (1923), p. 198.

Teubner pages, the latter five hundred. The *Prior*, as the title shows, was written first. We also have Boethius himself for corroboration. In the *Prior* he often refers to the *Secunda* as in the future, e.g., *Prior Editio*:[9] 'Secundae editionis series explicabit.' The *Secunda* was still unfinished after two years of work.[10] These works on interpretation themselves, though in mind, were not taken up till after the *Commentarii in Categorias*.[11] As the *Commentarii in Categorias* was being written in 510, the year of Boethius' consulship, we fix the dates of the works *Peri Hermeneias* roughly, *Prior*, 511, *Secunda*, between the years 511–514. To compare the two works, we have it from Boethius himself that the principal difference is one of brevity and simplicity. The *Prior* is for less advanced thinkers; the *Secunda*, for those who wish to go more deeply into the subject.

Two other works are the *De Syllogismis Categoricis* and the *Introductio ad Syllogismos Categoricos*. These have already been discussed as furnishing the problem of this paper. The former consists of two books; only the first of these deals with interpretation; the second book treats of categorical syllogisms. In compass the *Introductio* is about twice the length of the *De Syllogismis Categoricis*, Book I, and one-third the length of the *Prior Editio*. The *De Syllogismis Categoricis*[12] seems to have been written between the two editions of *Peri Hermeneias*. The *Introductio* was written shortly after the *Secunda Editio Peri Hermeneias*. Brandt[13] has made a careful analysis of the subject matter of the *De Syllogismis Categoricis* and the *Introductio*. The first book of the *De Syllogismis Categoricis* and the *Introductio* are almost replicas of each other. The thoughts, expressions, and manner of treatment are similar. Whole passages are often the same. With the progress of the discussion the *De Syllogismis Categoricis* treats the topics more cursorily than does the *Introductio*.

In phraseology the *Introductio* resembles the *Prior et Secunda Editiones Peri Hermeneias* more than does the first book of the *De Syllogismis Categoricis*, e.g., *Prior Editio*,[14] and *Secunda*[15] and *Introductio*,[16] *secundum placitum*, but *De Syllogismis Categoricis*[17] *ad placitum* and often. The second book of the *De Syllogismis Categoricis* treats of the method of handling categorical syllogisms. Its style in many observed phenomena

---

[9] K. Meiser, p. 225, l. 14.

[10] Cf. *Secunda Editio*, K. Meiser, p. 421, l. 5.

[11] *Op. cit.*, Migne, 271 D. The Migne references are to volume LXIV of his *Patrologiae Latinae*.

[12] If Brandt's conclusions are correct, *Entstehungszeit*, p. 255.

[13] *Entstehungszeit*, pp. 243–245.

[14] Meiser, p. 48, l. 5.

[15] Meiser, p. 54, ll. 30–31.

[16] Migne, 762 D.

[17] *Ibid.*, 794 D.

is more like that of the other works of Boethius than is the style of the first book.[18]

The remaining extant work that deals with the *Peri Hermeneias* is the *De Differentiis Topicis*. Its introduction[19] summarily sets forth the various kinds of sentences and the parts of a sentence.

It remains to speak of two works which are seemingly not extant. One, a *Breviarium* of Boethius' commentaries *Peri Hermeneias*, is known only from the following passage:[20]

Huius enim libri post has geminas commentationes quoddam *breviarium* facimus, ita ut in quibusdam et fere in omnibus Aristotelis ipsius verbis utamur, tantum quod ille brevitate dixit obscure nos aliquibus additis dilucidiorem seriem adiectione faciamus, ut quasi inter textus brevitatem commentationisque diffusionem medius ingrediatur stilus diffuse dicta colligens et angustissime scripta diffundens.

The other treatise has been thus far an *opus incognitum*. Brandt's[21] careful scholarship has shown that there may have existed a work entitled *Institutio Categorica*. It fell before the *De Syllogismis Hypotheticis* and probably after the *De Syllogismis Categoricis*. It consisted of two books. The former dealt with predicative sentences and the latter presumably with predicative syllogisms; for such syllogisms formed part of the treatise. See *De Syllogismis Hypotheticis*:[22] 'ac de simplicibus quidem, id est de praedicativis syllogismis duobus libellis explicuimus.'

It is not out of place at this point to refer to another non-extant work, a commentary on the *Analytica Priora*; for the second book of the *De Syllogismis Categoricis*, if I may hazard the supposition, seems to be a resumé of this commentary, as the first book is of the commentary *Peri Hermeneias*. The second book of the *De Syllogismis Categoricis* is supposed to refer[23] to this hypothetical work four times in the past and once in the future. I leave the discussion of the questions involved till later.

I pass on now to the theories that have been put forth in regard to these works. The previous presentation will cause many questions to arise in the mind of the reader; such as: 'Wherefore the existence of two such similar books as the *De Syllogismis Categoricis* and the *Introductio ad Syllogismos Categoricos*?'; 'How explain the disagreement of the former work in style from that of the other works of Boethius?'; 'What is the relation of these works to the non-extant *Institutio Categorica* and the

---

[18] Cf. *Stylistic Tests*, pp. 142–143.

[19] Migne, 1174–1175.

[20] *Secunda Editio*, Meiser, p. 251, ll. 8–15.

[21] *Entstehungszeit*, p. 259.

[22] Migne, 833 B.

[23] Supra, p. 210. Cf. Brandt, *Entstehungszeit*, pp. 252–253.

Breviarium?'; 'How may we reconcile the use of the past and future tenses in the second book of the *De Syllogismis Categoricis* if they refer to the same work?'

Prantl,[24] noticing the brevity of the *De Syllogismis Categoricis* as compared with the *Introductio*, thought the first book of the former was an epitome of the latter. But Professor Brandt has shown that this cannot well be. The *De Syllogismis Categoricis* preceded the *Introductio* unless indeed the titles have become confused in our manuscripts and editions. Also, as Brandt has shown, the two works do not cover exactly the same ground.

Rocco Murari,[25] noticing that the first book of the *De Syllogismis Categoricis* is so peculiar in style, would make it a medieval reworking of our author. He considers the second book to belong to the *Introductio*.

I have shown[26] in my previous article that there are strong stylistic grounds for believing the first book of the *De Syllogismis Categoricis* to be spurious; that the second book shows many points of agreement in style with the *Introductio;* that some early manuscripts refer to the former work by other titles than the one appearing in our editions. All of this leads us to suspect that the references to the *De Syllogismis Categoricis* in the works of Boethius are not references to the work in question but to the non-extant *Institutio Categorica.*

This latter work Brandt[27] differentiates from the *De Syllogismis Categoricis;* for Boethius uses the term *praedicativis* in regard to the *Institutio*, though only *categoricis* is found in the former work. I notice, however, that Boethius makes these terms synonymous in the *Secunda Editio*[28] *Peri Hermeneias:* 'Et illas quidem quas *categoricas* Graeci nominant, Latini *praedicativas* dicere possumus.' In the *De Syllogismis Hypotheticis* we find these terms often used synonymously. In fact *praedicativis* is the favorite word. We may accordingly conjecture that this work on the hypothetical syllogisms is a sequel rather to the *Institutio Categorica* than to the *De Syllogismis Categoricis*, at least in the form in which we have this latter work.

As to the *Breviarium* Usener[29] concluded that in this work Boethius fulfilled the promise he had made in the *Introductio*. Brandt,[30] however,

---

[24] Cited by Brandt, *Entstehungszeit*, p. 241. Cf. C. Prantl, *Geschichte der Logik im Abendlande* (Leipzig: Fock, 1927), I, p. 682, note 80.

[25] *Dante e Boezio*, p. 92.

[26] *Stylistic Tests*, pp. 140–144.

[27] *Entstehungszeit*, p. 259.

[28] Meiser, p. 186, ll. 21–22. Cf. *De Differentiis Topicis*, Migne, 1183 C, and the *De Syllogismis Hypotheticis*, Migne, 832 A–B.

[29] Brandt, *Op. cit.*, p. 258. Cf. H. Usener, *Deutsche Litteraturzeitung*, I (1880), 370.

[30] *Op. cit.*, p. 258.

has shown that the *Introductio* does not touch on certain portions of the *Peri Hermeneias*.

Now for the mooted question concerning the commentary on the *Analytica Priora*. The four passages from the second book of the *De Syllogismis Categoricis* which seem to refer to the work as completed and published are as follows: 'Quam in Analyticis diximus;[31] in resolutoriis dictum est;[32] hoc quoque in resolutoriis[33] diximus; sed in Analyticis[34] nostris iam dicta est.' One would naturally make these passages refer to a commentary on the *Analytica* and not merely to a translation. There is however a passage in the *Commentarii in Ciceronis Topica* which shows that Boethius uses *nostros* in a sense that may be taken to refer not to a commentary but merely to a translation—*Commentarii in Ciceronis Topica*,[35] 'qui priores posterioresque *nostros* Analyticos, quos ab Aristotele transtulimus, legit.' Accordingly I am not so sure that Professor Brandt is correct in denying a future meaning to the future tense in 830 D. All that we can be sure of is that Boethius intended to write such a commentary as is shown by the expression *calcatius exprimemus*. I think it barely possible that at least as late as the *De Differentiis Topicis* this intention was unfulfilled. As I have said above, the introduction of this treatise contains a brief resumé of the *Peri Hermeneias*. At the close of this resumé our author refers to the commentary on the *Peri Hermeneias* as follows:[36] 'sed de huiusmodi propositionibus in his commentariis, qui in *Peri Hermeneias* Aristotelis libro conscripsimus, diligentius disseruimus.' Notice that he does not refer to the brief review of the same subject contained in the first book of the *De Syllogismis Categoricis* or even in the *Introductio*. Then he takes up categorical syllogisms, informing us that he has discussed the matter more fully in the second book of the *Institutio in Syllogismos Categoricos*. I notice that we are not referred to the commentary on the *Analytica* of which the second book of the *De Syllogismis Categoricis* is supposed to be a brief, as the first book is of the *Peri Hermeneias*. Accordingly I take it as a slight proof of the non-existence of the commentary on the *Analytica* that in the one case we have a reference not to that work, but to the relatively unimportant *Institutio*,[37] whereas in the other case we are referred not to the lesser work, the first book of the *De Syllogismis Categoricis*, or even to the *Introductio*, but to the all important commentaries on the *Peri Hermeneias*.

[31] Migne, 812 A.
[32] *Ibid.*, 816 B.
[33] *Ibid.*, 816 C.
[34] *Ibid.*, 822 B.
[35] Migne, 1051 B.
[36] *Ibid.*, 1176 A.
[37] If the argument, *supra*, p. 213, is convincing.

Now for the interrelationship of the *De Syllogismis Categoricis*, Book I, of the *Introductio ad Syllogismos Categoricos*, and of the *De Syllogismis Categoricis*, Book II. Aside from stylistic tests, is it possible to gain any light on the subject from our author himself? In the *Introductio*[38] Boethius outlines his task. He will first take up propositions and then treat syllogisms. The phraseology used is noticeable, i.e., *de syllogismorum connexione*. He fulfills the first part of his promise in the extant *Introductio*. As for the second part we must presume: first, that he failed to finish his work; or second, that the second book has disappeared; or third, that the extant second book of the *De Syllogismis* is the work in question.

As to the possibilities, I note that there is no definite close to the *Introductio*, as we have it. Boethius merely passes over his final point with the observation that discussion would be futile for the purpose in hand. He says nothing about going on with his task. Consequently he may have become tired of the work and have failed to complete it. In contrast, the first book of the *De Syllogismis Categoricis* has a definite ending that would either be suitable for a finished work or imply that the author had accomplished part of his undertaking and was now ready for the remainder. Are there any other clues? From a passage at the beginning of the *De Syllogismis Categoricis:*[39] 'sed quoniam syllogismorum *structura* nobis est *hoc opere* explicanda, syllogismis autem prior est propositio, de propositionibus *hoc libello* tractatus habebitur'—we infer that a second book was intended. Turning to the second book we find passages, some of which seem to hark back to the first part of the *De Syllogismis Categoricis* and some to the *Introductio*. The first book of the *De Syllogismis Categoricis* characterizes[40] itself as an *Introductio*.[41] On the other hand the *Introductio* characterizes itself as an *Institutio*.[42] Again, the *De Syllogismis Categoricis*, Book II, in the elaborate figure, comparing the building of a syllogism[43] to that of a house, harks back to the metaphor in *structura*, Book I.[44] The corresponding metaphor in the *Introductio* is *connexio*.[45] This figure is taken up[46] in Book II. I conclude therefore from such evidence as is contained in the works in question, that both the *De Syllogismis Categoricis*, Book I, and the *Introductio* look forward to a

---

[38] Migne, 762 C–D.

[39] Migne, 794 D.

[40] Notice that the early manuscripts cited, *Stylistic Tests*, p. 143, have the title, *Introductio*, not *De Syllogismis Categoricis*.

[41] Migne, 793 C. Cf. also Lib. II: 809 B; 809 C; 829 D (bis); 830 D.

[42] *Ibid.*, 761 B. Cf. also C.

[43] *Ibid.*, 809 B.

[44] *Ibid.*, 794 D.

[45] *Ibid.*, 761 C; 762 C; 762 D.

[46] *Ibid.*, 831 A.

continuation; also that such direct evidence is not conclusive in assigning Book II either to Book I or to the *Introductio*.

With this clearing of the ground one may now assemble from other works of Boethius the evidence that bears on this question. The *De Syllogismis Hypotheticis* has an elaborate dedication to some friend of the writer. A passage[47] couples the work with a preceding one on categorical syllogisms. The author informs us that his affection for his friend has led him to undergo the *immensus labor* of his undertakings; for after the friend had got a most thorough—*amplissime notitiam percepisses*—knowledge of categorical syllogisms, he kept asking to be instructed in hypothetical syllogisms. One would hardly be so bold as to refer the expressions above to such an abbreviated work as the *De Syllogismis Categoricis*. *Immensus labor* is even somewhat of an hyperbole when applied to the *Introductio*. Consonant with this interpretation is the derogatory tone in which the author himself speaks of *De Syllogismis Categoricis*.[48] After a short introduction, lest he may waste any time, he makes haste to plunge into his subject. He disarms criticism in advance by acknowledging that his style will be *sterilis* and *incompte*. And he dubs the first part of his prospective work a tract, *libello*, a term little consistent with *immensus labor*. In fact, this term would be an exaggeration, even with the second book included, so that Professor E. K. Rand is led to suggest that in speaking of the undertaking as 'immense' Boethius was thinking also of the commentaries on the *Peri Hermeneias*.

A further proof of the existence of a second book belonging to the *Introductio* is gleaned from the *De Differentiis Topicis*:[49] 'Huius diffinitionis rationem secundus quidem liber eorum quibus *institutionem* in Categoricos scripsimus Syllogismos, plene continet.' Cf. also the *De Syllogismis Hypotheticis*:[50] 'Ut sicut in Categoricorum Syllogismorum *institutione* monstratum est.' The word *institutio* would refer these passages to the *Introductio*, not to the *De Syllogismis Categoricis*; for, as has been shown above,[51] the latter work refers to itself as an *Introductio*; whereas the corresponding term in the *Introductio* is *Institutio*.

By way of a summary I conclude: That the commentary on the *Analytica Priora* may not have been written at least as late as the *De Differentiis Topicis*. This interpretation would relieve the dilemma of Brandt with his references to the *Analytica* as past and present in the same work. The past would refer to the translation, admittedly done be-

[47] Migne, 831 B–C.
[48] *Ibid.*, 794 C.
[49] Migne, 1183 A.
[50] *Ibid.*, 841 B.
[51] P. 215.

fore the Second *Peri Hermeneias;* the future would refer to the projected
commentary on the same translation. The phraseology of the respective
passages lends color to this interpretation. The expressions referring to
the past are simple and brief, *viz.: diximus, dictum est, diximus,* and *dicta
est* as implying a simple treatment. The reference to the future, *calcatius
exprimemus,* is more pregnant with meaning as implying an extended
commentary.

To go on with my findings, I would deny the titles of the *Editio Princeps*
to the *De Syllogismis Categoricis* and the *Introductio ad Syllogismos
Categoricos.* I would transfer the latter title to the former work and would
call the latter *Institutio Categorica,* or better *Institutio ad* (or *in*) *Syllogismos Categoricos:* for first, the better manuscripts do not know such
a title as *De Syllogismis Categoricis;* they designate that work by *Introductio ad Categoricos Syllogismos.* As to the *Introductio* of our edition the
manuscript tradition needs further investigation. However I do not hesi-
tate to deny its right to the name considering that the manuscripts
ascribe that title to the former work and know the latter by *Liber ante
Praedicamenta* or *ante Periermenias.*[52] Secondly, aside from manuscript
authority, internal evidence and cross references lead me to the preceding
conclusion. The *De Syllogismis Categoricis* of our edition refers to itself
repeatedly—seven times in all—as an introduction. The *Introductio* of
our edition refers to itself only as an *Institutio.*

This distinction in the use of these two words is all the more noteworthy
in view of the fact that they occur in passages wherein whole sentences
and paragraphs of the two works are almost verbatim replicas of each
other. Furthermore if we are to allow the second work to choose its own
title and call it *Institutio,* then we are corroborated by references from
other works, *viz.,* the *De Syllogismis Hypotheticis* and the *De Differentiis
Topicis.* These treatises refer to our work five times as an *Institutio* and
never as an *Introductio.* This fact shows that by the time of the *De Syllogismis Hypotheticis* the *Institutio* (the *Introductio* of our edition) had
entirely displaced the *Introductio* (the *De Syllogismis Categoricis* of our
edition) as a work of reference. To this manuscript and cross reference
authority I would add the use of the figure *connexio* and kindred deriva-
tives. In the *Institutio* (the *Introductio* of our edition) this is the common
figure, whereas *structura* is the usage in the *De Syllogismis Categoricis.* In
the *De Syllogismis Hypotheticis* and the *De Differentiis Topicis* we meet
with the same figure dozens of times and especially in connection with
any reference to the *Institutio.*

Lastly the assumption of the identity of the *Introductio* of the edition
and Professor Brandt's *Institutio* is corroborated from Boethius himself.

[52] Cf. *Stylistic Tests,* p. 143, note.

The descriptions of the two works are identical. In the *Introductio*[53] of our edition Boethius proposes to treat: first, the setting forth (*propositio*) of categorical syllogisms; second, their logical conclusion (*connexio*). In the *De Syllogismis Hypotheticis*[54] he tells us that he is the author of such a treatise in two books on predicative syllogisms—synonymous with categorical syllogisms.[55] Again he says[56] that the first book of a work on categorical syllogisms dealt with their setting forth. In the *De Differentiis Topicis*[57] he says that the second book of his work on categorical syllogisms treated of their logical sequence.

Lest anyone may object to identifying the *Introductio* of our edition with the *Institutio* of the text on the ground that the latter had two books whereas only the first appears in our edition, I would reply that the extant work promised two books and that there is no reason to suppose that the author failed to live up to his promise. We may suppose the second book was lost or has come down to us in a somewhat abbreviated form as the second book of the *De Syllogismis Categoricis* of the edition.

Therefore, in view of the manuscript tradition and the internal evidence I conclude that the *Introductio* of our text should be entitled the *Institutio* and that the former title should be given to the *De Syllogismis Categoricis*.

In regard to the latter work I feel sure that in its present form it is not from the hand of Boethius, but is a late reworking either of the treatise on the same subject that fell between the two commentaries on the *Peri Hermeneias* or of the *Institutio* (the *Introductio* of our edition). The latter hypothesis is supported by the fact that the *Introductio* (the *De Syllogismis Categoricis* of our text) does not cover the ground in quite the same way as does the *Institutio*. The former theory on the contrary derives support from the fact that the earlier treatise was entirely superseded by the later and hence probably disappeared from the canon of our author's works. The correspondence in style of the second book of the *Introductio* (the *De Syllogismis Categoricis* of our edition) with the *Institutio* and the other works of Boethius affords another indication that the medieval author used the *Institutio* rather than the earlier work. He was probably some schoolmaster who wanted to introduce his students to the subject of categorical syllogisms. Hence he looked upon his pamphlet as an introduction, not as a treatise (*Institutio*). Consequently,

[53] Migne, 762 C–D.
[54] *Ibid.*, 833 B.
[55] *Ibid.*, 832 A–B.
[56] *Ibid.*, 835 A.
[57] Migne, 1183 A–B.

he used the former term to the exclusion of the latter. His crude and careless Latinity would show itself far more in the first book where there is much discussion than in the second book which consists mostly of model syllogisms. Therefore the second book could be changed but little and would keep its Boethian style. In his epitome he would pick up some Boethian traits: notable among these is the fondness for the *quidem-vero*, *sed*, and *autem* collocations, of which four appear in our text and three more have been gleaned from the manuscript through the kindness of Professor William A. Oldfather of the University of Illinois and Mr. Malcolm Burke Lawrence, *viz.:* 'sine tempore vero quod verba quidem voces sunt designativa et secundum placitum, sed distant, quod nomina sine tempore sunt, verba cum tempore, cuius vero[58] nulla pars extra designativa est'; 'hoc enim significat quidem[59] quiddam et secundum placitum impositum est enim sed dubium est.' This instance is very significant. Who but Boethius—here copied by the epitomizer—would have put in *quidem* before *quiddam?* And lastly: 'et quoniam non homo vox quidem[60] significat quiddam, quid autem significet in homine ipso non continetur.'

In reaching these conclusions I feel that I am standing on firm ground; for they solve so many problems. They account for the abnormality in style and the anomalous status of the *De Syllogismis Categoricis* of our edition. They give due weight to the manuscript authority and simplify the situation by identifying the *Institutio* of the manuscript with that of Professor Brandt instead of making the situation all the worse by assuming a third work that seemingly covers the same ground as the two we already have and whose *raison d'être* has so puzzled students of Boethius.

UNIVERSITY OF CALIFORNIA AT LOS ANGELES.

[58] Mss. reading Codex Monacensis, 6372, fol. 70ʳ, v. 9, Migne, 795 A.
[59] Mss. reading, *ibid.*, fol. 70ʳ, v. 24, Migne, 795 C.
[60] Mss. reading, Migne, fol. 70ᵛ, v. 3, Migne, 795 C.

TRE DETTATI UNIVERSITARI DELL'UMA-
NISTA MARTINO FILETICO SOPRA
PERSIO, GIOVENALE ED ORAZIO

Giovanni Card. Mercati

Fu buona ventura che i seguenti cenni dell'inventario, e quelli corris-
pondenti dell'indice alfabetico,[1] circa l'Ottoboniano latino 1256 (un
codice, o piuttosto tre codici affini,[2] scritti da una medesima mano del-
l'ultimo terzo del secolo XV e poi riuniti insieme in ordine diverso[3] dal
tempo della loro scrittura):

1256. Mariani Praenestini Publici Eloquentiae Professoris in Iuvenalis Satyras
Interpretatio, in Romano Archigymnasio ab eodem dictata. Semper ego. 1.

Leges Romanae Pompeja, Fabia et aliae nonnullae. Gn. Pompeius. 48.[4]

Mariani supradicti in Persium Expositio, publice pariter dictata, quam Alexandro Sfortiae nuncupavit. Quemadmodum. 50.

E. (ut videtur) in Horatii Artem Poëticam. Solent plerique. 102.

Cod. ex Pap. fol. c(hartae). s(criptae). 148.

non siano stati osservati da veruno di coloro che si sono occupati dei
professori della Sapienza e degli umanisti di Roma e dintorni e da nessun
palestrinese in particolare: altrimenti con grande probabilità sarebbe
toccato al buon Mariano l'onore di figurare, sia pure in seconda linea, fra
i cattedratici dell'Archiginnasio e fra gli umanisti del Lazio al tempo,
non infelice per le lettere e le arti, di Sisto IV, e magari di dare il nome ad
una via della patria; specialmente se a qualcuno della vetustissima cit-
tadina fosse venuta l'idea che egli potesse essere quel Mariano de Blan-
chellis prenestino, che solo per avere non molto dopo, nel 1515,[5] emendato
—non si sa in che—il supposto spropositatissimo[6] 'Pomponius Laetus de

---

[1] Ivi si fece anche peggio: all' 'Abbate' Mariano Prenestino del sec. XV, professore nell' Archiginnasio Romano, si attribuì inoltre la 'Interpretazione di una Iscrizione greca' dell' 'Ab⁰. Mariani'
Francesco, viterbese, scrittore nella Vaticana, del secolo XVIII!

[2] Lo rivela la composizione stessa dei fascicoli, specialmente dell'ultimo di ciascun codice, non
mai uguale ai precedenti e non mai interamente scritto, tanto che, o se ne ritagliarono i fogli bianchi
come in fine al Persio e all'Orazio, o si adoperarono a scrivervi altro, come dopo Giovenale le *Leggi*
romane e la dedica del Persio.

[3] Dalla dedica del Persio risulterà difatti che il commento di Giovenale è posteriore.

[4] Sono appunti senza relazione col resto, per non lasciar vane delle pagine bianche.

[5] Per lo meno questa sola edizione ha il titolo: 'Pomponius Laetus de / Romanae Urbis ve/tustate
noviter im/praessus / ac per Mari/anum de Blanche/llis Praene/stinum emen/datus.'

[6] G. B. De Rossi, 'Note di topografia romana' ecc., *Studi e documenti di Storia e Diritto*, III (1882),
51: 'indegnissimo della penna e della fama di tanto maestro;' Vl. Zabughin, *G. Pomponio Leto*, II
(1910), 171.

Romanae Urbis vetustate noviter impraessus' dal Mazochi venne presentato da L. Cecconi[7] e da P. A. Petrini[8] per un emulo del concittadino Andrea Fulvio, e forse come lui scolare del Leto, e detto 'uno dei più celebri letterati dell'età sua.'

D'altronde fu male che quei cenni non abbian colpito verun altro studioso e indottolo ad osservare il manoscritto, perchè sono così rimaste finora ignote tre opere dell'autentico professore della Sapienza, Martino di Filettino, dettosi Filetico, non ignobile collega nell'insegnamento, di Pomponio Leto, Gaspare Veronese, Domizio Calderini ecc., che pur gli odierni cattedratici non arossiscono di riconoscere quali predecessori non indegni rispetto al tempo: segnatamente ne sarebbe stato felice e se ne sarebbe servito B. Pecci, che al Filetico ha dedicato quasi cento pagine dell'opera *L'Umanesimo e la 'Cioceria.'*[9]

Invero a conoscere Mariano per un semplice uditore e copista avrebbe bastato uno sguardo alla sottoscrizione del commento di Giovenale (f. 47^v): 'Expliciunt Collectae Iuvenalis per me Marianum praenest. precipiti chalamo dum Auctor ex tempore dictavit;' e al riconoscimento dell'autore avrebbe senza pena condotto la rubrica a principio del commento di Persio, ritagliata bensì alquanto nella prima riga ma pur tuttora leggibile con sicurezza (f. 51^r):

Martinus Phileticus vir Clariss. ha⟨n⟩c Persii interp⟨re⟩tatione⟨m⟩ In gy⟨m⟩nasio / romano innumerabili auditorum multitudini ex tempore dictavit: et ego Mari/anus inter caeteros collegi precipiti calamo,

che rende chiara la sottoscrizione (f. 101^r):

Expliciunt Collecte Persii per me Mar/ianum M^{ari} [10] Praenestinum sub voc⟨e⟩ Phy^{ci} (=Phyletici) / precipiti chalamo.

Superfluo dopo ciò ricorrere alla dedica del commento ad Alessandro Sforza signore di Pesaro, di cui il Filetico educò i figli Battista, la futura

---

[7] *Storia di Palestrina* (1756), 317, dove per isbaglio di stampa il testamento appare dell'8 settembre 1519, (corr. 1529). Mariano 'Reliquit Capitulo et Canonicis (di Palestrina) omnes libros, qui reperiuntur in haereditate pro usu Sacristiae, et Bibliothecae ipsius Ecclesiae s. Agapiti;' libri che Cecconi, 318, n. 46, dice 'affatto smarriti.'

[8] *Memorie Prenestine* (1795), 201 sg., all'an. 1510. E' più esatto del Cecconi. Riferisce 'che il padre chiamavasi Stefano Antonio: ch'egli oltre il cognome *Blanchelli* portava quello de'*Leonardi:* ch'era Chierico, . . . familiare del Cardinal de Vio,' ecc. ecc. Annoto questo, perchè mi fa dubitare dell'identità di lui col nostro copista, che m'era parsa dapprima così probabile. Stando alla sottoscrizione del Persio esso avrebbe avuto un nome o di padre o di famiglia troppo lontano da quelli riferiti dal Petrini (v. la nota 10).

[9] Trani 1912, 113–208, ristampato con aggiunte dall' *Archivio della R. Società Romana di Storia Patria*, XIII (1890), 468–526.

[10] La lettera maiuscola, anzichè un semplice M, si direbbe un monogramma di ML legati insieme: le tre letterine in alto sono senza dubbio 'ari.' Perciò nella nota 8 l'ho detto troppo lontano dal nome paterno e dai cognomi del Mariano editore di Pomponio e familiare del card. Caietano. Un palestrinese probabilmente riconoscerà sotto quell'abbreviazione qualche nome o cognome cittadino.

consorte di Federico di Montefeltro, e Costanzo e restò sempre devoto;[11] dedica nella quale ricorda di avergli sempre dato, fino dalle primizie, i frutti dei proprî studi, e che conviene benissimo a quanto si sa della vita del Filetico da circa il 1456 in avanti.

Pertanto è sicurissimo che Martino di Filettino e non Mariano di Palestrina è l'autore del commento a Persio, e che lo dettò nel ginnasio romano ad un 'numero innumerevole di uditori';[12] ottimo segno questo e non l'unico, come si vedrà in seguito, del credito che il maestro godeva.

Che poi il Filetico sia l'autore anche degli altri due commenti, lo si può stabilire con sicurezza sufficiente.

Nel commento di Orazio mancano le iscrizioni, per il taglio (suppongo) della maggior parte del margine superiore, ridotto ora ad un centimetro, mentre il margine inferiore è alto quasi 5 centimetri. Ma c'è la dedica (f. 102) ad un uomo di primo ordine, anzi il primo d'allora, vuoi per le ricchezze, vuoi per le virtù e per il sapere, giurista, oratore, poeta ecc., che tutto ciò non ostante, finora non sono giunto a ravvisare con le mie conoscenze superficiali di quell'epoca;[13] ed essa dedica—un capolavoro di adulazione e di finto pudore—termina con una vita di Orazio in ventuno distici, riportata da un 'libro de poetis antiquis' non ancora pubblicato dal dedicante, che in un'opera stampata del Filetico è dichiarato apertamente di lui.

Ecco la dedica che a me dà modo di provare l'assunto e ai buoni conoscitori di Roma sul declinare del Quattrocento servirà a riconoscere l'illustre per me ignoto.

Solent plerique, vir omni reverentia et cultu dignissime, quos honori habent et magnifaciunt, eos gemmis donare caelato argento et auro. Hi autem mihi non secus ac illi viro excellenti ingenio et doctrina Isocrati[14] quandam facere[15] mercaturam videntur; qum eos huiusmodi munusculis condonant, munera[16] ab illis et plura et longe prestantiora conantur accipere. Ego vero etsi hoc agere

---

[11] Cf. Pecci, 124 sgg.

[12] Doveva ciò essere certo e notorio, perchè se ne vantò anche nella dedica del commento delle *Epistole* di Cicerone al card. Giovanni Colonna, romano: 'Concursus frequens erat innumerabilium et variae nationis et linguae personarum ad ea percipienda, quae in gymnasio legebantur' (Pecci, 164).

[13] Il tenore delle lodi non lo fa per nulla supporre un ecclesiastico, il quale, nell' ipotesi, non avrebbe potuto essere se non dei primi e più potenti: non si sciupa tanto inchiostro e tanta verità per uno . . . non arrivato. Che se fu un laico, e da lui il Filetico riconobbe in certo senso la vita stessa, sarebbe egli stato mai Antonio Colonna, principe di Salerno, prefetto di Roma sino dal 1459 e influentissimo, 'suo valido amico e protettore, che l'aveva chiamato a Roma, fattogli avere la cattedra di greco e affidata l'educazione di Giovanni suo figlio' (Pecci, 179; e cf. anche 161 e 164)? Nel qual caso commento e dedica sarebbero anteriori al 25 febbraio 1472, ultimo giorno di Antonio. Ma ad un tanto benefattore come mai la Musa del Filetico avrebbe avuto così paura di presentarsi, se non fu proprio su gl'inizî, verso il 1467? e chi altri fuori del Filetico gli ha attribuito tante e così alte qualità?

[14] *Orat.* 16.

[15] *fecer'* ms.

[16] *nunera* ms.

voluissem, non pateretur facultas mea: neque animo ducerem id esse libero homine dignum. Quamobrem alii gemmas tue humanitati, alii argenti et auri pondera deferant; ego autem verba solum ad te mittam, quae prudentie tue maiori oblectamento esse possunt quam munera: sunt enim haec fortunae, illa virtutis.[17] Es et Tu, vir etate nostra omnium optime, adeo dives, ut temporibus nostris vel Lucullus vel Crassus esse videaris. Nec eum tamen te animum habere dixero, qui neque expletur neque satiatur, sed qualem vel Stoici plurimum commendarent. 'Imperat,' ait Flaccus,[18] 'aut servit collecta pecunia quoique tortum[19] digna sequi potius quam ducere funem.' Ancilla est tibi, non domina. Nec huiusmodi muneribus indiges, sed novi aliquid in dies lectitare vehementer[20] exoptas.

O si esset mihi dignum aliquid eruditissimis auribus tuis, quod ad te mitterem. Ego non pauca poemata elusi:[21] multa etiam prosa oratione complexus sum. Horum tamen impresentia nil ad te audeo mittere. Veretur enim non parum[22] Musa nostra, qum sit admodum rudis et inepta, ad te venire, qui es omnium bonarum artium disciplinis ornatus et quidem, audeo[23] dicere, omnium etate nostra prestantissimus. Quid est enim per Deum inmortalem, quod non ita noris ut quisque manus et ungues suos? Tu optimus sanctissimarum legum[24] interpres, quoi vel Scaevola cederet, ex iunioribus autem quem in his tibi conferre possem non invenio. Tu poeta et orator excellentissimus, et historias scis omnis[25] et fabulas. Tu denique philosophus multa laude dignus. Sed desino commemorare preclarissimas virtutes tuas, in quas explicandas non venimus sed incidimus. Non adeo sum mentis expers ut illas crederem verbis meis exponi posse, quae praeseferunt splendorem quemdam maximum et inmortalitatem.

Quod cum ita sese habeat, his primum experiri placuit quem ad te aditum Musa nostra posset offendere: non autem quod mihi sit dubium quin eam benigne susciperes, sed vereor an digne satis et absque illo rubore rustico, quo perfusa genas interdum solet incedere, severos vultus tuos Catone dignos intueri possit. Omnia tamen, cum hec legeris, si quidem tue humanitati placuisse intellexero, propediem me tibi allaturum polliceor. Nam ita factus sum tuus qum amore in me tuo singulari, tum uti maxime virtutum tuarum excellentia, ut vel vitam hanc meam tibi debere cognoscam.[26] Nunc autem Acrona, quem a me dudum petivisti,[27] ea mente, qua quidem ad te perferendum curavi, suscipias vehementer

---

[17] Qui in marg. *hec sunt fortunae illa virtutis*, un 'notabile' (come ve ne ha altri in seguito), non un ritocco.

[18] *Epist.* I, 10, 48–49.

[19] *Totum* ms.

[20] *veherenter* ms.

[21] Così il ms.: preferirei *lusi*.

[22] *paurum* ms.

[23] *adeo* ms.

[24] Leggi canoniche? o piuttosto in genere?

[25] L'autore che usa *quoi* può avere usato anche *omnis* per *omnes;* perciò lo lascio.

[26] Niente meno! Che l'abbia salvato da qualche pericolo in una brutta occasione, come, puta, della famosa congiura del 1469? nella quale però non sembra che Martino sia stato impacciato (cf. Pecci, 174). Oppure solo da una grande strettezza, aiutandolo ad ottenere la cattedra, come appunto fece il Colonna prefetto di Roma (Pecci, 179)?

[27] E' curioso che quel ricchissimo amatore delle lettere non avesse pensato a comprarsene un esem-

obtestor. Sed quoniam non aepistolarum, non de institutione poetica interpretatio
apud me erat, sane quae lectitans viris quibusdam mea quidem sententia non
indoctis dictaveram in eo qui est de arte poetica libro, cum Acrone accipias
obsecro, et ea quidem ut Quintilianus[28] et tanquam precaeptor et pater atque
princeps meus legas etiam atque etiam rogo. Atque si haec ipsa probaveris et
iocunda et grata tibi fuisse cognoro, non modo quae poemata lusimus, sed epistolarum expositionem[29] in Flaccum aggrediar, et alterum opusculum in tuo
nomine apparebit. Haec autem qualia sint leges, et 'quid spei sit reliquum,' ut
Terentii verbis utar,[30] probe cognosces. Sed quae in libro de poetis antiquis de
Flacci vita complexi sumus hic primum ponere statui, ut quae de eo viro legimus
tu primum[31] a nobis accipias. Ea sunt huiusmodi.

> Si quis amat Quinti fortunam discere Flacci,
>   Me legat, et patriam norit et inde genus.
> Quicquid erat domina praeco venale sub hasta
>   Qui me progenuit vendere doctus erat.
> Sum libertino natus de semine, Cocta
>   Tempore quo Roma consul in urbe fuit.
> Viderunt idus nascentem quinque decembres
>   Paupere me tecto. Parca benigna fuit.
> Non me nobilitas generis, sed plurima virtus
>   Praeclarum toto reddidit orbe virum.
> Corpore parvus eram, celerique movebar ab ira,
>   Placabarque tamen: lumine lippus eram.
> Charus eram Phoebo, facili pergratus Iacho:
>   Me quoque dilexit dulcis et alma Venus.
> Itala me vidit tellus vigilasse Latinis
>   Et primum studiis maxima Roma suis.
> Hinc me quae sacrum caepit de Pallade nomen
>   Excepit docto terra beata sinu.
> Inter Aristippi sobolem[32] iocunda voluptas
>   Me traxit curvas inter habenda feras.
> Inde mihi favit veneranda ad cetera Pallas:
>   Qua[33] duce perdidici plurima digna Deo.
> Sum[34] quoque post studium civilia bella secutus,
>   Qum colerem Brutum, quippe tribunus eram.
> Fortia magnanimi vicerunt arma Quirini:
>   Victoris praeda[35] Caesaris ipse fui.
> Indulsit tamen ille[36] mihi te propter, amice

---

plare, trattandosi di commento non raro e ricopiato più volte nel secolo XV. Con tutto questo, poichè
esso commento fu stampato a Milano nel 1474 e a Roma circa il 1475 (Hain, 8876 e 8899), dedurrei
almeno da quel fatto che i nostri due uomini non sapevano ancora di una stampa e che dedica e commento dell'Arte poetica sono da ritenere anteriori, anche se per avventura non fu Antonio Colonna
il mutuatario dell'Acrone.

[28] Non so al momento indicare il luogo.

[29] *expositione* ms.

[30] *Andria*, v. 25.

[31] Così, non *primus*, come forse scrisse l'autore.

[32] *sobilem* ms.

[33] *Quae* ms.

[34] *Sun* ms.

[35] Così, contro il metro.

[36] *illa* ms.

Mecenas animae dimidiumque meae.
Lusimus inde tibi meritis pro talibus odas,
 Nomine sermones scripsimus inde tuo.
Plurima sub nostro gravis ivit epistola multis,
 Quae docuit, virtus queve ferat vitium.
Vos quoque, Pisones, vidistis carminis artem,
 Qua versus semper quisque regendus erit.
Ut sex labentis etas mea pertulit annos,
 Hec quoque bis quinas vidit olympiadas.[37]
Improba tum Lachesis rupit mea stamina vitae.
 Nunc sacros vates Elysiumque colo.
Inque meis rebus statui te, maxime Caesar,
 Omnibus heredem: tu mihi numen eras.
Mecenas, nostri solus pars altera sensus,
 Iussit in exequiis ossa tegenda mea.

Habes, vir clarissime, paucis verbis quae de Flacci vita sensimus. Nunc vero, antequam expositionem aggrediamur, titulum operis exponamus.

Orbene in capo all'edizione dei sette idilli di Teocrito tradotti dal Filetico, che uscì in Roma verso il 1482 presso il Silber,[38] si vede una simile vita del poeta in quindici distici col titolo in maiuscole: 'Phileticus de vita Theocriti in libro de poetis antiquis.'[39] La dedica adunque e il commento che segue della Poetica di Orazio sono del Filetico; ciò che potevamo aspettarci, leggendosi prima nel codice, e cioè nella dedica del Persio allo Sforza (f. 50^v; v.avanti), il proposito suo di commentare anche Orazio.

Lascio il libro *De poetis antiquis*, di cui il Pecci non conobbe altro avanzo fuori della vita di Teocrito, e lascio le questioni del tempo della dedica dell'Orazio e se il Filetico ne abbia poi realmente commentato anche le Epistole, perchè non so rispondere, e ritorno al commento di Giovenale.

Esso non ha dedica, almeno ora,[40] ma ha le iscrizioni affatto simili a quelle di Persio. La sottoscrizione ho già riferito: qui riporto la rubrica del principio, di cui purtroppo in una rilegatura fu per intero ritagliata col margine la linea prima.

/obscuros Iuvenalis locos hac extemporaria oratione claros fecit: cuius / Inter-

---

[37] Qui 'olimpiade' sta per quinquennio o lustro. [38] Hain, 15478. Pecci, 144, dice 'verso il 1480.'

[39] L'ha ristampata Pecci, 149, n. 3, dicendo il 'libro *De poetis antiquis*, libro f o r s e a p p a r - t e n u t o a l u i o da lui composto e che è andato smarrito.' La prima insinuazione è da escludere affatto: il Filetico compose, o almeno volle comporre, un poema sui poeti antichi, come ne compose uno, pure in distici, su 'gli avvenimenti dell'epoca dei re e della repubblica' romana per il suo discepolo Guido Antonio figlio di Federico di Montefeltro (v. Pecci, 128 sg.). I due saggi che rimangono non fanno rimpiangere la perdita di quel poema, se pure è perduto davvero.

[40] Il primo fascicolo è bensì completo, ma la dedica potè essere prefissa dopo in uno o due fogli supplementari, di poi caduti. Certo è che mancano i fogli antichi di riguardo, non rimanendo sul codice il solito numero del Sirleto, da cui viene il ms., nè il solito ex-libris Altempsiano con le varie segnature Altemps e Ottoboni: saranno stati gettati nel secolo XVIII, quando il ms. fu legato di nuovo.

pretationem ego Marianus inter alios innumerabiles scholasticos collegi. /

La linea recisa,—visto che il mediocrissimo catalogo della biblioteca del Sirleto[41] francamente dice del Filetico i commenti di Giovenale e di Persio, mentre tace affatto l'autore del commento d'Orazio,—dovette presentare ancora ben chiaro e nome e cognome, e perciò sarà stata questa all'incirca: 'Martinus Phileticus vir Clariss.,' con l'aggiunta forse d' 'in gymnasio romano' o una equivalente che l'empisse, 'obscuros' ecc.: insomma l'avrà apertamente mostrato autore.

Che se ciò non persuade, persuaderanno, credo, le undici strofe saffiche sulle Muse, che l'autore, il quale si compiaceva di ricordare le proprie opere e di riportarne dei trati (l'abbiamo visto in Teocrito e in Orazio), ha riferito nel commento della satira VIII, f. 25ᵛ sg.:

... Sed Musarum habitum et officia his nos lyricis carminibus complexi sumus:
Hic adest Clyo vario colore
Vestis inteste[42] variis figuris

. . . .

Fert decoram Calliope coronam
Diva triformis.

Esse difatti si trovano nel carme del Filetico al card. Bessarione, di cui ha riportato parecchi versi il Pecci a p. 154, con assai varianti dovute a ritocchi dell'autore.[43]

E ora ritorniamo alla dedica del commento di Persio per pubblicarla intera quale documento di certa importanza nella biografia del Filetico. Invero ne risulta anzitutto che egli cominciò l'insegnamento della retorica, di cui sono frutto i commenti dei classici latini, prima del 1473, fino al quale anno lo si credette invece professore soltanto del greco.[44] Difatti nella dedica, che non può mettersi dopo l'aprile 1473, essendo ai tre del mese morto Alessandro Sforza,[45] è detto apertamente che il corso sopra Persio e quello insieme sulle Tusculane erano stati tenuti nell'anno

[41] Vatic. lat. 6163, f. 317ʳ, fra i 'libri humanitatis . . . in folio in papiro,' al n. '129. Martini Philetici comment. in Iuvenalem. / Eiusdem comment. in Persium. / Comment. in artem poeticam Horatii' (senza ripetere l' 'Eiusdem').

[42] Anche il Laurenziano XXXVIII, 38 ha 'vestis intextae' e non 'vestes intexta' come ha stampato il Pecci contro la metrica. Mariano è talvolta scorretto o per la fretta o perchè non udì bene le parole del professore. Così omise, ad es., il verso successivo: 'Et tubam libro manibus coronam.'

[43] Per es., il ms. ha 'figere terrae (ed. iungere plantas), Tibiae inventrix manibus sonorae (tibiae gracilis repertrix), modulata sacros (reperit sonoros)' ecc. Ometto altri che dubito siano errori di stampa in Pecci, come 'ferendi (ms. serendi), colli (coeli), diros (divos).'

[44] Pecci, 165 sg. e 190: 'divenuto lettore di latino, commentò e spiegò' ecc.

[45] A. degli Abbati Olivieri, *Memorie di Aless. Sforza Signore di Pesaro* (1785), cx. Non occorrebbe appoggiarsi a questo e converrebbe riportarla ad un altro anno o due più addietro, se veramente fu dedicato ad Antonio Colonna il commento della *Poetica* di Orazio.

p r e c e d e n t e, quindi nel 1472 al più tardi, regolarmente e come di do-
vere, 'cum me ad id genus interpretationis[46] Gymnasium excepisset.'

Inoltre vi si attesta un tale buon successo quale almeno io non mi sarei
immaginato e quale forse non possono vantare molti cattedratici di
oggidì anche valentissimi: numero innumerabile di uditori e, ciò che più
monta, l'esito (diciamo così) di duecento copie del dettato dentro tempo
così breve. Onde ben si comprende che il Filetico, incoraggiato, abbia
pensato a continuare con Giovenale e con Orazio e che il card. Latino
Orsini ai 31 gennaio 1473, sulle 'buone informazioni di uomini fededegni'
ed a richiesta 'altresì di m o l t i d e g l i u d i t o r i,' i quali allora stu-
diavano l'arte rettorica,[47] lo abbia sostituito, senza togliergli l'insegnamento del greco, al lettore Gaspare Veronese in partenza da Roma.

Penso che le duecento copie siano state a mano, eseguite in parte
durante la dettatura e in parte ricavate dopo: non oso pensare che furono
a stampa, perchè non si conosce stampato nessun commento di Persio
prima del 1481[48] e nessun commento u m a n i s t i c o di classici prima del
1474.[49] E fu probabilmente quel tanto buon successo a dare il pensiero
di stampare i commenti stessi; ciò che principiava in Roma già del 1474
il giovane ed intraprendente Domizio Calderini, professore di valore e
di grido non comune, e continuò intrepidamente,[50] e lo seguirono qui
stesso il Cillenio nel 1475, e a Venezia il Calfurnio nel 1476,[51] provocando
quella gara di grossi commenti che si osserva nell'ultimo ventennio del
secolo XV ed è un fatto di rilievo non piccolo nella storia nostra letteraria
e della filologia e coltura classica e dell'arte tipografica; gara che a sua
volta non potè non produrre anche un effetto in contrario, in quanto la

[46] Che egli vi trovò già introdotto da alcuni uomini dottissimi e dovette seguire. Nella dedica al
card. Giovanni Colonna, già suo scolaro, delle lettere commentate di Cicerone, in Pecci, 164 sg., il
Filetico dichiara: 'Et quoniam tunc quidam sane doctissimi viri assuefecerant iuventutem, ut nil
audire cuperent, ni s u p e r u n a q u a q u e p r o p e m o d u m d i c t i o n e sensum et
e x p o s i t i o n e m a d i u n g e r e n t . . .Eorum ego instituta sequerer necesse fuit. Quare, quom
in d i v e r s o s a u c t o r e s non pauca d i c t a v e r i m, Ciceronis lectionibus non parum
delectatus, haec illius opera interpretatus sum: Paradoxa: Laelium: Senectutem: Officia: Tusculanas
quaestiones: Rhetoricos etiam libros: De oratore ad Brutum. Et quom tu, annos t u n c natus non
plures quam quindecim, et instituebaris bonarum artium disciplinis: quasdam tuo nomine Ciceronis
epistolas ad eruditionem tuam et eligendas et exponendas accepi, quae satis ad capessendum ingenii
cultum videbantur. Has nunc ideo edendas putavi . . . ' (nel 1480-81). Il Colonna essendo nato
nel 1456, il 'tunc' ci riporta al 1471 circa, sempre prima della nomina del 1473.

[47] Pecci, 189 sg.

[48] Hain, 12719 (il commento di Bartolomeo della Fonte) e 12729 (di Giovanni Britannico) ristam-
pati più volte dentro quel secolo (v. i numeri sgg. fino al 12744).

[49] V. le due note seguenti con dati fornitimi dal peritissimo Don Tommaso Accurti, il quale mi ha
pure riveduto il passo della nota 46.

[50] Cf. Hain, 4235 (Marziale; 1474), 4242 (*Ibi* d'Ovidio; 1474), 4244 (*Selve* di Stazio; c. 1475), 4239
(Giovenale; Brescia 1475).

[51] Hain, 15522 (Tibullo; Roma 1475), 15407 (*Heautontimorumen.*; Venezia 1476), 15408 (Id.;
Treviso 1487).

comparsa di un commento molto stimato e fortunato, per es. del Giovenale del Calderini, facilmente disanimò o autori o stampatori dal tentare l'alea della stampa di un altro commento e fu causa che restarono inediti più dettati; i quali naturalmente per una pubblicazione di concorrenza avrebbero dovuto essere completati e perfezionati. Probabilmente avvenne così che il Filetico, quantunque autore di molti commenti e tanto persuaso dell'eccellenza dei propri corsi da vantarsi ingenuamente che quello su Persio era sembrato non meno utile e gradevole dell'opera stessa del poeta, ne pubblicò solo tre, e forse dei minori, a Cicerone: quello di un certo numero di lettere,[52] del *De Senectute* e dei *Paradoxa*,[53]—i soli che il Pecci, p. 191, credette superstiti; gli altri rimasero inediti, e non si sa nemmeno se ancora esistano, all'infuori dei tre nostri dettati. Questi forse nessuno leggerà mai, ma pure si dovevano segnalare una volta a complemento della biografia del Filetico e della storia dell'Umanesimo Laziale, e per comodità di chi mai volesse servirsene da termine di confronto con altri dettati d'allora, quali di Pomponio Leto collega del Filetico nella Sapienza, dettati che potentemente concorsero a formare le nuove generazioni e rappresentano l'insegnamento universitario di quel tempo.

Ecco la dedica. Essa è scritta sull'ultima pagina del commento di Giovenale, ch'era rimasta vuota come lo sono ancora le due pagine precedenti. Mariano ne avrà ottenuto copia dal quasi compaesano Martino, il quale da buon uomo e buon maestro l'avrà trattato assai benevolmente. Attesi gli errori di scrittura e le omissioni costanti delle parole greche nel commento della *Poetica*, non direi che il Filetico abbia voluto copia del suo dettato e fatto aggiungervi la dedica senza guardare se quella era completa e corretta.

. . . .[54]

Magnanimo principi Alexandro Sphortiae S.P.D.

Quemadmodum memores grati et boni agricolae de messibus suis spiceas coronas parvosque uvae racemos Poenatibus afferre consueverunt, sic ego primitias studiorum meorum, Magnanime princeps, ad te dare iam dudum inceperam.

[52] Hain, 5223 e 12981. Si fa del 1482 circa. Pecci, 191, la pone 'tra il 1480 e il 1481, q u a n d o Giovanni Colonna . . . fu innalzato alla sacra porpora,' ciò che fu il 15 maggio 1480. Se nella dedica (che non ho intera sotto gli occhi) non c'è proprio 'quando' o altra espressione equivalente di quella occasione, mi atterrei piuttosto al parere dei conoscitori degli incunaboli, che propendono a farla del 1482.

[53] Hain, 5283, Venezia 1498, cc. 131ᵛ–157ʳ. Il nome del Filetico compare soltanto a c. 131ᵛ, dove dice di non esporre la vita di Cicerone 'cum eam ipsam pertractare alio loco decrevi [-vit sic l'ed.] Thusculanarum quaestionum libris,' il commento delle quali—uno dei primi con quello di Persio secondo la dedica allo Sforza—si direbbe non ancora composto o finito. Questa ed. però del 1498, al seguito del commento di Pietro Marso al *De officiis*, fu la prima o una ristampa? Il Filetico, a credere del Pecci, 120, era morto circa il 1490.

[54] Vi sarà stato *Martinus Phileticus*, con qualche titolo dell'officio o qualche termine esprimente devozione.

Sequar inceptum. Quodcumque e sensu manabit nostro, tibi soli dicare constitui;[55] sic enim facere me cogit clarissimarum virtutum tuarum prestantia, singularis humanitas, innata clementia, incredibilis beneficentia, amplitudo rerum gestarum vel pace vel bello: quibus omnibus tuum nomen inmortalitati commendatum est. Omne studium meum, curam, industriam, cogitationem in te convertam. Tibi serviet animus in omne tempus etatis meae. Faxit Deus, qui omnium est[56] optimus maximus, te dignum aliquid queam dare. Quodcumque a me nascetur, tibi erit. Tu vero, Invicte princeps, scripta nostra, qualiacunque venerint, obsecro laeta fronte suscipias: et cum erit ocium, fuerisque a Martiis muneribus aliquando liberatus, legas[57] postulo. Quod si feceris, maximam dabis auctoritatem scriptis meis: et si placere videbuntur, accensum animum in te colendo plurimum inflammabis.

Haec autem, quae nunc mittimus, anno superiori in hac urbe publice dedimus sub innumerabilium clarorum virorum censuris, cum me ad id genus interpretationis Gymnasium excepisset, ubi maxima doctissimorum virorum copia vocem cum in hac re meam tum in Tusculanis quaestionibus[58] audiebat: quam ut tu, etiam absens, sicuti princeps et dux meus rexque optimus, aliqua ex parte cognosceres, ad te perferendam curavi: et eo libentius hoc fecimus, quo te ita velle intelligebamus et meam in hoc opere sententiam vehementer optare significabas. Legebam equidem poetam hunc Persium; qui cum nimis durus videretur nec facilem se daret auditoribus meis, qui et docti erant et habebantur, hanc interpretationem ipsis ex tempore dictavimus: et plusquam bis centum huiusce expositionis huc usque quod scimus volumina exiverunt: quae quoniam non minus[59] utilis et iocunda—hoc ausim dicere—quam ipsum opusculum poetae visa est, volui ut in tuo nomine appareret. Quod si laudabis, i d e m i n I u v e n a l i s a t q u e F l a c c i o p e r i b u s f a c t i t a b o: quae non breviorem quam ista Persii scripta videntur exposcere.[60] Videbis quid in hoc poeta clarissimo sentiamus:[61] quem tanti facere sunt soliti et frequentissime lectitare Augustinus,[62] Hieronymus, Quintilianus, Martialis. Huius expositionis hoc fuit initium: Consueverunt plerique omnes etc.

BIBLIOTECA APOSTOLICA VATICANA,
   CITTÀ VATICANA.

[55] Se si potesse pigliare sul serio tale dichiarazione, converrebbe dirla posteriore alla dedica della *Poetica*, oppure che, quando questa fu scritta, lo Sforza era già morto.

[56] *Qui* . . . ÷ (= *est*) in marg. senza segno; non vedo altro posto vicino dove possa stare.

[57] *leges* ms., ma sopra *ges* c'è *a* di correzione.

[58] Cf. sopra, n. 46, e n. 53.

[59] *non nimis* ms.

[60] Manca *expositionem* o altra parola di tale senso.

[61] *sensiamus* ms.

[62] *Agustinus* ms.—'Suoi libri prediletti erano Cicerone, Teocrito, Sant' Agostino, Lattanzio, San Girolamo, i quali ultimi afferma egli stesso di aver letti e riletti più volte' (Pecci, 122).

DA PRATO'S SAIBANTIANUS OF SULPICIUS SEVERUS AND ITS HUMANISTIC CONNECTIONS

BERNARD M. PEEBLES

NEARLY ten years ago my teacher and friend, the recipient of this collection of essays, pointed out the need of a critical study of the works of Sulpicius Severus contained in the *Martinellus* and materially aided such a study by describing a group of Turonese copies of that collection.[1] Earlier, while reviewing recent contributions to that subject, Père Hippolyte Delehaye, S. J., had drawn attention to a special phase of Sulpician scholarship which merited prompt investigation[2]—a fresh analysis of the manuscripts used in his edition (1741) by a Veronese Oratorian, Girolamo Da Prato,[3] but since then, with one notable exception, the semiuncial *Capitularis* of Verona,[4] lost or forgotten. Addressing myself both to the larger task proposed by Professor Rand and to the immediate problem of Da Prato's sources, I was enabled, by the generosity of the American Academy in Rome, to prepare and in 1936 to publish a paper dealing expressly with the latter subject.[5] That presentation was incomplete in a number of ways,[6] and the present paper serves to fill out one of its gaps.

---

[1] E. K. Rand, *A Survey of the Manuscripts of Tours* (Cambridge, Mass.: The Mediaeval Academy of America, 1929), p. xiii; cf. p. 230, *s. v. Martinellus*.

[2] 'Saint Martin et Sulpice Sévère,' *Analecta Bollandiana*, XXXVIII (1920), 9.

[3] Tom. I (1741; hereinafter cited as *ed. Sulp.*, I) contains the Martinian writings of Sulpicius; II (1750), the *Historia Sacra*. Omitted in my account of Da Prato's literary activity (art. cit. below, n. 5) is a reference to his weighty contributions to the study of St Zeno's sermons. Cf. G. B. C. Giuliari's edition (ed. alt., Verona, 1900), p. x, cxxix, 30, 101–108 and elsewhere.—In *Cod. Venet. Marc. Lat. IX. 51* there are found one or more letters from Da Prato to Andrea Gallandi. See Valentinelli's catalogue, V, 281.

[4] Supplementing the notes in my article, pp. 16 f., 56, 61 f., are two chapters in a Harvard doctoral dissertation, *De Sulpici Severi operum Martinianorum textus priscis fontibus*, recently completed under Professor Rand's direction.

[5] 'Girolamo Da Prato and his Manuscripts of Sulpicius Severus,' *Memoirs of the American Academy in Rome*, XIII (1936), 7–65, Pls. 1–7; hereinafter cited as *Da Prato*.

[6] For the derivation, directly from the *Legenda Aurea*, of a non-Sulpician text (see *Da Prato*, p. 34, I) in Da Prato's *Venetus* (now *Vatic. lat. 13699*) and other manuscripts, see Dom André Wilmart, O.S.B., in *Ephemerides Liturgicae*, L (1936), 170–175, 195 f., 202–206. Likewise possibly traceable to the *Legenda Aurea* (ed. Th. Graesse [Leipzig, 1850], p. 749) is the paragraph (found in the same manuscripts) presenting Ioannes Beleth's brief account of the *cappa S. Martini*; cf. *Da Prato*, p. 34, O, and n. 4. Knowledge of this fact also I owe to Dom Wilmart, who refers further to B. Hauréau, *Notices et Extraits*, I (Paris, 1890), 88–99 (esp. 95). The chapter by Iacopo da Varagine on St Martin (*Leg. Aur.*, Cap. CLXVI [161]) opens with a series of interpretations of the name *Martinus* which stand in close relation with a passage in *MS. Florence, Bibl. Naz., Conv. Soppr. I. VI. 18*, fol. 2ʳ–4ᵛ (see

Of the seven manuscripts used by Da Prato two remained undiscovered when my article went to press.[7] What in his judgment was the more important of the two, a book at that time owned by the Theatine Fathers of Padua, still awaits identification.[8] The other, the *codex Saibantianus*,[9] has now come to light far from its native Verona and is the subject of this paper.

Among the many manuscripts older than 1600 owned by Miss Phyllis Goodhart and Mr Howard L. Goodhart of New York City,[10] *MS. 11* is a portly little codex of 323 parchment leaves[11] (180×125 mm.), arranged in gatherings of five.[12] The original binding of boards (7 to 8 mm. thick) bears a cover, added before 1821,[13] of tooled red velvet. The leaves, each carrying a single column (116×62 mm.), are ruled horizontally in a light brown ink on both sides; vertically in lead, now on one, now on both sides.[14] The script is a clear Humanistic minuscule of the fifteenth century, which is employed as well for titles etc. (though then in red)

Da Prato, p. 38, n. 3). The unpublished text of a metrical setting of the Saint's life contained in this manuscript, fol. 106[r]–123[v], is now being prepared for publication by me.

[7] See *Da Prato*, p. 58.

[8] To the clues brought together for its identification (*Da Prato*, pp. 27 f.) should be added Da Prato's statement (*ed. Sulp.*, I, 267) that the leaves are of parchment.

[9] See *Da Prato*, pp. 24–26.

[10] A description of the contents of the Goodhart collection as of the end of 1936 is found in Seymour de Ricci and W. J. Wilson, *Census of Medieval and Renaissance Manuscripts in the United States and Canada*, II (New York: H. W. Wilson Co., 1937), 1675–1684; description of *MS. 11*, pp. 1677 f. To Mr Goodhart I would express my deep obligation for placing the manuscript at my disposal and fostering its study. It is owing to his generosity that Mr Claude W. Barlow, fellow (1935–1938) of the American Academy in Rome was enabled to go to Verona (Sept., 1937) and make in my behalf certain investigations which will later be mentioned. For friendly coöperation I extend my thanks likewise to Mr de Ricci and to Mr Wilson, as also to their colleague, Miss Annie M. Nill, who described the manuscript when it was owned by Mr Voynich and recently re-examined it at my request.

[11] Fol. 323 (blank) is conjoint with fol. 324 (blank and unnumbered), pasted to the lower cover. Serving as flyleaves at the beginning of the book are fol. a+b, once blank and apparently original. Fol. a[v], extreme upper left-hand corner (in bold ink strokes): *321*, the oldest library number in the manuscript. For another, see below, p. 239, n. 60.

[12] Except fols. 151–154, a binion which brings to a close Part I of the manuscript.

[13] This cover has been described as 'early XIXth c. English' by de Ricci and Wilson, *Census, loc. cit.* That it had been added before 1821, when the manuscript made its first appearance in a public English booksale, is learned from the catalogue of that sale, *Saibanti and Canonici Manuscripts. A Catalogue of a Singularly Rare Collection of Manuscripts on Paper and Vellum . . . Brought to this Country by the Abbé Celotti and are Sold by Order of the Present Proprietor* (London, Sotheby, 26 Feb. 1821), p. 15, n. 182: 'Eusebii et alior. Epistolae, MS. on vellum with illuminated capitals, in crimson velvet.' For an examination of copies of this catalogue (Br. Mus.: S.-C. S. 123. [7], and Bibl. Nationale: Δ 34923) I am indebted to Mr de Ricci and to Mlle. Marthe Dulong, of whom the latter graciously undertook at the British Museum several investigations pertinent to this study.

[14] Precisely this arrangment is seen in *Cod. Veron. Bibl. Com. 1171–1179* (Catal. Biadego, No. 1359; *Da Prato*, p. 19 and n. 5), a fifteenth-century manuscript whose Sulpician text is closely allied with that in the Goodhart book. This *Veronensis*, possibly a local product, is almost identical in format with the New York manuscript: 188×124 (110×63) mm.

as for the text proper. A second hand enters in fol. 298^v, l. 3, and completes the book.[15] Initials for chapters and sections alternate red and blue, the latter decorated with red, the former with either (Hand A) brown-red or (Hand B) blue pen strokes. The initials which open the three chief divisions of the manuscript receive more elaborate decorative treatment: P, fol. 1^r; S, fol. 155^r; Ɋ, fol. 297^r. The first of these is set in an E-shaped frame,[16] in the lower arm of which is placed a crestless helmet, with mantling, somewhat defaced. The contents of the manuscript, exclusively hagiographical, are as follows:

(I.) Epistulae tres de S. Hieronymi morte, virtutibus, miraculis Eusebio Cremonensi (fols. 1^r–72^r; BHL, 3866), S. Augustino (fols. 72^r–86^r; BHL, 3867) S. Cyrillo Hierosolymitano (fols. 86^r–154^v; BHL, 3868) falso nomine adscriptae.[17]

(II.) Fols. 155^r–296^r (vacuo fol. 296^v). Martiniana.

A. Fols. 155^r–156^r. Sulpicii Severi ad Desiderium epistula Vitae S. Martini (BHL, 5610) praefixa.

B. Fols. 156^r–158^r. Eiusdem Vitae capitulatio (insunt 27 tituli).[18]

[15] According to de Ricci-Wilson, *Census, loc. cit.*, the second hand enters at fol. 297^r and transcribes the entire *Vita S. Zenonis.*

[16] There is some indication that the decoration on fol. 1^r is superimposed upon an earlier design.

[17] One of the numerous manuscript copies of these once much-read letters which are available for a critical edition to supplant the (not identical) recensions reprinted by Migne, *Patr. Lat.*, XXII, 239–326; XXXIII, 1120–1153. The three letters, followed by works of Caesarius, Cassian, etc., formed No. 25 (parch., in 8°, '*miniato*') in Ottavio Alecchi's catalogue of certain *Saibantiani* found in *Cod. Veron. Capit. CCCVII (282)*, pp. 29–32. For recent opinions as to the date of these *pseudepigrapha* see F. Lanzoni, 'La Leggenda di S. Girolamo,' in *Miscellanea Geronimiana* (Rome, 1920), p. 37 f.; F. Cavallera, *Saint Jérôme, sa Vie et son Œuvre*, Première Partie (Louvain, 1922), II, 144 f.

[18] The separate *tituli* are numbered, as are those below in F, in Arabic numerals. *Tit. 18* was first omitted, then supplied, probably by the first hand; the numerals *18–26* were then changed to *19–27*. There is no such alteration in *Cod. Veron. Capit. CXII (105)* [= *Biv*; cf. *Da Prato*, p. 18], with which manuscript ours, as well in the *capitulationes* as in other matters, closely agrees.

Although (see *Da Prato*, p. 19, n. 7) Tobias Eckhard (1723) alone has printed the *indices capitum* of Sulpicius's *Martiniana* from a manuscript surely associated with Tours, similar *capitulationes* are found in some of the first printed copies. The earliest instance which I can quote with confidence is a Zwolle printing (Petrus Os de Breda, c. 1480; Copinger, *Suppl.*, II, 5684), but for the *Vita S. Martini* only; so also, as it seems, Hain *15168 (*sine nota*). All four groups of *capitula* (cf. in the above description: B, F, H, K) are brought together at the end of Aldus's edition (Venice, 1501/2). The complete set, in four distinct groups, is also contained in an early printed book (*sine nota*) of which one copy is *Br. Mus. 4866. b. 43*, a volume recently examined for me by Mlle. Dulong. Copinger in two entries (II, 3893, 5685) seems to refer to this book, but its provenience and date have yet to be determined. The Br. Mus. printed catalogue (s.v. SEVERUS), tentatively though erroneously, refers it to J. Bernardi (Utrecht, 1514), for an account of whose edition see A. M. Ledeboer's description (1867) of the early printed books of the Deventer public library. A printed text of the *capitulatio* for the *Vita S. Martini* alone is found in F. N. Klein's Coblenz *Programm* (1820), *Aus Handschriften des Sulpicius Severus, zu dessen Lebensbeschreibung des heiligen Martinus und den angehängten Briefen*, pp. 13 f., a recension based upon three (or four) manuscripts (*saec. XIII* or later, as it seems) then in the Coblenz Gymnasium but now probably in the Staatsarchiv. A copy of this rare *Programm* is in the Princeton University Library.

C. Fols. 158ʳ–158ᵛ. Anonymi auctoris versus, *Martini meritum si quis vult noscere primum* etc.[19]

D. Fols. 158ᵛ–191ʳ. Vita S. Martini auctore Sulpicio (*BHL*, 5610).

E. Sulpicii de S. Martino epistulae tres (*BHL*, 5611–5613): I (fols. 191ʳ–194ᵛ); II (fols. 195ʳ–199ʳ); III (fols. 199ʳ–204ᵛ).

F. Fols. 205ʳ–207ʳ. Sulpicii Dialogi I capitulatio (insunt 20 tituli).[20]

G. Fols. 207ʳ–240ʳ. Sulpicii Dialogus I (*BHL*, 5614).

H. Fols. 240ʳ–241ᵛ. Sulpicii Dialogi II capitulatio (insunt 15 tituli).[21]

I. Fols. 241ᵛ–261ʳ. Sulpicii Dialogus II (*BHL*, 5615).

K. Fols. 261ʳ–262ᵛ. Sulpicii Dialogi III capitulatio (insunt 21 tituli).

L. Fols. 262ᵛ–283ᵛ. Sulpicii Dialogus III (*BHL*, 5616).

M. Fols. 283ᵛ–285ʳ. Fidei Catholicae expositio sine auctoris nomine,[22] alias vero S. Martino Turonensi perperam, ut videtur, adscripta:[23] *Clemens Trinitas est una divinitas . . . in sancta ecclesia nunc . . . seculorum amen.*

N. Fols. 285ʳ–291ᵛ. E Gregorii Turonensis opusculis quaedam de S. Martino excerpta (*BHL*, 5619–5623).[24]

O. Fols. 291ᵛ–295ᵛ. Auctorum diversorum tituli, magna ex parte metrici, in

---

[19] Published by me, *Da Prato*, pp. 62 f. Our manuscript corresponds letter for letter with *C* (= *Biv*), but does not have the marginal variant *caritatis* in l. 20.—After the verses and immediately before the incipit of the *Vita* are placed the words: *I.I.I. Idus nouembris.* Just so in *Biv*, fol. 15ʳ.

[20] *Biv* here shows nineteen *tituli*. Our scribe has reached the number *20* by erroneously assigning *I* to the heading of the *capitulatio*. As in *Biv* and the two other fifteen-century manuscripts at Verona which I have associated with it (see *Da Prato*, p. 19), *tit. xv* in the set published by Eckhard and regularly found in the ninth-century manuscripts of Tours is here omitted. The omission points to a community of origin for the four manuscripts. A correction in the enumeration in *Biv*, fol. 32ᵛ (*xvii–xx* changed to *xvi–xviiii*), suggests that the omission was first made by the scribe of *Biv*.—The heading of *Dial. I* takes an extended form which I can now match only in *Biv* (fol 32ᵛ): *Incipit dialogus seueri sulpicij postumiani et galli primus. Refert postumianus qualiter in orientem transmigrauerit (transnauigauerit* Biv) *et que ibi uiderit uel audierit et quod ante descriptam uitam beati martini secum portauerit et regressus ut pretermissa miracula scriberentur rogauit.*

[21] The rubricator, as below in K, has here failed to supply the *tituli* with their numbers. He has similarly neglected the section-numbers in the text of all three *Dialogues*.

[22] The rubricator failed to add the title but two lines had been left blank for it.

[23] On this text (cf. *Da Prato*, p. 18, n. 3) see the article by E. Amann in *Dict. de. Théol. Cath.*, Tome X, I. Partie, 213–214 and the literature there cited. Jérôme and not the more famous Josse is the Clichtove associated with the earliest printing (1511) there named by the Abbé Amann. (On Jérôme and his relation to Josse, who was probably his uncle, see J. C. Adelung, *Fortsetzung . . . zu C. G. Jöchers allg. Gelehrten-Lexicon*, II [Leipzig, 1787], 373; J.-Al. Clerval, *De Iudochi Clichtovei Vita et Operibus* [Paris, 1894], p. 2.) A rival claiment as editor is Guillaume Petit, O.P.; see J. Quétif and J. Échard, *Scriptores O. P. recensiti*, II (Paris, 1721), 101. The volume itself (Paris: J. Marchand and J. Petit, 1511 [cf. Brunet, *Manuel du Libraire*, V 1, 322 f; fol. XLʳ for the *Confessio*]) opens with a prefatory letter from Jérôme Clichtove to Père Petit which reveals the former as editor, the latter rather as instigator of the volume. For manuscript sources possibly used for this collection, see B. Krusch, *MGH, Scr. Rer. Merov.*, I, 480–481. What *codices impressi* lay behind Clichtove's edition of Sulpicius (fol. IIᵛ–XXXIIʳ)? Certain details point to Mombritius (Milan, 1479), but the matter needs careful study.

Another (earlier?) printing of the *Confessio* is that found at fol. 34ᵛ in *Br. Mus. 4866. b. 43* (for which see above, p. 233, n. 18).

[24] Our text of *BHL*, 5619+5620 (Greg. Tur., *H.F.*, I, 48) does not show the additional phrases observed by me (*Da Prato*, p. 47, n. 2) in certain manuscripts. In this point again it agrees with *Biv*.

Maiori Monasterio et in basilica S. Martini Turonensi olim inscripti (*BHL*, 5624 b).[25]

P. Fols. 295ᵛ–296ʳ. Basilicae S. Martini Turonensis descriptio (*BHL*, 5624 c).

Q. Fols. 296ʳ. Sollemnitatum eiusdem basilicae enarratio (*BHL*, 5624 d).[26]

(III.) Fols. 297ʳ–322ᵛ. Vita S. Zenonis Veronensis et alia de eodem, auctore anonymo (*BHL*, 9010 [fol. 297ʳ–311ᵛ], 9011 [311ᵛ–322ᵛ].[27]

That this Goodhart manuscript (*Gd*) is identical with Da Prato's *Saibantianus* (*Saib*) may, I think, be shown almost conclusively.

On Da Prato's published statement,[28] *Saib* resembled, *fere ad unguem*, another Veronese manuscript, the *Bivilaquius* above mentioned,[29] and so also does *Gd*.[30] Of the twelve readings from *Saib* which Da Prato printed[31] all appear in *Gd*,[32] but none was, among Da Prato's sources, unique to *Saib*. These two tests of identity are the only ones which Da Prato's edition supplies. *Gd* meets them perfectly, but so does another manuscript still at Verona.[33] We must look elsewhere for further criteria.

[25] To the improvement of the text of these inscriptions, edited by E. Le Blant, *Incriptions Chrétiennes de la Gaule*, I (Paris, 1856), Nos. 166–183 (pp. 227–245), the Goodhart manuscrpt (*Gd*) offers little that is not contained in two other fifteenth-century manuscripts of Italian provenience: that (*Biv*) used by Da Prato (*ed. Sulp.*, I, 385–397; cf. *Da Prato*, pp. 17 f.) and *Gd*'s close kinsman, Z, used by Gaetano Marini for the edition in Cardinal Mai's *Script. Vet. Nova Coll.*, V (Rome, 1831), 138–143, and now (see *Da Prato*, p. 62) *Cod. Venet. Marc. Lat. IX. 61 (3287)*. Common to *Biv Gd Z* is the error: Le Blant, No. 168, l. 5 *vallatu*] vallatu praeclaro; to *Biv Gd* (Z?): No. 176, l. 19 *furiosus et*] futuriositis. The family *Biv Gd Z* is, however, in some places superior to that represented by the much older books transcribed for the most part in France (see the incomplete list in Le Blant I, 227 f.). *Biv Gd*, for example, do not show a group of errors common to Le Blant's French sources (I, 228, n. 2). His contention that all known copies of the collection stem from a faulty archetype is borne out, however, by a passage in Le Blant, No. 176 (the work of Paulinus of Périgueux), l. 10: *scande polum angelicum scrutatus in aethera coetum*, where *angelicum* is omitted in the earliest French manuscripts (those of Tours): *Paris. lat. 5325, 5580, 10848, 13759; Quedl. 79*, as also in *Biv Gd Z*. De Prato supplied the omission in *Biv* by use of Juret's edition of the poems of Paulinus.

[26] This and the preceding section, both regularly found in our manuscripts after the *epigrammata*, appear to stem from Greg. Tur., *H.F.*, II, 14. Le Blant, *op. cit.*, I, 245 so believed and R. P. A. Lambert, O.S.B., in a recent article (*Revue Mabillon*, XXVI [1936], 15), reinforces this opinion, without, however, citing in support of the opposite view the weighty authority of G. B. De Rossi, *Inscr. Christ. Urb. Rom.*, II (Rome, 1888), 187 f.

[27] *BHL*, 9010 and the first part of 9011 were published, posssibly with the use of this manuscript (see below, p. 236, n. 38) by Scipione Maffei, *Istoria diplomatica* (Mantua, 1727), pp. 315–334; reprinted in his collected *Opere*, VIIII (Venice, 1790), 174–203.

[28] *Ed. Sulp.*, I, Praef., p. x; cf. *Da Prato*, p. 24.

[29] P. 233, n. 18. For an eighteenth-century account of *Biv*, see below, p. 241, n. 74a.

[30] In the note just cited and in those which follow it I have pointed out only a few of many resemblances. In the texts relating to St Martin *Biv* and *Gd* are of identical structure and agree in scores of significant readings. Both manuscripts contain the identical *Vita S. Zenonis*, but in *Biv* it precedes the *Martiniana*. Cf. *Da Prato*, p. 18, n. 3.

[31] *Ed. Sulp.*, I, pp. 1–8, *app. crit.*, passim.

[32] There is one slight exception. *Gd*, fol. 159ᵛ, shows *ad oram illius acta*, where Da Prato (p. 5, *ad* l. 22) reported for *Saib* and other manuscripts: *ad omnia illius acta*. The presence of *acta* was the important thing: *oram* as an easy miscopying of *oīa* (so *Biv*) was hardly worth noting.

[33] *Cod. Veron. Com. 463–465* (Catal. Biadego, No. 1228; paper, *saec. XV*); cf. *Da Prato*, p. 19, n.

Among the manuscripts owned by Giulio Saibante of Verona in 1734 an anonymous printed catalogue of that date[34] cites one and only one as containing Sulpicius Severus on St Martin of Tours; this, then, is surely the *Saibantianus* which Da Prato, before 1741 and probably after 1738,[35] examined for his forthcoming edition. To this item the author of the catalogue, probably Scipione Maffei,[36] devotes a paragraph of more than normal length:

B. Eusebii Epistola ad S. Damasium Portuen. Episc. & ad Theodosium Rom. Senator. de morte gloriosiss. Hieronymi. Severi Epistola de Vita S. Martini Episc. Vita S. Zenonis Episc. Veronen. Membr. Saec. 14. Ubi notatur prope initium Vitae S. Martini quod Ferrum sive ensem ejusd. Sancti Maddius de Madiis vidit, & tetigit Veronae in Domo Spect. de Bivilaquis die Sabathi IV. Augusti 1425. quodque postea servatur in Templo F. F. Minor. quod Carotae nuncupatur infra limites Paroeciae S. Jo. Bapt. de Quinzano Suburb. Veron. 8.

Without giving a full acount of the contents of Sig. Saibante's manuscript,[37] Maffei has indicated the three large divisions into which it fell, divisions which correspond with those which we have delimited in *Gd*.[38] In material, size and (closely enough) in date *Gd* corresponds to this description of *Saib*. Further it shows just the note which Maffei had be-

---

6.—*MS. 1171–1179* of the same library (parch., *saec. XV;* see above, p. 232, n. 14) shows at the front the loss of two leaves on which were once present the passages in which the first six of the readings cited by Da Prato were found. In the second group of six readings this manuscript also corresponds with *Saib.*

[34] Title in *Da Prato*, p. 22, n. 2. Copies in the Vatican and in the Verona Biblioteca Comunale.

[35] In that year Da Prato published a dissertation on Sulpicius Severus in [Calogerà's] *Raccolta d'Opuscoli Scientifici et Filologici*, XVIII, 69–131; cf. *Da Prato*, pp. 14 f. At p. 122 he enumerates four manuscripts which he will use in re-editing the text of Sulpicius's *Epist. III: Cap., Brix., Patav., Bivil.* He may, of course, already have seen and rejected *Saib.*

[36] See F. Doro, *Bibliografia Maffeiana* (Turin, 1909), I, No. 54.

[37] For a proof that he has done so, see *Da Prato*, p. 25.

[38] As possibilities for identification with *Saib* the two Verona manuscripts cited above, p. 235, n. 33, now drop out. Neither they nor any other of the manuscripts which I group with *Biv* (see below, p. 239 f.) contain the three letters about St Jerome.

That the Saibante library contained the very *Vita S. Zenonis* found in *Gd* is shown by the statement of the editor of that text, Scipione Maffei (see p. 235, n. 27): *Si trova questa Vita nell' avanzo de' codici del monastero Zenoniano, in quelli della libreria di s. Lonardo, in quelli di casa Bevilaqua, in quelli di casa Saibante, e nei miei* (edit. Mantua, p. 315; Venice, p. 175). Of his own manuscript Maffei later made mention, *Verona Illustrata*, III, vii (*Opere*, VIIII, 107). Maffei's edition gives no indication of the variant readings of his five manuscripts, of which the third is probably our *Biv* (fol. 4ʳ–13ʳ). If *Gd* is the *Saibantianus* here meant by Maffei, one of the remaining three may be *Phillipp. 6732*, recently purchased by Mr. Goodhart (see below, p. 240). The Marciana at Venice owns two manuscripts of this *Vita S. Zenonis: Lat. II. 83* (a. 1300) and *85* (*saec. XIII*). Incomplete manuscripts, at least one of them early, are at Munich (*1090, 19484*); see Andreas Bigelmair, *Zeno von Verona* (Münster i. W., 1904), p. 42. One of the Gianfilippi manuscripts sold at Paris in 1843 (cf. *Da Prato*, p. 26) contains a *Vita S. Zenonis* and other items of great interest for Verona. It is now at the University of Chicago: de Ricci-Wilson, *Census*, I, p. 593 f., No. 689.

fore him. This note is found in the margin of fol. 162ʳ, opposite the account of St Martin clothing the beggar outside the gates of Amiens. *Arrepto itaque ferro*, Sulpicius's text runs,[39] [*chlamydem suam*] *mediam diuidit*. Against this passage are set the following notes, the former in the hand of the text,[40] the latter in that of a later scribe:[41]

[*A*.] hoc ferru(m) q(uo)d gladiu(m) / u(e)l ensem uulgo ap- / pellamus uidi ⁊ te- / tegi ego madius / de madiis i(n) ciuitate / u(er)ona i(n) domo spec- / tabiliu(m) de biuilaq(ui)s / die sabbati quarto / augusti de. 1425.

[*B*.] Hodie uero seruat(ur) i(n) / Monaste(r)io fratru(m) / minor(um) i(n) templo / q(uo)d carrote uulgo / no(m)i(n)atur i(n) ag(r)o ueron(ensi).

If, as does not seem unlikely, Maffei did not attempt to reproduce exactly the note in *Saib*, or refuse to add an observation of his own,[42] the form of the double note in *Gd* corresponds sufficiently well with Maffei's account, and we leave his catalogue with increased confidence in the identity of *Gd* with *Saib*.

As has elsewhere been shown,[43] Da Prato also saw in *Saib* the note about the sword of St Martin. According to his testimony, that note was in two parts. Of these the first had been observed by him in *Biv* and may clearly be seen there today.[44] Of the second part Da Prato wrote: *In Saib. cod. sequitur alia manu. Hodie vero servatur in Monasterio Fratrum Minorum in templo q(uo)d carrotae vulgo nominatur in agro Veronensi.*[45] Aside from two trifling variations in spelling[46] Da Prato has furnished us with what is a perfect transcription of note [*B*] in *Gd* and, appropriately as regards that book, has noted the difference in hand between the two parts. The use of Da Prato's evidence, therefore, lends further support to the equation, *Saib=Gd*,[47] and it is Da Prato likewise who furnishes us with still other proof of this identity.

Not all the readings culled by Da Prato from the opening pages of

[39] Edit. C. Halm, (*C.S.E.L.*, I [Vienna, 1866]), p. 113, l. 9.

[40] With de Ricci and Wilson, *Census*, p. 1678, who assign this note to the hand of fols. 297 ff. (cf. above, p. 233, n. 15) I am unable to agree.

[41] Assigned plausibly by de Ricci and Wilson, *loc. cit.*, to a date around 1480.

[42] The words *infra limites—Suburb.* do not appear in *Gd.*, nor do they seem to have been present in the manuscript seen by Pellegrini (see below, n. 47).

[43] *Da Prato*, pp. 12, 22, 24. The information is drawn from the Da Prato miscellany described *ibid.*, pp. 11-14. To this assembly the Bibl. Comun. at Verona has now assigned the shelf-mark, *Manoscritti: Da Prato 189.*

[44] See *Da Prato*, pp. 19 f., Pl. 3.

[45] *Da Prato*, p. 22, n. 5, rests upon an assumption to which I no longer adhere.

[46] For *carrote* (*Gd*) Da Prato has *carrotae*; in his transcript *Veronesi* and not *Veronensi* may be the final word. But note the appearance of the *quod* symbol in both instances.

[47] We know, to be sure, that Pellegrino de' Pellegrini saw in Verona, about the year 1525, a parchment copy of Sulpicius carrying note [*A*.] and either [*B*.] or else an expanded form of it (see *Da Prato*, p. 21). If, as has seemed more probable (*ibid.*, p. 23), the latter alternative is the true one, then the book observed by Pellegrini is neither *Saib* nor *Gd* and is still to be identified.

Saib are registered in his edition. Fifteen more are found among his autograph notes,[48] and of these all but one is reproduced literally in *Gd.*[49] In regard to this single discrepancy we may remember that Da Prato, like other collators of manuscripts, occasionally nods.[50]

Finally, as evidence that the Goodhart manuscript passed through Da Prato's hands, I point to a note, the work surely of his time, which appears (fol. 283ᵛ) at the beginning of the creed, *Clemens Trinitas . . .* , which in this manuscript lacks a title. The note may be read as follows: *In aliis Manuscriptis inscribitur*[51] *Confessio S.ⁱ Martini de S.ᵃ Trinitate.* A passage in Da Prato's edition of Sulpicius[52] shows that he was familiar with this *Confessio,* and in his *Bivilaquius* the text carries (fol. 62ʳ) just the caption quoted in the note. The script of the note, moreover, shows various features (among them a form of majuscule *S*) quite characteristic of Da Prato's hand,[53] and I believe the annotation to be his.[54]

So far internal evidence. The list of successive owners of the manuscript has been carefully prepared[55] and leads us to North Italy, if not indeed to the very library of the Saibante family in Verona.[56] Before the manuscript

---

[48] In the miscellany cited above (p. 237, n. 43): *Da Prato,* p. 12, I (d) (2). The *Saib* readings entered by Da Prato in the margins of his copy of the Leipzig edition of 1709 (see *Da Prato,* p. 15, Pl. 2) add no new evidence. For an assembly of these *Saib* variants I am indebted to Mr Barlow.

[49] Edit. Halm, 110, 9 *auctorem*] autor *Gd;* here Da Prato's notes show *auctor* [= *Biv.corr.*] as the reading of *Saib.*

[50] See *Da Prato,* pp. 19, 35 and n. 1, 48, 52–54—In thirty cases where I had found *Biv* reported in Da Prato's edition as showing a reading not found in *Gd* a check made by Mr Barlow reveals that in a good half of these cases *Biv* actually agrees with *Gd.*

[51] The transcription *inscribitur* is not sure.

[52] *Ed. Sulp.,* I, 349.

[53] Examples of his script are reproduced in *Da Prato,* Pls 1, 2; photostats of others are in my possession.

[54] If Da Prato's examination of the manuscript proceeded as far as fol. 283ᵛ, it may well be wondered that he did not go farther and study the *tituli metrici* in fols. 291ᵛ ff., thus procuring a manuscript with which to compare (*Biv*) see above, p. 235, n. 25. Among various answers to which this objection is open I know none that is thoroughly convincing.

[55] By de Ricci-Wilson, *Census, loc. cit.*

[56] For documents relating to this library and its dispersion (cf. *Da Prato,* p. 24, n. 4; p. 26) see C. Frati-A. Sorbelli, *Dizionario Bio-bibliografico dei Bibliotecari e Bibliofili Italiani . . .* (Florence, 1933–1934), pp. 508 f. Further notes by Alecchi (*saec. XVIII in.*) on *Saibantiani* (cf. *Da Prato,* p. 24, n. 4) are found in *Cod. Venet. Marc. Ital. X. 102;* see Segarizzi, *op. cit.* (below, p. 241, n. 75), p. 95, n. 1. *Olim Saib. 358 = Veron. Com. 1366* (*ibid.,* p. 102, n. 4). See also Bethmann, in Pertz' *Archiv,* XII, 657; *Bibliofilia,* XIII (1911–1912), 299; XXII (1920–1921), 98–102.—E. S. Buchanan, *The Four Gospels form the Codex Veronensis* [*Old-Latin Biblical Texts*], VI] (Oxford, 1911), p. vii, errs in stating that the Saibante collection was dispersed in the seventeenth century. A. Spagnolo, in *Atti d. R. Accad. d. Scienze di Torino,* XXXIV (1898–1899), 769, n. 3, seems to doubt that the *Evangeliarium* (*b*) with which Buchanan dealt (*Veron. Capit. VI* [6]) was ever Saibante property. While members of the Saibante family do appear in the records of the Verona cathedral as Archpriests as early as 1664 and 1700 (see Conte Francesco Florio, *Nuova Difesa di Tre Documenti Veronesi* [Rome, 1755], p. 210 f.), this Verona *codex purpureus* was already owned by the Cathedral Chapter in 1625, the date of the (unpublished?) Rezano catalogue cited by Spagnolo.

was acquired by Mr W. M. Voynich, from whose estate its present owners purchased it, it had passed seventy years in the library of Sir Thomas Phillipps. In the Phillipps catalogue (1837) its entry[57] is one of some seventy referring to books purchased from the Rev. Henry Joseph Thomas Drury (1778–1841),[58] Lord Byron's teacher at Harrow and a collector of books highly esteemed by Dibdin.[59] Drury's ownership—he signed the book in 1823[60]—stands at only one remove from the first known appearance of the manuscript in the English book-trade, viz. in an auction[61] of 'Saibanti and Canonici manuscripts' brought to England by Abbate Luigi Celotti and put on sale at London by Sotheby, February 26, 1821.[62] Celotti's activity as a collector of books and art-objects[63] centered largely in Venice, Padua, and Verona, but the catalogue of 1821 unfortunately does not distinguish the *codices Saibantiani* from those brought together by Abbate Matteo Luigi Canonici.[64] Had it done so, there can be little doubt that Item No. 182 (=*Gd*) would have been assigned to the former class.

* * *

As a text of Sulpicius Severus, the Goodhart manuscript (*Gd*) is related not only to the *Bivilaquius* (*Biv*), but to two other Verona books above cited,[65] *Codd. Bibl. Com. 1171–1179 (V1)* and *463–465 (V2)*, all manuscripts of the fifteenth century and partially collated for the present study. Shar-

[57] P. 40, No. 3399. See also H. Schenkl, *Bibl. patr. lat. Britt.*, Part IV (Vienna, Akad. d. Wiss., Phil.-Hist. Cl., *Sitzungsb.*, CXXVI [1892], Abh. VI), p. 60, No. 1377.

[58] See the article in *Dict. Nat. Biogr.*, XVI (1888), 56.

[59] Drury was 'Menalcas' in Dibdin's bibliophile Arcadia.—See T. F. Dibdin, *Bibliomania* (London, 1842), pp. 605–609; also Seymour de Ricci, *English Collectors of Books and Manuscripts* (Cambridge, 1930), pp. 98, 122.

[60] On the recto of the first free fly-leaf (b) Drury has written a list of the contents of the manuscript. Then follows the sentence: 'I consider this as a very curious Monkish volume. 1823.' On the verso of this leaf, in the upper left-hand corner, is written in pencil *Nº 58*. In a onetime Drury manuscript of Tibullus and Ovid now at Harvard (*MS Lat 46*; parch., *saec. XV*) Drury has signed his name in the upper right-hand corner of the first free fly-leaf—this was his habit (see de Ricci, *English Collectors*, p. 98),—and again overleaf is written in pencil the numeral *48*. Drury's *8* (in *1823*) and those which appear in the two penciled numerals are identical or nearly so. Do these possibly refer to Drury's private catalogue?—In the de Ricci-Wilson *Census* a number of items are listed as formerly Drury property. Possibly others beside *Goodhart 11* were once *Saibantiani*.—According to a kind communication from the Librarian of Harrow School, the School archives contain no documents relative to Drury's library.

[61] The purchaser at this sale was, according to de Ricci-Wilson, *Census*, *loc. cit.*, Thorpe. A note in the Br. Mus. copy of the catalogue reveals as buyer (£5/6/0) a certain Cochran.

[62] Title of this catalogue quoted above, p. 232, n. 13.

[63] An excellent short account is that by Emil Jacobs, in *Zentralblatt für Bibliothekswesen*, XXVII (1910), 367 f., who suggests the desirability of an extended treatment; p. 368: items from the 1821 London sale now in Berlin. The de Ricci-Wilson *Census* reveals that not a few manuscripts auctioned at that sale are now found in the United States. Among them is probably more than one *Saibantianus*.

[64] See Frati-Sorbelli, *Dizionario*, pp. 134–136; de Ricci, *English Collectors*, p. 136.

[65] Above, p. 235, n. 33.

ing with these books various similarities of structure and also the verses, *Martini meritum . . .* ,[66] are three other manuscripts of like date which may prove to have closely related textual character:

B3 Brix. Quirin. L. III. 31. See *Da Prato*, p. *62* (=*B*).
Gp Alter Goodhartianus (olim Phillipp. 6732).[67]
Z Venet. Marc. L. IX. 61 (3287). See *Da Prato, ibid.* (=*M*).

That *Biv Gd V1 V2* show a common origin is indicated by numerous agreements in certain or probable error, among them the following:[68]

111, 10 legentes] *om.* 111, 16 omnia illius] acta *add.*[69] 112, 21 putaretur] crederetur 123, 13 salutis] salutiferae crucis 129, 14 penes quem tam incredibili euentu uictoria fuisset] penesque se iam incredibili euentu uictoriam fuisse 131, 23 nullam a Domino praestari posse clementiam] nullam misericordiam Domini praestare clementiam (clementia *V2*) 132, 27 omne monasterium loco] omnem monasterii locum 141, 15 temptatum] non solum temptatum 149, 19 caelo[70] reddidit] Deo reddidit 174, 4 birrum] bissum 199, 21 illa] illi autem 206, 24 uisam] uisam esse 210, 4 non] *om.* 211, 11 uasta solitudine] uasta solitudinis

Within this group, *Biv Gd V1* are bound together by certain places in which they err in common against *V2*:

121, 2 haut] haud *V2* autem *Biv Gd V1* 159, 3 fratres] *V2* sunt *Biv Gd V1* 165, 13 uti] *V2* uiuere *Biv Gd V1* 174, 4 rigentem] *V2* nitentem *Gd V1 et (teste De Prato) Biv* 174, 5 fluentem] *V2* fulgentem *Gd V1 et (teste De Prato) Biv*

The very close correspondence between *Biv* and *Gd* noted above suggests still further subdivision of the group, but more facts are needed before certainty in this matter can be reached.

The common appearance in all four manuscripts and in *B3 Gp Z* of the introductory verses, *Martini meritum . . .* , points to the derivation of all from a recension prepared, probably in North Italy, *ca.* 1400 or before. Since Da Prato's *Patavinus* is recorded as showing some of the errors common to *Biv Gd V1 V2*,[71] that manuscript may be tentatively assigned to the same group. Back of all would seem to stand a *Martinellus*

---

[66] See above, p. 234 (*C*) and n. 19.

[67] Acquired from Mr E. P. Goldschmidt of London; his *Catalogue 41* [1936], No. 175 (with facsimile, p. 59). In the Phillipps catalogue the book is dated *s. XII.*

[68] Reference is to page and line of Halm's text. Few readings from *V1 V2* are in my possession; otherwise the list would have been more striking. Among the scores of places in which Da Prato, in his edition, cites *Biv, Gd* agrees in all except nine, of which all but one or two are cases of no significance. For correcting Da Prato's report of *Biv* and gathering additional readings from *V1* and *V2* I am indebted to Mr Barlow.

[69] The *Dublinensis* (see E. A. Lowe, *Codices Latini Antiquiores*, II [Oxford, 1935], No. 270; and my *Da Prato*, p. 9, n. 7) here adds *opera* instead.

[70] In Halm's text *caelo* was omitted by oversight. It appears in *V* and generally elsewhere.

[71] Those at 111, 16; 123, 13; 131, 23; 132, 27; 211, 11.

of the type familiar at Tours[72] but studded with variants and glosses.

An item which, among the manuscripts just named, appears only in *Biv* and *Gd* is the marginal note (*Hoc ferrum—CCCCXXV*) on the sword of St Martin. It was surely the hand of the Veronese jurist, Maggio Maggi himself,[72a] which first entered that note into a manuscript of Sulpicius. That copy may be the book seen by Pellegrino de'Pellegrini[72b] or some other still undiscovered manuscript. But it seems worthwhile to bring forward again my earlier conjecture[73] that *Biv* contains the original note. Correcting my former opinion,[74] I now believe that the note in *Biv*, though in a different ink, was written by the hand of the adjacent text.[74a] Two noted scholars of Veronese Humanism have regarded *Biv* as written *propria manu* by Maggi.[75] But unless their opinion is based on solid evidence not brought forward, or until an undoubted autograph of Maggi's be adduced to confirm the identification,[76] there should be no dogmatic statement on the point.

Maggi knew the text of Sulpicius well enough to imitate it[77] and probably owned a copy, which may well have been written in his own hand. The note on the sword appears in *Biv* in a script rather more studied and meticulous than the somewhat cursive hand of the text proper. The scribe's consciousness of writing words that were his own would have tended to produce this effect.

On the assumption that *Biv* was once Maggi's own book, *Gd* emerges as either a direct copy of that manuscript or else a slightly later descendant. Such also would have been the codex seen by Pellegrini. Into both, Maggi's original note would have been copied, not unnaturally, along with the text itself.

Other first-hand marginalia found in *Biv* and *Gd* but not in *V1* and *V2*

[72] For a *Martinellus* of Reims as a likely source of the Sulpicius text in Da Prato's *Venetus* (now *Vatic. lat. 13699*), see *Da Prato*, pp. 36–38.

[72a] See below, p. 242, n. 84.

[72b] See above, p. 237, n. 47.

[73] *Da Prato*, p. 23.

[74] *Da Prato*, pp. 19 f. Cf. *ibid.*, Plate 3.

[74a] Mr Barlow informs me that Don Giuseppe Turrini, Librarian of the Bibl. Capit., shares this opinion. The same view had been expressed in 1704 by Ottavio Alecchi, in whose catalogue of Bevilacqua manuscripts (see Segarizzi, *op. cit.*, p. 78, n. 1) found in *Cod. Venet. Marc. Ital. X. 101*, there is a description (fols. 289r–291v) of our *Bivilaquius* (fol. 289v for the note on the sword). Alecchi's catalogue was examined for me by Mr Barlow.

[75] A. Segarizzi, 'Lodovico Sambonifacio e il suo Epistolario,' *Nuovo Archivio Veneto*, N. S., Tomo XX (1910), 93, n. 4 (where a well documented account of Maggi's career is found); R. Sabbadini, *Epistolario di Guarino Veronese*, III (*Miscellanea di Storia Veneta*, Serie Terza, XIV [1919]), p. 60 (comment on *Epist. 62*, l. 30).

[76] Mr Barlow, working from certain clues furnished by Segarizzi and Sabbadini (*locc. cit.*), generously carried out an extensive but vain search in Verona and (to a lesser extent) in Venice for Maggi's autograph.

[77] In a letter to San Lorenzo Giustiniani; see *Da Prato*, p. 20, n. 9.

serve to bind closer the former pair. Five such glosses appear in *Gd* and are found likewise in *Biv*.[78] The latter shows four others which are wanting in *Gd*.[79] This is a result which could well have arisen if *Gd* was derived from *Biv*.

Two of the five glosses shared by *Biv* and *Gd* are of a type not commonly found in manuscripts of Sulpicius. They are the work of one who could read the Classics and the Lives of the Saints with equal zeal and make profitable comparison between them. The first of these notes[80] recognizes the Terentian authorship of the line (*Andria*, 68) *obsequium amicos*, *ueritas odium parit*, tellingly used by Sulpicius himself in gentle rebuke to Gallus.[81] The second is set against the following passage: *miseratus est [libertum] potius quam insectatus abeuntem.*[82] The scribes of both manuscripts have commented marginally as follows:[83] *miseratus. etiam in oratione pro Murena.* The author of this note may have had sharper eyes than Merguet, who did not find *miseratus* anywhere in Cicero; or he may have read a version of the text in which some Humanist corrector had inserted the word; or else it may be that, more familiar with *misereo(r)* than *miseror*, he was calling attention, even if obliquely, to the two forms of the latter verb which do appear in the *pro Murena* (55, 88). It seems hardly likely, however, that the author of the note had not some knowledge of the text of that oration.

Can this be safely assumed of Maggio Maggi?[84] An eloquent jurist and

---

[78] *Biv*, fols. 14ʳ, 36ᵛ, 37ᵛ, 58ᵛ, 60ʳ; *Gd*, fols. 155ʳ, 217ʳ, 220ᵛ, 277ʳ, 280ᵛ.

[79] *Biv*, fols. 20ʳ, 22ᵛ, 25ʳ, 53ᵛ. Of these the first and the third are not surely in the hand of the text.

[80] *Biv*, fol. 36ᵛ; *Gd*, fol. 217ʳ.

[81] *Dial.*, I, 9, 3.

[82] *Dial.*, I, 12, 3.

[83] *Biv*, fol. 37ᵛ; *Gd*, fol. 220ᵛ.

[84] To supplement the imperfect account given of this distinguished Veronese patriot in *Da Prato*, p. 20, see especially the material assembled by Segarizzi and Sabbadini, *opp. cit.* (above, p. 242, n. 75). Among printed documents for Maggi's biography the chief are twenty-one letters written to him by Guarino of Verona, who grew up with Maggi and used his services at many points in his career. These have been admirably published (1915–1919) by Sabbadini, *Epistolario di Guarino Veronese* (three volumes: *Miscellanea di Storia Veneta*, Serie Terza, VIII, XI, XIV). The series ends with *Epist. 692* (A.D. 1436), written eight years before Maggi's assassination. In addition to Sabbadini's commentary (Vol. III) see the same author's *La Scuola e gli Studi di Guarino Veronese* (Catania, 1896), Indice, *s.v.* Maggi. A long, unsigned notice on Maggi, written in a hand of the seventeenth or eighteenth century is preserved with *Cod. Veron. Com. 1876*; in it Maggi is called 'Padre della Patria.' This notice, of which Mr Barlow sent me a copy, supplements Segarizzi's account at several points. On Mr Barlow's testimony, there is nothing in the text proper (*saec. XV*) of *Cod. Veron. Com. 1876* (a *Summa Notarile*) to prove Maggi's authorship; but see Biadego's catalogue and Sabbadini, *Epistolario*, III, 60. The letter cited by Sabbadini, *ibid.*, as found in *Cod. Venet. Marc. Lat. XIV. 221*, fol. 103, is, Mr Barlow reports, a copy made by Giacomo Morelli. Evidence of Maggi's friendship with Francesco Barbaro is found in Guarino's *Epistolario* and in a letter (Oct. 12, 1422) written by Barbaro to Maggi; published by Sabbadini, *Centotrenta Lettere Inedite di Francesco Barbaro* (Salerno, 1884), p. 67. In Italian Maggi's name appears also as Maio, Mazo (Sabbadini's final preference), and Mazzo.

man of affairs, he would naturally have found a guide in Cicero; and a reader of that author, well after his school days, he surely was. On one occasion we find his intimate friend Guarino of Verona and a group of disciples visiting him and finding him puzzled over the *tertia aetas* of Nestor in the *Cato Maior*.[85] Earlier (1418), when Guarino was still teaching in Venice, Maggio sent him a volume of Cicero's speeches to receive Guarino's emendations.[86] Small doubt then that the new-found *Mureniana* furnished a subject of common interest to the two friends. There is strong evidence that Guarino received at Venice, through Francesco Barbaro, a copy of this oration and of the *pro S. Roscio* shortly after Poggio discovered them (1415) in the *vetus Cluniacensis*.[87] By 1425 the *pro Murena* had surely come into Guarino's hands, for in the spring of that year he was arranging for his copy to be freshly transcribed[88] and was expounding the oration in his school at Verona.[89] It was during this period that, as my evidence points, the *Bivilaquius* was transcribed and with it the note professing to cite the *pro Murena*. The joy that Guarino then as always took in his association with Maggi is exhibited in a letter of June, 1424.[90] Guarino had been the guest at Zevio of Vitaliano Faella, whose entertainment had included a symposium in the ancient manner, *tibicines* and all. A fellow guest was Maggi. At such a meeting—and many like them there must have been—Guarino may well have interpreted the *pro Murena* and recited portions of its text.

[85] See Sabbadini, *La Scuola*, p. 137.

[86] See Guarino, *Epist. 124* and *126*; Sabbadini, *Storia e Critica di Testi Latini* (Catania, 1914), pp. 52 f.

[87] Sabbadini so held in more than one place; e.g. *Storia e Critica*, p. 32 (cf. p. 52 and *La Scuola*, p. 91). Ernst Walser, *Poggius Florentinus, Leben und Werke* (Leipzig-Berlin, 1914), p. 50, accepted his opinion. That Barbaro himself executed Guarino's copy is unlikely if we strictly interpret the former's statement about the illegibility of the *Cluniacensis*; see Sabbadini, *Storia e Critica*, p. 32; *La Scuola*, p. 91. Guarino's commentary on the *pro S. Roscio*, if (as Sabbadini maintained) a Venetian work, indicates the author's ownership of that text (and, in all probability, of the *pro Murena* as well) before 1419. Sabbadini finds in Guarino's *Epist. 34* (A.D. <1415>) and *62* (A.D. <1417>) quotations or reminiscences of the *pro S. Roscio*. If he is right in finding the *pro Murena* quoted in *Epist. 197* (A.D.<1421?>), we have Guarino's ownership of that oration reasonably well established for the early years of his school at Verona.

For Poggio's discovery, see A. C. Clark, *The Vetus Cluniacensis of Poggio* [*Anecdota Oxoniensia*, Classical Series, X] (Oxford, 1905) and the other works cited in Schanz-Hosius, *Gesch. d. röm. Lit.*, I (1927), 406 f., 424. See also Erich Reitzenstein, 'Cicero-Reden in einem Palimpsest zu Bologna,' *Nachrichten von d. Ges. d. Wiss. zu Göttingen*, Phil.-Hist. Kl., 1927, 38–52 (with his earlier statement, *Gnomon*, I [1925], 299 f.).

[88] Guarino, *Epist. 298.*

[89] Guarino, *Epist. 300.* I have adopted the interpretation of Sabbadini, *Storia e Critica*, p. 54. Possibly the *coetus* from which Vitaliano Faella, the addressee of the letter, had absented himself was one of the less formal gatherings which Guarino, wherever he was teaching, would bring together. (See an account of them in Sabbadini, *La Scuola*, pp. 137 f., 153 f.) In 1419, in any case, Faella appears to have been Guarino's pupil; see *Epist. 158.*

[90] *Epist. 259;* see Sabbadini, *La Scuola*, p. 154 (with the first publication of the letter, pp. 186–188).

In Maggi was a zeal as well for hagiography as for the Classics. A passage from Guarino's bread-and-butter letter to Faella reveals its author as a man of like temper.[91]

Ut enim primum tuas aedes intravimus oblatus est codex pervetustus, qui cum nostrum gratulari visus sit adventum, obviam nobis quibus poterat modis progrediebatur. Eius lectio cum sanctissimos patres nostros coram apposuisset, ad pulcherrima vitae instituta, probitate prudentia liberalitate fide, rerum mundanarum contemptu, imitatione invitabat et exemplis, id est virum bonum et magnum informabat.

With the adjective *pervetustus* Guarino could hardly, even as a joke, have referred to our *Bivilaquius*, then newly transcribed if yet in existence at all, but it may be that the volume of the Fathers read at Zevio was the exemplar of all or part of that codex.

Its kinsman, the *Saibantianus*, was four hundred years later called by Byron's teacher a 'very curious monkish volume,'[92] but the reunion at the home of Faella and the enthusiastic regard entertained for Sulpicius Severus by Petrarch,[93] Coluccio Salutati[94] and other laymen of the Renaissance[95] tend to give the lie to that description.

HARVARD UNIVERSITY.

[91] See Sabbadini, *op. cit.*, Cap. XV 'Studi Sacri.' In St Ambrose, St Jerome, and St Zeno, lives of whom are contained in *Biv* and *Gd*, Guarino had more than an ordinary interest; see Sabbadini, *op. cit.*, pp. 100, 139; *Epistolario*, III, 571 ff., Indice degli autori antichi. Of St Martin and Sulpicius Severus I have found no mention in Guarino's letters.

[92] See above, p. 239, n. 60.

[93] See Pierre de Nolhac, *Pétrarque et l'Humanisme* (Paris, 1907), II, 211: 'la vie de saint Martin de Tours, écrite par Sulpice Sévère, à qui Pétrarque faisait l'honneur d'une estime particulière.'

[94] The splendid Florentine *Martinellus* mentioned above (p. 231, n. 6) was Coluccio's property. Professor B. L. Ullman assures me that it was written at his order. Before coming to the friars of San Marco it passed through the hands of Cosimo de' Medici.

[95] See Sabbadini, *Le Scoperte dei Codici Latini e Greci*, II (Florence, 1914), 253, where, however, ecclesiastics, if not monks, are largely dealt with.

A MAGICAL TEXT FROM BEROEA
IN MACEDONIA

David M. Robinson

RECENTLY a silver tablet,[1] which was rolled up in a bronze tube (Plate 1B), came to me from the Ritsos Collection when it was sold in Paris. Mr. Ritsos, before he died, had said that it was found at Beroea, the modern Verria, in the northern district of Macedonia, which was called Emathia.[2] What concerns us particularly in considering the Jewish influence in our text is the fact that in the first century A.D. (54 or 55 A.D.) we find at Beroea a Jewish community and a synagogue to which St. Paul and Silas preached.[3] Even the Jews of Thessalonica came thither and stirred up the people. Paul left, but Silas and Timotheus abode there still. Beroea continued to be an important city during the first three centuries A.D.,[4] the time to which our text may belong.[5] The forms of the letters are in a crude script inclining slightly to the cursive, as so often in the third or early fourth century A.D. The syntax and the spelling are sometimes confused, as often happens in such texts. See the enlarged illustration on Plate 1A.

Ανοχ αι
Ακραμμαχαμαρι
Βαρβαθιαωθ

[1] Two pieces of the tube are preserved, one 0.082 m. high, the other (from the opposite side) 0.045 m. high. The diameter of the tube was 0.015 m. The silver foil is 0.073 m. high and 0.058 m. wide. The original edge is preserved on all sides. See Plate 1.

[2] Cf. A. Struck, *Makedonische Fahrten*, II: *Die Makedonische Niederlande* (Sarajevo: Kajon, 1908), pp. 27–44; M. G. Demitsas, Μακεδονία (Athens, 1896), pp. 59–89. Cf. W. M. Leake, *Travels in Northern Greece* (London: Rodwell, 1835), III, 292, where three inscriptions are mentioned; E. Cousinéry, *Voyage dans la Macédoine* (Paris: Imprimerie Royale, 1831), I, 57 ff. For other inscriptions from Beroea cf. *C.I.G.* II, 1957, Add. d-g; *C.I.L.* III, 596; A. Struck, 'Inschriften aus Makedonien,' *Ath. Mitt.* XXVII, 1902, 315–316; for coins cf. B. V. Head, *Historia Numorum* (2nd ed., Oxford Press, 1911), 242–243; Pauly-Wissowa, *Real-Encyclopädie* (Stuttgart, Metzler: 1899), III, cols. 304–306; C. F. Edson, 'The Antigonids, Heracles and Beroea,' *Harvard Stud. in Class. Phil.* XLV, 1934, 232–246. Cf. Strabo VII (330), frag. 26: ἡ Βέροια πόλις ἐν ταῖς ὑπωρείαις κεῖται τοῦ Βερμίου ὄρους. A list of Beroeans is given by Edson, *loc. cit.*, pp. 233–234, but it omits those in the inscriptions as given by Demitsas, *loc. cit.*; in *Ath. Mitt., loc. cit.*; and such names as that in *I.G.* III, 2395. For an original Greek bronze statuette in Munich, which comes from Beroea and because of its Polyclitan characteristics dates from the fifth century B.C., cf. D. M. Robinson, *The Art Bulletin*, V, 1922, 109–110, pl. XLV.

[3] *Acts*, XVII, 10–14; XX, 4: 'There accompanied him as far as Asia Sopater of Beroea.'

[4] Cf. Pliny, *Nat. Hist.* IV, 33; VI, 216.

[5] Cf. Head, *op. cit.*, p. 243. For Olympic games at Beroea in the third century A.D. cf. also *I.G.* III, 129.

Λαμψουηρ

Λαμηηρ

Λαμφορη Ἰάω

Ἀβλαναθαναλ-

βα, Κύριοι Ἄνγελοι,

σώσετε τὸν (= ὃν) ἐγέν-

νη⟨σ⟩εν Ἀταλάντη,

Εὐφήλητον

Such tablets of silver and even of gold have been found elsewhere and generally have magical texts.[6] The Greek expression for such amulet-inscriptions seems to have been φυλακτήριον εἰς πέταλον ἀργυροῦν, if we can argue from that published by Wessely,[7] though Preisendanz[8] cites a text

[6] In 1924 I excavated one in a bronze tube (when unrolled 0.093 m. high by 0.033 m. wide; tube 0.05 m. high as preserved) at Antioch-over-against-Pisidia, with twelve lines of Greek letters all mixed up so that I am unable to read it. The fourth line may have the word Αναξ unless this is part of a participle ἀναχωρέων. If any one wishes a photograph to study, the University of Michigan or I can furnish one. I have seen two such Greek silver leaf scrolls, which are unpublished, in the collection of Robert Garrett in Baltimore; two others of the second century A.D., also unpublished, in the Ashmolean Museum at Oxford (bought at the Amherst sale and inventoried as 1921. 1121 and 1921. 1122); and one from Syria in the Metropolitan Museum (18. 84. 2B) with bronze cylindrical case and an inscribed thin bronze foil with twelve lines of an Aramaic inscription invoking protection for an unborn child and the children of all her children and with a reference to 'the Holy Angels' (cf. *Bull. Met. Mus.* XIV, 1919, 94–95). Cf. also A. Wiedemann, 'Die gnostische Silbertafel von Badenweiler,' *Bonner Jahrbücher*, LXXIX, 1885, 215–234; M. Siebourg, 'Ein gnostisches Goldamulet aus Gellep,' *ibid.*, CIII, 1898, 123–153 (126–7, 135, 139 give parallels and a list of those known up to 1898); P. Perdrizet, 'Amulette Grecque trouvée en Syrie,' *Rev. Ét. Gr.*, XLI, 1928, 73–82. For the magic quality of silver cf. E. Riess in Pauly-Wissowa in article 'Aberglaube' (Stuttgart: Metzler, 1894) I, 51; and on such amulets in general cf. Daremberg-Saglio, *Dictionnaire des Antiquités*, I, 254–255. Cf. also Paribeni, *Le Terme di Diocleziano*, 1920, p. 231, no. 991 (65057), 'laminetta d'argento con iscrizione magica in lettere greche che non pare diano un significato'; Marshall, *Cat. of Jewellery, Gr. Et. and Rom. in the Brit. Mus.*, nos. 3150–3157; Conway, *From Orpheus to Cicero*, p. 9; Gulick, *Athenaeus* (Loeb Cl. Libr.), V, 486, note c, where Gulick suggests Ἐφεσήϊα γράμματα βαιά, not καλά, a likely correction in view of the small letters in such phylacteries as ours.

[7] Cf. K. Wessely, 'Griechische Zauberpapyrus von Paris und London,' *Denkschriften der kaiserlichen Akademie der Wissenschaften, Wien*, phil.-hist. Klasse, XXXVI, 2, 1888, p. 112, line 2705. Cf. also the πέταλον ἀργυροῦν found at Badenweiler and published by F. Kraus, *Die christlichen Inschriften des Rheinlandes* (Freiburg i. B.: Mohr, 1890–94) I, 13 and cf. M. Siebourg, *Bonner Jahrbücher*, CIII, 1898, 123–153, especially 135–137. Cf. Wessely, *op. cit.*, p. 90, no. 1847, χρυσοῦν πέταλον. Cf. especially T. Puschmann, *Alexander von Tralles* (Vienna: Braumüller, 1879) II, 583 (physician of 6th century A.D.): προφυλακτικὸν ποδάγρας. Λαβὼν πέταλον χρυσοῦν . . . γράφε ἐν αὐτῷ . . . εἶτα ὅμοιον τῷ πετάλῳ σωληνάριον ποιήσας κατάκλεισον. For the word φυλακτήριον cf. also F. G. Kenyon, *Greek Papyri in the British Museum* (1893), I, p. 91, 218; p. 94, 298; p. 100, 486; p. 102, 579; p. 111, 857; p. 125, 37; Wessely, *op. cit.*, Pap. 2391 of Louvre, lines 97, 127; large papyrus of the Bibliothèque Nationale, lines 78, 86, 257, 660, 708, 813, 1071, 1253, 1263, 1316, 1335, 1619, 1653, 1675, 1690, 2358, 2506, 2510, 2630, 2705, 2877, 2897, 3014, 3114, 3127; Kopp, *Palaeographia Critica* (Mannheim: 1817–1829), 55, 177, 342, 450, 555, 588, 688; *Arch. f. Religionsw.* XII, 1909, 26–27; Campbell Bonner, *Michigan Papyri*, III, 1936, p. 124, col. I, line 2; pp. 130, 131: ἐν τῷ φυλακτηρίῳ τούτῳ; also Plutarch, *De Iside et Osiride*, 68 (378 B).

[8] K. Preisendanz, *Papyri Graecae Magicae* (Leipzig, Teubner, 1931), II, p. 164, col. II. Cf. also Wessely, *op. cit.*, p. 51, lines 257–8: φυλακτήριον—εἰς λεπίδα ἀργυρᾶν. The Latin word is *lamella* or

A.

B.

PLATE I

A. A Magical Text from Beroea (enlarged).
B. The Tubular Container.

with λᾶμναν ἀργυρᾶν γράφε χαλκῷ γραφίῳ. Phylacteries were often worn by
the Jews and are referred to in the Old Testament.[9] These generally consist of a small leathern case[10] which contains slips of parchment with
passages from *Deuteronomy*. They were worn on the head or left arm. But
the term might be applied to a bronze tube with an amulet or prayer in it,
such as ours. The Jews still wear on their person tephillin or phylacteries.
Roman Catholics and even Mohammedans also today have similar amulets which are often attached to the door of the house, like the Jewish
mezuzoth, or hung on the necks of children to protect them from disease.
Such amulets were often worn on the person and buried with the dead.
Even from mediaeval times there is preserved an astrological text, translated from Aramaic into Hebrew, which says: 'If thou wishest to protect
a young babe from an evil spirit . . . write these angels on a tablet of gold
in Assyrian writing.'[11] Such texts have been found not only in Syria but
in Asia Minor, Greece, Carthage, Rome, and even southwestern Ger-
many. They are not necessarily Jewish, but many of the names are taken
from Hebrew or Aramaic as well as from Egyptian. Possibly sometimes
they represent the solar deity whom the syncretism of the last centuries
of paganism confused with the ancient gods. The formulas probably originated in the ghetto quarter of Alexandria, but this Judaic-Alexandrine
magic spread even to Macedonia, where it remained even after the Jewish
influence had waned. Let us now consider the text with its gibberish Greek.

Line 1: The reading after Ανοχ seems to be AI, and there may have
been other letters. In the Berlin papyrus no. 5025 (K. Preisendanz,
Papyri Graecae Magicae, I, 10, col. 2) we have ανοχα (= Ανοχ α or ω,
'the great Anoch'). It must be the Coptic word which is found so often
in magic papyri and which has been so well discussed by Adolf Jacoby
in his article, 'Ein Berliner Chnubisamulett,' *Arch. f. Religionsw.* XXVIII,
1930, 269–285. It certainly seems to be a proper name of a demon or
deity addressed in K. Preisendanz, *op. cit.*, I, p. 122 (*Pap. Par.* 1537–8),
'Ανοχω, 'Αβρασάξ, | Τρω etc.[12] This would be the great Anoch and his
name appears as Ανοχ,[13] Ανοκ,[14] Ανογ.[15] That he might be connected with

---

lamna or *lamina;* cf. Marcellus Empiricus, *De Medicamentis*, XXI, 8: lamella stagnea; *ibid.*, XXII,
10: in lamina stagnea scribe . . . laminam vero licio ligatam collo.

[9] *Exodus*, XIII, 1–10, 11–17; *Deuteronomy*, VI, 4–9, 13–22; 11, 18; *Numbers*, XV, 38–39. Cf. also
Marcellus Empiricus, XXX, 8: phylacterium . . . in collo ex licio suspendes.

[10] Cf. Athenaeus, 548 c (from the comic poet, Anaxilas): ἐν σκυταρίοις ῥαπτοῖσι φορῶν | Ἐφεσήια
γράμματα βαιά.

[11] Cf. M. Gaster, *Proceedings of the Society of Biblical Archaeology*, XXII, 1900, 340.

[12] Cf. T. Hopfner, *Griechisch-Ägyptischer Offenbarungszauber* (Leipzig: Haessel, 1921), I, 692;
Pap. Par. 1570 ff., 1577 (Preisendanz, *op. cit.*, I, 124); A. Dieterich, *Abraxas* (Leipzig: Teubner, 1891),
p. 203, 16.

[13] Preisendanz, *op. cit.*, II, p. 18, col. 11; p. 96, col. 5; p. 123, col. 18; p. 141 (P. XIX).

[14] *Ibid.*, II, p. 18, col. 11.   [15] *Ibid.*, II, p. 115, col. 13.

the Rising Sun seems to be implied in Preisendanz, *op. cit.*, I, p. 124 (*Pap. Par.*, ll. 1585-7): ἐπικαλοῦμαι καὶ σέ, τὸν τὸ πῦρ κρατοῦντα Φθαν ᾿Ανοχ, and in *ibid.*, II, p. 72, col. 7: ὦ θεοὶ ἐν μέσῳ μέρει κυκλούμενοι, τρεῖς ἥλιοι ᾿Ανοχ Μανε Βαρχυχ. There are several cases (Jacoby, *loc. cit.*, p. 271), however, where Anok or Anoch seems to be the Coptic pronoun of the first person. In one example[16] it is combined with the very Barbarioth which occurs on our tablet; but as so many other deities are named and the later part of the inscription is in Greek, it seems as if the Greek εἰμί and not the Coptic Anoch would have been used, if the meaning were, 'I am Akrammachamari, etc.,' though there are many examples (e.g. P. V, 146, 248) in which the operator identifies himself with such and such a deity or demon.[17]

Line 2: We find many different forms of this word: Ακραμμαχαμαρι,[18] Ακραμμαχαμαρει,[19] Ακραμμαχαμμαρι,[20] Ακραμμαχαμμαρει,[21] Ακραμαχαμαρι,[22] Ακραμμαχαρι,[23] Αγραμακραμαρ,[24] even Αγραμεχορρει.[25] This compound,[26] written usually as one word, may have been originally two words. At any rate in G. F. Kenyon, *Greek Papyri in the British Museum*, I, p. 95, line 328, we read Κραμμα and, *ibid.*, p. 100, line 496, Χαμαρι, surrounded by quite different magic words. Kopp[27] explains the word as Κραμ αχαμαρι, the Hebrew for liga amuletum meum, or Ακραμνι καμαρι, the Hebrew for protegit me amuletum meum. C. Schmidt, *Pistis Sophia* (Leipzig, Hinrich, 1925, p. 359) gives the word as the name of the first of the three ἀόρατοι θεοί, a triad standing high in the gnostic hierarchy of deities. He is the master of the heavenly firmament in A. Audollent, *Defixionum Tabellae* (Paris, Fontemoing, 1904, p. 325, lines 7-8): ὁρκίζω σὲ τὸν θεὸν

[16] *Ibid.*, I, p. 70 (*Pap. Paris*, IV, l. 91).

[17] Cf. also Campbell Bonner, *Michigan Papyri*, III, 1936, 126: ἐγώ εἰμι ᾿Ερεσχιγάλ or, p. 131: ἐγὼ γάρ εἰμι αβρασαξ.

[18] K. Wessely, 'Ephesia Grammata aus Papyrusrollen, Inschriften, Gemmen,' etc. (*Zwölfter Jahresbericht über das k. k. Franz-Joseph-Gymnasium in Wien*, Selbstverlag des Gymnasiums, 1886), no. 229; S. Eitrem, 'Papyri Osloenses' (Academy of Science and Letters of Oslo, 1925), I, p. 12, col. ix; I, p. 44; Preisendanz, *op. cit.*, I, p. 36, col. 3; p. 106, 981, 11; II, p. 65; p. 138; p. 143, no. 19 a, line 30; p. 164, col. 2; Hopfner, *op. cit.*, II, 214.

[19] Preisendanz, *op. cit.*, I, p. 54, col. 16; p. 182, 65; II, 10, col. 6; p. 14, col. 9; p. 44, col. 30: δὸς μοι ... [τὴν ἰσχὺν τοῦ Α]κρα[μ]μαχα[μ]αρεί; p. 48, col. 2; p. 54, col. 16; p. 68, col. 5; p. 70, col. 6: ὁ ἐπίχαρις θεός; p. 187 (P. LIX): ὁ καλὸς θεός; p. 78, col. 9. Cf. Hopfner, *op. cit.*, I, 735; F. G. Kenyon, *Greek Papyri in the British Museum*, I, p. 91, 220; p. 94, 311; p. 122, 28.

[20] G. Vitelli, Società Italiana, *Papiri Greci e Latini* (Florence, Ariani, 1912), p. 69, 57.

[21] Preisendanz, *op. cit.*, II, p. 10, col. 6.

[22] Soc. Ital., *Pap. Gr. e Lat.*, I, p. 70, 24; Preisendanz, *op. cit.*, II, p. 161.

[23] Preisendanz, *op. cit.*, I, p. 38, col. 6.

[24] Kenyon, *op. cit.*, p. 94, 316.

[25] R. Wünsch, *Arch. f. Religionsw.*, XII, 1909, p. 42, B 16.

[26] Cf. also *Pap. Leid.* V, col. 5, 18; 6, 9 (*Jahrbücher für classische Philologie*, Suppl. XVI, A. Fleckeisen, 1888, pp. 803-804); K. Wessely, *op. cit.*, p. 22, no. 216.

[27] U. Kopp, *Palaeographia Critica*, 681, 749; T. Hopfner, *op. cit.*, I, 735.

τὸν τῶν οὐρανίων στερεωμάτων δεσπότην Αχραμαχαμαρει (an inscription of the same date as ours).

Line 3: The form Βαρβαθιαωθ is unique, but very similar spellings occur frequently: Βαρβαθιαω,[28] Αρβαθιαω,[29] Αβραθιαω,[30] and even Μαρμαραωθ[31] or Μαρμαρανωθ or Μαρμαρεωθ.[32] In Kenyon, *Papyri in the British Museum*, I, p. 80, 479 we have Ιαωθ after Αρβαθιαω. In *Archiv für Religionswissenschaft*, XII, 1909, p. 25, line 9 we have Αβριαωθ. In *Archiv Orientální*, III, 1931, p. 337 we have Βαρβαρανω, Βαρβαριωθ, Σαβαρβαρβαθιωθ with Σαβαρβαρβαθιουθ and even Αβρατιαωθ, so that the ending ιαωθ in our text is possible. Perhaps we should divide the word into two parts, since the last part is surely Ιαô,[33] a solar deity, and the first part an epithet, possibly meaning "four" from the Hebrew *arba*. It would be easy for the beta to be repeated at the beginning and for the intervocalic θ (Hebrew *oth*) to be inserted. In any case the text of *Papyrus W. of Leiden*, 176, 21: Ἥλιε, . . . Αρβαθιαω, shows that *arbathiaô* may be a solar deity. Wessely, *Ephesia Grammata* (no. 36), speaks of τὸν Ἥλιον . . . Ιαο Σαβαωθ Αβραιαωθ. The large magical papyrus of Paris (Wessely, *Denkschriften der kaiserlichen Akademie der Wissenschaften in Wien*, phil.-hist. Klasse, XXXVI [1888], p. 69, line 990) has Αβραϊωθ τὸν τὰ πάντα φωτίζοντα καὶ διαυγάζοντα.

Lines 4–6: The forms in these three lines must be related and all may refer to some solar deity. The threefold repetition is a magical aid to power. Λαμψουηρ[34] occurs in Preisendanz, *Papyri Graecae Magicae*, II, p. 49, col. 2; Kenyon, *Greek Papyri in the British Museum*, I, p. 119, 82; λαμψουρη[35] by metathesis, Preisendanz, *op. cit.*, I, p. 182, 64; Kenyon, *op. cit.*, I, p. 67, 62; λαμψουωρ in *Archiv Orientální*, III, 1931, 342 (*Pap. Leid. W.*, col. XXI, 13); Preisendanz, *op. cit.*, II, p. 22, col. 13; p. 127,

[28] Preisendanz, *op. cit.*, I, p. 44, col. 10; p. 192, 356; Kenyon, *op. cit.*, I, p. 76, 355; T. Hopfner, 'Orientalisch-Religionsgeschichtliches aus den griechischen Zauberpapyri Aegyptens,' *Archiv Orientální*, III, 1931, pp. 337–8, also Βαρβαριωθ; *ibid.*, p. 358.

[29] T. Hopfner, *op. cit.*, II, 214; *Rev. Ét. Gr.*, XLI, 1928, 73, 77–8; Eitrem, *op. cit.*, I, p. 15, line 308; Kenyon, *op. cit.*, p. 69, 117; p. 76, 352; p. 80, 479; 82, 35; p. 92, 236.

[30] *Rev. Ét. Gr.*, XLI, 1928, 73, 78; Eitrem, *op. cit.*, I, p. 16, line 350.

[31] This is the name of an angel in Hopfner, *op. cit.*, I, 657; 746; cf. also Preisendanz, *op. cit.*, I, p. 84.

[32] *Pap. Par.*, 947 (Preisendanz, *op. cit.*, I, p. 84, 368; p. 104, 947).

[33] For Ιαω cf. Kenyon, *op. cit.*, p. 68, 90; p. 69, 128; p. 70, 176; p. 74, 300; p. 76, 341; p. 80, 472, 478; p. 82, 29, 41; p. 91, 220; p. 94, 309; p. 96, 375; p. 101, 521, 545; p. 102, 564, 584; p. 103, 596; p. 105, 649; p. 115, (b.) 7; p. 118, 60; p. 121, 6; Eitrem, *op. cit.*, p. 6, 42, 49; p. 11, 197; p. 15, 308; p. 16, 349. On *Iao*, not the Jewish Yahweh but the great god of the solar syncretism, cf. Perdrizet, *Rev. Ét. Gr.* XLI, 1928, pp. 76–7 and works there cited; Hopfner, *op. cit.*, II, 214; ὁρκίζω σέ, ἱερὸν φῶς, ἱερὰ αὐγή, etc. Cf. Campbell Bonner, *Michigan Papyri*, III, 1936, 130: μέγας οὐράνιος εἱλῶν τὸν κόσμον ὁ ὢν θεὸς ὁ Ἰάω κύριος παντοκράτωρ αβλαναθαλααβλα (*sic*).

[34] The same ending is found in Ἀρουήρ, *Pap. Par.* 1805 (Preisendanz, *op. cit.*, I, p. 128).

[35] Perhaps this form should be read for Χαμψουρη in *Pap. Berl.*, II, p. 168 (Preisendanz, *op. cit.*, I, p. 30).

col. 21; Kenyon, *op. cit.*, p. 99, 476; λαμψωρει in Preisendanz, *op. cit.*, II, p. 65, col. 4; λαμψηρ in *Archiv Orientální*, III, 1931, 338; λαμψυς in Preisendanz, *op. cit.*, II, p. 150, 36; λαμψτηρ, *ibid.*, II, p. 124, col. 18. Though undoubtedly there was confusion with the Greek word λάμπειν, the form developed out of the Hebrew or Coptic and is perhaps another name for the eternal sun.[36] Often he appears under the name Semesilamps,[37] Semesilampsa, Semesilamph, Semesilampe, or Semesilam. The first part is from the Hebrew *semes* = sun, and the second half is perhaps the same word with consonantal dissimilation of sigma into lambda or confusion with the Greek root, λαμπ-. Wessely, *Ephesia Grammata*, no. 36, has Ἥλιον . . . Σεμεσιλαμψα. In R. Wünsch, *Antike Fluchtafeln* (1907), p. 16, line 14, we have . . . ὁρκίζω σὲ τὸν θεὸν τὸν φωτίζοντα καὶ σκοτίζοντα τὸν κόσμον Σεμεσειλαμ. The variants in our text, Λαμηηρ and Λαμφορηιαω (with the name of Ιαô at the end) are unparalleled. A form with φ occurs, Λαμηηαφατουηγι in Dieterich, *Abraxas*, p. 200, 26; in Kenyon, *Greek Papyri in the British Museum*, XLVI, p. 76, line 350, we have Σεμεσιλαμφ . . . Αρβαθιαω. But, as I have said, the forms are probably fabricated to get anaphora or three-fold repetition of the syllable λαμ and the endings purposely changed, terminating with an appeal to Ιαô[38] to enhance the magic power of the amulet. Λαμφορη is used for Λαμφοήρ by metathesis.

Line 7: The word Ablanathanalba, which spells the same forwards as backwards, is frequent in papyri, on Gnostic charms, invocations, and magic monuments.[39] It is of Hebrew origin and would mean "Our Father" or "Father, come to us" (*ab* = father, *lanath* = to us).[40] In the *Revue des Études Grecques* XLI, 1928, p. 78, another explanation is proposed, that the four letters of *abla* stand for *atta, barouch, leolam, Adonaï* and then

---

[36] Cf. *Arch. f. Religionsw.* XXVIII, 1930, 276–284; *Rev. Ét. Gr.* XLI, 1928, 80; Dieterich, *op. cit.*, p. 52, n. 3; cf. also *ibid.*, p. 178, 4; p. 183, 49; p. 200, 14.

[37] Cf. Audollent, *Defixionum Tabellae*, p. lxx, n. 5; and the many examples from gems and papyri cited by A. Jacoby, *Arch. f. Religionsw.*, XXVIII, 1930, pp. 276–279. Cf. especially T. Hopfner, *Archiv Orientální*, III, 1931, 334.

[38] Preisendanz, *op. cit.*, I, p. 132, 1983: Λαιλαμ Ἰάω; p. 192, 366: Σεμεσιλαμ Ἰαεω; p. 196, 478: Λαιλαμ . . . Ἰάω.

[39] Preisendanz, *op. cit.*, I, p. 34, col. 3; p. 36, col. 3; p. 38, col. 6; p. 46, cols. 12, 13; p. 106, 983; p. 170, 3031; II, p. 14, col. 9; p. 44, col. 30: τὴν ἐπιτυχίαν τοῦ Ἀβλαναθαναλβα; p. 48, 62; p. 53, col. 2; p. 61, 24; p. 65, col. 4; p. 68, 157; p. 70, 184: ὁ τὸ δίκαιον ἔχων; p. 124, col. 18; p. 138; p. 140; p. 143; p. 159 (Pap. XXXIII); p. 161, 23; p. 164, col. 2; p. 170, col. 9; p. 179 (Pap. XLIII); p. 187, 2: δοῦλ[ος] τοῦ [ἐνδόξ]ου θεοῦ; *Rev. Ét. Gr.* XLI, 1928, 73; A. Delatte, 'Études sur la magie grecque,' in *Le Musée Belge*, XVIII, 1914, 28; *Archiv Orientální*, III, 1931, 337–338; F. Dornseiff, *Das Alphabet in Mystik und Magie*[2] (Leipzig: Teubner, 1925), p. 63; Audollent, *op. cit.*, p. lxxi. Cf. Kenyon, *op. cit.*, p. 67, 63; Eitrem, *op. cit.*, p. 6, 43; p. 12, 227; *Papyrus in the Bibliothèque Nationale* (Wessely, *op. cit.*), lines 982 and 3030. Cf. also Campbell Bonner, as cited in note 33.

[40] Cf. Kopp, *op. cit.*, 580–586, 681; Hopfner, *op. cit.*, I, 708: ἐγώ εἰμι ὁ ἐπικαλούμενός σε Συριστί θεὸν μέγαν Σααλαηριφρου καὶ οὐ μὴ παρακούσῃς τῆς φωνῆς Ἑβραϊστί Ἀβλαναθαναλβα (cf. also Dieterich, *op. cit.*, p. 69); Hopfner, *op. cit.*, pp. 731, 732 (28 varieties of spelling); *ibid.*, II, 264.

follows the name of the prophet, Nathan, which can be written backwards or forwards, and the *alba* is *abla* backwards. In any case the word is a palindrome, which increases its magic power. Such an anagrammatisation possibly refers to the sun, which according to ancient belief reversed its course during the night. In Wessely, *Ephesia Grammata*, no. 229, we have an oath by the sacred names, which include our Akrammachamari, Arbathiao, Iaô, and Ablanathanalba. It is worth while in connection with Akrammachamari, Iaô, Lampsouer, and Ablanathanalba to quote what T. Hopfner says in *Archiv Orientální*, III, 1931, 337–8: 'Natürlich sind gelegentlich an diesen oder jenen gebräuchlichen Namen auch noch andere ὀνόματα βαρβαρικά oder *Voces mysticae* angehängt, z. B. an ᾽Ιάω Σαβαώθ ᾽Αδωναί noch ᾽Ακραμμαχαμαρει (*Pap. Lond.* 121, 224 ff. [Amulett gegen Schüttelfrost]) . . . ja einmal wird ᾽Ιάω auf "Hebräisch" als Αβλαναθα-ναλβα Αβρασιλωα angerufen (*Pap. Lond.* 46, 475–476) . . . Auch beruft sich der Zauberer darauf, dass er die Kraft des Abraham, Isaak und Jakob und des grossen Gottes, *des Daemons* ᾽Ιάω, ᾽Αβλαναθαναλβα, Σιαβραθιλάω, Λαμψηρ, ᾽Ιηιωω sich noch hinzugenommen habe.'

Eitrem, *Papyri Osloenses*, I, 82, in the note to line 192, says that Ablanathanalba is ordinarily followed by Akrammachamari,[41] but that is certainly not the case in our text. Such phrases as that in *Papyri Osloenses*, I, 11, line 191, show that such a magic name was invoked in oaths: ὀργίζω σέ, τὸν μετὰ τῶν ὀνομάτου⟨ν⟩ Αβλαθανα . . . καὶ τὴν δύναμειν τοῦ ακραμαρι ὅτι σε ὁρκίζω.

Line 8: The Κύριοι ῞Αγγελοι[42] are often invoked in magical papyri, generally with the spelling ἄγγελοι. In *Revue des Études Grecques*, XLI, 1928, p. 74, we have Κύριοι ᾽Αρχάγγελοι Θεοί. Κύριος is a usual epithet applied to the deity invoked in magical papyri, as in Kenyon, *Greek Papyri in the British Museum*, p. 107 (*Pap.* CXXI), line 707: Θεοὶ Κύριοι; *ibid.*, p. 108, 743: Κύριοι Θεοί. *Ibid.*, p. 107, 710, we have only Κύριοι; in *Papyri Osloenses*, I, 10, 176 only ἄγγελοι; and Iaô, Sabaoth, etc. are all addressed as ἄγγελοι.[43] Kenyon, *Greek Papyri in the British Museum* (Pap. CXXI), p. 101, line 528, shows that κύριος can be applied to the sun: εἰσάκουσον μου τοῦ (δεῖνα) (ἥλιε) κύριε, θεὲ μέγιστε. Perhaps even the 'angels' here are heavenly bodies connected, like the other words above, with the sun. The writer of the text perhaps is calling on all the solar deities to protect him.

---

41 Cf. also Wessely, *op. cit.*, nos. 210 ff.

42 Cf. Preisendanz, *op. cit.*, II, p. 164, 45; p. 171, 246; Eitrem, *op. cit.*, p. 6, 44; Wünsch, *Arch. f. Religionsw.* XII, 1909, 38, where in addition to Κύριοι ῞Αγγελοι we have Κύριοι Θεοί (B. 3) with the same meaning. Epictetus (II, 16, 13) speaks already at the beginning of the second century A.D. of Κύριε ὁ θεός.

43 Cf. Hopfner, *op. cit.*, I, 154; Kenyon, *op. cit.*, p. 112, 893, where the angels seem to be identified with demons, though they can be archangels as we have seen.

Lines 9–10: The reading σώσετε seems to be certain, but there is much doubt how we should read the remaining words. The individual letters can be deciphered more easily on a good photograph than on the original, which is difficult to interpret. The writer seems first to have written φ, perhaps because he glanced down at the φ of the last line in his copy. Then, since erasing was almost impossible, he simply made an ε over φ or around the φ. In any case he meant epsilon and left out sigma. For σώσετε instead of σώσατε cf. for example κλαύσετε for κλαύσατε in H. A. Sanders, 'Manuscript No. 16 of the Michigan Collection,' in *The University of Missouri Studies,* XI, 1936, p. 176, V. 1. For similar expressions cf. σῶσον in Kenyon, *Papyri in the British Museum* (Pap. XLVI), p. 69, line 140. The large magical papyrus in the Bibliothèque Nationale (*Denkschriften Wiener Akad.* XXXVI, 1888), p. 74, lines 1211–1213, has: σῶσον με. ἀεὶ γὰρ πάντοτε χαίρεις τοὺς σοὺς σώζων. In *Papyri in the British Museum* (Pap. XLVI), p. 69, lines 139–142, we have κύριε βασιλεῦ δυναστὰ βοηθὲ, σῶσον, etc. In *Bonner Jahrbücher,* LXXIX, 1885, pp. 216–217, we have σερουα (=Latin *serva*), and σερουατε . . . υμ κουεμ πεπεριτ Λειβ . . . αβ ομνι περεκουλω (=*servate [Luciol]um quem peperit Leib[ia mater] ab omni periculo*). *Ibid.,* CIII, 1898, p. 135, we have σερουατε (=Latin *servate*).[44] In *Michigan Papyri,* III, 1936, p. 130, we have instead of σῶσον, φύλαξόν μοι ἀπὸ παντὸς κακοῦ πράγαμτος (*sic*) ὃν ἔτεκεν ἡ δῖνα ἐγέννησεν. The best reading in our text seems to be τὸν (for ὅν, due perhaps to the last word ending in -τον) ἐγέννη⟨σ⟩εν 'Αταλάντη, Εὐφήλητον ("preserve the one to whom Atalanta has given birth, Euphiletus"). Probably τον was written as the ending of Εὐφίλητον, and, when the writer discovered his mistake, he added the omitted name at the end, out of place. Euphiletus (the η is a mistake, due to itacism, for ι) is a good Greek name.[45] Sometimes these tablets refer to an unborn or new-born child which should be protected. The Aramaic tablet in the Metropolitan Museum[46] is a good example; and in *Revue des Études Grecques,* XLI, 1928, pp. 74, 81, we have ἀπελάσατε πᾶν κακὸν καὶ πᾶσαν [ἐπίλη]μψιν καὶ πᾶσαν [κοιλι]αργίαν ἀ(μ)πὸ [παιδί]ου ἣν ἔτεκεν [ἡ δεῖνα], evidently a prayer to protect the new-born child from the terrible infantile diseases. In *Exodus,* XIII, 1, in the Septuagint Greek version we have 'Αγίασόν μοι πᾶν πρωτότοκον πρωτογενές, etc. But it is much more likely that an

[44] Cf. also *Arch. f. Religionsw.,* XII, 1909, p. 26; *Rev. Ét. Gr.,* XLI, 1928, p. 82.

[45] Cf. Pape-Benseler, *Greichische Eigennamen, s.v.;* F. Preisigke, *Namenbuch* (1922), p. 115; J. Kirchner, *Prosopographia Attica,* nos. 6046–6077; *L'Antiquité Classique,* V, 1936, p. 88, no. 10. For help in deciphering this name and for other suggestions I am indebted to Professors Campbell Bonner and Herbert C. Youtie of the University of Michigan.

[46] Cf. note 6 above.

adult is meant and is appealing for protection. In magic the persons concerned are usually identified as sons of their mothers and not of their
fathers.[47]

THE JOHNS HOPKINS UNIVERSITY
  BALTIMORE, MARYLAND.

[47] Cf. Eitrem, *op. cit.*, p. 6, lines 44–45; also the inscription cited above, p. 252: quem peperit
Leib[ia mater]; also *Arch. f. Religionsw.*, XII, 1909, 44: ἣν ἔτεκεν μήτηρ Ακεσα. Cf. *Rev. Ét. Gr.*, XLI,
1928, pp. 74, 81. It is not necessary to name the child; cf. R. Wünsch, *Sethianische Verfluchungstafel
aus Rom* (Leipzig, Teubner, 1898), p. 64, where a list of mothers' names is given; "Deisidaimoni-
aka," *Arch. f. Religionsw.*, XII, 1909, p. 45. In *Michigan Papyri*, III, 1936, p. 131, we have ἐγέννησεν as
referring to the father, but it can also refer to the mother. There Campbell Bonner cites Audollent,
Defixionum Tabellae, p. 272, no. 198, 14, 27, 32, a curse tablet from Cumae where the father's name
appears.

THE EASTERN QUESTION IN LUCAN'S BELLUM CIVILE

Eva Matthews Sanford

THE EASTERN question is an important secondary theme in Lucan's epic, and is closely associated with the primary motif of the civil war between Caesar and Pompey. It is handled in a fashion which reflects the influence of Lucan's intransigeant republicanism and of the discussion of current foreign policy among the members of the Pisonian conspiracy. Lucan subscribed to the popular opinion that Rome was on the verge of actual world-monarchy when her triumphant progress was interrupted by the disasters of civil war. He represented partisans on both sides in the conflict as considering Pharsalia the prelude to the universal power of the victor. So Curio of the venal tongue cried to Caesar at the Rubicon

> . . . facili si proelia pauca
> gesseris euentu, tibi Roma subegerit orbem,[1]

and the stanch republican Cato explained to Brutus his reasons for entering the war on Pompey's side:

> . . . nec, si fortuna fauebit,
> hunc quoque totius sibi ius promittere mundi
> non bene compertum est: ideo me milite uincat,
> ne sibi se uicisse putet.[2]

The great power which lay within the reach of Rome in the middle of the first century was further suggested by the exaggerated account of universal participation in the war; here the strong forces which Pompey recruited from the eastern dependencies of Rome are multiplied to include all the oriental peoples. The very depths of the East were stirred; the Ganges, Indus and Hydaspes sent their men; the Cappadocians and Armenians, the Arabs and all the Libyan tribes, and the Bosporan peoples from the borders of Europe and Asia came to fight on Pompey's side and

---

[1] *Bellum Ciuile*, I, 284-285. References hereafter are to Lucan's poem, unless otherwise designated.

General bibliography has been deliberately omitted in this article, since it is readily available elsewhere and the background material is familiar. The pertinent chapters and bibliographies in *Cambridge Ancient History*, X, are very useful. The present paper supplements my previous studies of Lucan: 'Lucan and his Roman Critics,' *Classical Philology*, XXVI, 233-257; 'Lucan and Civil War,' *ibid.*, XXVIII, 121-127; 'Quotations from Lucan in Mediaeval Latin Authors,' *American Journal of Philology*, LV, 1-19; 'The Manuscripts of Lucan: *Accessus* and *Marginalia*,' *Speculum*, IX, 278-295.

[2] II, 320-323.

to give rich opportunity for the geographical descriptions which Lucan so enjoyed. Even this list, more inclusive than the historical roll of the peoples who sent embassies to Augustus, was not sufficient, perhaps because these races had figured in the account of Antony's allies at Actium in the works of the Augustan poets. The Essedonians, Arimaspians, Massagetes and Geloni were added to give a rich Herodotean flavor to Pompey's army. Thus the whole East witnessed the fraternal strife of Rome, which, despite their aid to Pompey, was to give the world to Caesar by a single battle.[3] If Lucan's muster-roll had been correct, there would have been no exaggeration in Pompey's boast before the battle;

> pars mundi mihi nulla uacat; sed tota tenetur
> terra meis, quocumque iacet sub sole, tropaeis.[4]

After the catastrophe Lentulus warned Pompey that posterity would reproach both him and Caesar for engaging in civil war while Crassus was unavenged, at a time when all Roman generals should have combined against Parthia.[5] Lucan's epic opened with the same charge against the folly of the Romans who exhausted in a war which could win no triumphs the military strength that might have gained them control over Scythians, Seres, Parthians, and Ethiopians. The world should have been brought under Latin law and every foreign foe should have been overcome before civil war was considered.[6] But instead of the conquest of Parthia, civil war had sprung from the disaster at Carrhae.[7] Lucan viewed the Parthian victory only, of course, as an immediate occasion for the civil conflict in Rome; individual ambition and the degeneracy of Roman *mores* were contributory factors, and he stated the underlying cause in terms like those which Livy and Horace, among others, had used before him, and which Augustine was to copy, in a characteristic classical interpretation of historical cycles:

> inuida fatorum series, summisque negatum
> stare diu; nimioque graues sub pondere lapsus
> nec se Roma ferens.[8]

---

[3] III, 229–297, esp. 296–297:

> acciperet felix ne non semel omnia Caesar,
> uincendum pariter Pharsalia praestitit orbem.

[4] II, 583–584, from Pompey's speech to his soldiers before the battle, in which he gave a similar account of his allies to that summarized above; cf. also VII, 360–362:

> ... primo gentes oriente coactae
> innumeraeque urbes, quantas in proelia numquam
> exciuere manus. *toto simul utimur orbe.*

[5] VIII, 420–426.

[6] I, 8–23.

[7] I, 98–111.

[8] I, 70–72; cf. 81–82:

Lucan emphasized the actual losses in the civil war no less than the poets who experienced them had done; and his conviction of the lasting ruin thus wrought gains emphasis from the century which had elapsed before he wrote:

> maius ab hac acie quam quod sua saecula ferrent
> uolnus habent populi; plus est quam uita salusque
> quod perit; in totum mundi prosternimur aeuum.[9]

Though Virgil and Horace had outlived the desolation of the civil wars to praise the culmination of Rome's imperial destiny in the achievements of Augustus at home and on the frontiers, Lucan admitted no recovery of her lost glories. The Roman soldiers who protested that civil war would hardly have been justified even if it had prevented both rivals from ruling expressed the poet's conviction also when they announced their readiness to fight on all the borders of the Empire at once, if only civil strife might be averted.[10] Since all the enemies whom they cited, except those in the West threatened the frontier in Lucan's time also, it is not surprising that the poet gave no hint of the glories of the Augustan peace, emphasis on which would have weakened his general argument. Aside from the progressive degeneracy of Roman society, he seems to have ascribed Rome's continued weakness, especially on the western frontier, to the contempt engendered among her neighbors by her civil dissensions,[11] to the establishment of the monarchy, and in some measure to the orientalization of Rome.

Rome had grown great through the liberty of her citizens; since liberty was exiled by civil crime, the Romans were in worse case than the eastern peoples who had never known freedom:

> ex populis qui regna ferunt sors ultima nostra est,
> quos seruire pudet.[12]

It is characteristic of Lucan's political sympathies that this lost liberty was not vested in the citizen-body as a whole, but in the aristocratic adherents of Pompey; hence the curious scene in which Caesar ordered that the senators alone should be put to death:

> in plebem uetat ire manus monstratque senatum;

---

in se magna ruunt; laetis hunc numina rebus
crescendi posuere modum.

See also Livy, praef.: quae ab exiguis profecta initiis eo creuerit, ut iam magnitudine sua laboret; Horace, Epod. 16, 1-2; Augustine, Ciu. Dei, XVIII, 45: Roma late orbi terrarum imperans tanquam se ipsa fine non ualens sua se quodammodo magnitudine fregerat.

[9] VII, 632–640; lines 638–640 are quoted.

[10] II, 47–56.

[11] Cf. esp. I, 9: gentibus inuisis Latium praebere cruorem; VIII, 352–353; X, 47–48.

[12] VII, 432–445; lines 444–445 are quoted.

> scit, cruor imperii qui sit, quae uiscera rerum,
> unde petat Romam, *libertas ultima mundi*
> quo steterit ferienda loco.[13]

By this interpretation the Roman authority over other nations became a tyranny which should have been resisted to the last extremity,[14] and the expansion of the republican rule of Rome was transformed into imperial despotism over citizens and subjects alike.

The most definite statement which Lucan gives of his attitude toward orientalization as a token of Roman degeneracy is in the prayer that Fortune might choose either Romans or barbarians as the victims at Pharsalia, with the pessimistic suggestion that the Cappadocians, Armenians, Syrians, and the unromanized peoples of the far West should be spared rather than the Romans:

> . . . nam post ciuilia bella
> hic populus Romanus erit.[15]

The example of Alexander is used not only for the boast that Roman influence in the last days of the republic had reached the limit of Macedonian advance in the far East:

> hic ubi Pellaeus post Tethyos aequora ductor
> constitit et magno uinci se fassus ab orbe est,[16]

but also for an indictment of monarchy, and of conquests dictated by the insane ambition of a single man:

> nam sibi libertas umquam si redderet orbem,
> ludibrio seruatus erat, *non utile mundo*
> *editus exemplum, terras tot posse sub uno*
> *esse uiro.*[17]

The destructive victories of the *rex uaesanus* are described in terms drawn from the Stoic criticism of Alexander, very different from the praise of the triumphs which might have been won by republican Rome. Lucan only censured imperialism when it sprang from what he considered a despotic government.

Caesar's plans for the Parthian war strengthened the popular demand for complete conquest of the East, often coupled with the subjugation of Britain, which could not be overlooked by any serious ruler, as the many references in the Augustan poets show, and which would naturally form

---

[13] VII, 578–581.
[14] Cf. IV, 575–579, ending:
> ignorantque datos, ne quisquam seruiat, enses.
[15] VII, 535–543; lines 442–443 are quoted.
[16] III, 233–234.
[17] X, 25–28.

a part of any revolutionary program that was intended to win general support. The attainment of *imperium sine fine* dominated patriotic interpretation of Rome's proper position in the world before Virgil immortalized the phrase in the *Aeneid*. Augustus, with the aid of well-chosen subordinates and of poets who supported his imperial policies even when they were urging their preference for themes of love as against those of empire, could substitute diplomacy for war and the attainment of defensible frontiers for boundless conquest. Thus the surrender of the Parthian standards was acclaimed by the poets who had recently prophesied glorious campaigns and magnificent triumphs. But the later members of the Julio-Claudian line were less successful, and the weakness of their eastern policy in the eyes of a people to whom successful wars were still a source of immediate material profit as well as of glory may have seemed to Lucan sufficient excuse for overlooking the achievement of Augustus.

Nero, however, could not be omitted from an epic written during his reign, and the extravagant praise accorded to him in the proem of Lucan is difficult to reconcile with the general tenor of the *Bellum Ciuile*.[18] Better knowledge of Lucan's method of work and of the order in which the different parts of the epic were composed would help to solve this and other critical problems.[19] It is not easy to accept such fulsome flattery as sincere; in fact, as some mediaeval annotations remind us, it is almost impossible to read it without the impression of a *double entendre*, which the vain emperor alone might be expected to overlook. One is tempted to suggest that the proem may have been formally presented to Nero to allay any suspicions which he might otherwise form about the *Tendenz* of a young republican's epic about the civil wars, and that his subsequent prohibition of Lucan's work was prompted as much by intimations of its true character as by professional jealousy. In any case, the lines to Nero have little to do with the *Bellum Ciuile* as a whole.

Attacks on the imperial policy of the Julio-Claudian rulers had most justification in the case of Armenia and Parthia. The crucial importance of the Armenian question at Nero's accession lends added interest to Lucan's estimate of Parthian strength and of the danger to Rome of Parthian independence. While Seneca helped to direct Roman policies, his young nephew must have heard much discussion which affected his maturer views of the eastern question. Roman patriots in the time of Augustus resented the attitude of certain Greek historians who claimed that Parthia was as great a power as Rome, and Strabo asserted that

[18] I, 33–66. Cf. A. D. Nock, 'The Proem of Lucan,' *Classical Review*, XL, 17–18.

[19] The rhetorical character of Lucan's style supports the theory that the earlier parts of the poem were subject to constant revision while the later books were being written, and that the increased republicanism of the latter is a climax in the general development of the poet's thesis rather than a fundamental change in his attitude toward the emperor.

the Parthians were about to accept Roman sovereignty.[20] A more rational view of the question was that of Trogus, who described the world as divided into Parthian and Roman spheres, and stated that the Parthians alone among the nations were not only a match for Rome, but had sometimes defeated her.[21] The most eloquent interpretation of this view is found in Milton's *Paradise Regained*, when Satan tempts Christ by showing him first Parthia and then Rome under Tiberius, as the only 'kingdoms of the earth' that were worthy of consideration as a basis for universal power.[22]

References to the East in the Augustan poets emphasize its wealth in incense, pearls and gold, with corresponding expectations of glittering triumphs to be won in adventurous campaigns[23] on the farthest borders of the world among strange rivers and Hyrcanian tigers, where Medes, Persians, Parthians, Seres, Indians, Sabaeans and Ethiopians mingle in a romantic confusion despite the painted maps which ladies eagerly con while their lovers are at the wars.[24] Milton correctly reproduced the attitude of the gilded youth of Rome when he compared the Parthian 'chivalry' with the forces of Agrican in one of the romances of the 'peers of Charlemain.'[25] Whether the young gallant sought to exercise his powers in armed warfare or in the lists of love,[26] he drew his metaphors from the East and thought of the *fugax Parthus* as *magni noua causa triumphi*.[27] The men who dreamed of the laurels to be won in the great Parthian campaign saw themselves as makers of history.[28] Though the conquest of Parthia was denied by the wisdom of Augustus, the phrases coined before the surrender of the standards were firmly embedded in the Roman vocabulary, and reappear as stock expressions in the works of later poets. Lucan, to whom the Parthian question was a grim and unromantic reality, and Statius, with his intimate knowledge of Domitian's plans, are the chief exceptions among the later poets to the conventional use of eastern allusions.[29]

---

[20] *Geog.* VI, 4, 2. In this passage Strabo attributes Armenian risings to the preoccupation of Rome with more important affairs, and describes the independent peoples of the East as nomads of no use to the Empire, who therefore only required watching.

[21] Justin, *Epitome*, XLI, 1. Cf. Fronto, *Princ. Hist.*, 7 (ed. Haines). For a brief summary see W. Schur, 'Die orientalische Frage im römischen Reiche,' *Neue Jahrbücher für Wissenschaft und Jugendbildung*, II, 270–282.

[22] *Paradise Regained*, III, 244—IV, 153.

[23] Ovid, *Ars Amat.*, I, 170 ff.

[24] Propertius, IV, 3, 35–38.

[25] *Paradise Regained*, III, 337–343.

[26] Propertius, II, 14, and elsewhere.

[27] Ovid, *Rem. Am.*, 155–156.

[28] Propertius, III, 4; esp. l.10: ite et Romanae consulite historiae.

[29] A full list of references to Parthia in the Roman poets is given by Neilson C. Debevoise, *A Political History of Parthia*, (Chicago University Press, 1938).

The men who forfeited their lives by joining in Piso's attempt to provide a better government for Rome than the principate of Nero were seriously concerned about the safety of the Empire, and had good reason for anxiety about the East. Antony's 'retreat from Moscow' in the ill-fated campaign of B.C. 36 had left a lasting impression. The full consequences of Caligula's bungling of the Armenian question were delayed by civil wars in Parthia, but before Nero's accession Vologases seized Armenia without opposition from Rome, and Corbulo's first command against Parthia was rendered futile by the need for intensive training of his undisciplined troops. The gains made by his subsequent victories were lost by the consummate folly of Paetus, and the overwhelming disaster to the Roman army in 62, the year in which plans for the Pisonian conspiracy were probably initiated, must have confirmed the resolution of the conspirators to provide for the sound conduct of eastern affairs. The peoples of the East had feared the Macedonian pikes more than they now feared the Roman javelins:

> . . . licet usque sub Arcton
> regnemus Zephyrique domos terrasque premamus
> flagrantis post terga Noti, cedemus in ortus
> Arsacidum domino. non felix Parthia Crassis
> exiguae secura fuit prouincia Pellae.[30]

The Arsacids had created a stronger power in the East than any which had opposed Alexander, and Romans who were either ignorant of the dynastic weakness of Parthia or consciously forebore to consider it might well echo the words of Pompey:

> o utinam non tanta mihi fiducia saeuis
> esset in Arsacidis! *fatis nimis aemula nostris*
> *fata mouent Medos*, multumque in gente deorum est.[31]

Lucan's analysis of the Parthian strength is contained in his account of the conference of the fugitive Pompeians in Cilicia after their defeat at Pharsalia. Pompey set before the senators his plan to seek the mighty world beyond the Euphrates, and make its warlike hosts his instruments of revenge on Rome.[32] The movements of defeated leaders in a civil war

[30] X, 48–52.

[31] VIII, 306–308. On the last phrase note Lucan's scorn of the Roman worship of Osiris, whose rites confessed him mortal (VIII, 831–833), and of the ruler-cult which made men gods (VII, 445–446, 457–459):

> . . . sunt nobis nulla profecto
> numina . . .
> bella pares superis facient ciuilia diuos;
> fulminibus manes radiisque ornabit et astris
> inque deum templis iurabit Roma per umbras.

[32] VIII, 256–455. Cf. Quintilian, *Inst. Or.*, III, 8, 33 for this theme as a subject of *triplex suasoria*.

were fraught with danger to the Empire; non-Roman lands offered military opportunities which the Roman victor would deny to his foes.[33] Labienus proved what a Roman general could accomplish with Parthian support,[34] an example rendered the more impressive by reports of Antony's intrigues in the East, and by the current prophecies that a world-conqueror should lead the armies of Asia to triumph over Rome.[35] Nero himself meditated flight to Parthia in 68,[36] when he could no longer rule in Rome. Pompey counted on his *nomen, quod mundus amat*,[37] to win the support of the Parthians, whose only joy was in war, and whose poisoned arrows were sure and deadly in effect. He called on Rome herself to favor his enterprise:

> . . . quid enim tibi laetius umquam
> praestiterint superi, quam, si ciuilia Partho
> milite bella geras, tantam consumere gentem
> et nostris miscere malis?[38]

But Lentulus answered this consummate audacity with more prudent counsels, which the senators wisely accepted. Even if Pompey's fall had not destroyed his prestige in the East, his proposals involved as much disgrace for Rome as the defeat of Crassus:

> . . . quid uolnera nostra
> in Scythicos spargis populos cladesque latentes?
> quid Parthos transire doces? solacia tanti
> perdit Roma mali, nullos admittere reges
> sed ciui seruire suo.[39]

The Parthians, he declared, cannot be counted on for an aggressive campaign; they are a soft people bred under the mild eastern skies, invincible only where the great plains leave them room for flight, and incapable of warfare in difficult terrain. They have no siege-engines, and no strong battle array to enable them to dislodge the enemy:

[33] Cf. IV, 143–147:

> . . . postquam omnia fatis
> Caesaris ire uidet, celsam Petreius Ilerdam
> deserit et noti diffisus uiribus orbis
> indomitos quaerit populos et semper in arma
> mortis amore feros, et tendit in ultima mundi.

[34] Dio XLVIII, 24.

[35] See W. W. Tarn, 'Alexander Helios and the Golden Age,' *Journal of Roman Studies*, XXII, 135–160, and my article on 'Nero and the East,' *Harvard Studies in Classical Philology*, XLVIII (1937), 75–103.

[36] Suetonius, *Nero*, 47.

[37] VIII, 276; note the effective contrast between this boast after Pharsalia, and the famous *magni nominis umbra* of the description of Pompey before the war began (I, 135).

[38] VIII, 322–325.

[39] *Ibid.*, 352–356.

> pugna leuis bellumque fugax turmaeque uagantes,
> et melior cessisse loco quam pellere miles.[40]

Strength in battle belongs to men who wield the sword, not to those who trust in poisoned arrows. Parthian customs are as alien to the Romans as their stars and their religion, and Parthia is the natural enemy against whom all the Roman forces should be combined. This part of Lentulus' plea ends with a prayer to Fortune:

> Assyriae paci finem, Fortuna, precamur;
> et si Thessalia bellum ciuile peractum est,
> ad Parthos, qui uicit, eat. *gens unica mundi est,*
> *de qua Caesareis possim gaudere triumphis.*[41]

Lucan's interest in the conquest of Parthia did not blind him to the other dangers of Rome; only the grace of the gods, he said, prevented the Sarmatians, Dacians, and Getae from attacking the city when the Pompeians fled,[42] though Lentulus thought that Rome could afford to expose her other frontiers to their attack for the sake of the conquest of Parthia.[43]

Lucan's account of the disasters due to Pharsalia is an extreme illustration of the catastrophe theory of history. In spite of the happy turn of affairs in 64, when Corbulo's successes induced Vologases to open negotiations, and the Empire enjoyed such undisturbed peace as it had seldom known,[44] Lucan could still write with unshaken pessimism of Pharsalia as the fatal check to the world-power of Rome and to her security and freedom:

> haud multum terrae spatium restabat Eoae,
> ut tibi nox, tibi tota dies, tibi curreret aether
> omniaque errantes stellae Romana uiderent.
> sed retro tua fata tulit par omnibus annis
> Emathiae funesta dies. hac luce cruenta
> effectum, ut Latios non horreat India fasces,
> nec uetitos errare Dahas in moenia ducat
> Sarmaticumque premat succinctus consul aratrum,
> quod semper saeuas debet tibi Parthia poenas,
> quod fugiens ciuile nefas redituraque numquam
> libertas ultra Tigrim Rhenumque recessit
> ac, totiens nobis iugulo quaesita, uagatur,

[40] *Ibid.*, 380–381.
[41] *Ibid.*, 427–430.
[42] III, 93–96; cf. II, 54–55.
[43] VIII, 423–426.
[44] Tacitus, *Ann.* XV, 46; XVI, 28.

Germanum Scythicumque bonum, nec respicit ultra
Ausoniam. . . .[45]

Though the peace was widely celebrated[46] it was not yet firmly established, and the need of a firm eastern policy without the danger of such
disastrous commands as that of a Paetus could still be an important plank
in the conspirators' platform. Had they lived to see the coronation of
Tiridates in 66, they would probably have interpreted it as a sign of the
servile adoption in Rome of oriental ceremonies rather than as the long-
awaited settlement of the Armenian issue.

Lucan's view of the eastern question, like his account of the civil war
itself, is too much colored by his political sympathies to rank as an objec-
tive historical study, but the old argument that he should be considered
a historian rather than a poet was formulated by men ignorant of Ranke's
definition of historical objectivity. His work throws more light on the
interpretations of Roman history current in his circle than on the events
themselves, and this interpretation influenced the historical judgment of
many later writers, especially during the Middle Ages. If the conspirators
had been successful, the political theory of the *Bellum Ciuile* might for
a time have supplanted that of the *Aeneid*, despite the manifest inferiority
of Lucan's talent to the genius of Virgil. It would then have remained
for the leaders of the new government to inaugurate, as best they could,
a golden age to justify their denial of that of Augustus.

Sweet Briar College.

[45] VII, 423–436.
[46] Note the many commemorative coins issued in 64–66.

AN OLD IRISH VERSION OF LAODAMIA AND PROTESILAUS

JOHN J. SAVAGE

WE ARE indebted to the late Professor Kuno Meyer for many contributions to the study of Irish poetry of the older period. One of the choicest specimens of this literature is the love story of Liadain and Cuirither,[1] which, though found in two late manuscript copies, must, according to Meyer, have had its origin in the Old Irish period. The reasons given for this claim are twofold: (a) the fact that in the Old Woman of Beare, a song of undisputed antiquity (tenth century), Liadain is mentioned as one of the celebrated women of Corkaguiney; (b) one of the quatrains of the poem of Liadain and Cuirither is cited as an example of its meter—*treochair*—in a metrical treatise of the tenth century.[2] The story is told in the form of a *chantefable*.[3] Both the prose and verse belong to the ninth or early tenth century.[4]

The story may be summarised thus:[5]

Liadain of Corkaguiney, a poetess, went visiting[6] into the country of Connaught. There Cuirither, Otter's son, himself a poet, made an 'ale-feast' for her. 'Why should not we two unite, Liadain?' said Cuirither, 'a son of us two would be famous.' 'Do not let us do it now,' said she, 'lest my round of visiting be ruined for me. If you will come for me again at my home, I will go with you.' And so it happened. Southward Cuirither went and a single servant followed him with his poet's dress in a bag upon his back. There were spear-heads in his bag also. He reached a well beside the court of Liadain. There he put on his crimson dress and brandished his spears. A youth named 'Boy of Two Arts' (*Mac Da Cherda*) is sent to

---

[1] K. Meyer, *Liadain and Cuirithir, an Irish Love Story of the Ninth Century* (London: David Nutt, 1902). This publication gives the full text with an English translation. A summary of the story and a condensed English version is printed by Meyer in his *Selections from Ancient Irish Poetry* (New York: E. P. Dutton and Company, 1911), 65 f.

[2] Cf. E. Windisch, *Irische Texte*, III, p. 16 and p. 45, cited by Meyer, *Liadain and Cuirithir*, p. 9.

[3] Cf. J. R. Reinhard, "The Literary Background of the Chantefable," *Speculum*, 1 (1926), 157 f.

[4] Meyer, *ibid*.

[5] I have made use of part of Meyer's own summary given on page 65 of his *Selections from Ancient Irish Poetry*.

[6] On the "visitations" of Irish poets see P. W. Joyce, *A Social History of Ancient Ireland* (London: Longmans, Green and Co., 1903), I, 449 f. The transformation of the classical hero and heroine into poet and poetess may be due, if I am right, to a Christianising process. The Irish order of *fili* or poets seemed to have formed part of the original orders of Druids (cf. W. K. Sullivan, *Encyclopedia Britannica*, ninth ed., V, 303).

summon Liadain to the well. She is addressed as the 'Grey Lady' by the boy, while Cuirither is called the 'Son of the Beast' (=Otter) that stays at night under pools.[7]

Meanwhile Liadain made a vow of chastity; but faithful to her word she went with him. They proceeded to the monastery of Clonfert, where they put themselves under the spiritual direction of Cummin. 'The power of soul-friendship be upon you. Whether for you shall it be seeing or talking together?' said Cummin. 'Talking for us!' said Cuirither. 'What may come of it will be better. We have ever been looking at each other.'

Her cell was closed while Cuirither went the rounds of the grave-stones of the saints and his was closed when Liadain's turn came. Then follows a number of quatrains between the two lovers. Cummin proposed a chastity-test for them. As a result Cuirither was banished to another church. Thereupon he gave vent to his feelings in verse (Meyer, p. 21, 19–22):

> Of late I parted from Liadain.
> Since I parted from Liadain,
> Long as a month is every day,
> Long as a year each month.

Liadain made an observation such as would not have ill become Ovid himself:

> If Cuirither to-day
> Is gone to the scholars,
> Alas for the sense he will make
> For any who do not know!

He went on a pilgrimage until he came to Kil-Letrech in the land of the Dessi. She went seeking him and spoke some beautiful verses, in which she uttered the intensity of her grief (p. 25, 19 f.):

> Conceal it not!
> He was the love of my heart,
> If I loved every other.
> A roaring flame
> Has dissolved this heart of mine—
> However for certain it will cease to beat![8]

---

[7] I am not competent to pass upon what appear to be folk-lore elements here as elsewhere in the story. For wells leading to the Underworld, see A. B. Cook, "The European Sky-God," Folklore, XVIII (1907), 29.

[8] The finest lines in this poem, it seems to me, are those which immediately precede this lament. The descriptive adjective for the sea found in one of these verses may well be a classical reminiscence. Virgil, following Homer (*Il.* XVI, 391), uses *purpureum* of the sea (cf. *Geor.* IV, 373). Here are the verses of the Irish poet (*Selections*, p. 66):

> The music of the forest
> Would sing to me when with Cuirither,
> Together with the voice of the purple sea.

Cuirither was hurt by the haste with which she had entered the religious life. When he heard that she was coming from the west, he went in a coracle over the sea to strange lands and pilgrimages, so that she never saw him more. Until the day of her death she stayed upon the flagstone on which she was wont to pray. 'Her soul went to heaven and that flagstone was placed over her face. Thus far the meeting of Liadain and Cuirither.'

There is mention of a Liadain, wife of Cuirither, in the tenth-century *Old Woman of Beare*, to which reference has already been made. It would be well to cite here the prose introduction to that poem which Meyer[9] found in a manuscript in Trinity College, Dublin (H.3.18, p. 42):

The Old Woman Beare. Digdi was her name. Of Corcaguiney she was, i.e. of the Ui Maic Iair-Conchinn. Of them also was Brigit, the daughter of Iustan, and Liadain, the wife of Cuirither (*Liadain ben Chuirither*). For a hundred years she wore a veil, which Cuimine[10] had blessed, upon her head.

There is a hint of a story of a Lladdon, the daughter of the stream, in W. F. Skene's *Four Ancient Books of Wales*.[11] The verses which concern us here are brief, but, if I am right, they tell a tale which seems to have been inspired by a classical model. This model, I shall attempt to show, is that which furnished the basis for the Irish love story. I refer to the well-known tale of Laodamia and Protesilaus. Here is Skene's translation of the verses from the Welsh poem:

> Lladdon, the daughter of the stream,
> Little was her desire
> For gold and silver.
> Who was the living one that left her?
> Blood on the breast;
> He will probably be spoken of,
> He will be greatly praised.[12]

---

[9] "Stories and Songs from Irish Manuscripts" (reprinted from *Otia Merseiana*, 1899), 121.

[10] Meyer, *ibid.*, notes that this may have been Cummine, bishop of Clonfert, who died in 661. He is called Cummin, son of Fiachna, in the poem *Liadain and Cuirithir*.

[11] There are two volumes to this work. The first contains the English translation, the second, the text (I, 526; II, 131). The verses cited are part of the 'Hostile Confederacy' (Book of Taliesin, VII).

[12] I do not profess to have any first hand acquaintance with either the Welsh or Irish texts here discussed. I am aware that a new text and translation have been offered since Skene's work was published. The new text is found in J. Gwenogvryn Evans' 'The Text of the Book of Taliesin,' *Series of Old Welsh Texts* (Llanbedrog, N. Wales, 1910) IX, 19, verse 19 f. In a companion volume published in the same place in 1915, *Poems from the Book of Taliesin*, we are presented with another edition, 'amended' (*sic*) and translated by the same scholar. The following is his version from his new text. 'Latona, daughter of the Ocean, had small desire for gold and silver. What living person has shed blood on her sacred island? The fact has hardly been mentioned, though it is worthy of great praise.' In his notes to the original volume of the text (p. 87) Evans would identify Lladdon with Latona, daughter of Oceanus and 'her sacred island' with the island of Delos. I fail to see how this classical

In a celebrated passage in Virgil's *Aeneid* (vi, 445 f.) Laodamia is listed among the famous women who died of *durus amor*:

> His Phaedram Procrimque locis maestamque Eriphylen,
> crudelis nati monstrantem volnera, cernit,
> Evadnenque et Pasiphaen, his Laodamia
> it comes . . .

The Commentary on Virgil attributed to Servius[13] has a note on *Aen.* vi, 447:

Laodamia uxor Protesilai fuit. quae cum maritum in bello Troiano primum perisse cognovisset, optavit ut eius umbram videret: qua re concessa non deserens eam, in eius amplexibus periit.

Now let us examine these two stories, the Irish and Welsh, to see whether they have any theme in common. Liadain is separated from Cuirither twice; Lladdon from an unknown "living one" on just one occasion, very vaguely sketched. Cuirither fell in love with Liadain when the latter was visiting in his country of Connaught. She invited him to her home in the south (Co. Kerry, in Munster). They held a rendezvous near the well[14] near Liadain's court. At this point there is a Christian— or rather a Celtic-Christian—elaboration: a vow of chastity on the part of Liadain and life together in a monastery under a bond of "soul-friendship' (*anmchairde*[15]), with Cummin[16] as director, in the monastery of Clonfert.

---

hypothesis can shed much light on these Welsh verses, especially since emendation seems to have been resorted to in order to attempt to square the sense with the equation, Lladdon = Latona.

[13] *Servii grammatici qui feruntur in Vergilii carmina commentarii*, ed. G. Thilo and H. Hagen, (Leipzig: Teubner, 1878–1887), ii, 69. The readings of the manuscripts of Servius Danielis do not differ essentially from those of Servius. For the probable Irish (or Insular) provenience of both these bodies of comment on Virgil, see my articles in *Harvard Studies in Classical Philology*, XLIII (1932), 120 f., and XLV (1934), 157 f. Some years ago Sophus Bugge in his *Home of the Eddic Poems* (translated by W. H. Schofield, London: David Nutt, 1899), in his discussion on the sources of the Lay of Helgi ventured to state (p. 253) that the story of Laodamia, as related by Servius, was known in Ireland at an early date. From this he argues for a common source for certain Irish poems and for the Lay of Helgi. The element in common is the story of a dead husband (or lover) who returns to his surviving wife (or betrothed). This is the theme too of another Old-Irish poem, 'The Tryst after Death,' translated in Meyer's *Selections*, p. 9 f. This has been pointed out by Eleanor Hull, 'The Helgi Lay and Irish Literature,' *Mediaeval Studies in Honor of Gertrude Schoepperle Loomis* (New York: Columbia University Press, 1927), 265–276. Alan Seeger's well-known poem, 'I have a Rendezvous with Death,' may have been suggested by Meyer's translation which was published in 1911. Seeger, when a student at Harvard, studied Celtic literature with Professor F. N. Robinson.

[14] For fountains as lovers' rendezvous in folk literature, see K. Malone, *Pub. Mod. Lang. Assoc.*, XLIII, 402, cited by Stith Thompson, 'Motif Index of Folk Literature,' *Indiana University Studies*, XXII, 5, 258.

[15] Cf. Dom Louis Gougaud, *Les Chrétientés Celtiques* (2nd ed., Paris, 1911), 92 f., chapter on "La Femme et le Monachisme." See also James F. Kenney, *The Sources for the Early History of Ireland*, Records of Civilisation, Sources and Studies (New York: Columbia University Press, 1929), I, 420 f. for bibliography on *virgines subintroductae*.

[16] Cf. Thomas P. Oakley, 'A Great Irish Penitential and its Authorship,' *Romanic Review*, XXV

Here, if I am right, there seems to be a reminiscence of the account which Servius gives of Laodamia and Protesilaus. In the original story her lover, it appears, is slain (cf. 'blood on the breast' in the Welsh version) and the visit of the poet Cuirither would seem to have been a ghostly one in the tale from which both the Irish and Welsh versions were derived. Servius states that Laodamia wished to *see* the shade of Protesilaus after he was slain in the Trojan war: *optavit ut eius umbram videret*. In the Irish story Cummin, the spiritual director, asks the pair 'whether for you shall it be *seeing* or talking together' 'Talking for us!' said Cuirither . . . '*We have ever been looking at each other.*'

After the chastity-test there is another separation. In the Welsh version there is only one hinted at ('Who was the living one that left her?'). we may safely conclude, therefore, that the rest of the narrative, which relates Cuirither's pilgrimage[17] and Liadain's penitential grief, is a later appendage of a moralising nature.

Recent investigation points towards the British isles for the provenience of many of the manuscripts of Ovid.[18] Interesting is the fact that the codex of Ovid, written in Welsh script, now in the Bodleian library at Oxford (Auct. F 4.34), contains the *Ars Amatoria*. There are several Welsh glosses on this poem. According to Lindsay[19] there is no clue to the date of this part of the manuscript, which is a composite volume, formerly belonging to the Glastonbury Abbey library.

The *Heroides* may have been read in Celtic Wales and Ireland. The thirteenth *Epistula* is an imaginary letter written by Laodamia to Protesilaus on the occasion of his going to the wars of Troy. It would be tempting to search for possible influences of Ovid's poem on both the Welsh and Irish love songs, in which the lover's plaint too is from a woman who has been left desolate by her beloved. True that in the Irish version of the tale, the hero has become a monk and is relegated to another convent. In the Welsh, there occur some curious parallels with Ovid, which may be more than mere coincidences. What does the verse 'Lladdon, daughter of the *sea*' mean? The Roman poet (*Heroides* XIII, 19 f.)

(1934), 25 ff. Cummean (a variant of Cummin?) was abbot of Clonfert, *ibid.*, p. 26, n. 18. On p. 30 Professor Oakley cites from the 'Penitential of Cummean' a passage which ordains a punishment of *peregrinatio perennis* for the sin of incest. See also John Ryan, S. J., *Irish Monasticism* (London: Longmans, Green and Co., 1931), p. 38.

[17] Cf. Oakley, *loc. cit.* Servius merely says *periit* of Laodamia. In the Irish poem she is depicted as doing penance.

[18] Cf. the summaries of the dissertations of Dr. Walter H. Freeman and Dr. William F. Smith in *Harvard Studies in Classical Philology*, XXIII (1912), 168 f. and XXXVI (1925), 183 f. on the MSS of the *carmina amatoria* and of the *Metamorphoses* respectively.

[19] W. M. Lindsay, *Early Welsh Script*, University of St. Andrews Publications, no. x (Oxford, 1912), 7. These glosses were first edited by Zeuss; cf. Zeuss-Ebel, *Grammatica Celtica* (2nd ed., Berlin: Weidmann, 1871), 1054.

pictures Laodamia in a state of collapse, when the ship on which her lover sailed has passed out of sight (23–24):

> Lux quoque tecum abiit, tenebrisque exanguis obortis
> succiduo dicor procubuisse genu.

With difficulty does her mother, aided by her father-in-law and her grandfather, revive her with cold water (25–26):

> Vix socer Iphiclus, vix me grandaevus Acastus,
> vix mater gelida maesta refecit aqua.

Did the imagination of the Welsh poet run riot here by regarding *aqua*, here, of course, in the ablative, as a nominative in apposition with *mater?* This would be a very tenuous argument in itself, but the verses which follow soon after in Ovid (29 f.) have in them an idea that might well have been the inspiration for 'Little was her desire for gold or silver.' When Laodamia regained consciousness, we are told, she was wholly indifferent to her personal adornment (31–32):

> Nec mihi pectendos curast praebere capillos,
> nec libet aurata corpora veste tegi.

'She had no desire for her gowns, gold embroidered' becomes in the Welsh 'gold or silver.'

In the verses embedded in the Irish *chantefable* there is no verbal reminiscence of Ovid, as far as I am aware, but there is discernible, I venture to say, beneath their native charm something of the exotic *spirit* of the poet of the *Heroides*.[20]

Let me review at this point the main contentions for my identification of Liadain and Cuirither as Laodamia and Protesilaus. The relation between the classical prototypes is one of faithful love, reaching even beyond the bounds of death. Such was the relationship which the Irish poet seems to have visualised and to have put into an appropriate Christian setting. The facts of the classical story, as related by Virgil and his commentators, are supported by the details given in the *Heroides* of Ovid, which may have helped to give form to the faint sketch of Lladdon in the Welsh book of Taliesin. Now Ovid was known as a didactic poet in the later Middle Ages. Sedlmayer[21] shows that the scholia in one manuscript point to the interpretation of the story of Laodamia as an example

---

[20] Professor E. K. Rand in his delightful little book *Ovid and his Influence* (Boston: Marshall Jones Company, 1925), 20 f., writes *inter alia* of Ovid's humorous treatment of the letter of Laodamia to Protesilaus. There is real humor too in the Irish poet's dramatic picture of Cuirither doling out nonsense to his pupils after his break with his beloved. Shades of Abelard and Heloise!

[21] Cited by A. Palmer, *P. Ovidi Nasonis Heroides* (Oxford: Clarendon Press, 1898), introd., p. xxvii, n. 1, from Sedlmayer, *Prolegomena critica*, p. 101.

of *castus amor*. From another codex of the fourteenth century[22] it appears that Ovid was regarded, erroneously of course, as having written his *Heroides* in exile, in quo [libro] castas extollendo et incestas deprimendo ponit, ut earum [epistularum] benevolentia recepta ad statum pristinum reducatur. Behold Ovid the penitent!

What of the name Liadain (Liadin), if this form was borrowed from the Latin? Thurneysen[23] does not appear to give any instances of formation in Irish from the Latin diphthongs -ao-, -au-. We have, however, *pían* from *poena*, *riagol* from *rēgula*,[24] *srian* from *frēnum*.[25] It should be noted that the Latin manuscripts varied in their spelling between Laodamia, Laodomia, and Laudamia.[26] In the Middle Irish version of the *Aeneid*[27] the spelling is Ludamia. The -i- of the original word is long, but Thurneysen adduces instances, as might be expected, of false quantities in borrowed words.[28] The antepenult in that case would have been stressed and lengthened with loss of the two final syllables in both Welsh and Irish.

Initial p- or qu- in Latin became regularly c- in Irish.[29] Latin *presbyter* is *cruimther* in Irish, *premter* or *primter* in Old Welsh.[30] Cuirither (Curithir) would then, if it is a loan word from the Latin Protesilaus, presuppose a dropping of the two final unstressed syllables, followed by assimilation of final -l to -r.[31] Next -s- between vowels -e- and -i- became -h- and tended to disappear in pronunciation.[32]

The identification of Cuirither as Protesilaus, if my reasoning is correct, seems to be further attested by the story called 'The Sword of Oscar' in the Middle Irish *Dunaire Finn*.[33] The sword passed through the hands of gods and heroes, Greek and Roman, down to certain Irish chiefs. 'The *first* man whose head thou didst take off was sturdy Crithir, son of Dubh

---

[22] Codex Laurent. xxxvi, 27; cf. Sedlmayer, 'Beiträge zur Geschichte des Ovidstudien im Mittelalter,' *Wiener Studien*, vi (1884), 146. Cf. E. K. Rand, *op. cit.*, p. 112 ff., chapter on 'Ovid in Middle Ages,' especially on *Ovidius Ethicus*, p. 131 f.; on *Ovidius Theologus*, p. 134 f.

[23] R. Thurneysen, *Handbuch des alt-Irischen*, I Teil: Grammatik (Heidelberg, 1909). Cf. however H. Pedersen, *Vergleichende Grammatik der Keltischen Sprachen* (Göttingen, 1909), I, p. 211: Irish *or* from Latin *aurum*, and a possibly later *cál* from *caulis*.

[24] Thurneysen, sect. 51.

[25] J. Vendryes, *De Hibernicis vocabulis quae a Latina lingua originem duxerunt* (Paris, 1902), p. 61.

[26] Cf. R. Ewald, *P. Ovidius Naso* (Leipzig: Teubner, 1916), I, p. xxii; Thilo and Hagen, *op. cit.*, II, 69.

[27] *Imtheachta Aeniasa, The Irish Aeneid*, ed. and transl. by George Calder (Irish Texts Society vi, 1907), p. 86.

[28] Thurneysen, *op. cit.*, Anhang, sect. 907.

[29] *Ibid.*, sect. 909.

[30] *Ibid.*, sect. 222.

[31] Cf. J. Morris Jones, *A Welsh Grammar, Historical and Comparative* (Oxford, Clarendon Press, 1913), sect. 102, ii (1).

[32] *Ibid.*, sect. 94, ii and iii: Welsh *caws* from Latin *caseus*.

[33] *Dunaire Finn*, ed. Eoin MacNeill (Irish Texts Society, vii, 1908), text, p. 49; transl., p. 153.

Greann; Minelus justly passed thee to the hand of Saturn, son of Pallor.'
The setting here is certainly classical: 'Minelus' at least is recognisable.
Is there here also a reminiscence of the tale of Protesilaus, the *first* man
to fall at Troy, and of his death by the sword of Hector?[34] 'Oscar,' it seems,
may here well have been a corruption of 'Hector.'[35]

FORDHAM GRADUATE SCHOOL.

[34] The Greek hero's death at the hands of Hector is foreshadowed by Laodamia in *Heroides* XIII,
63 ff. Crithir seems to be a variant of Cuirither (Curithir). It would be idle to conjecture whether
the Irish Dubh Greann, father of Crithir, is a corruption of Iphiclus, father of Protesilaus (cf. *Heroides*
XIII, 25). In a study of 'Classical Tradition in Mediaeval Irish Literature,' *Philological Quarterly*, III
(1924), 267 ff., by E. G. Cox, due account is given of 'The Sword of Oscar.' On page 273 he states
that in Irish literature 'the omission of Ovid is puzzling.'

[35] The classical tale of Laodamia may have had its echoes in the great mass of legend that centered around King Arthur. It would be rash to make any claims for this without deeper investigation.
However I cannot refrain from mentioning the well-known story, 'The Lady of the Fountain' in
the Welsh *Mabinogion*, in this connection. The story has been summarised by A. B. Cook, 'The
European Sky-God,' *Folklore*, XVIII (1907), 35 f., from A. C. L. Brown, *Iwain*, p. 13 f. Note the following (p. 36): 'Lunete's mistress, *whose name is Laudine*, a most beautiful lady, now enters, *weeping
for her lord*, who is carried on a bier. When the corpse is brought into the hall where Iwain is, *it begins to bleed*,' I have italicised the most significant points of this tale. The reader, I venture to say,
cannot fail to see some points of resemblance between what is related of Laudine and the brief sketch
of Lladdon in the Welsh poem cited above. The Lady of the Fountain is first wedded to the Black
Knight (cf. Laodamia and her Other-World lover, the shade of Protesilaus) and then to Owein,
brother of Peredur. Owein is a 'white divinity,' according to Rhys, *The Arthurian Legend*, (1891),
p. 96.

ABBREVIATIONS IN CLM 6272 FROM FREISING ABBEY

Alexander Souter

My attention was directed to this manuscript, which may be assigned to the first third of the ninth century, by the fact that it contains the commentary of Jerome on Matthew's Gospel, of which I am preparing the Vienna edition. In the course of perusing the manuscript *sur place* in 1931, I noticed some rather unusual abbreviations. By the generosity of the British Academy and the kind permission of the authorities at Munich, I have come into possession of a complete set of rotographs, from which my list of abbreviations is derived. If it was a far cry from Freising to Tours, with which the name of our *cher maître* will be lastingly connected, the two places have this in common that they were both powerfully influenced by Anglo-Saxon teachers at the same period, and were both great centres of scholarship.[1] The very abundance of the available material has probably hindered the publication of an adequate study of the early work of the Freising scriptorium. I offer this as a small contribution to that study.

To save difficulty in printing, I leave out the superposed horizontal strokes, and I have modelled the arrangement of the list on Professor Lindsay's well-known *Notae Latinae*. It should be mentioned that *Clm 6272* was not studied by Lindsay, though he naturally takes account of twenty other Freising manuscripts. Its general palaeographical characteristics are interesting, and C. H. Turner was of the opinion that its text is likely to be good.[2] It will naturally be collated for my edition.

The Anglo-Saxon influence is clear in a number of the abbreviations, but the continental influence is also apparent; the absence of certain Anglo-Saxon abbreviations is perhaps equally significant.[3]

WORD SYMBOLS

autem: usually aut, rarely au, almost as rarely h with the hook

Christus, etc.: xps, etc.; also wrongly xpos, antixpos, of unholy persons

deus, etc.: ds, etc.

dicens: dcs, dics

dicentem: dictm

dicentes: dicts

---

[1] The names of Aribo (764–783) and Hatto (810–835) deserve to be remembered in connexion with Freising (W. Wattenbach, *Deutschlands Geschichtsquellen im Mittelalter,* I⁷ (Stuttgart u. Berlin, 1904), 171, 287.

[2] *Early Worcester Mss.* (Oxford, 1916), p. xviii.

[3] Cf. the case of Lorsch (*Palaeographia Latina,* III, 1–48).

dicit: dic

dicitur: dr, dcr, dicr

dicunt: dict

dixerunt: dixt

dixit: dix

dominus, etc.: dns, etc.

ecce: ec

eius: ei, with comma above the i

enim: the old nota, rarely

esse: ee

esset: e&

essent: eent

est: e with horizontal stroke above

frater, etc.: fr, frem, fris, frm (*gen.pl.*), frum, fribus

gloria, etc.: gla, glẹ, glam

Hierusalem: hierlm

homo: ho (once)

Iesus, etc.: ihs, ihus (rarely), ihm, ihu

illo tempore(?): ill (should mean *illis*)

Israhel, etc.: isrl, irl, isrlis (*gen.*), isrlitarum

meus, meum: ms, mm

mihi: m with superposed i

misericordia, etc.: miscrda, miscrdia, miscdia, miscrdm

nihil: nil (thrice)

{*nobis:* nob, nb (rarer)

{*vobis:* uob, ub (rarer)

nomine: nnẹ (with o above first n)

non: n

{*noster*, etc.: nr, nra, nm (=*nostrum*)

{*vester*, etc.: ur, urm, uros uris

omnis, etc.: oms (once or twice for *omnis*, generally for *omnes*), omis, oma

per: p with usual stroke across lower part

populus, etc.: ppls, pplm, ppli, pplo, pplis; popls, poplm; ppulo (once)

post: p with the comma at right top corner

prae: p with the stroke above

pro: p with the usual curve to the left

propter: ppr (usually), pp with cross bar cutting both letters, ppt (once)

qua: q with superposed a

quae: q with the line above; q with triangular dots (once)

quam: q with the slanting stroke hooked at each end (*m.2* adds m in one case)

-que: q followed by semicolon

quem: q with bar across stem below (four times)[4]

qui: q with i above

quia: q plus the usual angle (ancient nota)

quis (after *si*): q with short stroke above

quo: q with o superposed

quod: qd with short stroke above the q only (usually); rarely crossing the d; also the insular symbol (in latter part of ms. d often added to this by another hand)

quomodo: qm, each with o above

quoniam: qm

quoque: qq, with one stroke crossing both lower shafts; also q with o above, followed by q with semicolon

reliqua: rel, rl, reliq

saeculum, etc.: sclm, etc.; so *saecularia:* sclaria

sanctus, etc.: scs, etc. (e.g., scorum); so *sanctificans*, etc.: scificans, etc.

secundum: scdm, scd, secdm, secund; so with adj., *secundus*, etc.: scds, scda, scdo

sed: s, followed by comma (once)

sequitur: seqr

sicut: sic

spiritalis, etc.: spalis, etc.; spitalis, etc.

spiritus, etc.: sps, etc. (contrast spituu [f. 44ᵛ], spiritibus [f. 69ᵛ] of the unholy)

sunt: s

supra: sup, with supraposed a

---

[4] This is perhaps the most notable of all these symbols.

(*suus*) *suis:* ss (once)
tempore: tempr
tibi: t with i above
vel: ul; l; u (flanked by one or two dots or none, with horizontal stroke above)

vero: u with o above; uo (o on line)

SYLLABLE SYMBOLS

ae: e with hook
con: reversed c (only once, by corr.)
men: m with horizontal stroke above
bitur: br(thrice, near end of line)[5]
ter: t with horizontal stroke above
ber: b with cross bar
bis: b with cross bar
it: horizontal stroke above preceding letter
m, n: suprascript stroke
ri: i above the letter preceding the r in the full form of word

runt, bunt, lunt, gunt: rt, bt, lt, gt; r with line above
tur: t with suprascript comma; changed once or twice to the 2 form by another hand
bus: b with semicolon
mus, pus, nus, tus: m, p, n, t, with comma at right top corner, or with horizontal stroke or line, crossed angularly

OTHER ABBREVIATIONS[6]

Abraham: abhm, abrhm
aliter: al
angelus, etc.: angls, anglm, anglrm[7] (*gen. plur.*)
apostolus, etc.: apos; much oftener apls; also aplus, apl*, aplm, aplo, aplis, aplrm, apls (*corr.* aplos) (*acc. plur.*)
apostolica: aplica
David: dd(with bar across the two d's)
discipulus, etc.: discpls, discplm, discpli, discplos, discplrm, discplis
ecclesia (or rather *eclesia,* for this ms. never has the double c), etc.: ecla, etc.
ecclesiasticus(ecl-): eclasticus
episcopus, etc.: eps, epm, epi (*nom. plur.*), epis (=episcopis), epos (*acc. plur.*), epis (=*episcopi, but corr.* epi)
epistula: epla
evangelium, etc.: euanglo, euglo

Iohannes, etc.: ioh (*nom., gen., acc.*); iohs (*nom.; corr. m.2* iohes), iohm (*acc.*), iohis (*nom., gen.*), iohem (*acc.*), iohes (*nom.*)
milia: mil (once)
mulier: mlr (end of line, once)
mundus: muds (end of line, once)
omnipotens, etc.: omps, omptis (*gen.*)
presbyter, etc.: presbit (end of line; =presbyteri); prbr; prbi, prbri (*both nom. plur.*); prbos (*acc. plur.*)
propheta, etc.: ppha, pphas (*acc. plur.*), pph (*nom. sing.*), pphm (*acc.*),pphrm (*gen. plur.*), (in all cases the first p is to be understood as the *pro* symbol)
psalmo: psalo (once, end of line)
sempiternum: sepitm (once)
templum, etc.: tplm, tplo, teplm
voluntatem: uoltatem (once, not ending a line)

UNIVERSITY OF ABERDEEN.

[5] If Lindsay knew this contraction, I cannot discover where he refers to it.

[6] These are of a kind not placed in Lindsay's final lists; some of them he would have called 'capricious,' 'technical,' and some are quite unrecorded in his book.

[7] This type of abbreviation for the gen. plur. is quite characteristic of this ms.: cf. *apostolus, discipulus, propheta,* in this list.

ENNODIUS AND POPE SYMMACHUS

PART I

W. T. TOWNSEND

How COMPLETELY the controversy that raged around the Henotikon dominated ecclesiastical politics at the beginning of the sixth century has been shown in another connection.[1] There were various causes for division in the Rome of that day, but a definite issue was needed to crystallize them, and this issue was supplied by the Henotikon schism. It is not too much to say that but for the struggle between Constantinople and Rome thus engendered Laurentius would never have been elected anti-pope.

As by-products of the Symmachus-Laurentius schism there arose many interesting historical incidents (perhaps even the *Liber Pontificalis* had its beginnings in the rival lines of popes put forth by the opposing factions), and many famous characters were directly or indirectly involved. In fact from 498 till the final settlement of the schism by the elimination of Laurentius in 504 or 505, when by the order of Theoderic he withdrew to the country estates of the Senator Festus, it was practically impossible for a man of any prominence in Rome to abstain from taking sides. Evidence of the bitterness with which the campaign was waged on both sides meets us on every hand as we read the documents of the period. Cudgels and pens were both wielded with good effect, but, when all is considered, it was the pen which was as ever the mightier. The anonymous authors of *The Symmachian Forgeries*[2] wrote popular pamphlets for the man in the street, while writers with greater claims to scholarship supplied a more learned, if not a more dignified, approach.

It seems that the supporters of Symmachus were largely clerical. The Roman aristocracy, led by the Senators Festus and Probinus, were mainly on the side of Laurentius the imperial nominee. In fact the author of the life of Symmachus in the *Liber Pontificalis* complains that 'Only Faustus, an exconsul, fought for the church.' This, however, can be shown to be somewhat of an exaggeration. The Senator Symmachus, father-in-law of Boethius, was a papal supporter. It was to him, along with Faustus, that Saint Avitus Bishop of Vienne wrote in the name of the bishops of Gaul, denouncing the trial of a pope by any council what-

[1] See my article 'The Henotikon Schism and the Roman Church,' *The Journal of Religion*, 16 (1936), pp. 78 ff.

[2] See my article in *The Journal of Religion*, 13 (1933), pp. 165 ff.

soever.[3] Symmachus' famous son-in-law does not himself appear in the controversy during the years of struggle (perhaps because of his youth), but, as will be seen later, he was called in council by the pope, along with Symmachus the Senator and other famous men of the time, when a letter from some Eastern bishops was under consideration, so he was probably a loyal supporter of Pope Symmachus from the beginning.[4] But as far as our information goes Symmachus' greatest literary supporter was Magnus Felix Ennodius.[5]

Much more important than *The Symmachian Forgeries* was a tract entitled *Adversus Synodum Absolutionis Incongruae.* This work is unfortunately lost. It was evidently an appeal to the better classes of the community in the form of an able attack on the synod which absolved the pope without investigation. So important a work could not be allowed to go unanswered, so Ennodius set himself to compose a reply. The result was his famous *Libellus Apologeticus pro Synodo.*[6] It was, perchance, the beginning of Ennodius' career. It is easy to imagine the young scholar presenting his defence of the papal party and springing at once into prominence, just as a chance remark in the presence of Gardiner and Fox brought young Thomas Cranmer to the notice of his king, to the archepiscopal throne, and finally to the stake.[7] Ennodius' work was received with great enthusiasm and placed after the acts of a previous synod, thus assuring its immortality.

The author of the *Adversus Synodum* had contended that the whole trial of Symmachus was a farce and the acquittal of the pope illegal for the following reasons:—(1) The synod was not representative, and even

[3] Mansi VIII, 293 ff. For a discussion see Auguste Charaux, *Saint Avite, évêque de Vienne*, Paris, 1876, pp. 95 ff.

[4] For a full discussion of Boethius' relation to the Symmachus-Laurentius struggle and the Henotikon controversy, see P. Dr. Viktor Schurr, *Die Trinitätslehre des Boethius im Lichte der 'skythischen Kontroversen,'* Paderborn, 1935.

[5] Saint Ennodius became bishop of Pavia in 510 or 511, probably as a reward for his staunch support of the legitimate pope. His *Libellus Apologeticus pro Synodo* was accepted by the papal party as their official defence, and incorporated among the acts of the synods. His wide and varied correspondence is second only to that of Cassiodorus, and is indispensable for a study of the times. The student of Ennodius is fortunate in the fact that his writings have been ably edited. Besides the collection given in Migne, which is only a reprint of one of the two editions which appeared in 1611, there are two complete editions by modern scholars; one by W. Hartel in the *Corpus Scriptorum Ecclesiasticorum,* the other by F. Vogel in the *Monumenta Germaniae Historica.* There is no manuscript of Ennodius which is entirely satisfactory, and a good deal of reconstruction has been necessary. The letters of Ennodius were published with a French translation by S. Léglise in 1906.

[6] Ennodius quoted so extensively from the *Adversus Synodum* that it can practically be reconstructed from his citations. For such a reconstruction see A. Thiel, *Epistolae Romanorum Pontificum Genuinae* I, 1868, pp. 735 ff.

[7] It has generally been held that the *Libellus* of Ennodius was first presented at a synod assembled in Rome in 503. I at one time looked on this as a genuine synod of which the acts had been rewritten by a later hand, but now I reject it altogether. The Pseudo-Isidore simply built the synod around the *Libellus* of Ennodius. For a full discussion see my article in *Church History,* 6 (1937), 233 ff.

all those present had not voted for the absolution.[8] The bishops who did attend were by their own statement old and imbecile.[9] (2) The assembled bishops had not followed the intention of the king, and had questioned his right to call a council. (3) The council had advanced the false proposition that no one was able to remedy the disorderly conduct of the pope, as if the privilege of the successors of Saint Peter were to have a full license to sin. (4) The proposition that a pope cannot be judged by his inferiors is very dangerous, because if this were the case, it was useless to assemble the council in the first place, and the council when called had no right to cite the pope to appear, or to summon his accusers; nor ought the pope to have come or to have approved the assembly. But others had been judged greater far than Symmachus; the Lord and Redeemer submitted to judgement, of whom it was prophesied, *O man of Judah and inhabitant of Jerusalem, judge between me and my vine*; Peter and Paul had not repudiated judgement; while Samuel had asked the whole nation to judge his administration. (5) The pope had only been absolved and never cleared of the charges laid against him. (6) The bishops had advanced the false proposition that councils must be assembled by the pope, yet year by year provincial assemblies met and passed laws. Were these of no value because the pope was not present? (7) The mere fact of the king having appointed a visitor to the Roman Church showed that he recognized that the conduct of the pope needed to be reformed. Anyway the pope, who appointed visitors for other bishops, had no right to complain when one was appointed for Rome.

Ennodius answered these charges point by point. (1) To the first he

---

[8] This was the last synod held for the trial of Symmachus. A marginal rendering in one of the manuscripts gives the following caption:—*Quarta synodus habita Romae Palmaris*, which I believe sets the synod in the portico of St. Peter's. Because of its importance I append a translation of the final decision of this synod. 'Pope Symmachus, bishop of the apostolic see, has been charged with certain misdemeanors. Because for reasons set forth above, the whole affair has been reserved for divine judgement: as far as this affair concerns men, let him be free and without blame, and let him give the divine mysteries to the Christian people without let or hindrance in all churches which belong to the jurisdiction of this see; because we, for reasons designated above, perceived that no obligation could be imposed on him by the petition of his assailants. Wherefore, according to the fundamental precepts which concede this to our power, we place back in his hands whatever of ecclesiastical jurisdiction is within or without the sacred city of Rome; and reserving the whole cause to the judgement of God we exhort, that, as occasion demands, people receive the sacred communion from him, and be mindful of God and their own souls, because he is both a lover of peace and himself peace, who thus admonishes us: *My peace I give unto you, my peace I leave with you*, and affirming that peace must be established in every state he says, *Blessed are the peace makers*. Whoever after our arrangement, which we do not think will happen, either will not admit [these things], or believes that the case ought to be reopened, let him take heed, for as we trust in God, when he shall come to render his account he shall be lightly esteemed in the divine judgement.' A. Thiel I, pp. 665 f.

[9] To avoid sitting in judgement on the pope the bishops, when called by Theoderic, had pleaded that they were *debilitate corporis invalidos*. This statement was seized upon by the author of the *Adversus Synodum*.

replied that it was not essential to the legality of a council that all the bishops be called, but it was false that this particular synod was 'packed.' It was ridiculous to speak of the bishops of the council as foolish and incapable just because of their bodily weaknesses. (2) The bishops were right in pointing out to the king that the synod ought to be summoned by the pope, because they had this privilege. (3) There was no need to reform the pope, for who would doubt the sanctity of one who held such a high position? God would not permit such a one to become corrupt.[10] Strictly speaking the pope had not been judged by the council, but had voluntarily submitted himself to its judgement. To illustrate how local prejudices often made it difficult for a man to get a fair hearing in his own vicinity, Ennodius took the example of the African controversy and the appeal to Pope Zosimus in 418.[11] Thus by analogy Symmachus was justified in refusing to be tried by a synod in Rome, as soon as he saw that local prejudices made justice impossible. (5) To the charge that after submitting to the judgement of the synod the pope had withdrawn, Ennodius made a very bitter rejoinder, showing how impossible it was for Symmachus to reach the synod through the streets of the hostile city.[12] (6) Ennodius admitted that it was true that provincial councils might be lawfully assembled without the consent of the pope, but not a council to try the pope himself. If his opponents would only read they would not make such ridiculous statements. He then proceeds to quote, or rather to give in substance, the third canon of Sardica:—

Any bishop deposed by a provincial judgement, may, if he please, appeal to the pope of Rome; and he, if it seem right to him, may give a new trial, thus assisting the condemned.[13]

[10] It is well for the soundness of Ennodius' reasoning that he did not know some of the later popes. This part is the weakest of the whole work.

Maurice Dumoulin says of the *Libellus:*—'Il y a plus de personnalité dans la *Dictio* que dans le *Libellus*, qui est une oeuvre officielle. Ces opuscules sont tous deux des ouvrages de polémique dont la véracité n'a jamais été mise en doute, parce que Symmaque a été reconnu comme l'unique et véritable pontife, comme l'évêque régulièrement élu.'

'Le gouvernment de Theodoric et la domination des Ostrogoths en Italie, d'après les oeuvres d'Ennodius,' *Revue Historique* 78 (1902), p. 4.

[11] For a full account of this incident see Hefele-Leclercq, *Histoire des conciles* II, Paris, 1908, pp. 197 ff.; also T. Scott Holmes, *The Christian Church in Gaul*, London, 1911, pp. 356 ff.

[12] The papal party had been attacked in the streets on its way to the synod and some of its members killed. After that the pope refused to leave the precincts of Saint Peter's.

[13] 'Si quis episcoporum iudicio provinciali depositus fuerit, Romanum papam, si placet, rursus appellet, et ipse, si videtur, reparet iudicia in opitulatione damnati.' (Vienna Corpus VI, p. 312.)

The canon of Sardica on which this is based is not quite so definite, and has given rise to a good deal of discussion. It reads in part:—'Quod si aliquis episcoporum iudicatus fuerit in aliqua causa, et putat se bonam causam habere, ut iterum concilium renovetur; si vobis placet, sancti Petri apostoli memoriam honoramus, ut scribatur ab his, qui causam examinarunt, Iulio Romano episcopo, et si iudicaverit renovandum esse iudicium, renovetur et det iudices.'

The fourth canon of the same council provides that if a bishop, deposed by a local council, desires

(7) In dealing with the question of the visitor Ennodius makes his best contribution. He was quite ready to admit that the pope by right appointed visitors for other churches, but claimed that the present case was no parallel. He then appropriates for the pope, the highest ruler in the Church, the theories which had already been formulated for the emperor, 'But I claim,' he writes, 'that the proposer of a law is not, unless he wish, under the law which he has made, and unless the prince is set above all criticism it is useless to call upon him to enforce the law which he has given. There is of course the law of conscience and of the heart, which corrects men who live without law; by customs of its own it checks men who do not owe discipline to necessity. God wishes, perchance, the causes of other men to be judged by men, but has reserved the bishop of this see, without examination, to his own tribunal.'[14] Note that he makes no appeal to the past, no appeal to authority, but seems to found this amazing claim on reason alone. But when we turn to the pages of Roman law we find that he is only making, in different words, the same claim that had already been made long before for the emperor. The statement of Ulpian is well known, *Princeps legibus solutus est*,[15] with which should be compared the following extract from an edict of Theodosius and Valentinian:—*Digna vox maiestate regnantis legibus alligatum se principem profiteri: adeo de auctoritate iuris nostra pendet auctoritas.*[16]

It is at first surprising to find such theories at this early date; but it must be remembered that Ennodius was pleading a cause, and would turn as a matter of course to those arguments most ready to hand. What was more natural than that being himself familiar with Roman law, and arguing against men skilled in that law, he should ascribe to the pope, now by far the most important person in Rome, the same exalted position in ecclesiastical affairs that had been claimed for the emperor in secular? It was a natural tendency that prompted Ennodius to place the bishop of Rome ecclesiastically on the throne of the Caesars, but just because the tendency was natural it was likely to be developed.[17]

---

to appeal, no appointment shall be made to the vacant see till the bishop of Rome has decided on the case. Ennodius had good backing for his claim.

See Hefele-Leclercq, *op. cit.*, I, pp. 762 f.

[14] This is much stronger than the claim made by Gelasius:—'Et si cunctis generaliter sacerdotibus recte divina tractantibus fidelium convenit corda submitti, quanto potius sedis illius praesuli consensus est adhibendus, quem cunctus sacerdotibus et Divinitas summa voluit praeeminere, et subsequens Ecclesiae generalis iugitur pietas celebravit?' (A. Thiel I, p. 351 f.) On the other hand it is well to remember that papal supporters generally went farther than popes themselves.

[15] *Digest* I, 3, 31. *Ulpianus libro XIII ad Legem Iuliam et Papiam.*

[16] *Codex* I, 14, 4. *Impp. Theodosius et Valentinianus AA. ad Volusianum P. P.*

[17] That Ennodius was by no means far ahead of his time may be seen by a glance at a letter from Avitus, bishop of Vienne, to the senators Faustus and Symmachus. 'Quasi senator ipse Romanus, quasi Christianus episcopus obtestor . . . ut in conspectu vestro non sit ecclesiae minor, quam re-

It is very unlikely that Pope Symmachus, having discovered such a ready pen, would not have put it to permanent use. One would naturally expect to see Ennodius become to the papacy what Cassiodorus was to the court at Ravenna. This is a subject that has never been thoroughly probed, and I open it up hoping thereby to direct criticism. In several instances we know that Ennodius did write letters in the pope's name, just as Cassiodorus did for Theoderic; such were a letter to the African bishops victims of Vandal persecution,[18] and a letter to Liberius confirming Marcellinus in the see of Aquileia.[19]

It would be of much greater interest, however, if it were possible to see the pen of Ennodius in the longer letters of Symmachus, namely the answer to the Eastern bishops, and his reply to Emperor Anastasius. Difficulties meet us in the very beginning owing to the fact that even at this early date there is a set style developing in papal correspondence, especially when treating of the same or similar subjects. This is particularly noticeable when comparing the letters of Gelasius and Symmachus to Emperor Anastasius on the question of the schism. The letter to the Eastern bishops is the more obvious point of departure, mainly because we have some hint as to the manner in which the content, if not the form, was determined.

There were in the Eastern Church, and especially in that part of it that lay nearest to the Latin jurisdiction, many who were just as opposed to the Henotikon as the pope himself; but placed as they were within reach of imperial resentment, it was not so easy for them to show their opposition. A few of these had stood out and gone into exile, but the great majority had bowed to the storm. These latter were very grieved to find themselves classed as heretics, and regarded at Rome as little better than open enemies. About the year 512 a group of these bishops addressed a letter to Pope Symmachus in the name of the *Oriental Church*.[20] The letter is undated, but the reply was written October the eighth, 512,[21] so that it could not have been received many months before.

Boethius in his *Contra Eutychen et Nestorium* has left us an outline picture of the assembly called to consider the letter of the *Oriental Church*.[22]

---

publicae status; . . . nec minus diligatis in ecclesia vestra sedem Petri, quam in civitate apicem mundi.' Mansi VIII, 293 ff.

[18] *Ennodii Ep.* ii, 14. Sundwall (*Abhandlungen zur Geschichte des ausgehenden Römertums*, Helsingfors, 1919) places this letter in the year 503, or about the same date as the *Libellus*. However I am not sure that Sundwall's dating is always very accurate.

[19] *Ennodii Ep.* v, 1.

[20] A. Thiel I, pp. 709 ff.

[21] Data octavo Idus Octobris post consulatum Felicis viri clarissimi. This letter was addressed to all the bishops, presbyters, deacons, archimandrites, and to the whole order and populace throughout Illyricum, Dardania, and both the Dacias.

[22] Boethius, *Loeb Classical Library*, Stewart and Rand, London and New York, 1918, pp. 72 ff.

Boethius' description leads us to infer that the assembly was a large one, not just a few prominent men called in to advise the pope. Boethius speaks of 'Sitting a long way from the man whom I especially wished to watch' (no doubt his father-in-law, the Senator Symmachus), and that he was 'Much put out and overwhelmed by the mob of ignorant speakers.'[23] These are not expressions that one, as careful of his language as was Boethius, would use of a small select circle. Still in all that large group we can name only the pope, Boethius, John the Deacon,[24] and probably Boethius' father-in-law Symmachus the Senator. Was Ennodius there? The duties of his new see of Pavia would be no bar if the pope needed his services. Three years later he headed a legation to Constantinople in an unsuccessful attempt to settle the same controversy. As we have just seen the reply made to the Eastern bishops was not the work of the pope alone, but the whole question was thrashed out in an assembly. The problems discussed seemed so important to Boethius that he made them the basis of a special study. It is almost certain that a secretary would be chosen to communicate the findings of the Roman Church in council assembled to their Eastern brethren. Of course it would be written and sent in the pope's name, but it would be the answer of the assembly none the less. As far as known there was absolutely no one in the circle around the pope so well fitted for this work as Ennodius, and every probability points to him. It only remains to examine the text of the letter and compare it with the known writings of Ennodius, and see if their style can throw any light on our problem. This has been done by Professor Wyatt in Part II of this article.

Pawtucket, Rhode Island.

[23] Boethius held a very low opinion of the theologians of his day. See the Introduction to *De Trinitate, Loeb Classical Library*, p. 4.

[24] Schurr (*Die Trinitätslehre*, pp. 115 f.) thinks there was only one John the Deacon who changed sides twice, Duchesne claims there were two, one on each side. (*L'Église au VIe Siècle*, p. 125, *n.* 4.) Schurr makes the better case.

PART II

William F. Wyatt

It has been suggested in Part I that the author of the Letter to the Eastern Bishops may have been Ennodius, and a number of facts have been cited in support of this thesis. The following may be added. Symmachus was a provincial from Sardinia. He did not become a Christian until he went to Rome. He must therefore have felt hesitancy in the already complicated field of Christian reasoning and perhaps in the use of the Latin language itself. So far as I know the schools of Sardinia were not of high order. Symmachus must have felt it necessary to enlist the aid of some one whose standing as a man of learning was secure. Ennodius was also a provincial, but he came from Gaul where the schools had always been famous; and besides he was taken early to Milan where the schools were good. Of these he had taken advantage. Ennodius was a lawyer and a teacher of rhetoric and also a churchman. His provincialism and his churchmanship were a point of unity with Symmachus and his training and professional gifts provided exactly what Symmachus may have lacked.

Farther examination of the matter may best be made by a comparison of the Letter with work that is known to be by Ennodius. It happens that we have among the works of Ennodius a Dictio[1] (number six in Hartel) whose theme is just that of the Letter to the Eastern Bishops. I shall therefore make a somewhat detailed comparison of these two documents.

Both the Letter and the Dictio open with a short introductory sentence.

Ep. 1. Quod fieri plane cupimus, si quae scribimus, impleantur.

Dct. 1. Pro ratione solvendum est quod pro ratione tacuimus. The content of the two is different, but the tone is similar, the one a wish or a command, the other an obligation—the one more fitting to one in authority, the other better suited to one not immediately concerned with the situation who is writing as it were unofficially.

Then follows in both an explanatory paragraph. Both are concerned with the question of silence as against speech, lines 2–15 of the Letter and lines 1–9 of the Dictio.

Ep. 2, 3. Nullus stupeat servatum hactenus nos nunc solvisse silentium. The phrase 'solvisse silentium' takes up the 'solvendum est quod

---

[1] For convenience of reference I have numbered the lines in each document; the Dictio as printed in Vol. VI of the Vienna Corpus (Ed. Hartel). Other references to Ennodius are given by page and line in Hartel. The line numbers for the Letter are according to the text given in Migne, *Patrologiae Cursus Completus*, LXII, col. 61 ff.

tacuimus' of the Dictio. The sentence of the Letter beginning 'Nullus stupeat' corresponds fairly closely to the following:

Dct. 1-3. Nam ut pateat et linguae nostrae officia et silentium ordinatis servisse temporibus, fide hortante in officium sermonis erumpimus.

Ep. 3, 4. Most wise Solomon says, 'Tempus loquendi et tempus tacendi', (Eccl. III, 7). In the Dictio 5, 6 the 'tempus loquendi' appears in a much more elaborate form: To speak without cause is the same as to say nothing when necessity presses; in the words of the apostle, '"Vae enim mihi est, nisi evangelizavero," et alibi, "tempus tacendi."' The thought is the same in both, but the Dictio presents it with clumsy rhetoric and confused quotation; the Letter by simple direct quotation.

Ep. 5-14. The present time forbids silence. In other matters one might not be stirred by the goads of the faith, 'fidei stimulis' (cf. 'fide hortante' of the Dictio), now even the gentle must become aggressive. . . . To instruct you is unpleasant but necessary; 'Et vos quidem docere quod doceatis, grave onus pudoris sed necessarium.'

Dct. 6-9. It becomes us who are moved by the weight of duty, 'pondus obsequii,' to support the doers of good and to crush the doers of evil. To instruct you is but to apply goads to runners: 'Et quidem vos docere non aliud est quam stimulos admovisse currentibus.' Strikingly similar are the phrases 'onus pudoris' of the Epistle and 'pondus obsequii' of the Dictio.

Lines 15-17 of the Letter and 9-11 of the Dictio serve in each case as a transition to what follows, but do not appear to provide further basis for consideration.

Then follows in each a list of heretics of the Eastern Church: Nestorius, Eutyches, Dioscorus, Peter, Timotheus, and Cyrus (mentioned only in the Dictio), Ep. 18-41, Dct. 11-31. There is considerable similarity in the mode of presentation, especially in the first three sentences:

Ep. 18. Cui incognitum . . . ? About Nestorius.

22. Ubi terrarum non praedicatur . . . ? Referring to the Council of Chalcedon.

27. Quis Petrum et Timotheum . . . ignorat?

Dct. 11. Stat apud conscientias . . . Statement about Nestorius and Eutyches.

20. Apud quem Chalcedonensis non vivit commemoratio . . . ? On the Council of Chalcedon.

25. Ubi gentium Timotheus ignoratur . . . ?

Compare also the constructions following the first examples in each of the groups given above.

Ep. 18-20. Cui incognitum qua Constantinopolitana Ecclesia Nestorii contagione laboravit.

Dct. 11–14. Stat apud conscientias vestras quanta Nestorius et Eutyches
. . . disciplinam perfidiae fornicatione corruperint.

In both these an indirect question appears introduced by an interrogative
adjective in the ablative separated widely from the noun with which it
agrees:

Ep. qua . . . contagione laboravit.

Dct. quanta . . . perfidiae fornicatione corruperint.

The phrasing of the Dictio appears strained; 'perfidiae fornicatione' is a
strange expression. But 'contagione' of the Letter expresses the same
notion more concisely. The term 'perfidiae' is employed in the next sentence in the Letter.

Ep. 24. Eutyches and Dioscorus are called 'duo nomina famosa et magnae perfidiae'.

Dct. 12–13. Nestorius and Eutyches are called 'gemina diabolicae informationis ostenta'.

Here 'famosa' and 'ostenta,'[2] though differing as parts of speech, carry
a similar suggestion of things conspicuous for evil; and the thought contained in the phrases, 'magnae perfidiae' and 'diabolicae informationis'
is the same.

Ep. 29. Peter and Timotheus are described as 'auctores ac magistros
suos saevo errore vincentes'—outdoing their teachers.

Dct. 28. It is said that Timotheus 'sacri persecutione pontificis et genera
criminum vicit et nomina'—outdid kinds and names of offenses. The use
in both of 'vinco' in the sense of outdo is notable: i.e. 'vinco' for 'supero.'
Timotheus is spoken of as a parricide or more in both:

Ep. 30–34. Illum Timotheum loquimur patricidam qui . . . effusionem
pii sanguinis ad crimen pervasionis adiecit.

Dct. 26, 27. Where is Timotheus not known 'qui propter . . . caedem
fieri plus quam parricida non horruit'?

After this there is in both documents a sort of break which comprises
lines 42–46 of the Letter and 31–46 of the Dictio.

Ep. 42–46. Are the troubles of Antioch because of another Peter not to
be mentioned? Who could worthily bewail the sorrows of Apamea and
Tyre?

Dct. 31–46. Exhortation and statement. Figures from war and surgery
are used. There are some points of similarity between this and parts of
the Letter, but since they do not fit into the formally corresponding section of the Letter, I will consider but one part of the Dictio which connects with an earlier passage in the Letter.

Dct. 35–38. Alluding to heretics already mentioned, Ennodius using
a figure drawn from surgery says, 'Scimus quia qui in putribus membris

[2] Cf. Boethius Cons. II m. 1.8.

non utitur ferri medicina serpentibus morbis praestat obsequia; nam
nisi secentur tabefacta, contaminant'.

Ep. 18–22. Cui incognitum Constantinopolitana Ecclesia qua Nestorii
contagione laboravit? Nestorii, inquam, qui quasi putre corporis membrum a societate catholicae communionis excisus est.

The 'scimus' of the Dictio corresponds to 'cui incognitum' of the Letter,
'in putribus membris' (Dct.) corresponds to 'putre membrum' (Ep.).
And perhaps it would not be too far fetched to regard 'secentur' (Dct.)
as corresponding to 'excisus est' (Ep.). At any rate the idea in the one
is that an offending member had been cut out, and in the other, that all
such should be so treated. The Letter presents the matter in a straightforward statement; the Dictio strains rhetorically.

Next in both documents—Ep. 46–56 and Dct. 46–54—comes the case
of Acacius, the man who had once been a defender of the faith but had
fallen away. Both agree in stating the character of Acacius' behavior, but
the Letter adds to this the necessity for others to avoid him. The wording
differs considerably, as does the tone—the Letter being deeply serious
and the Dictio rhetorically or formally so—yet the two agree in the type
of person and the situation that occasions their words.

There follow in the Letter nearly a hundred lines that are pretty much
outside the content of the Dictio. For these I will give the substance,
calling attention as I go to places and expressions in Ennodius that offer
parallels or similarities.

Ep. 57–81. This section contains a general reflection: disaster will follow
if established things can be easily overthrown. 'nam ubi facilis dissolutio
est rationabilis constituti, ibi omnis sanctitatis forma corrumpitur,
Christus impetitur, et (quis hoc fidelium patienter accipiat?) instituta
Patrum reverenda calcantur.'

Dct. 34, 35. Patienter ferre non possumus vana in Christum nostrum et
blasphema ructantes.

'Quis hoc patienter accipiat' (Ep.) corresponds to 'patienter ferre non
possumus' (Dct.). 'Christus impetitur' (Ep.) corresponds to 'vana in
Christum nostrum et blasphema ructantes' (Dct.). Also the verb 'calcare'
is a favorite with Ennodius. Again the Dictio is rhetorical and the Letter
simple and direct. The Dictio is less concerned with the institutes of the
Fathers.

Ep. 81–84. Et ideo qui pro ea (fide) periculum persecutionis subire
meruerit, dignum se coelestis ostendit esse militiae.

Afris Epistola, Hartel, p. 55, lines 4 and 5. Quos habeat Christus milites
certamen ostendit; qui triumphum mereantur per bella cognoscitur.
Suffering as a test of worth is the common idea here. Also the word
'ostendit' occurs in both passages, and the 'meruerit' of one corresponds

to 'mereantur' in the other. 'Se ostendit' (Ep.) equals 'cognoscitur' (*Afris*). The idea is of wide occurrence and is often expressed in much the same language, but I cite this case as offering some confirmation of my thesis, or at least not contradicting it.

Ep. 89–96. One should choose any disaster rather than be separated from the people of Christ. The time is opportune; the reward great. 'Ecce tempus optabile, ecce fructuum congregatio desiderata fidelium, parvis passionibus munera magna compenset.'

Dct. 39–44. In similar vein: 'Quis a bellis talibus timoris revocetur obstaculo, de quibus vitali possit morte gaudere? . . . "Non sunt condignae passiones huius mundi ad superventuram gloriam, quae revelabitur in nobis?" ' (Rom. VIII, 18).

In both these passages the 'passiones' of this world win great rewards. The Letter states simply what the Dictio accomplishes by quotation.

Ep. 97–103. This contains a direct address to the bishops. I should like to say more, but what need? We have the examples of the Apostles and the Fathers. 'Quid opus est vocis stimulis?'

Compare Ep. 7. . . . 'nec fidei stimulis excitari', and

Dct. 9. . . . 'stimulos admovisse currentibus'.

There is here a common fondness for the word 'stimulus'.

Ep. 103–113. Hortatory. Let us declare the teachings fearlessly; the enemy is strengthened if convictions are not delcared boldly: '. . . magnum robur ad impugnantium fidem, quandiu adversus eos (the enemy) prolatae sententiae non viriliter asserunter.'

Compare *Libellus* p. 289, line 3. 'Ad lucrum hostis sui procedit qui in conflictibus non prius causas quam aliud expendit.'

In both the thought is that he who holds back contributes to the strength of the enemy.

Ep. 113–115. Direct address: I wish to say better things of you that through you remedy may be found for harm done by evil men. There is no parallel in the Dictio.

Ep. 115–117. An aphoristic sentence: 'Non est tam durum decipi quemquem, quam deceptum in errore persistere.'

Dct. 51–52. (Said in connection with Acacius): 'Gravius enim est degustata bona quam intacta calcasse'.

In both the idea is, to continue in an evil state is worse than merely to fall into error.

Ep. 117–121. The language is here figurative: all parts of the body should be in harmony; otherwise disease gradually involves the whole body; 'malum hoc et malis omnibus gravius, cum a corpore suo membra dissentiunt. Nam etsi non sigillatim occupet omnia lineamenta debilitas, necesse est tamen iuxta apostolicam vocem, totum corpus ex parte prae-gravari'.

And anticipating a little:

Ep. 127 ff. Let us avoid communion with those men, 'qui nunc quasi morbum et contagium Ecclesiis partium vestrarum tentant irrepere'. Heresy, like disease, beginning with parts of the Christian body creeps on and gradually involves the whole. This idea appears in the part of the Dictio cited above:

Dct. 35–38. Who does not use the knife does service to insinuating dis-eases—'serpentibus morbis'—and if the diseased parts are not cut out, they communicate their poison—'nisi tabefacta secentur, contaminant.'

Ep. 122–137. Reflections: we must avoid the communion of the dis-credited. What I say is said in love, for correction in bad spirit is not effective. There is no parallel to this in the Dictio.

This brings us to the opening of the concluding paragraph of the Letter and at this point there are marked similarities in the Dictio.

Ep. 138, 139. Propter quod, fratres, illius bonae Ecclesiae desiderantes unitatem.

Dct. 31–34. Here is an expression of a similar conclusion, not, how-ever, in the last paragraph. 'Proinde, fratres, . . . tenete sententiam, quia nos mundae Ecclesiae et non habentis maculam optamus unitatem.' 'Proinde' of the Dictio corresponds to 'propter quod' of the Letter. Both are addressed to the brethren. In both, unity is the conditioning motive.

Ep. 144–148. Donec enim unitas non redeat, nullus ambigat eadem ni-hilominus esse ventura quae in Constantinopolitana nuper Ecclesia contigerunt; de quibus mihi pariter ingemiscere necesse est et tacere.

Dct. 54–56. De his quae praefati sumus natum est, quod in Constantino-politana nuper Ecclesia fertur admissum. Unde patimur sine vocis usura tristitiam: . . .

'Ingemiscere' of the Letter corresponds to 'tristitiam patimur' of the Dictio. 'Tacere' of the Letter corresponds to 'sine vocis usura'; and again we have in the Dictio the thought of the Letter expressed in rhetorical phrase while the Letter is direct and simple.

Ep. 148–150. Nam qui apostolicae sedis admonitionem neglegendam esse crediderunt, merito inciderunt in ea quae evenire solent solatio destitutis.

Dct. 56–58. . . . qui enim oblatis remediis non oboediunt, merito nihil consolationis tempore quo premuntur habuerunt.

The Letter makes the direct assertion of papal authority and the result of its neglect; the Dictio makes the same kind of statement, but in-directly and figuratively—those who do not follow the doctor's directions have no recourse when they get sick.

Heretical teaching is spoken of as poison:

Ep. 154–159. We gladly welcome those who separate themselves from the poisons of Eutyches, etc.; 'illos qui se a suprascriptorum . . . venenis dissociant, libentur amplectimur.'

Dct. 53–54. Nihil defensionis superest homini . . . ad mortifera schismatum venena redeunti.

Libellus p. 288, 16, 17. Adversus quos sibilantium effusa sunt venena linguarum.

Besides the similarity in diction and arrangement of topics, there are certain peculiarities of style that are common to the Letter and Dictio and are absent or not so marked in the other letters of Pope Symmachus. One of the most striking is the wide separation of noun and adjective, the adjective and noun being the first and last words of what may be an independent sentence, an infinitive phrase, or an adjective and noun with various modifiers between, the whole forming a noun or adjective phrase. Examples of the first class are:

Ep. 7. magni constat esse fastidii.

102. coelestium nobis ostenderunt argumenta virtutum.

110. manifestum latet sub veritatis colore mendacium.

Dct. 7. praelati ceteris hortatur pondus obsequii.

21. Chalcedonensis non vivit commemoratio veneranda concili?

Afris p. 55, 12. prolixis non est opus fervorem in vobis caelestem animare conloquiis.

32, 33. manentem in supernis patrum et adhaerentem beato Petro tenete sententiam.

Examples of the second class:

Ep. 2. servatum hactenus nos nunc solvisse silentium.

16. religiosae adferre dogmata disciplinae.

There is but one example in the Dictio and that not impressive.

Dct. 2, 3. ordinatis servisse temporibus.

Examples of the third class:

Ep. 11. spiritualis quaedam Deo accepta congressio.

54. designato superius damnatorum agmini.

103. claras Ecclesiae cum magna fiducia disciplinas.

Dct. 40. quibus mundi huius potestatibus.

46, 47. diro diaboli a sententia sua motus imperio.

48. clari deserens ornamenta certaminis.

It does not seem likely that the Dictio is a rhetorical exercise based on the Letter,—a possibility that has been suggested. For, if such were the case, the Epistle should be more free from the rhetorical quality that belongs both to it and to the Dictio. There should be a much wider gap than there is between the two documents. The Letter as it stands in relation to the Dictio seems rather a toning down of a rhetorical model than the Dictio a rhetoricism of the Letter. The fact, too, that this letter shows stylistic qualities that approach those of the Dictio and depart from the usual letters of Symmachus indicates that the order is Dictio to Letter rather than Letter to Dictio.

The comparisons given above seem to me sufficient to indicate that Ennodius did write the Letter to the Eastern Bishops. I believe that in Dictio VI we have actually a first rough draft of the communication as it came from the hand of Ennodius. In the Letter we have the final form which it took after consultation and deliberation with the Pope himself and other advisors. The Letter is more clearly informed with the spirit of authority appropriate to a papal document; the Dictio shows rather the spirit of rationality or perhaps of legal reasoning. The style of the Letter is simpler and more direct; the Dictio is rhetorical and inclined to center the attention upon the manner of expression sometimes obscuring the meaning. But back of these differences the framework and the manner of thought is strikingly similar in the two documents. The differences show what happened to the Dictio in the process of its becoming the Letter to the Eastern Bishops.

Tufts College.

L'ODYSSÉE DU MANUSCRIT DE SAN PIETRO QUI RENFERME LES ŒUVRES DE SAINT HILAIRE

Dom André Wilmart, O.S.B.

Peu d'anciens manuscrits sont plus souvent cités et méritent davantage leur renom que l'insigne *Basilicanus* qui renferme une portion considérable des œuvres dogmatiques et polémiques de saint Hilaire, l'évêque de Poitiers.[1]

Composé pour une part, la moins étendue, en lettres onciales,[2] et pour tout le reste,[3] dans le nouveau style semioncial qu'un texte récemment publié permet de regarder comme un produit original de l'Afrique chrétienne,[4] il a de plus le prix inestimable, à nos yeux, de se présenter sous une référence expresse qui, longtemps obscure, désormais élucidée,[5] garantit son âge et son origine tout ensemble. Mais cette souscription même, qui nous reporte à la quatorzième année du roi des Vandales Thrasamond (Sept. 509–Sept. 510)[6] et à Cagliari en Sardaigne, reçoît aussitôt, tant du

[1] Pour l'ensemble de la bibliographie, voir E. A. Lowe, *Codices Latini Antiquiores*, I (Oxford, 1934), p. 38: No. 1.—Je dois ajouter que la phototypie publiée par D. Amelli en 1922 est très imparfaite et ne laisse pas voir la plupart des notes marginales.

[2] Voir *ibid.*, p. 2, le facsimilé marqué 1[b].—La partie onciale commence au bas du fol. 288 et aussitôt après la célèbre note chronologique, avec le titre et la première ligne du prétendu premier traité *Ad Constantium*; toute la suite, depuis fol. 288[v], est donnée en lettres onciales régulières. Le cahier XXXVIII s'achève avec ce même fol. 288[v]. Il n'y a donc pas lieu de distinguer les deux parties, semionciale et onciale, eu égard à la date. La partie onciale continue la partie semionciale et doit être tenue pour contemporaine. On observe un changement de main et de style; rien de plus. En certains ouvrages, l'on peut constater que le même copiste se sert concurremment des deux styles; ce n'est pas ici le cas. Nous avons certainement affaire à deux copistes différents; mais cette substitution des personnes ne signifie pas que le travail de transcription ait été proprement interrompu. Si les traités *Ad Constantium* et ceux qui les escortent avaient été ajoutés après un certain laps de temps, le nouveau copiste n'aurait pas songé à commencer ce supplément au terme du cahier XXXVIII et dès le bas d'une page. Tout indique, au contraire, qu'il avait sous les yeux le même modèle qui avait fourni le *De Trinitate* et le livret intitulé *In Constantium*.

[3] Hors les additions postérieures, bien entendu; mais, au vrai, celles-ci sont presque toutes sur des pages de remplacement, destinées à compenser les pertes qu'avait subies la partie onciale.

[4] Cf. Bernhard Bischoff, 'Die alten Namen der lateinischen Schriftarten', *Philologus*, LXXXIX (1934), 462. sqq.

[5] Cette souscription, de première importance, a été souvent reproduite. On peut la lire, parfaitement nette, dans les *Specimina codicum Latinorum Vaticanorum* d'Ehrle-Liebaert (1927), p. 6[a]. Pour l'interprétation depuis le XVIIe siècle, voir *Revue Bénédictine*, XXIV (1907), 153, n. 1, et XXIX (1912), 381.

[6] 'Trasamundus' succéda à son frère 'Gutamundus,' qui avait régné deux ans et un mois; lui-

caractère des ouvrages copiés que des circonstances historiques, un sens d'une grande force évocatrice. Le recueil, du même coup, passe au rang des documents d'histoire les plus significatifs ou, pour mieux dire, doit être classé parmi les reliques émouvantes du passé.

Car à Cagliari, en ces années-là, plus de soixante évêques de la Byzacène étaient exilés pour leur fidélité au catholicisme, par ordre du roi Thrasamond. Dès son élection au siège de Ruspe en 507, l'illustre Fulgence avait dû les rejoindre, accompagné de son futur biographe, le diacre Ferrand.[7] Il n'est donc pas douteux que le manuscrit des oeuvres de saint Hilaire provient de ce milieu de confesseurs, et qu'il a été rédigé par deux clercs africains qui souffraient pour leur foi, auprès de Fulgence. Qui sait même si celui-ci, qui fut mandé à Carthage peu après (vers 510 ou plus tard encore),[8] par le souverain, pour y disputer en sa présence sur la doctrine trinitaire, n'a pas médité longuement, voire annoté les pages du même volume, afin d'y trouver et souligner les arguments les plus favorables à sa cause? Qui sait si ces traités n'ont pas été transcrits à son intention, et si le beau et clair manuscrit dont finirent par hériter les chanoines de San Pietro ne fut pas tout d'abord en sa possession et ne resta point entre ses mains jusqu'à sa mort (1 Janvier 532)? Il n'y a rien là que de très vraisemblable, si l'on tient compte des divers faits rappelés. En voici un autre d'ailleurs, qui est précis et d'ordre littéraire: Ferrand, le disciple fidèle, adressa en 546, à propos des 'Trois Chapitres,' une lettre aux diacres romains, Pélage et Anatole, où la même collection des écrits de saint Hilaire relatifs à l'empereur Constance est employée.[9]

Que devint le manuscrit par la suite des temps? C'est ce que l'analyse de ses parties peut seule nous apprendre de quelque manière. Même si nous n'arrivons qu'à des approximations ou ne pouvons énoncer que de frêles conjectures, il n'est pas moins utile que convenable de rechercher les *fata* d'un livre de cette espèce, en l'étudiant tel qu'il s'offre à nos

---

même, qui fut un homme supérieur au demeurant, hors la préjugé anticatholique, tint le sceptre vingt-six ans, huit mois et quatre jours. Nous sommes renseignés à ce sujet par le *Laterculus regum Wandalorum et Alanorum* (éd. Th. Mommsen, *Chronica minora saec. IV–VI*, III [= MGH, *Auct. ant.*, XIII (Berlin, 1898)], 459: nᵒˢ 11–12). D'après L. Schmidt, *Geschichte der Wandalen* (Leipzig, 1901), p. 115, Guntamond serait mort vraisemblablement le 3 septembre 496. Thrasamond décéda le 28 mai 523. Tout cela s'ajuste à peu près. A s'en tenir au *Laterculus*, Thrasamond aurait commencé de régner le 24 septembre 496.

[7] Cf. la *Vita Fulgentii*, XX, 40 et 41, (*P. L.*, LXV, 137 sq.).

[8] Peut-être seulement en 515; deux ouvrages de Fulgence sont de ce temps-là et représentent sa propre défense à Carthage: le *Contra Arianos* (*P. L.*, LXV, 205–224) et les trois livres *Ad Trasamundum* (*ibid.*, 223–304). Fulgence fut renvoyé alors en Sardaigne, sur les instances des évêques ariens, et y demeura jusqu'à la mort du roi. Après la conférence, Ferrand put se fixer à Carthage.

[9] Cf. *P. L.*, LXVII, 922 D l. 9 sq.; rapprocher le bref commentaire de la *Revue Bénédictine*, XXIV (1907), 155.

regards. Mon dessein est, en effet, d'en faire humblement la description technique, selon les règles qui sont passées en usage dans les nouveaux catalogues de la Bibliothèque Vaticane. On verra mieux ainsi, je l'espère, l'intérêt profond de ce recueil et l'on saisira sa réalité, tout en distinguant ses différents articles et notant les accidents dont il fut victime. Comme il ne s'agit pas toutefois d'établir une rédaction latine sèche et serrée, je prendrai la liberté d'adjoindre de brefs commentaires et de ménager quelques transitions.

Quant aux détails les plus extérieurs, l'on voudra bien se reporter en outre aux indications succinctes d'E. A. Lowe, qui, suivant le plan de son répertoire déjà cité, comblent les vœux des paléographes. Ma propre direction va plutôt dans le sens de l'histoire littéraire; mais je ne puis négliger tout à fait les données matérielles qui concourent au même but.

Les dimensions du manuscrit *D. 182* de San Pietro ne dépassent guère celles du format dit moyen (275×205 mm.); soit, à peu près, la taille de l'in-quarto moderne. Les marges, sans doute, ont été diminuées par les relieurs du XVIIe siècle, peut-être même dès avant; mais il ne semble pas, à en juger par le faible espace laissé de chaque côté du pli, qu'elles aient été larges. Le cadre de la partie écrite varie entre 210 et 220 mm., pour la hauteur, et maintient, d'ordinaire, la longeur des lignes à 160 mm. Celles-ci sont au nombre constant de 30 par page. Il y a donc bien encore unité sous cet aspect, en dépit du changement de main et de style qui s'accomplit vers la fin de l'ouvrage. Les rédacteurs des portions plus récentes ont eux-mêmes tâché, visiblement, de respecter cette disposition générale; un nombre égal de lignes se présente dans leur travail, à cela près que les feuillets du début (ff. 1–9) proposent une ligne en plus. Dans son état original, le volume comprenait certainement quarante-quatre cahiers réguliers, de huit demi-feuilles chacun; la note de compte, uniforme, est marquée au terme de ceux qui subsistent, dans la corne de droite. Les deux premiers ont été remplacés, ainsi que le premier feuillet du cahier suivant; soit les ff. actuels 1–12, dont l'écriture minuscule a resserré beaucoup la matière; pareillement, le cinquième cahier, auquel correspondent nos ff. 28–33. Le vingt-sixième, qui aurait trouvé place après le f. 192, s'est perdu complètement; il manquait déjà vers le XVIe siècle, suivant une inscription de ce temps-là, après la référence originale du quaternion XXV au bas de f. 192^v. Enfin, il est aisé de calculer que trois cahiers de la dernière partie font encore défaut, qui complèteraient, après celui qui est noté XLI, le texte du *De synodis*. L'ouvrage intact devait donc être formé de 352 feuillets semblables. Selon le compte établi groissièrement, au XVIIe siècle, semble-t-il, nous n'avons plus que 311 feuillets; mais il faut ajouter à ce total deux feuillets sautés par oubli: 139^a et 292^a. Le parchemin étant fin et souple, d'excellente qualité, l'ensemble constituait un volume d'emploi facile, tel, par exemple, qu'on pouvait l'emporter en voyage sans encombrement.

J'en viens à la description littéraire, sauf à rappeler, autant qu'il sera nécessaire, les changements accidentels qui se superposent à l'analyse. Nous avons à distinguer six articles, mais fort inégaux, la copie du *De Trinitate* en douze livres remplissant de fait presque tout le manuscrit et pouvant, de ce chef, lui être identifiée. Le succès qu'on fit, au cours des Ve et VIe siècles,[10] à cet ouvrage, d'une théologie encore archaïque et d'une forme souvent difficile, doit être remarqué en passant, d'autant plus curieux au premier abord que les lecteurs cesseront bientôt de prendre goût à ces développements solennels, périmés par la force des choses. La necessité de faire opposition à l'arianisme des peuples barbares suffit en définitive à expliquer cette faveur provisoire. Nous trouvons encore de l'attrait aux pages du *De Trinitate* de saint Augustin, qui s'accordent dans leur profondeur avec le train de la pensée moderne; au terme de la période antique et devant la menace des ruines prochaines, les clercs éprouvaient surtout le besoin de maintenir les conquêtes doctrinales encloses dans le symbole de Nicée.

I.–1. Le premier livre du *De Trinitate* est presque tout entier, matériellement, l'œuvre des reviseurs; soit, après une page restée blanche:

a) ff. 1[v]–11[v]. *Circumspicienti mihi*[11]—*et uniuersis carnis nostrae passionibus functus ad deum*//(= *P.L.*, X, 25 D–46 C l. 10). A ces pages, deux copistes contemporains paraissent avoir collaboré. Le premier, qui a mené la tâche jusque vers le bas du fol. 9 (ligne 19 inclusivement), écrit d'une manière irregulière; à deux reprises (f. 2–2[v] et f. 7–7[v]), il abandonne le style calligraphique pour tomber dans les modes négligés du style cursif, qui devaient lui être plus familiers; nous y gagnons de pouvoir reconnaitre le milieu où lui-même et son compagnon travaillaient; car les parties lâches de cette copie sont nettement italiennes. Le second copiste, au contraire, garde une très bonne tenue littéraire, et les pages qu'on lui doit depuis la reprise (ff. 9–11[v]) portent leur date, à savoir environ le milieu du IXe siècle, plutôt un peu en deçà (vers 840), si nos catégories actuelles permettant de dater les écritures sont recevables.[12]

[10] On peut compter pour le moins sept exemplaires du traité de saint Hilaire qui remontent à ces temps-là, plus ou moins bien conservés (cf. *Revue Bénédictine*, XXIX [1912] 299): de quoi produire une excellent édition critique. Celle du Mauriste Pierre Coustant, revue par Maffei, (*P. L.*, X, 25 sq.) est bonne assurément; nos ressources permettraient pourtant de l'améliorer encore. Coustant avait connaissance du manuscrit de San Pietro et il a pu employer des notes de Bandini (cf. *P. L.*, IX, 220 D); néanmoins, l'étude complète de la tradition doit être reprise selon une méthode rigoureuse.

[11] Aucun titre littéraire n'a été joint à ce début; mais on lit, sur deux lignes, une sorte d'invocation trinitaire qui doit provenir du modèle employé. Une partie de cette phrase demeure inexpliquée: *In nomine patris et filii et spiritus sancti amen. pater noster ses fas/quas nus nis in xpo filio dei amen*. Les cinq syllabes intermédiaires qui font difficulté pourraient à la rigueur correspondre à des mots grecs qui ont été mal lus et déformés.

[12] Pour rejoindre exactement la portion suivante du texte, une dizaine de lignes du texte original

b) ff. 12–12ᵛ//*aut quum in stagnis domesticis nauem—Et ante omnia natum esse. Quum ubi nati*//(=*P.L.*, X, 47 A l. 10–48 A l. 15). Ces deux pages jettent un flot soudain de lumière sur le manuscrit et ses aventures possibles; elles ont été transcrites en effet par une main wisigothique, fort appliquée, de la fin du VIIIᵉ siècle; du reste, la seule orthographe du mot *quum*, qui se présente dans les réclames de part et d'autre, démontrerait l'origine de ce morceau.

A ce point du texte, nous avons enfin le raccord de la copie originale; mais le premier livre est presque achevé: ff. 13–14//*uitatis significatio est—et eum praedicare ne falsum* (=*P.L.*, X, 48 B l. 1–49 C). Le terme est donc marqué par cette simple souscription, dont les trois mots sont espacés sur le bas de la page: *expl(icit) liber primus*, et le livre suivant est annoncé pareillement au dessous: *Inc(i)p(it) liber secundus*. Aussitôt après ces formules, on lit une note contemporaine, tracée en une très fine écriture cursive: *Contuli in nomine d(omi)ni ih(es)u xpi*. Cette même note revient telle, régulièrement, à la fin de chaque livre.[13] En outre, au bas de la plupart des cahiers de la partie semionciale, après le numéro d'ordre du quaternion, on lit, dans les mêmes caractères, la déclaration abrégée: *Contuli*. Au terme de la partie semionciale, on retrouvera pour la dernière fois cette écriture, dans la souscription complète qui mentionne la date et l'endroit. La teinte de l'encre est exactement celle de la copie; mais il y a lieu surtout d'observer qu'aucune correction n'apparaît, au cours des pages du texte, qui dénote la main propre d'un reviseur; tous les mots qui ont été ajoutés par occasion, mais d'ailleurs rarement, soit dans l'interligne soit dans la marge inférieure, sont bien autant de retouches imputables au copiste lui-même, lequel emploie, pour les introduire, des caractères semionciaux plus menus.[14] Il me semble inévitable

---

font défaut: ⟨*et patrem nostrum—ad tribunalium pugnas*⟩ (=*P. L.*, X, 46 C l. 10–47 A l. 10). Ce bref morceau fut-il copié par les reviseurs italiens du IXᵉ siècle sur une bande de parchemin jointe au f. 11, ensuite perdue? Ou bien les reviseurs se sont-ils mépris sur l'étendue du texte à remplacer? Ce sont là de petites questions désormais insolubles; nous ne pouvons que constater la susdite lacune.

13 Variante *domini n(ostr)i . . .* : f. 82.

14 Voici un relevé d'ensemble de ces retouches et reprises. Il n'est pas tout à fait complet, et ne pouvait l'être. Seule, une édition critique serait capable de présenter la somme de ces petits faits, en les signalant au fur et à mesure. Mais il reste que la 'collation' originale a été faite avec soin, et que la copie première, au surplus, offrait peu de défauts. Le plus souvent, un mot omis est ajouté dans l'interligne: ff. 20ᵛ, 35ᵛ, 111, 112ᵛ, 136, 149ᵛ, 150ᵛ, 151, 152, 152ᵛ, 155ᵛ, 161ᵛ, 168ᵛ, 175, 175ᵛ, 186, 193, 236, 237. Quelquefois, deux mots sont transposés au moyen de légers traits: ff. 64ᵛ, 76ᵛ, 194ᵛ; une lettre est barrée: f. 151; deux lettres sont exponctués: f. 210ᵛ. L'addition d'une phrase entière dans l'interligne est exceptionnelle: ff. 149ᵛ et 166ᵛ. Enfin, une phrase a été restituée dans la marge inférieure, avec la référence: *h(abemu)s*, au terme; une note correspondante est marquée dans le texte courant: *h(aben)d(um)*. J'aurai à indiquer, en son lieu (f. 136), une autre correction de même nature, qui porte sur le début d'un livre, mais n'est plus parfaitement intelligible. La page qui offre le plus de retouches, pour quelque raison qui nous échappe, est le f. 149ᵛ; la précédente fait voir la restitution marginale notée ci-dessus; celle-ci réunit huit insertions dans l'interligne, dont une prolixe. Tout ce travail est donc imputable à l'unique copiste africain de la partie semionciale. Le cas des grattages,

de conclure qu'il n'y a pas eu d'autre 'collation' que celle qui fut faite par le copiste responsable, c'est à dire qu'après avoir transcrit le texte il l'a relu de nouveau, afin de pouvoir garantir sa conformité au modèle. Par suite, toutes les notes de souscription, y compris la dernière, sont dues au copiste des pages semionciales, et la date impliquée est à prendre d'une manière tout à fait stricte, visant tout le travail de copie qui la précède.

2. Le second livre du *De Trinitate*, dont le titre original est inscrit au bas du f. 14, débute à la page suivante (f. 14^v), toute la première ligne en rouge vif, mais dans le même style semioncial, devant mettre en évidence le point de départ et y suffisant; la lettre initiale est à peine agrandie, tout comme au principe de chaque phrase du texte courant; car les anciens copistes des Ve et VIe siècles ne sentaient pas, d'ordinaire, le besoin d'orner davantage leurs travaux; leur unique souci était apparemment de faire large et clair:
Sufficiebat credentibus dei sermo qui in au/res nostras etc. (=*P.L.*, X, 50 C). L'admirable transcription se poursuit, régulière, jusqu'à la fin du quatrième cahier (f. 27^v): *est enim spiritus sanctus unus ubique omnes patriarchas//*(=*P. L.*, X, 73 A l. 10). Les pages suivantes nous ramènent en effet un nouveau supplément, destiné à compenser la parte du cinquième cahier; elles sont toutes l'œuvre du second calligraphe du IXe siècle, fort habile, qui avait déjà remplacé une partie du premier livre (ff. 9–11^v). Cette réfection porte donc tout d'abord sur les derniers chapitres du second livre (f. 28–28^v): *//Profetas et omnem chorum—observatione retinendus* (=*P. L.*, X, 73 A l. 11–75 A). La souscription est reportée à la page suivante, jointe selon l'usage commun à l'annonce du livre voisin.

3. *Expli(cit) Lib(er) II. Incip(it) Lib(er) III S(an)c(t)i Hilari./Adfert pleris que obscuritatem sermo domini* etc.: f. 29 (*P. L.*, X, 76 A l. 4). Sans avoir bien évalué l'étendue des lacunes qu'il devait combler, le réviseur avait fait choix d'un cahier complet de huit feuilles. Arrivé au bout de son texte, il n'avait rempli exactement que onze pages: *opere consummato quod dedisti mihi ut fatiam:* f. 33 (*P. L.*, X 84 B l. 4) Rien n'était plus simple que de supprimer les derniers demi-feuillets, devenus inutiles; ce qui fut fait, vraisemblablement, sans délai. Mais le revers du feuillet 33 demeurait libre et devait tenter tôt ou tard un lecteur entreprenant. La principale partie de f. 33^v a servi en effet, sur la fin du Xe siècle, à l'in-

---

peu nombreux, est à part; je croirais qu'ils sont dus, d'ordinaire, à des lecteurs de l'époque carolingienne. Enfin, j'ai remarqué quatre brèves additions ou corrections d'une autre main tantôt minuscule tantôt onciale, qui pourraient avoir été faites au VIe siècle: *afferret* (f. 178), *ut fundata* (f. 271^v), *dispensationum* (f. 272^v), *Dona mihi* (275^v). On peut négliger quelques corrections du XIe siècle (ff. 3, 12, 20^v–21^v, 22^v, 38, 38^v), ou du XVIe (f. 4 et 4^v), et les essais de plume (ff. 3, 6, 22, 62, 143, 160^v, 216).

sertion d'une séquence en l'honneur de saint Benoît, composée par le doyen de Saint-Gall, Ekkehart I († 973): *Qui bene dici cupitis/huc festini currite/Benedicti patris/opem q(uae)rite//* etc.[15] Cette pièce adventice semble indiquer que le manuscrit se trouvait alors dans un monastère, non loin de Saint-Gall. Les traits et détails de l'écriture sont bien ceux qui avaient cours sous l'influence germanique dans les régions au sud des Alpes, dont Milan, Pavie, Padoue, Vérone étaient les principaux centres de culture. C'est, au reste, la plus récente addition que l'on ait à signaler, en parcourant les pages du volume; mais elle est instructive.

Avec le sixième cahier, nous retrouvons le texte original; l'analyse des parties n'offre plus désormais aucune difficulté, et peut être accomplie rapidement. La seconde partie du troisième livre est tout d'abord restituée: ff. 34–40ᵛ//*laus patris omnis a filio est—et testis et auctor exsistat* (= P. L., X, 84 B l. 4–95 A). /*sancti hilari trinitatis liber tertius/ expl!(icit) inc(i)p(it) liber quartus.*

4. f. 41: *Quamquam anterioribus libris quos iam pridem/conscribsimus* etc. (= P. L., X, 97 A). La première ligne du livre IV est rubriquée comme celle du second; la même distinction sera constamment observée, et je ne la rappellerai plus. Le livre est intact, ainsi que tous ceux qui suivent, le neuvième excepté; des corrections de première main n'y apparaissent que très rarement, comme j'ai déjà noté. Je puis me borner à marquer les limites de chacun, avec l'indication des titres connexes et des références à l'édition: *non sinit profeta quod deus est/liber quartus explicit/ inc(i)p(it) liber quintus.* f. 62ᵛ (= P. L., X, 129 A).

5. ff. 63–82: *Respondentes inpiis et uesanis hereticorum/institutionibus —deum in deo esse non confitens* (P. L., X, 129 B–157 A). /*Expl(icit) liber quintus/inc(i)p(it) liber sextus.*

6. ff. 82ᵛ–110: *Non sum nescius difficillimo me asperrimoque / tempore scribere—nec qui crucifixerat denegaret* (P. L., X, 158 A–198 A). /*liber sextus expli(cit)/inc(i)p(it) liber septimus.*[16]

7. ff. 110ᵛ–136: *Septimus hic nobis aduersus nouae hereseos/uesanam temeritatem—naturam in se dei se gignentis exhibuit* (P. L., X, 199 B– 234 C). /*liber septimus expl(icit)/inc(i)p(it) liber octauus.*

[15] Voir la nouvelle édition de G. Dreves, *Analecta hymnica medii Aevi,* L (Leipzig, 1907), 272 sq.: (n° 205). L'éditeur cite une douzaine de témoins, parmi lesquels le manuscrit de San Pietro ne figure pas; ce sont tous des tropaires ou recueils d'origine allemande, hors les deux tropaires de Saint-Benoît de Mantoue, conservé à Vérone, et du Mont-Cassin (n° 546), l'un et l'autre du XIᵉ siècle. L'attribution de cette ancienne séquence au doyen de Saint-Gall est certifiée par Ekkehart IV dans ses *Casus Sancti Galli,* c. IX (cf. *Monumenta Germaniae Historica, Scriptores,* II [Hannover, 1829], 118). Notre texte doit être l'une des plus anciennes copies, postérieure de peu à la publication.

[16] Aussitôt après l'annonce du nouveau livre, le copiste, croyant sans doute avoir affaire à un titre, a tracé sur une dernière ligne le début du texte: *septimus . . . uesanam;* il n'a pas moins recommencé en rouge à la page suivante: *Septimus,* etc. A remarquer que l'erreur, flagrante, n'est pas corrigée; c'est une nouvelle preuve du sens que j'ai cru devoir donner ci-dessus à la note réitérée 'contuli.'

8. ff. 136–160: *Beatus apostolus paulus formam constituendi/episcopi fi[n]gens*[17]—*corporaliter diuinitatis inhabitet plenitudo* (P. L., X, 236 A–278 B). /*Expl(icit) liber octauus/inc(i)p(it) liber nonus.*

9. ff. 160ᵛ–194ᵛ: *Tractantes superiore libro de indifferenti natura/dei patris et dei fili—intellegatur inscientia.* /*Expl(icit) liber nonus/Inc(i)p(it) liber decimus.* Pour que le texte du livre IX soit complet, il s'en faut toutefois d'un cahier, le vingt-sixième, enlevé très probablement vers la fin du moyen âge.[18] Nous ne lisons donc plus maintenant que les parties correspondant aux colonnes 280 A–328 C l. 5, et 340 A l. 11–343 A de l'édition; autrement dit, le défaut d'un cahier (après f. 192) nous prive de la portion de texte qui commençait selon l'édition: *dominus Christus non ignorat* (P. L., X, 328 C l. 5), et se terminait: *omnia quae patris* (P. L., X, 340 A l. 11).

10. ff. 194ᵛ–228: *Non est ambiguum omnem humani eloquii sermonem/contradictioni obnoxium—est professus et mortuum* (P. L., X, 344 C–398 C)./ *expl(icit) liber decimus/Inc(i)p(it) undecimus liber.* Dans l'intervalle, à savoir sur la marge supérieure du fol. 201, qui commence le cahier XXVIII, et par suite en une place quasi centrale du volume, une note stylisée, tracée nettement au IXᵉ siècle ou au Xᵉ siècle[19] par quelque main habituée à la copie des chartes solennelles, requiert l'attention: *liber iste sanctus est.* Par ces termes, l'on entendait sans doute exprimer les sentiments qu'inspirait l'antique manuscrit, et cet hommage, rendu au nom de ses détenteurs, est des plus touchants. Mais la forme graphique de la déclaration ne devrait pas égarer le lecteur moderne. De l'écriture de Corbie dite *ab*, à cause de la tenue particulière de ces deux lettres, elle n'offre qu'un simulacre. Il est bien vrai que le *b* du premier mot porte à droite l'épisème ou petit trait de ligature qui fut admis comme une sorte d'ornement dans le style factice de Corbie vers l'an 800; mais quantité de chartes de l'époque carolingienne, en Italie aussi bien qu'en France, présentent le même signe. L'intéressante addition nous laisse donc encore sur le sol italien, et l'on n'a point, heureusement, à faire intervenir le nom de Corbie en cette histoire, assez compliquée déjà.

[17] Le copiste avait bien écrit du premier coup, c'est à dire suivant son modèle: *fingens;* le premier *n* a été ensuite gratté. Coustant a noté que *figens* est la leçon des manuscrits récents (cf. P. L., X, 235 note *a*). Le grattage pourrait être ici tardif; toutefois, on aperçoit encore, sur la coupure de la marge inférieure, une longue addition ou correction de première main, accompagnée du signe '*h(abemu)s*,' qui paraît se rapporter à la première phrase du livre. Ces retouches pourraient être connexes; j'incline pourtant à croire que *figens* doit sa réalité à un lecteur du moyen âge, le même qui, par exemple, a effacé l'*n* de *thensauri* f. 169.

[18] Si la perte avait été consommée avant le IXᵉ siècle, elle aurait été certainement réparée par les copistes qui ont complété ces premiers cahiers. D'autre part, il y a quelques signes, çà et là, que l'ouvrage trouva encore des lecteurs au XIᵉ siècle.

[19] Il est très difficile de préciser, vu le caractère de l'écriture; mon impression est que cette note remonte plutôt à la fin du IXᵉ siècle ou au commencement du Xᵉ.

11. ff. 228-251ᵛ: *Totum atque absolutum fidei euangelicae / sacramentum —creatoris sui imago mansurus* (P. L., X, 399 B-433 A). /Expl(icit) *hilari detrinitate/liber unde cimus/Inc(i)p(it) liber duodecimus.*

12. ff. 252-275ᵛ: *Tendimus tandem iam sancto spiritu prosequente / ad tutum securae fidei tranquillumq(ue) portum—qui est benedictus/in saecula saeculorum amen* (P. L., X, 434 B-472 A)./sancti hilari de trinitate/ *liber duodecimus expl(icit).*

II. Le grand traité doctrinal de l'évêque de Poitiers est suivi, dans ce contexte, de divers opuscules, soit polémiques soit iréniques, qui forment la fin du recueil. Ma tâche n'est guère que de les énumérer d'une façon précise. Les trois premiers sont associées de quelque manière par la mention du nom de l'empereur Constance dans l'énoncé de leur titre; ils n'en sont pas moins bien distincts, surtout le second et le troisième, étroitement appariés par un vice étrange de la tradition, duquel, au début même du Vᵉ siècle, Sulpice Sévère paraît être déjà le témoin.[20] Le premier est une invective vibrante, courageuse et célèbre, rendue publique en l'année 360; nos éditions l'appellent 'Contra Constantium' (P. L., X, 577-603). Le titre du manuscrit de San Pietro, joint à la dernière souscription du *De Trinitate*, est exprimé un peu différemment:

ff. 275ᵛ-288: *Inc(i)p(it) Eiusdem liber/in Constantium imperatorem/ feliciter./ Tempus est loquendi quia iam praeterit tempus tacendi/Christus expectetur quia obtinuit antichristus—et paternae pietatis rebellem. Expl(icit) liber inconstantium.*

C'est immédiatement avant ces derniers mots que le copiste de la partie semionciale, parvenu au terme du travail qui lui avait été assigné, ou bien encore voulant marquer un temps de repos après sa propre revision, a tracé le fameux 'colophon,' sans lequel l'érudit moderne se serait débattu désespérément parmi les incertitudes de sa courte science. Il suffit, après en avoir tant dit, de le rapporter une fois de plus, en détachant les mots, presque tous liés entre eux:

/Contuli in nomine d(omi)ni ihū x͞pi aput karalis constitutus
anno quarto decimo trasamund(i) regis./

III. C'est donc maintenant que commence la partie onciale, le nouveau titre et la première ligne étant disposés au bas de la même page, l'un et l'autre en rouge:

ff. 288-291ᵛ: *inc(ipit) eiusdem ad constantium/Benignifica natura tua domine beatissime//Auguste cum benigna uoluntate concordat—de se loquitur ipsa* (P. L., X, 557 A-564 A). /Expli(cit) li(ber) I s(an)c(t)i

---

[20] *Historia sacra*, c'est à dire la Chronique, II, 45 (P. L., XX, 154 D l. 12 sq.). Cf. *Revue Bénédictine*, XXIV (1907), 155.

hilari ad constantium imp(eratorem).—Il y a quelque trente ans, j'ai eu l'occasion de montrer que cette prétendue lettre d'Hilaire n'est autre chose qu'un morceau détaché de la collection des 'Fragments historiques,' et qu'il reprend sa place avec la plus grande aisance dans cette collection, sorte de dossier composé et publié par l'évêque de Poitiers à la veille de son exil contre les prélats illyriens Valens et Ursace, puis brouillé par ses héritiers littéraires dès la fin du IVe siècle.[21] De cette étrange confusion, tout autant que de la fiction qui en est résultée, de manière à produire deux livres conjoints sous le nom de Constance, l'exemplaire de San Pietro se trouve être, matériellement, le plus ancien témoin.

IV. ff. 291ᵛ–294. *inc(i)p(it) lib(er) II eiusdem ad eundem*[22] *quem et constan/tinupoli ipse tradidit./Non sum nescius piissime imp(erator) ea quae de plerisque/de nonnullis negotiis—ab ea iuxta ista non/dissonans* (*P. L.,* X, 563 D–572 A). *expl(icit) s(an)c(t)i hilari ep(i)s(cop)i et conf(essoris) ad constantium/liber II.* Cette requête polie, rédigée et présentée à l'empereur, qui n'est pas encore 'l'Antéchrist,' au début de l'année 360, justifie les titres qui l'entourent, à part la fausse relation avec le précédent morceau, lequel était d'une tout autre nature.

V. ff. 294–299ᵛ: *incipi(t) eiusd(em) aduersus arrianos uel auxen-tium/mediolanensem//d(ilectissimis)*[23] *fratribus in fide paterna manenti-bus/et arrianam heresim detestantibus—christum deum uerum praedica-bunt./Expl(icit) s(an)c(t)i hilari. inc(ipit) blasphemiae/exemplum aux-enti./Beatissimis et gloriosissimis imp(eratoribus) ualentiniano/et ualenti augustis—haec retractari non oportere. / exp(licit) blasp(hemia) auxenti*

---

[21] Voir *ibid.,* pp. 151–179, 291–317.— Quoique Bardenhewer et Labriolle m'aient rendu pleine justice, les faiseurs de manuels, en France et ailleurs, ont pris l'habitude de mettre au compte d'A. L. Feder S. J. ma petite découverte (en partie liée a l'explication littéraire des *Tractatus Origenis*), et de lui attribuer par suite ma propre reconstruction des 'Fragments historiques.' Il est vrai que, chargé d'éditer ces textes pour le *Corpus* de Vienne, et tout d'abord beaucoup déconcerté par mes remarques, l'habile auteur s'arrangea pour limiter ma part d'invention le plus possible, et aussi bien les travaux d'autres chercheurs, à tel point que Dom John Chapman crut devoir s'élever fortement contre pareils procédés (cf. *Revue Bénédictine,* XXVII [1910], 350 sq.). Je ne puis sans doute que me féliciter d'assister au succès de ma démonstration; mais l'on comprendra que je ne me désintéresse pas tout à fait des droits de la vérité. J'ai gardé le silence longtemps à cet égard; devant la persistance de la mauvaise foi, il me semble préférable de protester moi aussi, si odieux que soit le plaidoyer personnel. Qu'on lise par exemple tel chapitre sur l'Arianisme, signé G. Bardy, dans l'*Histoire* Fliche-Martin en cours de publication, on sera pleinement édifié. Ces gens-là n'ont qu'un souci: écouler aux moindres frais leur pacotille.

[22] Le scribe avait écrit (en rouge) *euadem,* et dans la première ligne *piisme* (également en rouge): les corrections sont faites au dessus de la ligne par une autre main, ici onciale, qui doit être contemporaine. Diverses autres menues corrections se présentent çà et là de même, ou légèrement variées, dans cette partie des ff. 238ᵛ–311ᵛ. Je croirais que c'est encore la main, tout à la fois minuscule et onciale, dont j'ai signalé l'intervention en quelques endroits de la première partie, et qui reparaît maintenant un peu plus souvent (ff. 291ᵛ, 292ᵃ, 292ᵃᵛ, 293, 294, 294ᵛ, 295ᵛ, 296ᵛ, 298). C'est encore elle qui a pu inscrire en marge plusieurs titres secondaires: *in enceniis factum* (f. 285ᵛ), *c(ontra) ancyr(en-sem) syn(odum) et arium* (f. 302ᵛ), *de osio et potamio* (f. 303), *exemp(lum) blasph(emiae)* (f. 303ᵛ).

[23] Dans le manuscrit deux *d,* surmontés d'un trait.

arriani. Cette lettre adressée aux évêques d'Italie, avec une pièce à conviction, est le dernier témoignage que nous ayons de la vigilance d'Hilaire à l'égard de l'orthodoxie. (*P. L.* X, 609 B—618 C).

VI. ff. 299ᵛ–311ᵛ: *inc(ipit) s(an)c(t)i hilari ep(i)s(cop)i / pictabensis lib(er) fidaei catholicae contra arrianos et praeuaricatores arri / anis adquiescentes inc(ipit) feliciter / D(ilectissimis) et beatissimis fratribus et coepixcopis / prou(inciae) germaniae primae* etc. */Constitutum mecum habebam f(ratres) k(arissimi)*[24] *in tanto silen / tii uestri tempore—hisque nominibus non simpliciter //* Le plus bel ouvrage, à notre sens, de saint Hilaire pour établir l'entente entre Occidentaux et Orientaux en matière de foi complétait ainsi le recueil; malheureusement, nous n'en avons plus que la première partie (*P. L.*, X, 479 B–503 B l. 7) dans cette rédaction.

* *

Nous ignorons jusqu'à présent par suite de quelles circonstances le manuscrit des œuvres de saint Hilaire est devenu la propriété des chanoines de San Pietro. La plus ancienne mention qui est faite de sa présence dans l'archive de la basilique est ce titre d'un inventaire de l'année 1567: *Hilarius de Trinitate;*[25] il ne semble pas en effet qu'un autre volume ait pu être désigné en ces termes. C'est vers ce temps-là aussi que Latino Latini[26] recueillit quelques-unes de ses variantes. Peut-être un examen plus minutieux des anciens registres du Chapitre apportera-t-il d'autres renseignements. Mais, des faits précédement consignés, il résulte sans le moindre doute que le recueil était déjà conservé en Italie, plus précisément dans la région septentrionale, depuis le IXᵉ siècle. De plus, l'insertion de la séquence d'Ekkehart autorise à croire que l'Église, ou plutôt l'abbaye, qui le possédait et dans laquelle, vers la fin du IXᵉ siècle, on lui rendit un témoignage exprès de vénération, était sise dans le ressort de Milan, eu égard aux échanges littéraires qui se poursuivaient sans cesse à travers les Alpes, entre Milan et la Suisse.

Au delà du IXᵉ siècle, qu'imaginer pour rejoindre, depuis l'Italie, la transcription faite en Sardaigne par les Africains proscrits?—Deux itinéraires se laissent concevoir sans difficulté, l'un et l'autre capables de correspondre aux données du problème. Un troisième en effet, où l'on voudrait inclure la France à cause de la note en style de charte, est pur mirage, et doit disparaître de la perspective.

La route la plus directe serait assurément de passer droit de Sardaigne en Italie. Pour justifier ce transfert, deux conditions sont requises; il faut admettre, d'une part, que l'ouvrage africain était resté à Cagliari après le

---

[24] Comme tout à l'heure, deux *f* et deux *k*, avec le signe de l'abréviation.

[25] Manuscrit *A.* 77 de l'Archive, f. 18.

[26] Cf. *P. L.*, IX, 220 D.

départ des évêques exilés, en 523, et d'autre part, que les pages suppléées par un Wisigoth à la fin du VIIIe siècle l'ont été en Italie, dans le lieu même où le manuscrit fut conservé jusqu'aux abords du XIe siècle, et peut-être encore jusqu'au XVIe. Des deux parts, une certaine invraisemblance apparaît, moins grave pourtant concernant la rédaction des pages wisigothiques; car nous avons des traces certaines de la présence d'Espagnols dans l'Italie septentrionale, au début du moyen âge.[27] Il serait beaucoup plus naturel en effet, quant au premier point, que le personnage pour lequel le recueil fut composé, l'évêque Fulgence avant tout autre,[28] ait

[27] Cf. *Bulletin d'ancienne littérature et d'archéologie chrétiennes*, IV (1914), 187.

[28] A partir d'un certain endroit (f. 150), les marges du volume, à droite et à gauche, commencent d'être parsemées d'inscriptions; assez nombreuses ensuite (depuis f. 202ᵛ), elles représentent évidemment des notes de lecture. Seul le possesseur légitime a pu s'accorder pareille licence. Le répertoire de M. Lowe offre deux exemples de ces additions (*op. laud.*: n°s 1ᵃ et 1ᵇ, ff. 159ᵛ et 298). Il y aurait grand intérêt à les reproduire sur une seule planche. Elles sont tracées en lettres onciales ou parfois minuscules, mais rapidement,—d'où leur inclinaison à droite,—et comportent de fréquentes et curieuses abréviations qui leur donnent un caractère personnel. Graphiquement, cette rédaction doit avoir le même âge que le manuscrit. En attendant que le vœu émis tout à l'heure soit exaucé, je crois utile de publier la suite de ces petits textes, dont plusieurs, fort effacés, revivent aisément à l'aide d'un réactif; j'ai donc pu les lire tous à coup sûr. On y discerne le travail intérieur de celui qui les a notés, pour tirer profit des pensées et arguments du docteur gaulois.

1. *t(e)st(imonium) apostoli uos estis corp(us) xp̄i et m(em)bra:* f. 150.
   unus d(eu)s pat(er) ex quo omnia: f. 151.
   q̃ sit plenitudo diuinitatis in xp̄o corporalit(er) i(n)habitare: f. 159ᵛ.
   q̃ sentiat de anima: f. 202ᵛ.
5. *q(uo)m(odo) de passione xp̄i sentiat:* f. 204.
   exp̄ tristis e(st) anima mea usq(ue) ad morte(m): f. 209ᵛ.
   q(uid?) de ponendo anima(m) xp̄i: f. 220ᵛ.
   id e(ss)e anima(m) q(uod) et sp(iritu)m: f. 22.
   soluta q(uae?) de anima: f. 222ᵛ.
10. *fr⟨e⟩q(ue)nt(er) unus:* f. 224.
    c(on)t(ra) nesthorianos et euthicianos: f. 231.
    q(uo)m(odo) i(n)tell⟨e⟩g⟨a⟩t(ur) d(eu)m m(eum) et d(eu)m uest⟨rum⟩et cetera. f. 234ᵛ.
    nemo uenit ad patre(m) n(isi) p(er) f⟨i⟩l(iu)m et nemo uenit ad me n(isi) q(uem) p⟨a⟩t(e)r ad tracxerit. f. 224.
15. *de subiectione fili d(e)i:* f. 245.
    q̃ s(it) tradere r(e)gn(um) patri: f. 246.
    q(uo) m(odo) sapientia i(n) initio uiaru(m) d(o)m(in)i creatus accipiat(ur): f. 270.
    secundus si debeat recte dici: f. 274.
    Synodus arrianorum in seleucia orientis celebratur: f. 281ᵛ.
20. *quid antiochia p(rae)sens audierit:* f. 282.
    eusebiu(m) caesariensem et eusebi(u)m nicomediensem arrianos affirmat: f. 289ᵛ.
    q(uod) xp̄s d(eu)s e(st): f. 294.
    c(on)t(ra) eos qui negant xp̄m d(eu)m esse: f. 295ᵛ.
    xp̄m d(eu)m ueru(m): f. 296ᵛ.
25. *xp̄m d(eu)m ueru(m):* f. 297.
    calliditas arrianoru(m): f. 297.
    perfidia arrianoru(m) c(om)posita: f. 297ᵛ.
    antixp̄s q(ui) xp̄m d(eu)m negat N(ota): f. 298.
    mi/ra/bili/t(er): f. 301ᵛ.

rapporté en Afrique un livre auquel il devait attacher quelque prix. Pourquoi l'eût-il laissé à Cagliari et à qui, surtout si le modèle avait été fourni, comme il semble indiqué, par l'Église de Cagliari?

Dès lors, l'odyssée du volume s'oriente assez nettement. Revenu en terre d'Afrique, il aurait émigré de là, quand la civilisation chrétienne commença d'y périr sous les coups des Arabes musulmans, tout d'abord en Espagne, où il put recevoir un premier supplément en la seconde moitié du VIIIᵉ siècle; puis, peu après, par suite d'événements impossibles à déterminer, il aurait trouvé son dernier refuge en l'autre péninsule.

C'est ce voyage par escales successives qui me paraît expliquer le mieux l'ensemble des particularités révélées par l'examen paléographique. S'il en fut ainsi, n'aurait-on pas raison de dire que le bassin de la Méditerranée a été, bien avant nos jours, le théâtre de croisières variées? Mais celle-là, que nous apercevons en tournant les pages d'un vieux livre, fut toute pacifique, nonobstant le sérieux des incidents qui marquèrent l'année 509–510 et les années voisines, pour les sujets de Thrasamond le Vandale.

BIBLIOTECA VATICANA.

---

30. *de synodo sermiensi ad eorum blasphemia:* f. 303.
    impie dicta patrum c(on)uellere statuitis: f. 303ᵛ.
    male: f. 304.
    pessima: f. 304.
    N(ota) quid sit essentia exponit: f. 304.
35. *mirabilit(er):* f. 304ᵛ.
    N(ota) definitiones orientalium: f. 304ᵛ.
    N(ota) q(uo) m(odo) accipiatu(r) d(omi)n(u)s condidit me: f. 306.
    de ueritate disputat: f. 307ᵛ.
    un(um) s(unt) et unus: f. 309.
40. *s(an)c(t)i* [*Hilarii* de première main] *dicta:* f. 310ᵛ.
    recapitulatio: f. 310ᵛ.
    nonaginta ep(i)sco(po)rum antiochena synodus in encaeniis facta: f. 311.

LIST OF SUBSCRIBERS
UNITED STATES

Agnes Scott College
American Council of Learned Societies
Prof. Maurice W. Avery
Prof. Fernan Baldensperger
Prof. Allan P. Ball
Mr. Claude W. Barlow
Barnes and Noble, Inc.
Prof. LeRoy C. Barret
Prof. W. J. Battle
Prof. Paull F. Baum
Mr. Goodwin B. Beach
Prof. C. H. Beeson
Mr. Alfred Bettman
Prof. Robert P. Blake
Hon. Carroll T. Bond
Mr. Spencer Borden
Mr. Edward C. Bradlee
Mrs. Anna Cox Brinton
Prof. Carroll N. Brown
Brown University Library
Bryn Mawr College Library
Mr. Chandler Bullock
Prof. George L. Burr
Prof. Harry Caplan
Prof. Frederick M. Carey
Prof. Zechariah Chafee, Jr.
Dean George H. Chase
Prof. J. E. Church
Columbia University Library
Connecticut College Library
Prof. Lane Cooper
Cornell University Library
Mr. Charles Henry Coster
Mr. George M. Cushing
Prof. C. W. David
Dr. Lincoln Davis
Mr. Frederic J. DeVeau
Rev. Francis P. Donnelly, S. J.
Prof. George H. Edgell

Dr. Benedict Einarson
Mr. J. Peter Elder
Prof. Elizabeth C. Evans
Feehan Memorial Library, St. Mary of
    the Lake Seminary
Prof. John V. A. Fine
Prof. John D. Fitz-Gerald
Prof. Francis H. Fobes
Mr. Edward W. Forbes
Prof. J. D. M. Ford
Fordham University Library
Prof. Tenney Frank
Prof. James Geddes
Prof. Russel M. Geer
General Library, University of Michi-
    gan
Miss Phyllis W. Goodhart
Mr. Sidney P. Goodrich
Prof. Florence Alden Gragg
Prof. Charles H. Grandgent
Dr. Robert M. Green
Prof. William Chase Greene
Hamilton College Library
Prof. Jacob Hammer
Prof. Mason Hammond
Mr. William P. Hapgood
Harvard College Library
Harvard Coöperative Society
Prof. Charles H. Haskins
Haverford College Library
Dean George N. Henning
Prof. Arthur W. Hodgman
Prof. Herbert B. Hoffleit
Hunter College of the City of New
    York, Library
Indiana University Library
Prof. Leslie W. Jones
Mr. Carl T. Keller
Prof. Wilhelm R. W. Koehler

307

Prof. Franklin B. Krauss
Prof. M. L. W. Laistner
Dr. Austin Lamont
Mr. Thomas W. Lamont
Prof. Floyd Seyward Lear
Lehigh University Library
Mrs. Arthur Lehman
Dr. Waldo G. Leland
Prof. Harry J. Leon
The Library of the College of the City of New York
Library of Dartmouth College
Library of Duke University
The Library, Johns Hopkins University
Library of New York University
Library of Occidental College
The Library of Princeton University
The Library, Southwestern College
The Library, State University of Iowa
The Library of Swarthmore College
Library of the University of Akron
Library of the University of Arizona
Library, University of Colorado
Library, University of North Carolina
Library of the University of Virginia
Library, University of Wisconsin
The Library, West Virginia University
Mr. George L. Lincoln
Mr. Alan MacNaughton Gordon Little
Prof. Dean P. Lockwood
Prof. Louis E. Lord
Dr. Elias Avery Lowe
Prof. Stephen B. Luce
Miss Cora E. Lutz
Prof. L. C. MacKinney
Prof. R. V. D. Magoffin
Prof. Kemp Malone
Prof. Nelson G. McCrea
Prof. Walton Brooks McDaniel
Prof. A. P. McKinlay
Dean Clarence W. Mendell
Dr. A. Bertha Miller
Mr. Knower Mills
Mr. James K. Moffitt

Prof. Charles R. Morey
Prof. S. E. Morison
The Newberry Library
The New York Public Library
Prof. William A. Nitze
Prof. Arthur D. Nock
Oberlin College Library
Mr. George Oenslager
Prof. W. A. Oldfather
Dr. John Rathbone Oliver
Oliver Wendell Holmes Library, Phillips Academy
Prof. Brooks Otis
Prof. Howard R. Patch
Prof. Arthur Stanley Pease
Dr. Bernard M. Peebles
Prof. Edward Delavan Perry
Pierpont Morgan Library
Prof. William K. Prentice
Prof. Lester M. Prindle
Mr. Lewis I. Prouty
The Public Library of the City of Boston
Prof. G. Payn Quackenbos
Redwood Library and Athenaeum, Newport, R.I.
Mr. J. F. C. Richards
Prof. Rodney P. Robinson
Prof. William Walker Rockwell
Mr. Walter T. Rosen
Prof. Paul Sachs
Prof. Eva Matthews Sanford
Lt.-Col. Winthrop Sargent, Jr.
Dr. George Sarton
Prof. John J. Savage
Prof. Alfred C. Schlesinger
Miss Dorothy M. Schullian
Mr. Ellery Sedgwick
Prof. W. T. Semple
Prof. Herbert Weir Smyth
Prof. Taylor Starck
G. E. Stechert and Company
The Steiger Company
Mr. Ernest N. Stevens
Mr. Arthur F. Stocker

Dean Selatie Edgar Stout
Dom Anselm Strittmatter, O. S. B.
Prof. Helen H. Tanzer
Dr. Henry Osborn Taylor
Prof. James Westfall Thompson
Prof. S. Harrison Thomson
Mr. Ward Thoron
Prof. B. L. Ullman
Union College Bookstore
The University of Buffalo
University of California Library, Berkeley
The University of Chicago Libraries
University of Illinois Library
Prof. John Van Horne
Vassar College Library
Mr. George Byron Waldrop
Mr. Reginald Washburn

Prof. Robert H. Webb
Wellesley College Library
Wesleyan University Library
Dean Andrew F. West
B. Westermann Company, Inc.
Prof. M. N. Wetmore
Dr. Frederic M. Wheelock
President Ernest H. Wilkins, Oberlin
Mr. Sydney M. Williams
Williston Memorial Library, Mt. Holyoke College
Prof. Margaret B. Wilson
Prof. H. A. Wolfson
Mr. Philip W. Wrenn
Yale University Library
Prof. H. H. Yeames
Prof. Karl Young

FOREIGN COUNTRIES

Balliol College Library, Oxford
Biblioteca Apostolica Vaticana
Département des Manuscrits, Bibliothèque National, Paris
Bibliothèque de l'Université, Louvain
Bibliothèque de l'Université de Toulouse
Bodleian Library, Oxford
Prof. Albert Bruckner, Basel
Le Gabinetto di Paleografia dell'Universitá di Padova
The Gennadius Library, Athens
Gerold and Company, Vienna
Glasgow University Library
E. P. Goldschmidt and Company, Ltd., London
Göteborgs Stadsbibliotek
Dr. Ludwig Häntzschel and Co., Göttingen
Otto Harrassowitz, Leipzig
Hans Hartinger Nachf., Berlin
The Institute of Mediaeval Studies, Toronto
Dean W. A. Kirkwood, Trinity College, University of Toronto

Kungl. Universitets Biblioteket, Lund
Kungl. Universitetets Bibliotek, Uppsala
Librairie E. Droz, Paris
The Library of the American Academy in Rome
The Library, Kings College, University of Durham
Mr. R. A. B. Mynors, Balliol College, Oxford
The National Library of Scotland, Edinburgh
The National Library of Wales, Aberystwyth
N. V. Martinus Nijhoff, The Hague
Dr. Carl Nordenfalk, Göteborg
Oeffentliche Bibliothek der Universität, Basel
Mr. James M. Paton, Paris
Miss Lucy Allen Paton, Paris
Queens University Library, Kingston, Ontario
Prof. Alexander Souter, Aberdeen
B. F. Stevens and Brown, Ltd., London
Universitäts-Bibliothek, Bonn

Universitäts-Bibliothek, Münster i.   University of Toronto Library
  Westfalen   Workers' Educational Association,
Universitäts-Bibliothek, Würzburg   University, Adelaide, South Australia